Learning Pentaho Data Integration 8 CE

Third Edition

An end-to-end guide to exploring, transforming, and integrating your data across multiple sources

María Carina Roldán

BIRMINGHAM - MUMBAI

Learning Pentaho Data Integration 8 CE

Third Edition

First published: April 2010

Second edition: October 2013

Production reference: 1011217

Published by Packt Publishing Ltd.
Livery Place
35 Livery Street
Birmingham
B3 2PB, UK.

ISBN 978-1-78829-243-6

www.packtpub.com

Credits

Author
María Carina Roldán

Reviewers
Diethard Steiner
Paulo Pires
Miguel Gaspar

Commissioning Editor
Amey Varangaonkar

Acquisition Editor
Tushar Gupta

Content Development Editor
Tejas Limkar

Technical Editor
Sayli Nikalje

Copy Editor
Tasneem Fatehi

Project Coordinator
Manthan Patel

Proofreader
Safis Editing

Indexer
Rekha Nair

Graphics
Tania Dutta

Production Coordinator
Shraddha Falebhai

About the Author

María Carina Roldán was born in Argentina; she earned her Bachelor's degree in Computer Science at the **Universidad Nacional de La Plata** (**UNLP**) and then moved to Buenos Aires, where she has lived since 1994.

She has worked as a BI consultant for almost twenty years. She started working with the Pentaho technology back in 2006. Since then, she has been dedicated full time to developing BI solutions, mainly as an ETL specialist using Pentaho tools. In all these years, she worked for different companies, including Assert Solutions, a Pentaho partner company based in Argentina, and Webdetails, a Portuguese company acquired by Pentaho in 2013. Currently, she works as an independent consultant.

Carina is the author of the first and second edition of *Pentaho Data Integration Beginner's Book*, Packt Publishing and the co-author of the first and second edition of *Pentaho Data Integration Cookbook*, Packt Publishing.

I'd like to thank my colleagues and friends who gave me encouraging words throughout the writing process. I would also like to thank the technical reviewers for the time and dedication that they put into reviewing the book. I dedicate this book to my kids, Camila and Nicolás.

About the Reviewers

Diethard Steiner is one of the very early Pentaho adopters. He has implemented business intelligence projects for various clients for more than a decade, covering everything from data integration to multi-dimensional cubes and dashboards. Over the last few years, he has gained in-depth experience in utilizing Pentaho tools in the big data world. These days, he is running his own independent consultancy company called Bissol Consulting Ltd in London.

Diethard has been a very active Pentaho community member and regularly publishes articles on Pentaho and the wider business intelligence world on his GitHub blog (`http://diethardsteiner.github.io/`).

Paulo Pires is a Geographical Engineer, who in his early thirties decided to apply his skills in the business intelligence area. He started working in Webdetails more than 6 years ago and specialized in building dashboards with CTools and Pentaho, along with doing some ETL work when needed.

2 years ago Webdetails became a Pentaho company, and last month Hitachi Data Systems, Hitachi Insight Group, and Pentaho joined into a single company, called Hitachi Vantara, where Paulo Pires is a Senior Consultant.

Miguel Gaspar started working at Webdetails about 3 years ago, some time before the acquisition of Webdetails by Pentaho. He was a consultant in the Implementation team and his work involved developing dashboard solutions as part of services. He is now acting as the technical owner of some of the Implementations projects as part of the Webdetails team in Pentaho.

He likes to be as professional as possible, but in an informal way. One of his favorite hobbies is learning and his particular areas of interest are: business analytics, predictive analysis and big data, augmented reality, and cloud computing. He likes to play and is a huge martial arts fan and also one of the worst soccer players ever. He is married and a parent of two young and lovely daughters, who would like to spend more time playing like crazies with him. He also likes to spend time with friends or just having a drink and a good talk with someone else, if possible with his family at his side. He really hates liars.

www.PacktPub.com

For support files and downloads related to your book, please visit `www.PacktPub.com`.

Did you know that Packt offers eBook versions of every book published, with PDF and ePub files available? You can upgrade to the eBook version at `www.PacktPub.com` and as a print book customer, you are entitled to a discount on the eBook copy. Get in touch with us at `service@packtpub.com` for more details.

At `www.PacktPub.com`, you can also read a collection of free technical articles, sign up for a range of free newsletters and receive exclusive discounts and offers on Packt books and eBooks.

`https://www.packtpub.com/mapt`

Get the most in-demand software skills with Mapt. Mapt gives you full access to all Packt books and video courses, as well as industry-leading tools to help you plan your personal development and advance your career.

Why subscribe?

- Fully searchable across every book published by Packt
- Copy and paste, print, and bookmark content
- On demand and accessible via a web browser

Customer Feedback

Thanks for purchasing this Packt book. At Packt, quality is at the heart of our editorial process. To help us improve, please leave us an honest review on this book's Amazon page at `https://www.amazon.com/dp/178829243X`. If you'd like to join our team of regular reviewers, you can email us at `customerreviews@packtpub.com`. We award our regular reviewers with free eBooks and videos in exchange for their valuable feedback. Help us be relentless in improving our products!

Table of Contents

Preface

Pentaho Data Integration (also known as Kettle) is an engine, along with a suite of tools, responsible for the processes of **Extracting**, **Transforming**, and **Loading**, better known as the **ETL** processes. **Pentaho Data Integration** (**PDI**) not only serves as an ETL tool, but it's also used for other purposes, such as migrating data between applications or databases, exporting data from databases to flat files, data cleansing, and much more. PDI has an intuitive, graphical, drag and drop design environment, and its ETL capabilities are powerful. However, getting started with PDI can be difficult and confusing. This book provides the guidance needed to overcome that difficulty, by covering the key features of PDI. Learning Pentaho Data Integration 8 CE explains the new interactive features of the graphical designer—Spoon, and its revamped look and feel. It also covers the newest features of the tool including Transformations and Jobs executors and the invaluable metadata injection capability.

The content of the book is based on PDI 8 **Community Edition** (**CE**). However, it can be used with the **Enterprise Edition** (**EE**) as well. Besides, if you are currently working with an earlier version of the tool, you should know that most of the content is also valid for PDI 6 and PDI 7.

By the end of the book, not only will you have experimented with all kinds of examples, but will also have gained the knowledge about developing useful, portable, reusable, and well-designed processes.

What this book covers

`Chapter 1`, *Getting Started with Pentaho Data Integration*, serves as an introduction to PDI, presenting the tool. This chapter includes instructions for installing PDI and gives you the opportunity to play with the graphical designer (Spoon).

`Chapter 2`, *Getting Started with Transformations*, explains the fundamentals of working with transformations, including learning the simplest ways of transforming data and getting familiar with the process of designing, debugging, and testing a Transformation. This chapter also explains the basics of handling errors.

`Chapter 3`, *Creating Basic Task Flows*, serves as an introduction to the processes in PDI. Through the creation of simple Jobs, you will learn what Jobs are and what they are used for.

`Chapter 4`, *Reading and Writing Files*, explains how to get data from several files formats as spreadsheets, CSV files, and more. It also explains how to save data in the same kind of formats.

`Chapter 5`, *Manipulating PDI Data and Metadata*, expands the set of operations learned in the previous chapters. Besides exploring new PDI steps for data manipulation, this chapter introduces the **Select Value** step for manipulating metadata. It also explains how to get system information and predefined variables for being used as part of the data flow. The chapter also explains how to read and write XML and JSON structures.

`Chapter 6`, *Controlling the Flow of Data*, explains different options that PDI offers to deal with more than one stream of data: It explains how to combine and split flows of data, filter data and more.

`Chapter 7`, *Cleansing, Validating, and Fixing Data*, offers different ways for cleansing data, and also for dealing with invalid data, either by discarding it or by fixing it.

`Chapter 8`, *Manipulating Data by Coding*, explains how JavaScript and Java coding can help in the treatment of data. It shows why you may need to code inside PDI, and explains in detail how to do it.

`Chapter 9`, *Transforming the Dataset*, explains techniques for transforming the dataset as a whole; for example, aggregating data or normalizing pivoted tables.

`Chapter 10`, *Performing Basic Operations with Databases*, explains how to use PDI to work with databases. The list of topics in this chapter includes connecting to a database, previewing and getting data. It also covers other basic operations as inserting, looking up for data, and more.

`Chapter 11`, *Loading Data Marts with PDI*, explains the details about loading simple data marts. It shows how to load common types of dimensions (SCD, Junk, Time, and so on) and also different types of fact tables.

`Chapter 12`, *Creating Portable and Reusable Transformations*, explains several techniques for creating versatile transformations that can be used and reused in different scenarios or with different sets of data.

`Chapter 13`, *Implementing Metadata Injection*, explains a powerful feature of PDI, which is basically about injecting metadata into a template Transformation at runtime. Pentaho team has put in huge effort to highly support this feature in the latest PDI versions, so it's worth to explain in detail how this feature works.

`Chapter 14`, *Creating Advanced Jobs*, explains techniques for creating complex processes; for example, iterating over Jobs or manipulating lists of files for different purposes.

`Chapter 15`, *Launching Transformations and Jobs from the Command Line*, is a reference not only for running transformations from a Terminal, but also for dealing with the output of the executions.

`Chapter 16`, *Best Practices for Designing and Deploying a PDI Project*, covers the setup of a new project and also the best practices that make it easier to develop, maintain, and deploy a project in different environments.

What you need for this book

PDI is a multiplatform tool. This means that no matter which operating system you have, you will be able to work with the tool. The only prerequisite is to have JVM 1.8 installed. You will also need an Office suite, for example, Open Office or Libre Office, and a good text editor, for example, Sublime III or Notepad ++. Access to a relational database is recommended. Suggested engines are MySQL and PostgreSQL, but could be others of your choice as well.

Having an internet connection while reading is extremely useful too. Several links are provided throughout the book that complements what is explained. Besides, there is the PDI forum where you may search or post doubts if you are stuck with something.

Who this book is for

This book is a must-have for software developers, business intelligence analysts, IT students, and everyone involved or interested in developing ETL solutions, or more generally, doing any kind of data manipulation. Those who have never used PDI will benefit the most from the book, but those who have will also find it useful. This book is also a good starting point for data warehouse designers, architects, or anyone who is responsible for data warehouse projects and needs to load data into them.

Conventions

In this book, you will find a number of text styles that distinguish between different kinds of information. Here are some examples of these styles and an explanation of their meanings.

Code words in text, database table names, folder names, filenames, file extensions, pathnames, dummy URLs, user input, and Twitter handles are shown as follows: Unzip the downloaded file in a folder of your choice, as, for example, `c:/util/kettle` or `/home/pdi_user/kettle`.

A block of code is set as follows:

```
project_name,start_date,end_date
Project A,2016-01-10,2016-01-25
Project B,2016-04-03,2016-07-21
Project C,2017-01-15,???
Project D,2015-09-03,2015-12-20
Project E,2016-05-11,2016-05-31
Project F,2011-12-01,2013-11-30
```

Any command-line input or output is written as follows:

```
kitchen /file:c:/pdi_labs/hello_world.kjb
```

New terms and **important words** are shown in bold. Words that you see on the screen, for example, in menus or dialog boxes, appear in the text like this: Open Spoon from the main menu and navigate to **File** | **New** | **Transformation**.

Warnings or important notes appear like this.

Tips and tricks appear like this.

Reader feedback

Feedback from our readers is always welcome. Let us know what you think about this book-what you liked or disliked. Reader feedback is important for us as it helps us develop titles that you will really get the most out of. To send us general feedback, simply email `feedback@packtpub.com` and mention the book's title in the subject of your message. If there is a topic that you have expertise in and you are interested in either writing or contributing to a book, see our author guide at `www.packtpub.com/authors`.

Customer support

Now that you are the proud owner of a Packt book, we have a number of things to help you get the most from your purchase.

Downloading the example code

You can download the example code files for this book from your account at http://www.packtpub.com. If you purchased this book elsewhere, you can visit http://www.packtpub.com/support and register to have the files emailed directly to you. You can download the code files by following these steps:

1. Log in or register to our website using your email address and password.
2. Hover the mouse pointer on the **SUPPORT** tab at the top.
3. Click on **Code Downloads & Errata**.
4. Enter the name of the book in the **Search** box.
5. Select the book for which you're looking to download the code files.
6. Choose from the drop-down menu where you purchased this book from.
7. Click on **Code Download**.

Once the file is downloaded, make sure that you unzip or extract the folder using the latest version of:

- WinRAR / 7-Zip for Windows
- Zipeg / iZip / UnRarX for Mac
- 7-Zip / PeaZip for Linux

The code bundle for the book is also hosted on GitHub at https://github.com/PacktPublishing/Learning-Pentaho-Data-Integration-8-CE. We also have other code bundles from our rich catalog of books and videos available at https://github.com/PacktPublishing/. Check them out!

Downloading the color images of this book

We also provide you with a PDF file that has color images of the screenshots/diagrams used in this book. The color images will help you better understand the changes in the output. You can download this file from https://www.packtpub.com/sites/default/files/downloads/LearningPentahoDataIntegration8CE_ColorImages.pdf.

Errata

Although we have taken every care to ensure the accuracy of our content, mistakes do happen. If you find a mistake in one of our books-maybe a mistake in the text or the code-we would be grateful if you could report this to us. By doing so, you can save other readers from frustration and help us improve subsequent versions of this book. If you find any errata, report them by visiting `http://www.packtpub.com/submit-errata`, selecting your book, clicking on the **Errata Submission Form** link, and entering the details of your errata. Once your errata are verified, your submission will be accepted and the errata will be uploaded to our website or added to any list of existing errata under the Errata section of that title. To view the previously submitted errata, go to `https://www.packtpub.com/books/content/support` and enter the name of the book in the search field. The required information will appear under the **Errata** section.

Piracy

Piracy of copyrighted material on the internet is an ongoing problem across all media. At Packt, we take the protection of our copyright and licenses very seriously. If you come across any illegal copies of our works in any form on the internet, do provide us with the location address or the website name immediately, so that we can pursue a remedy. Contact us at `copyright@packtpub.com` with a link to the suspected pirated material. We appreciate your help in protecting our authors and our ability to bring you valuable content.

Questions

If you have a problem with any aspect of this book, you can contact us at `questions@packtpub.com`, and we will do our best to address the problem.

1
Getting Started with Pentaho Data Integration

Pentaho Data Integration (**PDI**) is an engine along with a suite of tools responsible for the processes of **Extracting**, **Transforming**, and **Loading** (also known as **ETL** processes). This book is meant to teach you how to use PDI.

In this chapter, you will:

- Learn what Pentaho Data Integration is
- Install the software and start working with the PDI graphical designer (Spoon)
- Explore the Spoon interface
- Set up your environment by installing other useful related software

Pentaho Data Integration and Pentaho BI Suite

Before introducing PDI, let's talk about Pentaho BI Suite. The **Pentaho Business Intelligence Suite** is a collection of software applications intended to create and deliver solutions for decision making. The main functional areas covered by the suite are:

- **Analysis**: The analysis engine serves multidimensional analysis. It's provided by the **Mondrian OLAP** server.

- **Reporting**: The reporting engine allows designing, creating, and distributing reports in various known formats (HTML, PDF, and so on), from different kinds of sources. In the Enterprise Edition of Pentaho, you can also generate interactive reports.
- **Data mining**: Data mining is used for running data through algorithms in order to understand the business and do predictive analysis. Data mining is possible thanks to **Weka project**.
- **Dashboards**: Dashboards are used to monitor and analyze **Key Performance Indicators** (**KPIs**). **CTools** is a set of tools and components created to help the user to build custom dashboards on top of Pentaho. There are specific CTools for different purposes, including a **Community Dashboard Editor** (**CDE**), a very powerful charting library (CCC), and a plugin for accessing data with great flexibility (CDA), among others. While the Ctools allow to develop advanced and custom dashboards, there is a **Dashboard Designer**, available only in Pentaho Enterprise Edition, that allows to build dashboards in an easy way.
- **Data integration**: Data integration is used to integrate scattered information from different sources (for example, applications, databases, and files) and make the integrated information available to the final user. PDI—the tool that we will learn to use throughout the book—is the engine that provides this functionality. PDI also interacts with the rest of the tools, as, for example, reading OLAP cubes, generating Pentaho Reports, and doing data mining with R Executor Script and the CPython Script Executor.

All of these tools can be used standalone but also integrated. Pentaho tightly couples data integration with analytics in a modern platform: the PDI and Business Analytics Platform. This solution offers critical services, for example:

- Authentication and authorization
- Scheduling
- Security
- Web services
- Scalability and failover

This set of software and services forms a complete BI Suite, which makes Pentaho the world's leading open source BI option on the market.

You can find out more about the of the platform at `https://community.hds.com/community/products-and-solutions/pentaho/`. There is also an Enterprise Edition with additional features and support. You can find more on this at `http://www.pentaho.com/`.

Introducing Pentaho Data Integration

Most of the Pentaho engines, including the engines mentioned earlier, were created as community projects and later adopted by Pentaho. The PDI engine is not an exception; Pentaho Data Integration is the new denomination for the business intelligence tool born as **Kettle**.

The name Kettle didn't come from the recursive acronym Kettle Extraction, Transportation, Transformation, and Loading Environment it has now. It came from KDE Extraction, Transportation, Transformation and Loading Environment, since the tool was planned to be written on top of KDE, a Linux desktop environment.

In April 2006, the Kettle project was acquired by the Pentaho Corporation, and Matt Casters, the Kettle founder, also joined the Pentaho team as a data integration architect.

When Pentaho announced the acquisition, James Dixon, the Chief Technology Officer, said:

> *We reviewed many alternatives for open source data integration, and Kettle clearly had the best architecture, richest functionality, and most mature user interface. The open architecture and superior technology of the Pentaho BI Platform and Kettle allowed us to deliver integration in only a few days, and make that integration available to the community.*

By joining forces with Pentaho, Kettle benefited from a huge developer community, as well as from a company that would support the future of the project.

From that moment, the tool has grown with no pause. Every few months a new release is available, bringing to the user's improvements in performance and existing functionality, new functionality, and ease of use, along with great changes in look and feel. The following is a timeline of the major events related to PDI since its acquisition by Pentaho:

- **June 2006**: PDI 2.3 was released. Numerous developers had joined the project and there were bug fixes provided by people in various regions of the world. The version included, among other changes, enhancements for large-scale environments and multilingual capabilities.

- **November 2007**: PDI 3.0 emerged totally redesigned. Its major library changed to gain massive performance improvements. The look and feel had also changed completely.
- **April 2009**: PDI 3.2 was released with a really large amount of changes for a minor version: new functionality, visualization and performance improvements, and a huge amount of bug fixes.
- **June 2010**: PDI 4.0 was released, delivering mostly improvements with regard to enterprise features, for example, version control. In the community version, the focus was on several visual improvements.
- **November 2013**: PDI 5.0 was released, offering better previewing of data, easier looping, a lot of big data improvements, an improved plugin marketplace, and hundreds of bug fixes and features enhancements, as in all releases. In its Enterprise version, it offered interesting low-level features, such as step load balancing, Job transactions, and restartability.
- **December 2015**: PDI 6.0 was released with new features such as data services, data lineage, bigger support for *Big Data*, and several changes in the graphical designer for improving the PDI user experience. Some months later, PDI 6.1 was released including **metadata injection**, a feature that enables the user to modify Transformations at runtime. Metadata injection had been available in earlier versions, but it was in 6.1 that Pentaho started to put in a big effort in implementing this powerful feature.
- **November 2016**: PDI 7.0 emerged with many improvements in the enterprise version, including data inspection capabilities, more support for *Big Data* technologies, and improved repository management. In the community version, the main change was an expanded metadata injection support.
- **November 2017**: Pentaho 8.0 is released. The highlights of this latest version are the optimization of processing resources, a better user experience, and the enhancement of the connectivity to streaming data sources—real-time processing.

Using PDI in real-world scenarios

Paying attention to its name, Pentaho Data Integration, you could think of PDI as a tool to integrate data.

In fact, PDI does not only serve as a data integrator or an ETL tool. PDI is such a powerful tool that it is common to see it being used for these and for many other purposes. Here you have some examples.

Loading data warehouses or data marts

The loading of a data warehouse or a data mart involves many steps, and there are many variants depending on business area or business rules.

However, in every case, with no exception, the process involves the following steps:

1. Extracting information from one or more databases, text files, XML files, and other sources. The extract process may include the task of validating and discarding data that doesn't match expected patterns or rules.
2. Transforming the obtained data to meet the business and technical needs required on the target. Transforming includes such tasks such as converting data types, doing some calculations, filtering irrelevant data, and summarizing.
3. Loading the transformed data into the target database or file store. Depending on the requirements, the loading may overwrite the existing information or may add new information each time it is executed.

Kettle comes ready to do every stage of this loading process. The following screenshot shows a simple ETL designed with the tool:

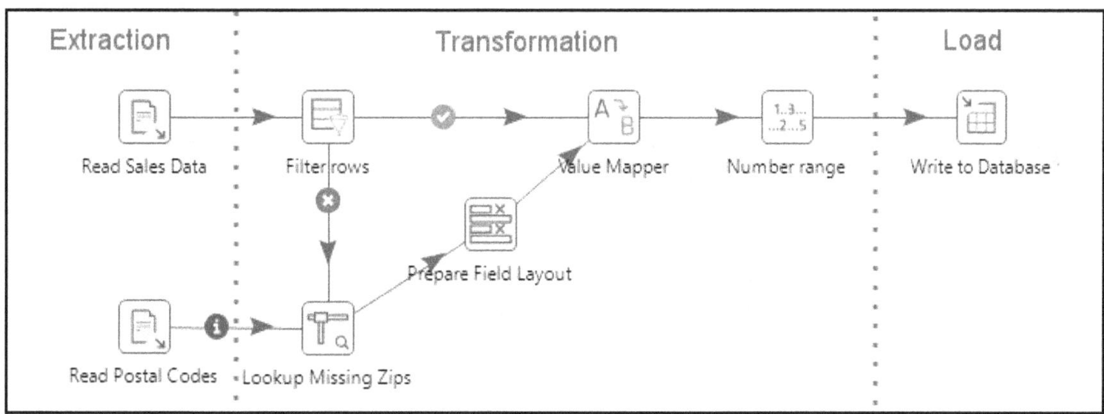

ETL process

Integrating data

Imagine two similar companies that need to merge their databases in order to have a unified view of the data, or a single company that has to combine information from a main **Enterprise Resource Planning** (**ERP**) application and a **Customer Relationship Management** (**CRM**) application, though they're not connected. These are just two of hundreds of examples where data integration is needed. The integration is not just a matter of gathering and mixing data; some conversions, validation, and transfer of data have to be done. PDI is meant to do all these tasks.

Data cleansing

Data cleansing is about ensuring that the data is correct and precise. This can be achieved by verifying if the data meets certain rules, discarding or correcting those which don't follow the expected pattern, setting default values for missing data, eliminating information that is duplicated, normalizing data to conform to minimum and maximum values, and so on. These are tasks that Kettle makes possible, thanks to its vast set of transformation and validation capabilities.

Migrating information

Think of a company, any size, which uses a commercial ERP application. One day the owners realize that the licenses are consuming an important share of its budget. So they decide to migrate to an open source ERP. The company will no longer have to pay licenses, but if they want to change, they will have to migrate the information. Obviously, it is not an option to start from scratch or type the information by hand. Kettle makes the migration possible, thanks to its ability to interact with most kind of sources and destinations, such as plain files, commercial and free databases, and spreadsheets, among others.

Exporting data

Data may need to be exported for numerous reasons:

- To create detailed business reports
- To allow communication between different departments within the same company
- To deliver data from your legacy systems to obey government regulations, and so on

Kettle has the power to take raw data from the source and generate these kinds of ad hoc reports.

Integrating PDI along with other Pentaho tools

The previous examples show typical uses of PDI as a standalone application. However, Kettle may be used embedded as part of a process or a data flow. Some examples are preprocessing data for an online report, sending emails in a scheduled fashion, generating spreadsheet reports, feeding a dashboard with data coming from web services, and so on.

The use of PDI integrated with other tools is beyond the scope of this book. If you are interested, you can find more information on this subject in the *Pentaho Data Integration Cookbook - Second Edition* by Packt Publishing at `https://www.packtpub.com/big-data-and-business-intelligence/pentaho-data-integration-cookbook-second-edition`.

Installing PDI

In order to work with PDI, you need to install the software.

The only prerequisite to install the tool is to have JRE 8.0 installed. If you don't have it, download it from `www.javasoft.com` and install it before proceeding.

Following are the instructions to install the PDI software, irrespective of the operating system you may be using:

1. Go to the **Download** page at `http://sourceforge.net/projects/pentaho/files/Data Integration`.

2. Choose the newest stable release. At this time, it is 8.0, as shown in the following screenshot:

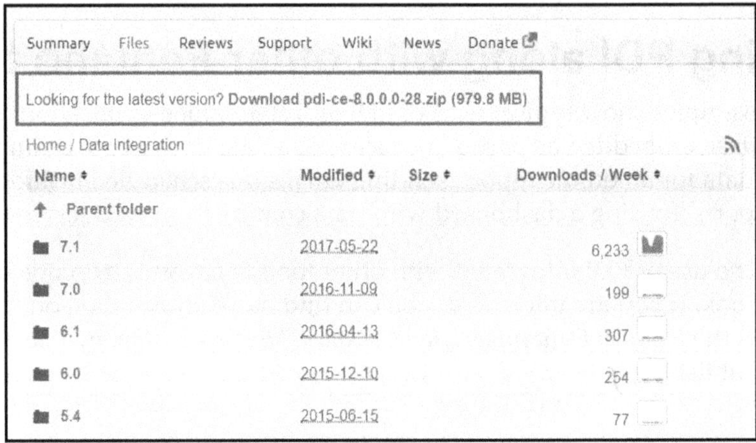

PDI on SourceForge.net

3. Download the available `zip` file, which will serve you for all platforms.

4. Unzip the downloaded file in a folder of your choice, as, for example, `c:/util/kettle` or `/home/pdi_user/kettle`.

And that's all. You have installed the tool in just a few minutes.

The version of PDI that you just installed corresponds to the **Community Edition** (**CE**) of the tool. The book, however, can be also used for learning to use the **Enterprise Edition** (**EE**). Excepting for minor differences if you work with repositories, most of the examples in the book should work without changes. Also, if for any reason you have to use a previous version of PDI, the good news are that most of the content explained here also applies to PDI 6 and PDI 7.

Launching the PDI Graphical Designer - Spoon

Now that you've installed PDI, you're ready to start working with the data. That will be possible only inside a graphical environment. PDI has a desktop designer tool named **Spoon**. Let's launch Spoon and see what it looks like.

Starting and customizing Spoon

Spoon is PDI's desktop design tool. With Spoon, you design, preview, and test all your work, that is, transformations and jobs. When you see PDI screenshots, what you are really seeing are Spoon screenshots. The other PDI components, which you will learn about in the following chapters, are executed from Terminal windows.

Here is how you launch the tool:

1. Start Spoon. If your system is Windows, run `Spoon.bat` from within the PDI install directory. In other platforms, such as Unix, Linux, and so on, open a Terminal window and type `spoon.sh`.
2. The main window shows up. The **Welcome!** window appears with some useful links for you to see:

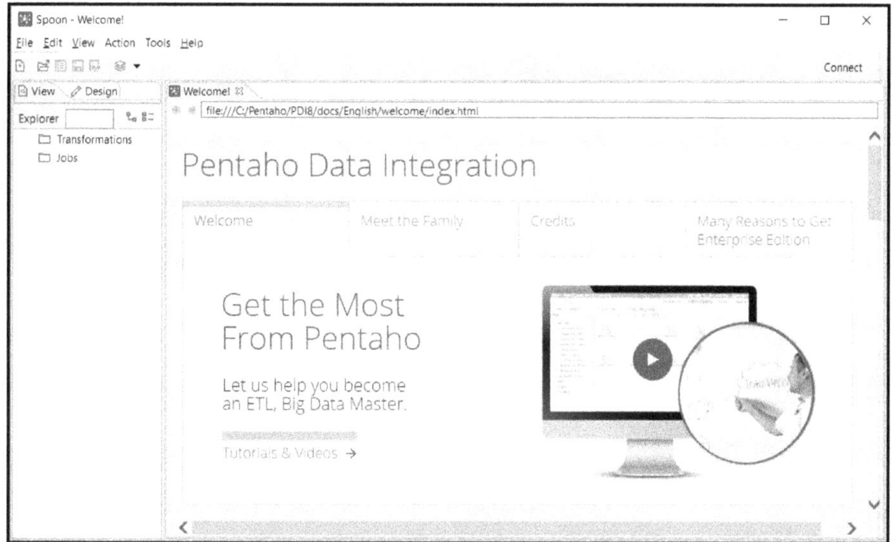

Welcome page

If Spoon doesn't start as expected, launch `SpoonDebug.bat` (or `.sh`) instead. This utility starts Spoon with a console output and gives you the option to redirect the output to a file. By inspecting this output, you will be able to find out what happened and fix the issue.

These simple steps would be enough to start working, but before that, it's advisable to customize Spoon to your needs. For doing that:

1. Click on **Options...** from the **Tools** menu. A window appears where you can change various general and visual characteristics. Uncheck the highlighted checkbox, as shown in the following screenshot:

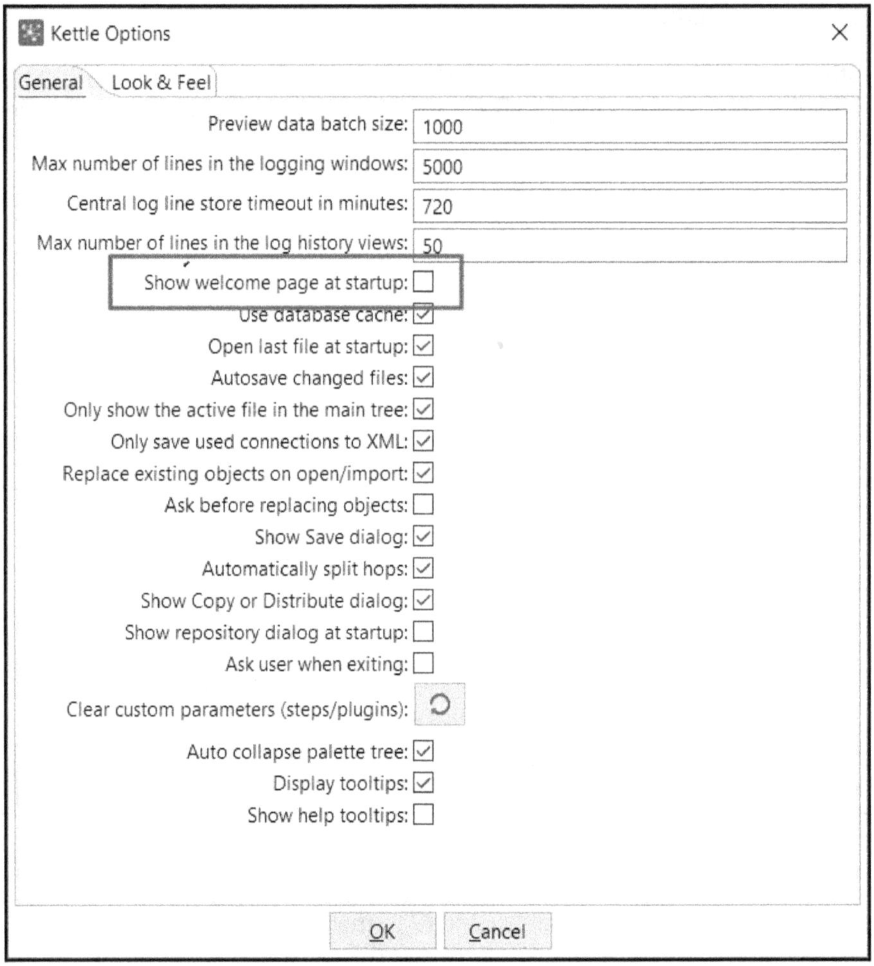

Kettle options

2. Select the tab window **Look & Feel**.

3. Change the **Font for notes, Show Canvas Grid**, and **Preferred Language** settings as shown in the following screenshot:

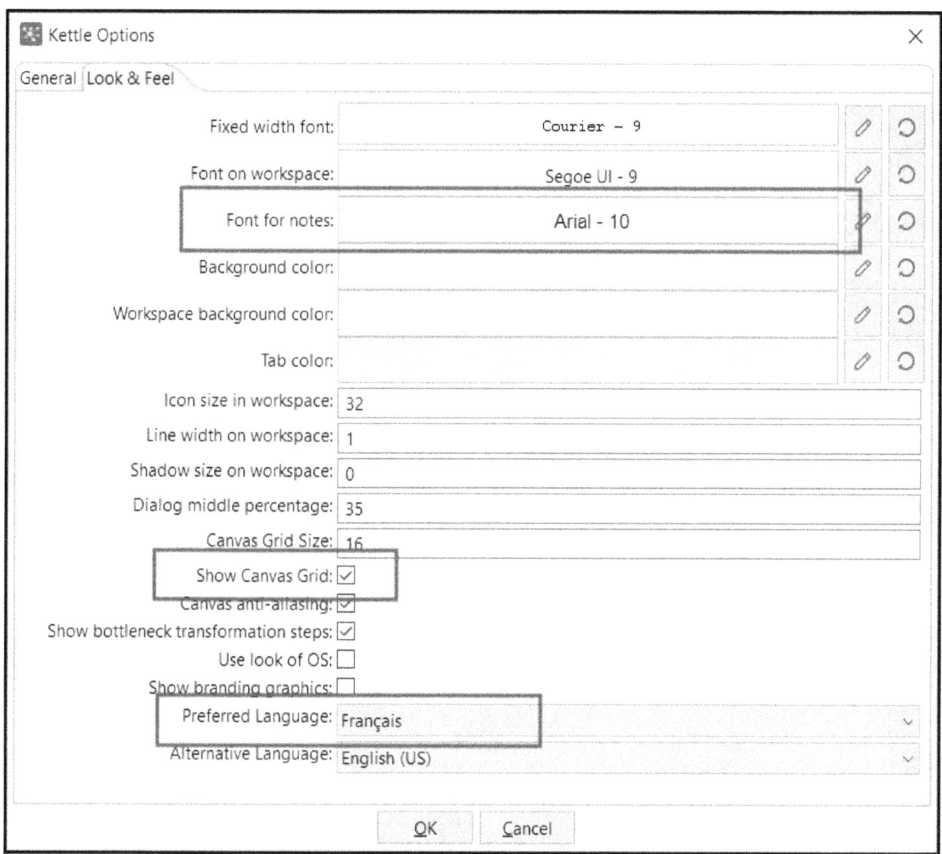

Look and Feel options

4. Click on the **OK** button.

5. Restart Spoon in order to apply the changes. You should not see the **Welcome!** window. You should see the following screenshot full of French words instead:

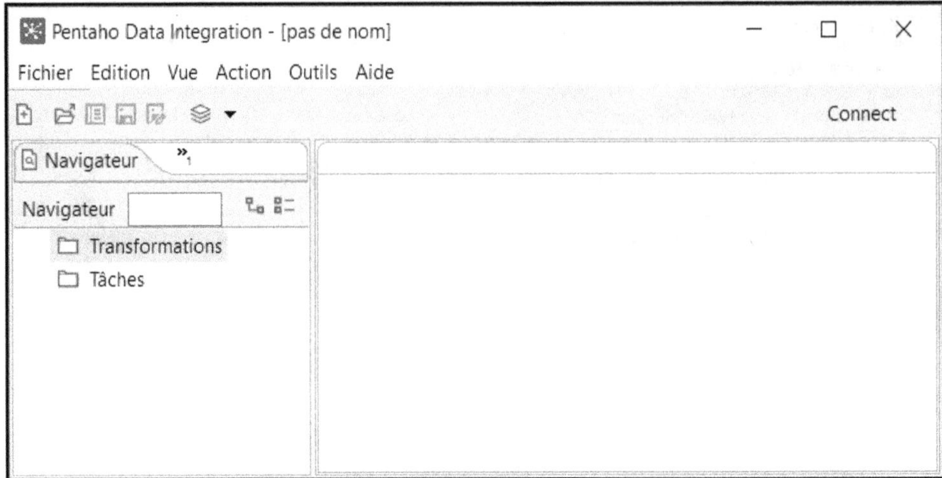

French as preferred language

As you can see, the **Options** window has a lot of settings. We changed only a few, just to show the feature. Feel free to change the settings according to your needs or preferences.

Remember to restart Spoon in order to see the changes applied.

In particular, take note of the following tip about the selected language.

If you choose a preferred language other than English, you should select a different language as an alternative. If you do so, every name or description not translated to your preferred language will be shown in the alternative language.

One of the settings that you changed was the appearance of the **Welcome!** window at startup. The **Welcome!** page is full of links to web resources, blogs, forums, books on PDI, and more. Following those links, you will be able to learn more and become active in the Pentaho community. You can reach that window anytime by navigating to the **Help** | **Welcome Screen** option.

The **Welcome!** page redirects you to the forum at `https://forums.pentaho.com/forumdisplay.php?135-Data-Integration-Kettle`. Since November 2017 there is a new collaboration space. You can reach the PDI space at `https://community.hds.com/community/products-and-solutions/pentaho/data-integration`.

Exploring the Spoon interface

As explained earlier, Spoon is the tool with which you create, preview, and run transformations. The following screenshot shows you the basic work areas: **Main Menu**, **Main Toolbar**, **Steps Tree**, **Transformation Toolbar**, and **Canvas** (**Work Area**). Note that there is a sample Transformation opened; it allows you to see how the tool looks when you are working with it:

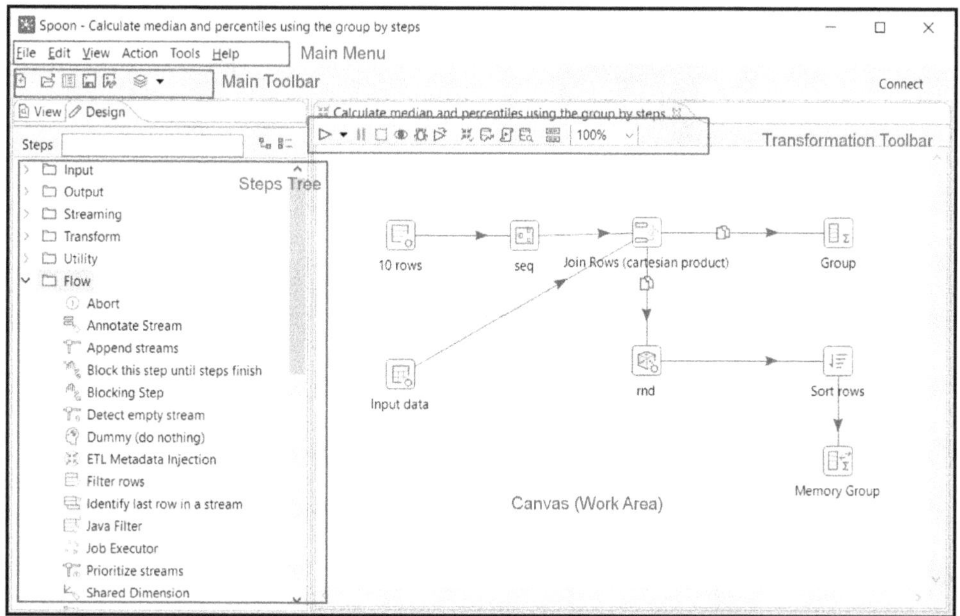

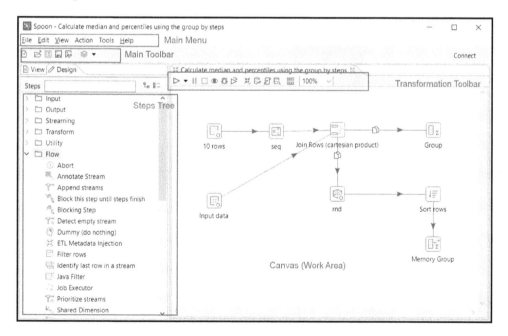

Spoon interface

The terms *Canvas* and *work area* will be used interchangeably throughout the book.

The Steps Tree option is only available in **Design** view. There is also an area named **View** that shows the structure of the Transformation currently being edited. You can see that area by clicking on the **View** tab at the upper-left corner of the screen:

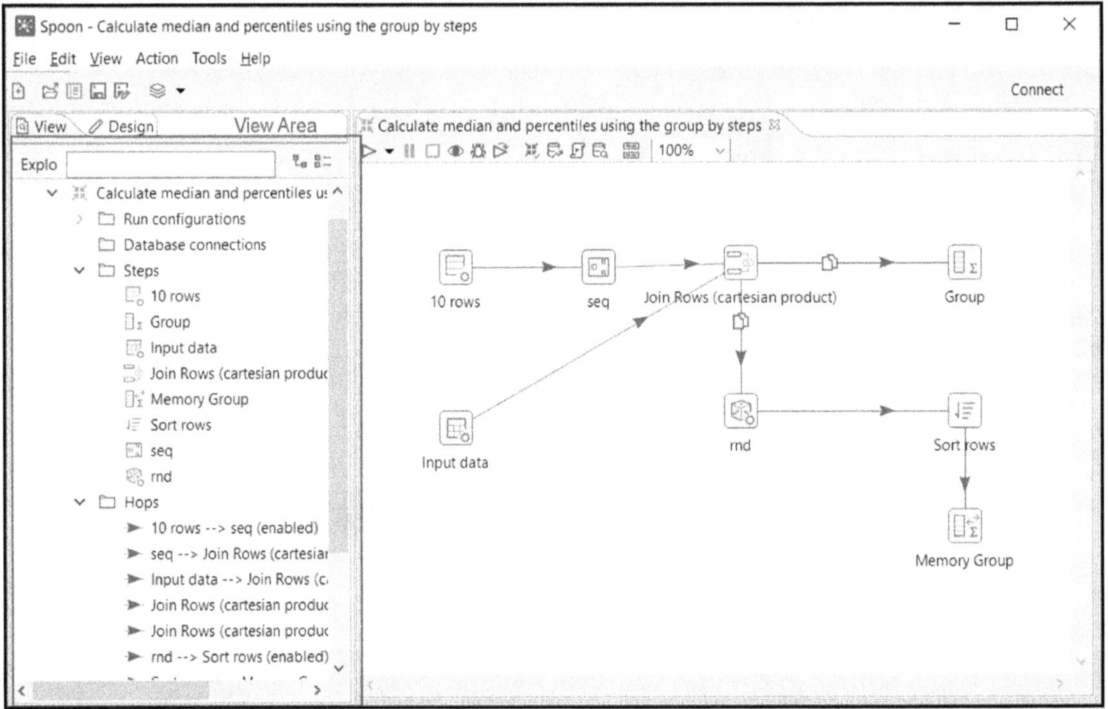

Spoon view area

Extending the PDI functionality through the Marketplace

Pentaho Data Integration is built on a pluggable architecture. This means that it can be extended to fulfill needs not included out of the box. The **Marketplace**—a plugin itself—emerged as a straightforward way for browsing and installing available plugins, developed by the community or even by Pentaho.

In PDI, you will find plugins for connecting to a particular database engine, for executing scripts, for transforming data in new ways, and more. According to the purpose, the plugins are classified into several types: big data, connectivity, and statistics, among others. In particular, there is a type named **Experimental**, which you will not use except for playing around. There is another type named **Deprecated**, which we don't recommend you use unless you need it for back compatibility.

An important point to highlight about plugins is the **maturity** stage. The maturity classification model consists of two parallel lanes:

- **Community Lane**: For Community and customer-sponsored projects.
- **Customer Lane**: For projects which are part of the official Pentaho offering. Projects in the *Customer Lane* can start as projects developed in the Community Lane that create value for Pentaho subscription customers.

There are four stages in each lane. To put it simply, stage 1 means that the plugin is under development (it is usually a lab experiment), while stage 4 indicates a mature state; a plugin in stage 4 is successfully adopted and could be used in production environments. Stages 2 and 3 are stages in between these two.

For a full explanation of the model and the maturity stages, you can refer to `https://community.hds.com/docs/DOC-1009876`.

That said, let's go back to Spoon. You can access the Marketplace page by clicking on **Marketplace** from the **Tools** menu. The page is quite simple, as shown in the following screenshot:

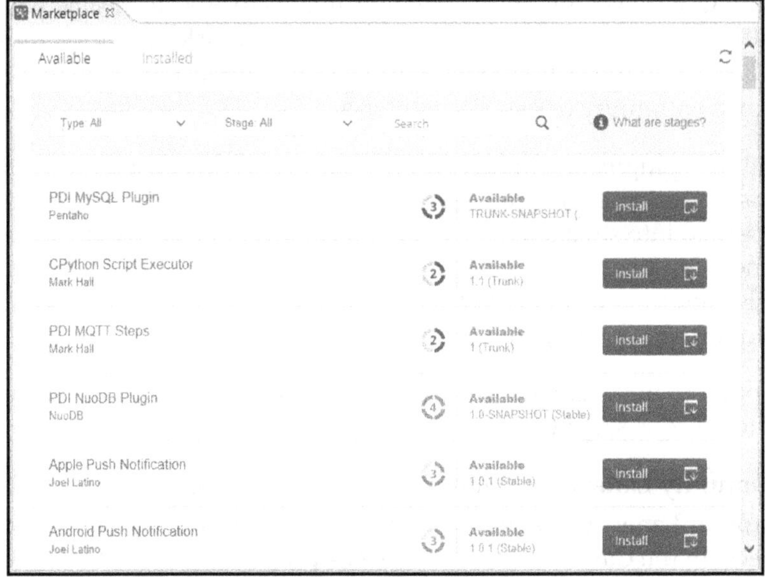

Marketplace

By default, you see the list of all the **Available/Installed** plugins. There is a secondary tab where you can filter just the installed ones.

Also, you can filter by plugin **Type** and by maturity **Stage**. And if you are looking for a particular plugin, there is also a **Search** textbox available.

Once in the Marketplace page, for every plugin you can see:

- The name
- The author
- The maturity stage
- The status: **Available** or **Installed**
- The branch and version
- A button for installing the plugin or a check telling that the plugin is already installed

If you click on the plugin name, a pop-up window shows up displaying the full description for the selected plugin, as shown in the following example:

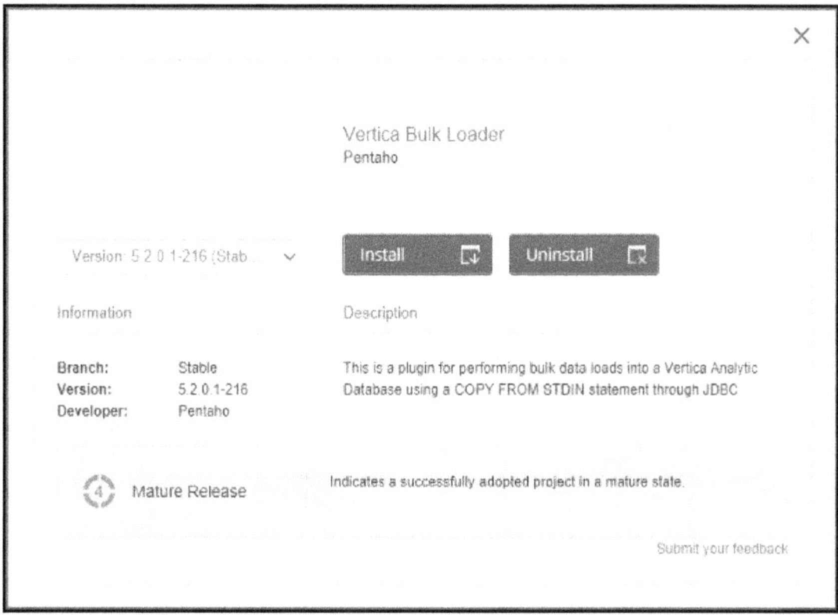

Sample plugin in Marketplace

Besides browsing the list of plugins, you can install or uninstall them:

- In order to install a plugin, there is an **Install** button in the plugin list and also in the pop-up window
- If the plugin is already installed, the pop-up window will also offer the option for uninstalling it, as in the previous example

Note that some plugins are only available in Pentaho Enterprise Edition. For a particular plugin, you can find this information as part of its full description.

It's premature to decide if you need to install a plugin for your work. So let's put this subject aside for a while; we will get back to this feature later in the book.

Introducing transformations

Till now, you've just opened and customized the look and feel of Spoon. It's time to do some interesting tasks beyond looking around. As mentioned before, in PDI we basically work with two kinds of artifacts: transformations and jobs. In this section, we will introduce transformations. First of all, we will introduce some basic definitions. Then, we will design, preview, and run our first Transformation.

The basics about transformations

A Transformation is an entity made of steps linked by hops. These steps and hops build paths through which data flows: the data enters or is created in a step, the step applies some kind of Transformation to it, and finally, the data leaves that step. Therefore, it's said that a Transformation is **data flow oriented**. Graphically, steps are represented with small boxes, while hops are represented by directional arrows, as depicted in the following sample:

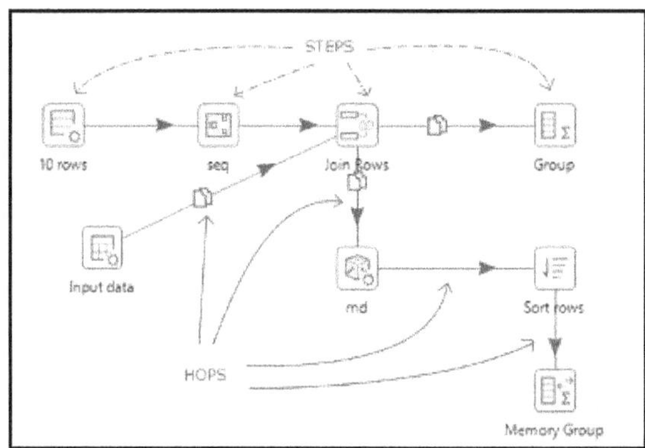

Steps and hops

A Transformation itself is neither a program nor an executable file. It is just plain XML. The Transformation contains metadata, which tells the Kettle engine what to do.

A **step** is a minimal unit inside a Transformation. A big set of steps is available, either out of the box or the Marketplace, as explained before. These steps are grouped in categories, as, for example, input, output, or transform. Each step is conceived to accomplish a specific function, going from a simple task as reading a parameter to normalizing a dataset.

A **hop** is a graphical representation of data flowing between two steps: an origin and a destination. The data that flows through that hop constitutes the output data of the origin step and the input data of the destination step.

That's enough theory for now. Let's see it in practice.

Creating a Hello World! Transformation

In this section, we will design, preview, and run a simple Hello World! Transformation; simple, but good enough for our first practical example.

Designing a Transformation

Here are the steps to start working on our very first Transformation. All you need for starting is to have PDI installed:

1. Open Spoon.From the main menu and navigate to **File** | **New** | **Transformation**.
2. On the left of the screen, under the **Design** tab, you'll see a tree of **Steps**. Expand the **Input** branch by double-clicking on it.

Note that if you work in Mac OS, a single click is enough.

3. Then, left-click on the **Data Grid** icon and without releasing the button, drag and drop the selected icon to the main canvas. The screen will look like the following screenshot:

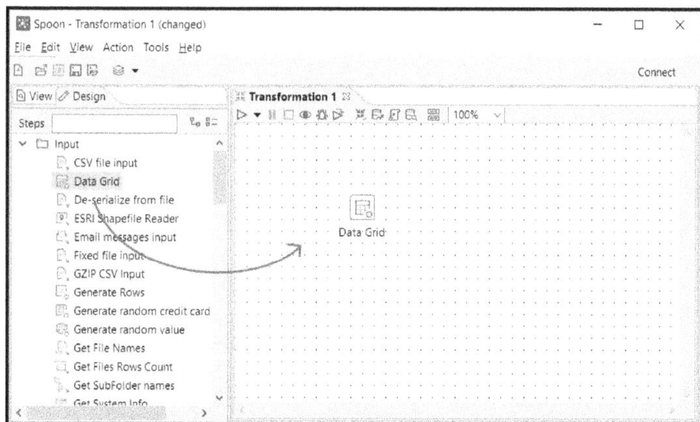

Dragging and dropping a step

The dotted grid appeared as a consequence of the changes we made in the options window. Also, note that we changed the preferred language back to English.

4. Double-click on the **Data Grid** step you just put on the canvas, and fill the **Meta** tab as follows:

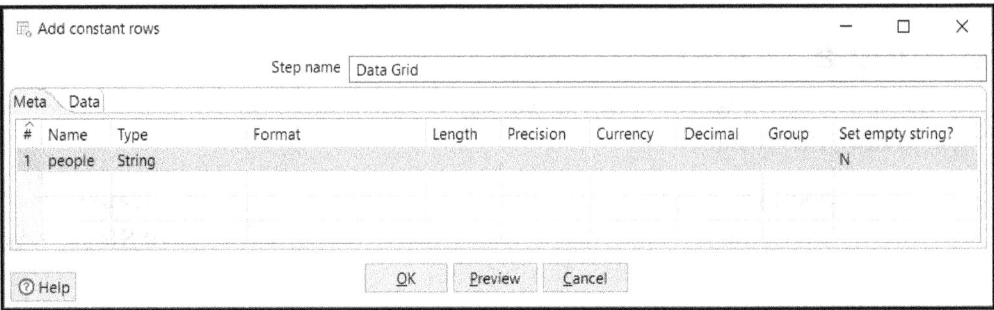

Configuring a metadata tab

5. Now select the **Data** tab and fill the grid with some names, as in the following screenshot. Then click on **OK** to close the window:

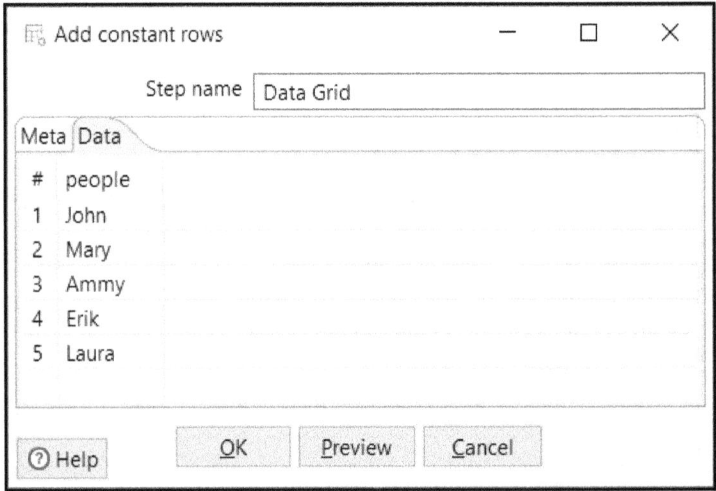

Filling a Data tab

6. From the Steps tree, double-click on the **Scripting** branch, click on the **User Defined Java Expression** icon, and drag and drop it to the main canvas.
7. Put the mouse cursor over the **Data Grid** step and wait until a tiny toolbar shows up succeeding the **Data Grid** icon, as shown next:

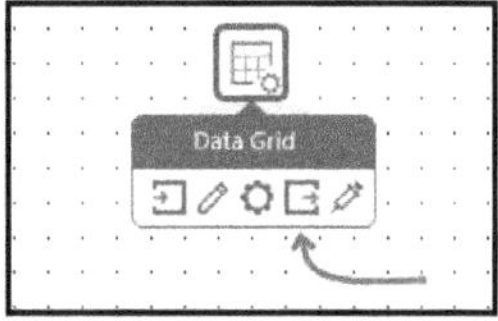

Mouseover assistance toolbar

8. Click on the output connector (the icon highlighted in the preceding image) and drag it towards the **User Defined Java Expression** (**UDJE**) step. A greyed hop is displayed.

9. When the mouse cursor is over the **UDJE** step, release the button. A link—a hop from now on is created from the **Data Grid** step to the **UDJE** step. The screen should look like this:

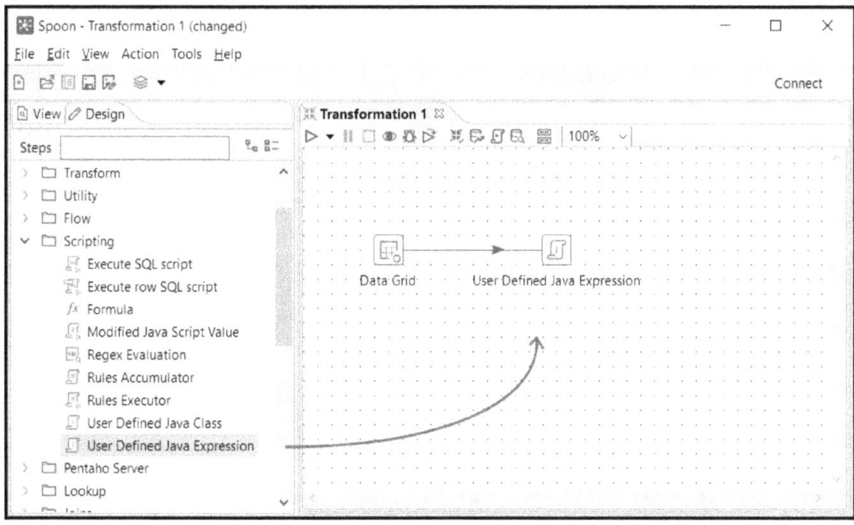

Connecting steps with a hop

10. Double-click the **UDJE** icon and fill the grid as shown. Then close the window:

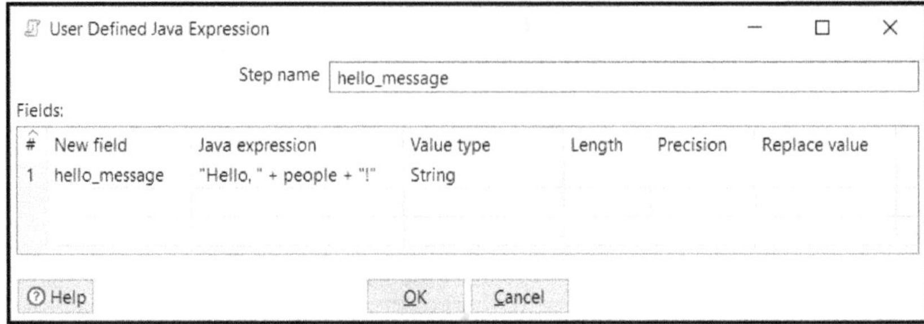

Configuring a UDJE step

Done! We have a draft for our first Transformation. A **Data Grid** with the names of a list of people, and a script step that builds the `hello_message`.

Before continuing, let's just add some color note to our work. This is totally optional, but as your work gets more complicated, it's highly recommended that you comment your transformations:

1. Right-click anywhere on the canvas to bring a contextual menu.
2. In the menu, select the **New note** option. A note editor appears.
3. Type some description, such as `Hello, World!`. Select the **Font style** tab and choose some nice font and colors for your note, and then click on **OK**. This should be the final result:

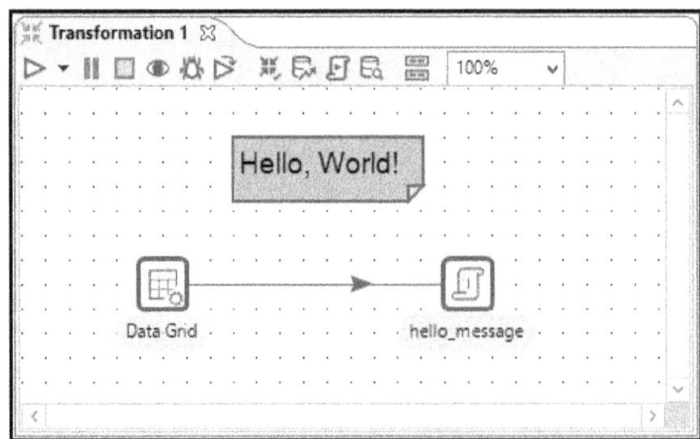

Hello World Transformation

The final step is to save the work:

1. From the main menu, navigate to **Edit** | **Settings...**. A window appears to specify Transformation properties. Fill the **Transformation name** textbox with a simple name, such as `hello world`. Fill the **Description** textbox with a short description, such as `My first transformation`. Finally, provide a more clear explanation in the **Extended description** textbox, and then click on **OK**.
2. From the main menu, navigate to **File** | **Save** and save the Transformation in a folder of your choice with the name `hello_world`.

Next step is to preview the data produced and run the Transformation.

Previewing and running a Transformation

Now we will preview and run the Transformation created earlier. Note the difference between both:

- The **Preview** functionality allows you to see a sample of the data produced for selected steps
- The **Run** option effectively runs the whole Transformation

In our Transformation, we will preview the output of the **User Defined Java Expression** step:

1. Select the **User Defined Java Expression** step by left-clicking on it.
2. Click on the **Preview** icon in the bar menu preceding in the main canvas:

Preview icon in the Transformation toolbar

3. The **Transformation debug dialog** window will appear. Click on the **Quick Launch** button.

4. A window will appear to preview the data generated by the Transformation, as shown in the following screenshot:

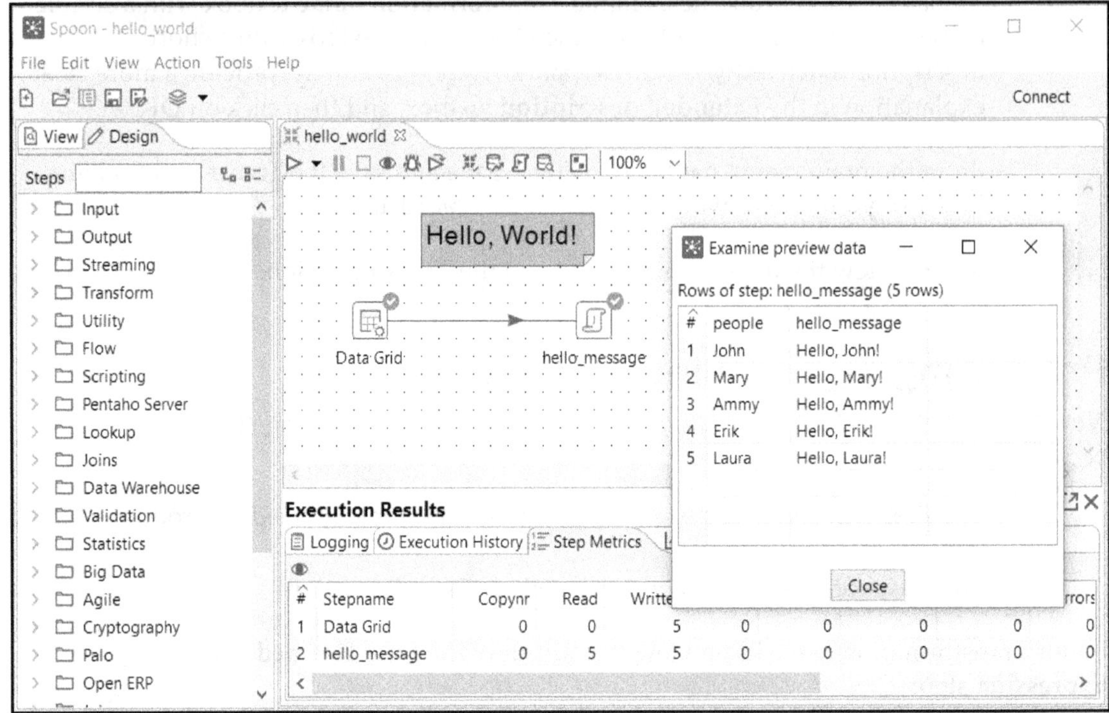

Previewing the Hello World Transformation

5. Close the preview window.

You can preview the output of any step in the Transformation at any time of your designing process. You can also preview the data even if you haven't yet saved the work.

Once we have the Transformation ready, we can run it:

1. Click on the **Run** icon:

Run icon in the Transformation toolbar

2. A window named **Run Options** appears. Click on **Run**.

You need to save the Transformation before you run it. If you have modified the Transformation without saving it, you will be prompted to do so.

3. At the bottom of the screen, you should see a log with the result of the execution:

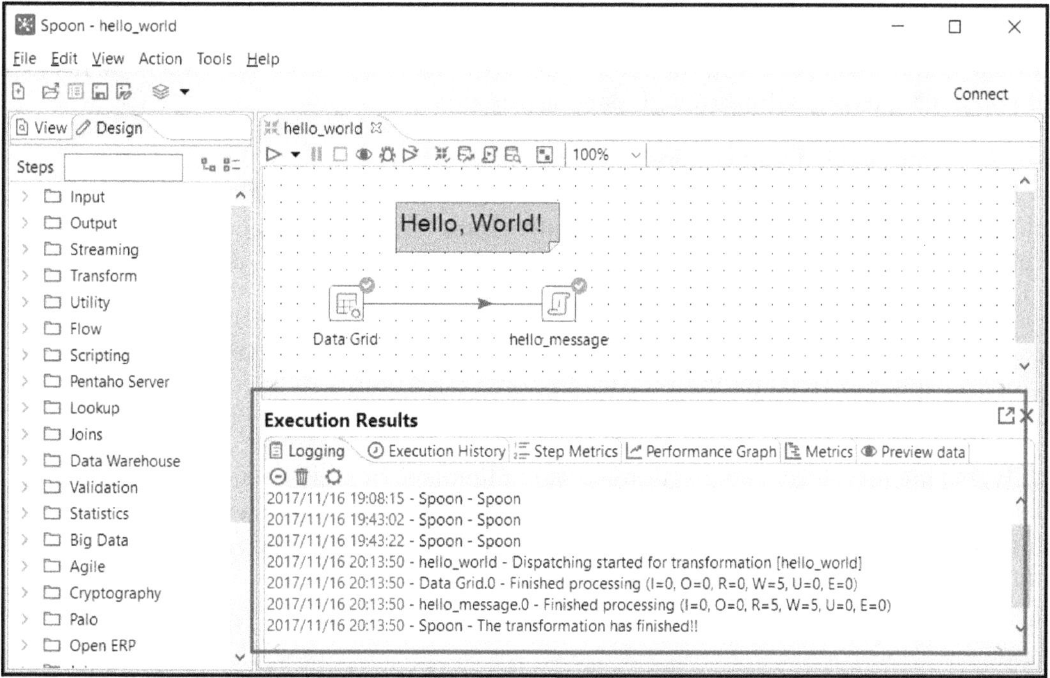

Sample execution results window

Whether you preview or run a Transformation, you'll get an **Execution Results** window showing what happened. You will learn more about this in `Chapter 2`, *Getting Started with Transformations*.

Installing useful related software

Before skipping to the next chapter, let's devote some time to the installation of extra software that will complement our work with PDI.

First of all, it is really important that you have a nice text editor. You will need it for preparing testing data, for reading files before ingesting them with PDI, for viewing data that comes out of transformations, and for reviewing logs. A couple of examples of good text editors are Notepad++ and Sublime Text.

You will be working with spreadsheets, so another useful software will be a spreadsheet editor, as, for example, OpenOffice Calc.

In `Chapter 10`, *Performing Basic Operations with Databases*, and `Chapter 11`, *Loading Data Marts with PDI*, you will work with databases. As PostgreSQL has become a very used and popular open source database, it was the database engine chosen for the database-related tutorials in this book. So, if you intend to work with databases from PDI, it will be necessary that you have access to a PostgreSQL database engine.

Also, it's recommended that you install some visual software that will allow you to administer and query the database. For PostgreSQL, you can install PgAdmin. Another option would be to install a generic open source tool, for example, SQuirrel SQL Client, a graphical program that allows you to work with PostgreSQL as well as with other database engines.

If you don't have access to a PostgreSQL server, it's fine to work with a different database engine, either commercial or open source. In some cases, you will have to slightly adapt the samples, but in general, you will be fine with the explanations of the book.

Finally, having an Internet connection while reading is extremely useful as well. Several links are provided throughout the book that complements to what is explained. Additionally, there is the PDI forum where you may search or post doubts if you are stuck with something.

Summary

In this chapter, you were introduced to Pentaho Data Integration. Specifically, you learned what PDI is and you installed the tool. You also were introduced to Spoon, the graphical designer tool of PDI, and created your first Transformation.

Now that you have learned the basics, you are ready to begin experimenting with transformations. That is the topic of the next chapter.

2
Getting Started with Transformations

In the previous chapter, you used the graphical designer Spoon to create your first Transformation, *Hello World*. Now you're ready to begin transforming data, and at the same time get familiar with the Spoon environment.

In this chapter, you will:

- Learn the simplest ways of transforming data
- Get familiar with the process of designing, debugging, and testing a Transformation
- Explore the available features for running transformations from Spoon
- Learn basic PDI terminology related to data and metadata
- Get an introduction to handling runtime errors

Designing and previewing transformations

In the previous chapter, you created a simple Transformation, previewed the data, and also ran the Transformation. That allowed you to get your first contact with the PDI graphical designer. In this section, you will become more familiar with the editing features, experiment the **Preview** option in detail, and deal with errors that may appear as you develop and test a Transformation.

Getting familiar with editing features

Editing transformations with Spoon can be very time-consuming if you're not familiar with the editing facilities that the software offers. In this section, you will learn a bit more about three editing features that you already faced in the previous chapter:

- Using the mouseover assistance toolbar
- Adding steps and creating hops in different ways
- Working with grids

Using the mouseover assistance toolbar

The mouseover assistance toolbar, as shown in the following screenshot, is a tiny toolbar that assists you when you position the mouse cursor over a step. You have already used some of its functionalities. Here you have the full list of options:

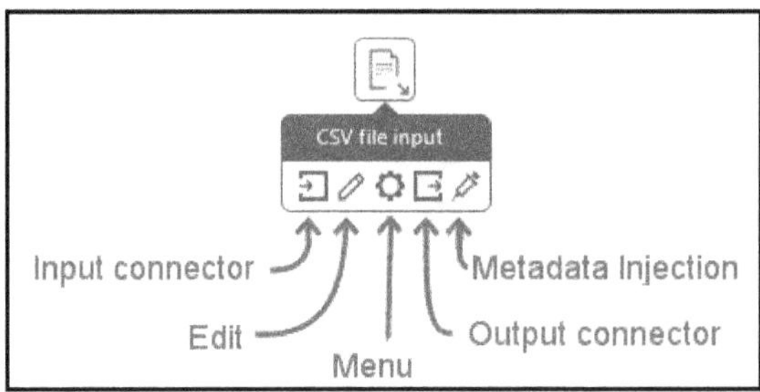

The mouseover assistance toolbar

The following table explains each button in this toolbar:

Button	Description
Edit	It's equivalent to double-clicking on the step to edit it.
Menu	It's equivalent to right-clicking on the step to bring up the contextual menu.
Input connector	It's an assistant for creating hops directed toward this step. If the step doesn't accept any input, the input connector is disabled.
Output connector	It's an assistant for creating hops leaving this step. It's used just like the input connector, but the direction of the created hop is the opposite.

Metadata Injection	If you see this button, it means that the step supports metadata injection, a capability meant for creating dynamic ETL processes. If you click the button, a pop-up window shows up, just informing that the step supports that feature.

Adding steps and creating hops

In the previous chapter, you designed a Transformation with just two steps and one explanatory note. You learned to drag and drop steps to the work area and to link steps by using the mouseover assistance toolbar. There are alternative ways to do the same thing.

For adding a new step to the work area, you can use any of the following:

- Drag and drop the step from the Steps tree to the work area.
- Double-click the step in the Steps tree. In this case, if there is a step selected in the work area, a new hop will automatically be created from that **Step** to the new one.
- *Shift*-double-click the step in the Steps tree. The step will appear in the work area and its configuration window will be opened, ready for being filled with data. If there is a step selected in the work area, a new hop will automatically be created from that step to the new one.

For linking two steps, you can either:

- Use the output or the input connectors in the mouseover assistance toolbar
- Click on a step and drag it toward the second step while holding down the middle mouse button
- Click on a step and drag it towards the second step while pressing the *Shift* key and holding down the left mouse button
- Double-click or *Shift*-double-click when adding a new step, as explained previously

When linking two steps, then depending on the kind of source step, you might be prompted for the kind of hop to create. For now, just select the **Main output of step** option. You will learn about the second option by the end of this chapter.

Among all the ways explained for adding steps and hops, you can use the one that you feel most comfortable with. As an addition, there are several shortcuts, very useful as your transformations become more complex. You can find them all in the different menus in Spoon.

If you are a Mac user, be aware that a mixture of Windows and Mac keys are used. In general, the *Ctrl* key should be replaced with the *command* key, and we use the name option for referring to the *Alt* key. For example, for copying, you do not use *Ctrl* + *C* but *command* + *C*; instead of creating a Job with *Ctrl* + *Alt* + *N*, you do it with *command* + *option* + *N*.

Working with grids

Grids are tables used in many instances in Spoon to enter or display information. You have already edited grids in the configuration window of the **Data Grid** and the **UDJE** steps.

Grids can be used for entering different kinds of data. No matter what kind of grid you are editing, there is always a contextual menu that you may access by right-clicking on a row. That menu offers editing options such as copying, pasting, or moving rows of the grid.

When the number of rows in the grid is high, use shortcuts! Most of the editing options of a grid have shortcuts that make editing easier and quicker.

The following is a full list of shortcuts for editing grids. The value between brackets is the option for Mac users:

Action	**Windows shortcut**
Move a row up	*Ctrl* + up arrow
Move a row down	*Ctrl* + down arrow
Resize all columns to see the full values (header included)	*F3 (fn + F3)*
Resize all columns to see the full values (header excluded)	*F4 (fn + F4)*
Select all rows	*Ctrl + A*
Clear selection	*Esc (fn + esc)*
Copy selected lines to clipboard	*Ctrl + C*
Paste from clipboard to grid	*Ctrl + V*

Cut selected lines	*Ctrl + X*
Delete selected lines	*Delete*
Keep only selected lines	*Ctrl + K*
Undo	*Ctrl + Z*
Redo	*Ctrl + Y*

Grids are usually accompanied by a **Get Fields** button. The **Get Fields** button is a facility to avoid typing. When you press that button, PDI fills the grid with all the available fields.

Every time you see a **Get Fields** button, consider it as a shortcut to avoid typing. PDI will bring the fields available to the grid, and you will only have to check the information brought and do minimal changes.

Designing transformations

The PDI design process is not only about putting steps, configuring them, and linking them with hops. It also involves previewing data as you add more steps, hitting and fixing errors along the way, and going back and forth until everything works as expected. Now you will start getting familiar with all these tasks.

Putting the editing features in practice

You were just introduced to the basic editing features. Now we will create a new Transformation and put all that into practice. At the same time, you will learn to use new PDI steps.

The prerequisite for this exercise is to have a file with the source data. So, open your text editor, create a new file, and type the following:

```
project_name,start_date,end_date
Project A,2016-01-10,2016-01-25
Project B,2016-04-03,2016-07-21
Project C,2017-01-15,???
Project D,2015-09-03,2015-12-20
Project E,2016-05-11,2016-05-31
Project F,2011-12-01,2013-11-30
```

Save the file as `projects.csv` and proceed with the PDI work.

This new Transformation will read the list of projects from the file, and then it will calculate the time that it took to complete each project.

First of all, we will read the file so its content becomes our input dataset. Here are the instructions:

1. Start Spoon.
2. From the main menu, navigate to **File** | **New** | **Transformation**.
3. Expand the **Input** branch of the Steps tree. Remember that the Steps tree is located in the **Design** tab to the left of the work area.
4. Drag and drop the **CSV file input** icon on the canvas.

At any time, feel free to use a different method for adding steps or creating hops.

5. Double-click on the **CSV file input** icon and enter `projects` in the **Step name** field.
6. Under **Filename**, type the full path to your project's file, as, for example, `D:/PentahoLearningSamples/files/projects.csv`. Alternatively, click on **Browse...** and look for the file on your disk.
7. Fill in the grid, as shown in the following screenshot:

#	Name	Type	Format	Length	Precision	Currency	Decimal	Group	Trim type
1	project_name	String							none
2	start_date	Date	yyyy-MM-dd						none
3	end_date	Date	yyyy-MM-dd						none

Configuring the fields of a CSV file input step

In the previous chapter, you tried the Preview functionality for the first time. This feature allowed you to get an idea of how the data was being transformed. Inside an **Input** step, the functionality allows you to see how the input data looks. Let's try it now:

1. Click on **Preview**, and in the small window that appears, click on **OK** to see the defined dataset. You should see a preview window with the six rows of data coming from the file:

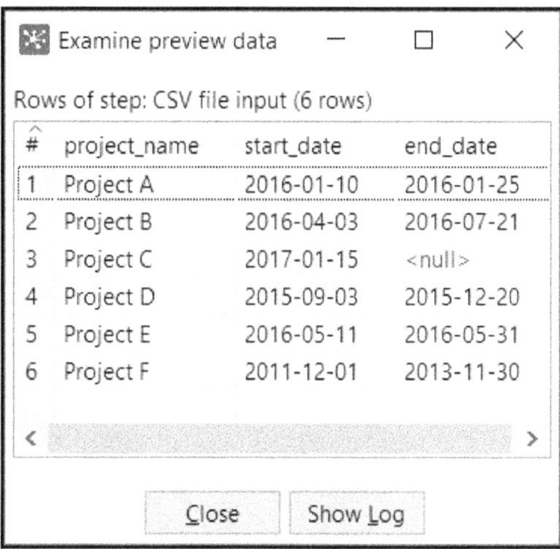

Examine preview data
Rows of step: CSV file input (6 rows)
project_name start_date end_date
1 Project A 2016-01-10 2016-01-25
2 Project B 2016-04-03 2016-07-21
3 Project C 2017-01-15 <null>
4 Project D 2015-09-03 2015-12-20
5 Project E 2016-05-11 2016-05-31
6 Project F 2011-12-01 2013-11-30
Close
Show Log

Previewing input data

If you don't see the same results, go back to the instructions and verify that you configured the step properly.

2. Close the window.

Now that we have some data to work with, we have to calculate the time that each project took. For doing that, let's introduce the **Calculator** step. This step allows you to create new fields by applying some calculations to the source data. In this case, we will use it for calculating the difference between two dates. In order to do that, we will have to provide the following:

- A name for the new field: `diff_dates`
- The calculation to apply, which will be the difference between dates (in days)
- The parameters for the calculation: `start_date` and `end_date`
- The type for the result: `Integer`

Proceed as follows:

1. Expand the **Transform** branch of steps. Look for the **Calculator** step and drag and drop it to the work area.
2. Create a hop from the **CSV file input** step towards the **Calculator** step by using any of the methods explained. A tiny menu will appear prompting you for the kind of hop. Among the options, select the **Main output of step**.

Make sure you create the hop as explained. If you don't do it, the fields will not be available in the next dialog window.

3. Double-click on the **Calculator** step and fill the first row in the grid with the following information:

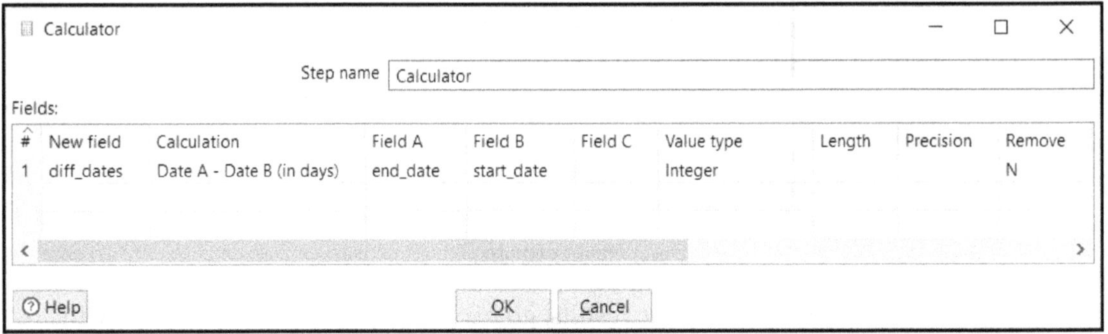

Configuring a Calculator step

4. Click on **OK** to close the window.

Instead of using the **Calculator** step, it is also possible to do the math with the **User Defined Java Expression** step.

The main difference between a **Calculator** and a **UDJE** step is that while the **Calculator** has a list of predefined formulas, the **UDJE** allows you to write your own expressions using Java code.

Feel free to experiment and compare both alternatives: One using a **Calculator** and another using a **UDJE**.

For using a **UDJE** step in this exercise, you can enter the following Java expression that does the calculation: `(dateB.getTime() - dateA.getTime())/ (1000 * 60 * 60 * 24)`

Finally, we will evaluate the performance of the project:

1. Add a new step, **Number Range**, and link the **Calculator** step to the **Number range** step with a new hop. Make sure that the arrow goes from the **Calculator** step toward the **Number range** step and not the other way.

If you have difficulty in finding a step, you can type the search criteria in the text box on top of the Steps tree. PDI will filter and show only the steps that match your search.

2. With the **Number ranges** step, you will create a new field, `performance`, based on the value of an incoming field, `diff_dates`. Double-click on the step and fill in the grid as shown in the following screenshot. Then click on **OK**:

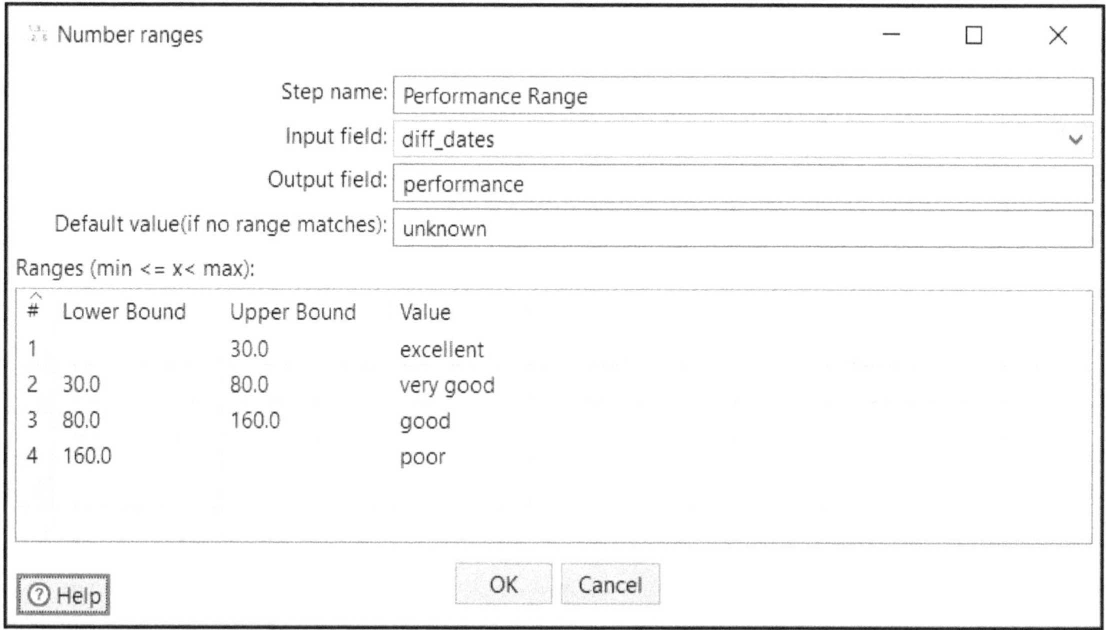

Configuring a Number ranges step

3. Now from the **Scripting** branch, add a **User Defined Java Expression** step, and create a hop from the **Number range** step towards this new step. When you create the hop, you will be prompted for the kind of hop. Select **Main output of step**.

If you unintentionally select the wrong option, don't worry. Right-click on the hop and a contextual menu will appear. Select **Delete hop** and create the hop again.

4. With the **UDJE,** you will create two informative messages: `duration` and `message`. As in the **Calculator** step, this step also allows you to create a new field per row. Double-click on the step and fill in the grid as shown in the following screenshot:

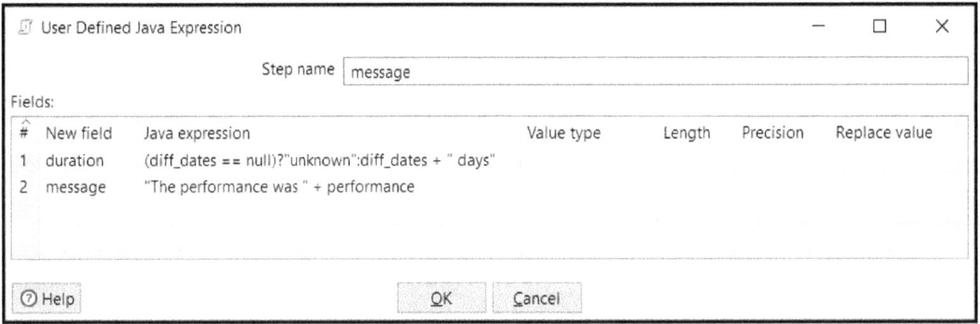

Configuring a UDJE step

5. Click on **OK** to close the window and save the Transformation. Your final Transformation should look like the following screenshot:

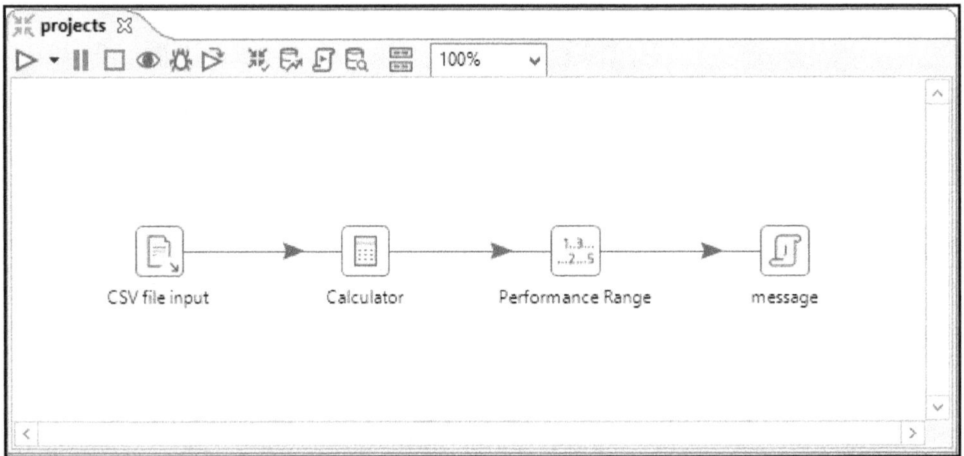

Transformation of projects

Previewing and fixing errors as they appear

Now that you have completed the design of the Transformation, let's run some previews:

1. Select the **UDJE** step and run a preview. You already know how to do it: click on the **Preview** icon in the Transformation toolbar and then click on **Quick Launch**. You'll see the following screenshot:

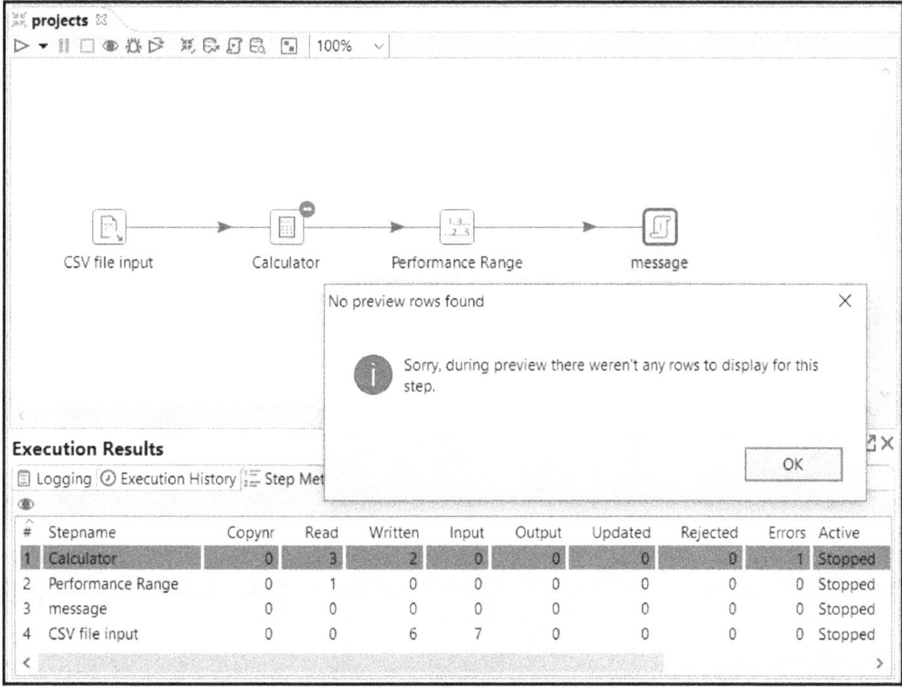

Errors while previewing a Transformation

Something is wrong. A pop-up window tells us that there are no rows to preview, but we can also see that an error has occurred. We know that because:

- The background of the **Calculator** row in the **Step Metrics** tab changed to red (highlighted)
- The border of the **Calculator** step also became red (highlighted)
- If you click on the **Logging** tab, you will see the error explained, also in red (highlighted) text

All of these indicators tell us which step caused the error. In this case, it was **Calculator**.

By reading the log, we can see the source of the error. In the file, we have an invalid value (`???`) in a place where a `Date` is expected. Let's retry the preview, but this time on the **Calculator** step:

2. Click on the **Calculator** step and run a preview. This time a popup with results appears, but we only see two rows:

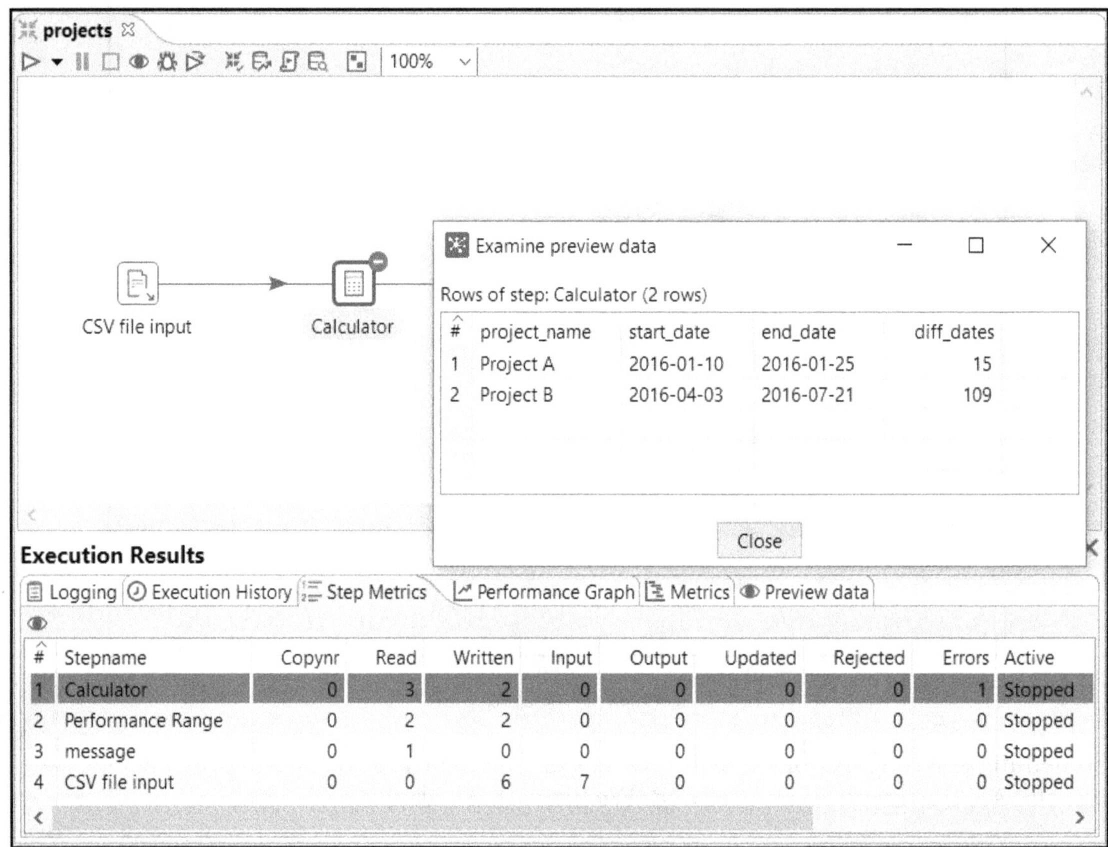

Partial Preview of a Transformation

Again, we have the same error. How do we fix this? For now, we will bypass the error by deleting in the file the row that is causing the error. Don't worry! Very soon we will learn to deal with it and put that line back in the file.

3. Edit the `projects.txt` file and remove the row that is causing the error.
4. Click on the **Calculator** step and run the preview one more time. This time, you will see all the rows and a new column with the new field `diff_dates`:

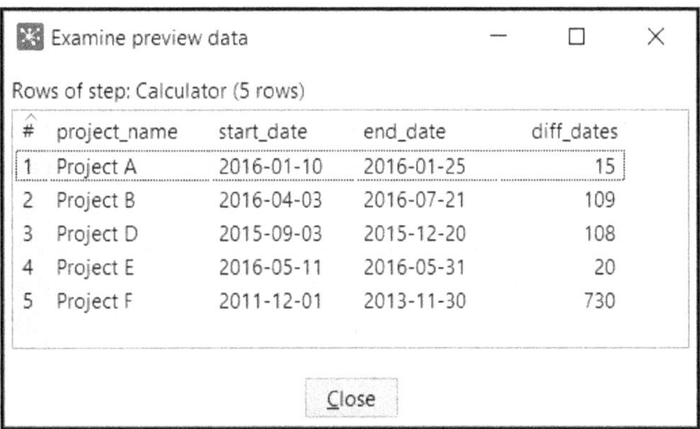

Preview of a Transformation

5. Close the window and click on the **UDJE** step. Run a new preview. You will see this:

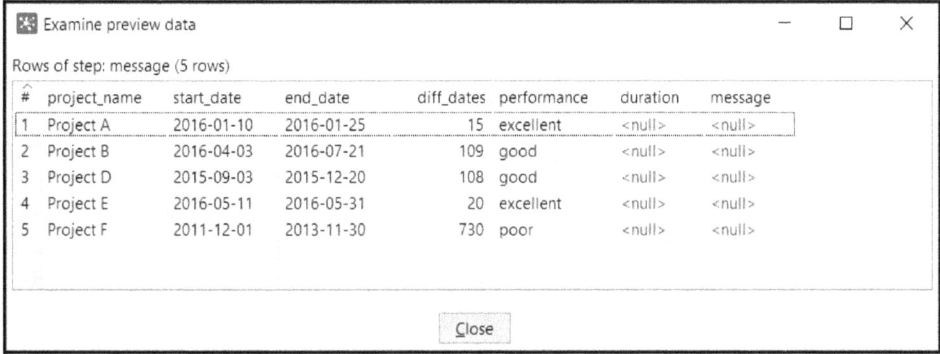

null values in a Preview

Clearly, this is not what we expected. Instead of a text with duration and performance, we only see null values. There are no visible errors, but if you click on the **Logging** tab, you will find out the problem: Among all the lines in red containing the full description of the error, you will find this:

```
Row Preview - duration None : Unknown type 0 specified.
```

This error is telling you that you didn't specify the type for the field `duration`.

At the beginning, it may be tricky to understand some error messages, but it's just a matter of time to get familiar with them.

6. Edit the **UDJE** step. Under the **Value Type** column, select `String` for both the `duration` and `message` fields. Close the window.
7. Make sure the **UDJE** step is selected, and run a final preview. The error should have disappeared from the **Logging** tab, and the window should display the final data:

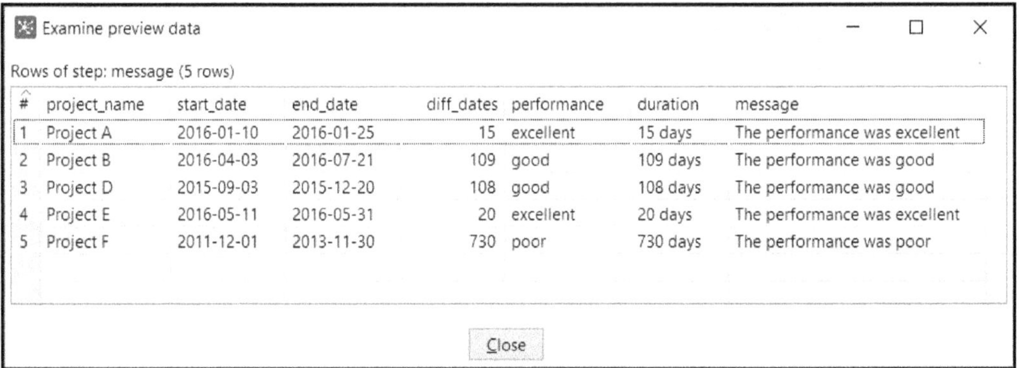

Examine preview data

Rows of step: message (5 rows)

#	project_name	start_date	end_date	diff_dates	performance	duration	message
1	Project A	2016-01-10	2016-01-25	15	excellent	15 days	The performance was excellent
2	Project B	2016-04-03	2016-07-21	109	good	109 days	The performance was good
3	Project D	2015-09-03	2015-12-20	108	good	108 days	The performance was good
4	Project E	2016-05-11	2016-05-31	20	excellent	20 days	The performance was excellent
5	Project F	2011-12-01	2013-11-30	730	poor	730 days	The performance was poor

Close

Final preview of a Transformation

There is something important to note about the preview functionality you experimented with in this section.

When you select a step for previewing, the objective is to preview the data as it comes out from that step. The whole Transformation is executed unless you disable a part of it. Don't feel intimidated if you don't understand completely how the used steps work. Right now, the objective is not to fully dominate PDI steps, but to understand how to interact with Spoon. There will be more opportunities throughout the book to learn about the use of the steps in detail.

Looking at the results in the execution results pane

The **Execution Results** pane shows you what happens while you preview or run a Transformation. This pane is located succeeding the work area. If not immediately visible, it will appear when a Transformation is previewed or run.

If you don't see this pane, you can open it by clicking the last icon in the **Transformation** toolbar.

The Logging tab

The **Logging** tab shows the execution of your Transformation, step by step. By default, the level of the logging details is basic logging but you can choose among the following options:

- **Nothing at all**
- **Error logging only**
- **Minimal logging**
- **Basic logging**
- **Detailed logging**
- **Debugging**
- **Rowlevel (very detailed)**

The names of the options are self-explanatory and they are sorted by **Nothing at all** to **Rowlevel (very detailed)**, which is the most detailed level of a log. Among them, you should choose the option depending on the level of detail that you want to see. In most situations, however, you will be fine with the default value.

This is how you change the log level:

- If you are running a Transformation: Once the **Execute a transformation** window shows up, select the proper option in the **Log level** drop-down list.
- If you are previewing a Transformation: Instead of clicking on **Quick Launch**, select **Configure**. The **Execute a transformation** window appears, allowing you to choose the level. Choose the log level and then click on **Run**.

The Step Metrics tab

For each step in the Transformation, the **Step Metrics** tab shows several status and information columns. For now, the most relevant columns in this tab are:

Column	Value
Read	Number of rows coming from previous steps
Written	Number of rows leaving this step toward the next
Input	Number of rows read from a file or table
Output	Number of rows written to a file or table
Errors	Number of errors in the execution; if there are errors, the whole row will become red
Active	Current status of the execution

To better understand the content of the **Read** and **Written** columns, let's explain them with an example. As said in the previous chapter, data flows from one step to other (or others). In our sample Transformation, data is read from a file and flows toward the **Calculator** step, the **Number range** step, and the **UDJE** step, in that exact order. The **Step Metrics** column allows us to see the number of rows that effectively flowed in that way. For example look at the **Calculator** row in the screenshot *Partial Preview of a Transformation*. Three rows came from the previous step (we see it in the **Read** column), while, due to the error in the third row, only two rows left toward the **Number range** step (this is visible in **Written** column). This also explains the difference between the two previews that we ran:

1. The preview on the **UDJE** step didn't show up any data. The error occurred before any row could reach this step. We can see it in the **UDJE** row in the **Step Metrics** tab.
2. The preview on the **Calculator** step showed only those two rows that left the step (those that count for the **Written** column).

Running transformations in an interactive fashion

So far, you have learned some basics about working with Spoon during the design process. Now you will continue learning about interacting with the tool.

First, we will create a Transformation, aiming to learn some new useful steps. After that, we will adapt that Transformation for inspecting the data as it is being created.

As you progress, feel free to preview the data that is being generated, even if you're not told to do so. This will help you understand what is going on. Testing each step as you move forward makes it easier to debug and craft a functional Transformation.

Let's start with the creation of the Transformation. The objective is to generate a dataset with all dates in between a given range of dates:

1. Create a new Transformation.
2. From the **Input** group of steps, drag to the canvas the **Generate Rows** step, and configure it as shown:

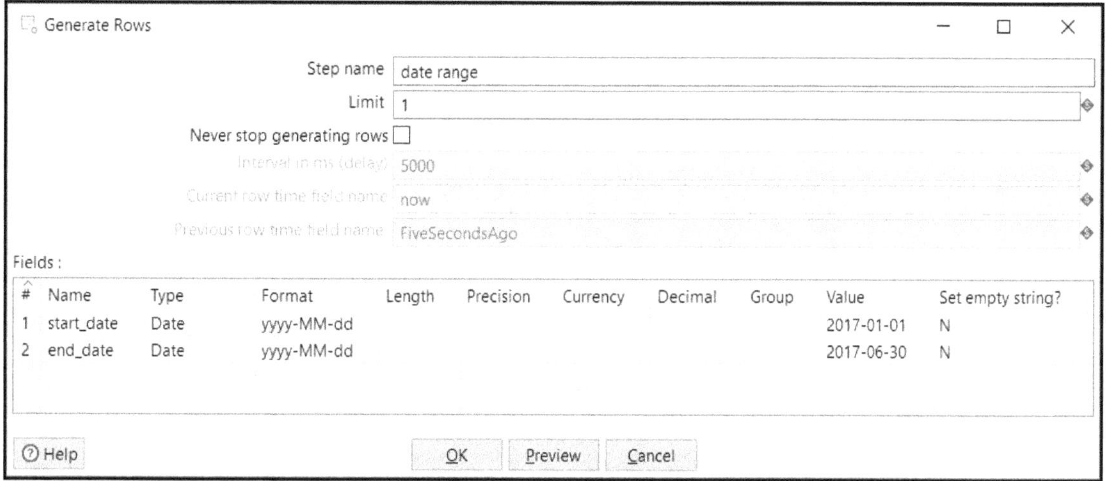

Configuring a Generate Rows step

Note that you have to change the default value for the **Limit** textbox, from `10` to `1`.

3. Close the window.

4. From the **Transform** category of steps, add the **Calculator** step, and create a hop that goes from the **Generate Rows** step to this one.
5. Double-click on the **Calculator** step and add the field named `diff_dates` as the difference between `end_date` and `start_date`. That is, configure it exactly the same way as you did in the previous section.
6. Run a preview. You should see a single row with three fields: the `start date`, the `end date`, and a field with the number of days between both.
7. Now add the **Clone row** step. You will find it inside the **Utility** group of steps.
8. Create a hop from the **Calculator** step towards this new step.
9. Edit the **Clone row** step.
10. Select the **Nr clone in field?** option to enable the **Nr Clone field** textbox. In this textbox, type `diff_dates`.
11. Now select the **Add clone num to output?** option to enable the **Clone num field** textbox. In this textbox, type `delta`.
12. Run a preview. You should see the following:

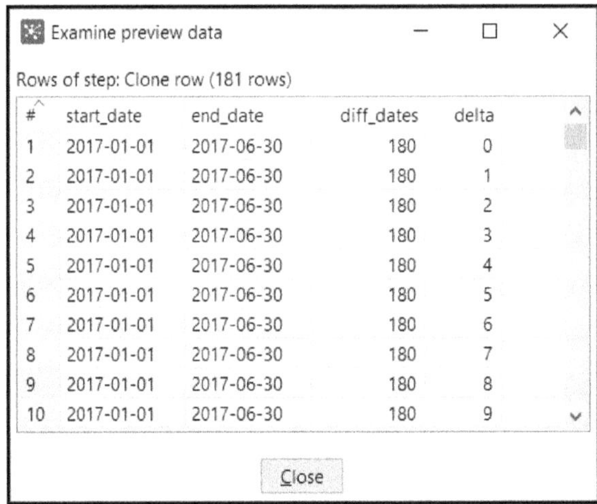

#	start_date	end_date	diff_dates	delta
1	2017-01-01	2017-06-30	180	0
2	2017-01-01	2017-06-30	180	1
3	2017-01-01	2017-06-30	180	2
4	2017-01-01	2017-06-30	180	3
5	2017-01-01	2017-06-30	180	4
6	2017-01-01	2017-06-30	180	5
7	2017-01-01	2017-06-30	180	6
8	2017-01-01	2017-06-30	180	7
9	2017-01-01	2017-06-30	180	8
10	2017-01-01	2017-06-30	180	9

Previewing cloned rows

13. Add another **Calculator** step, and create a hop from the **Clone row** step to this one.
14. Edit the new step, and add the field named `a_single_date`. As **Calculation**, select **Date A + B Days**. As **Field A**, select **start_date** and as **Field B**, select **delta**. Finally, as a **Value type**, select **Date**. For the rest of the columns, leave the default values.

15. Run a final preview. You should see this:

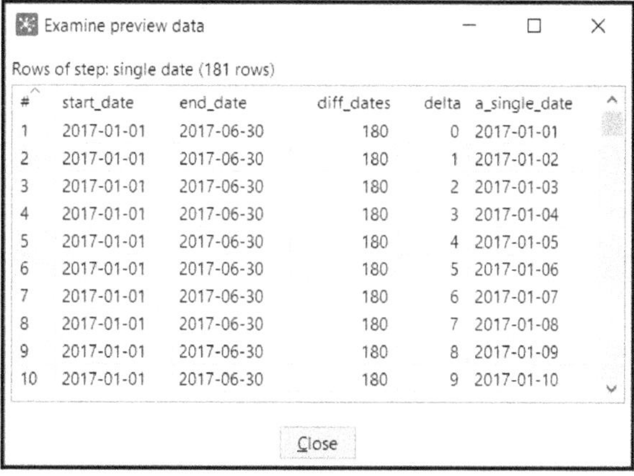

#	start_date	end_date	diff_dates	delta	a_single_date
1	2017-01-01	2017-06-30	180	0	2017-01-01
2	2017-01-01	2017-06-30	180	1	2017-01-02
3	2017-01-01	2017-06-30	180	2	2017-01-03
4	2017-01-01	2017-06-30	180	3	2017-01-04
5	2017-01-01	2017-06-30	180	4	2017-01-05
6	2017-01-01	2017-06-30	180	5	2017-01-06
7	2017-01-01	2017-06-30	180	6	2017-01-07
8	2017-01-01	2017-06-30	180	7	2017-01-08
9	2017-01-01	2017-06-30	180	8	2017-01-09
10	2017-01-01	2017-06-30	180	9	2017-01-10

Previewing a range of dates

If you don't obtain the same results, check carefully that you followed the steps exactly as explained. If you hit errors in the middle of the section, you know how to deal with them. Take your time, read the log, fix the errors, and resume your work.

Now you will run the Transformation and inspect the data as the Transformation is being executed. Before doing that, we will do some changes to the Transformation so it runs slow, allowing us to see in detail what is happening:

1. Edit the **Generate Rows** step and change the date range. As `end_date`, type `2023-12-31`.
2. From the **Utility** group of steps, drag to the work area the **Delay row** step. With this step, we will deliberately delay each row of data.
3. Drag the step to the hop between the **Clone row** step and the second **Calculator** step, until the hop changes the width:

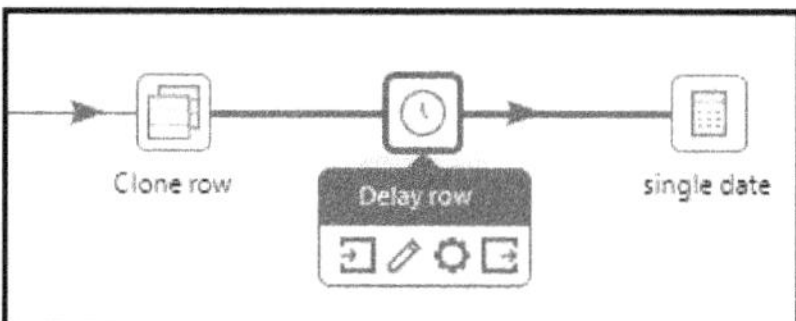

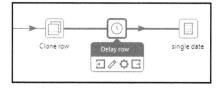

Inserting a step between two steps

4. A window will appear asking you if you want to split the hop. Click on **Yes**. The hop will be split in two: one from the **Clone row** step to the **Delay row** step, and the second one from this step to the **Calculator** step.

You can configure PDI to split the hops automatically. You can do it by selecting the **Don't ask again?** checkbox in this same window, or by navigating to the **Tools | Options...** menu and checking the option **Automatically split hops.**

5. Double-click on the **Delay row** step, and configure it using the following information: as **Timeout**, type `500`, and in the drop-down list, select **Milliseconds**. Close the window.
6. Save the Transformation and run it. You will see that it runs at a slower pace.

Now it is time to do the sniff testing, that is, looking at the rows that are coming into or out of a step in real time:

1. Without stopping the execution, click on the second **Calculator** step. A pop-up window will show up describing the execution results of this step in real time. **Ctrl**-click two more steps: the **Generate Rows** step and the **Clone row** step. For each selected step, you will see the **Step Metrics** at runtime:

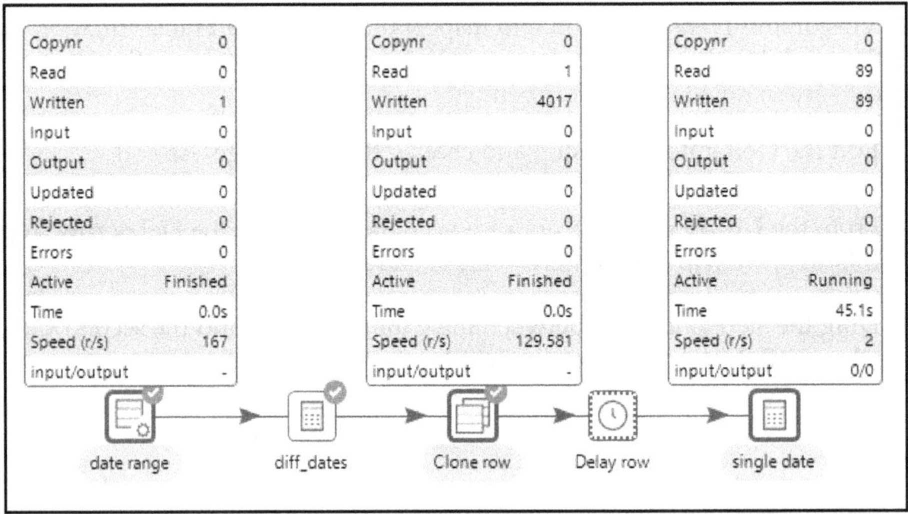

Runtime Step Metrics

2. Now, let's inspect the data itself. Right-click on the second **Calculator** step and navigate to **Sniff Test During Execution | Sniff test output rows**. A window will appear showing the data as it's being generated.

In the **Execution Results** window, it's worth noting a column that we didn't mention before:

Column	Description
Speed (r/s)	The speed calculated in rows per second

As you put a delay of 500 milliseconds for each row, it's reasonable to see that the speed for the last step is two rows per second.

Note that sniff testing slows down the Transformation and its use is recommended just for debugging purposes.

While the Transformation was running, you experimented with the feature for sniffing the output rows. In the same way, you could have selected the **Sniff test input rows** option to see the incoming rows of data.

As an alternative to run previews on individual steps, you can use the **continuous preview mode**. Instead of running a preview, you can run the Transformation and see the output in the **Preview data** tab of the **Execution Results** window.

Understanding PDI data and metadata

By now, you have already created three transformations and must have an idea of what a dataset is, the kind of data types that PDI supports, and how data is modified as it goes through the path of steps and hops. This section will provide you with a deeper understanding of these concepts:

- We will give formal definitions for PDI basic terminology related to data and metadata
- We will also give you a practical list of steps that will expand your toolbox for Transforming data

Understanding the PDI rowset

Transformation deal with datasets or **rowsets**, that is, rows of data with a predefined **metadata**. The metadata tells us about the structure of data, that is, the list of fields as well as their definitions. The following table describes the metadata of a PDI dataset:

Metadata Element	Description
Field name	Name of the field; it can be any (not null) text
Type	One of the supported types, as, for example, String or Integer
Length	Length of the field
Precision	Applicable for numeric fields
Position	Position of the field relative to the other fields, starting at 1

These metadata concepts shouldn't be new to you. Let's look at some examples:

- Recall the *Hello World* Transformation. You created a dataset with a **Data Grid** step. In the main tab, you defined the metadata (in that case you had only one field) and in the second tab, you entered the rows with data.
- In the Transformation of projects, you defined the dataset with a **CSV file input** step. In the grid, you defined the metadata: one string and two dates. In this case, the data was read from a file.

In Spoon, data is presented in a tabular form, where:

- Each column represents a field.
- Each row corresponds to a given member of the dataset. All rows in a dataset share the same metadata definition, that is, all rows have the same fields in the same order.

The following screenshot is an example of this. It is the result of the preview in the **Calculator** step in the Transformation of projects:

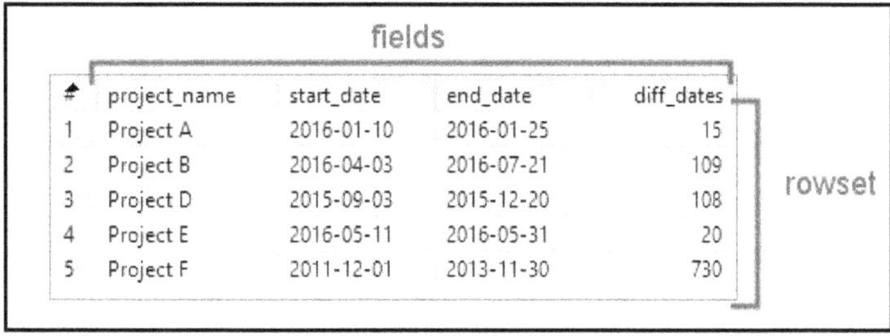

#	project_name	start_date	end_date	diff_dates
1	Project A	2016-01-10	2016-01-25	15
2	Project B	2016-04-03	2016-07-21	109
3	Project D	2015-09-03	2015-12-20	108
4	Project E	2016-05-11	2016-05-31	20
5	Project F	2011-12-01	2013-11-30	730

Sample rowset

In this case, you have four columns representing the four fields of your rowset: `project_name`, `start_date`, `end_date`, and `diff_dates`. You also have five rows of data, one for each project.

In the preview window of a rowset, you can see the field name and the data itself. If you move the mouse cursor over a column title (or click on any value in that column) and leave it there for a second, you will see a small pop up telling you the data type of that field:

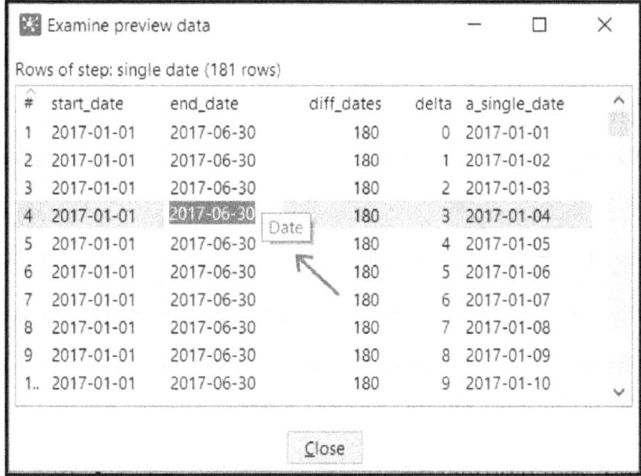

#	start_date	end_date	diff_dates	delta	a_single_date
1	2017-01-01	2017-06-30	180	0	2017-01-01
2	2017-01-01	2017-06-30	180	1	2017-01-02
3	2017-01-01	2017-06-30	180	2	2017-01-03
4	2017-01-01	2017-06-30	180	3	2017-01-04
5	2017-01-01	2017-06-30	180	4	2017-01-05
6	2017-01-01	2017-06-30	180	5	2017-01-06
7	2017-01-01	2017-06-30	180	6	2017-01-07
8	2017-01-01	2017-06-30	180	7	2017-01-08
9	2017-01-01	2017-06-30	180	8	2017-01-09
1..	2017-01-01	2017-06-30	180	9	2017-01-10

Column data type

For getting full details of the metadata, there is another option. Move the mouse cursor over the first of the **Calculator** steps and press the spacebar. A window named **Step fields and their origin** will appear:

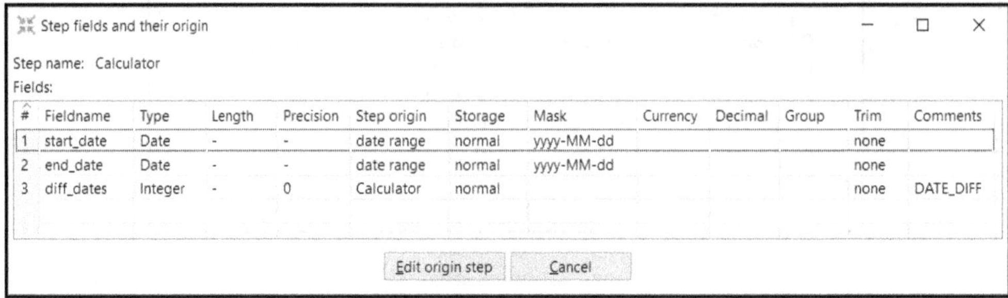

Step fields and their origin

Alternatively, you can open this window from the contextual menu available in the mouseover assistance toolbar, or by right-clicking on the step. In the menu, you have to select the **Show output fields** option.

As the name of the option suggests, it describes the fields leaving the step towards the next step. If you selected **Show input fields** instead, you would see the metadata of the incoming data, that is, data that left the previous step.

One of the columns in these windows is `Step origin`. This column gives the name of the step where each field was created or modified. It's easy to compare the input fields against the output fields of a step. For example, in the **Calculator** step, you created the field `diff_dates`. This field appears in the output field of the step but not in the input list, as expected.

Adding or modifying fields by using different PDI steps

As you saw in the last Transformation, once the data is created in the first step, it travels from step to step through the hops that link those steps. The hop's function is just to direct data from an output buffer to an input one. The real manipulation of data, as well as the modification of a stream, by adding or removing fields, occurs in the steps. In the last Transformation that you created, you used the **Calculator** step to create new fields and add them to your dataset.

The **Calculator** step is one of the many steps that PDI has to create new fields. You create the fields from scratch or by combining existent ones. Usually, you will find these steps under the **Transform** category of the **Steps** tree. In the following table, you have descriptions of some of the most used steps. The examples reference the first Transformation you created in this chapter:

Step	Description	Example
Add constants	Adds one or more fields with constant values.	If the start date was the same for all the projects, you could add that field with an **Add constants** step.
Add sequence	Adds a field with a sequence. By default, the generated sequence will be 1, 2, 3 ... but you can change the start, increment, and maximum values to generate different sequences.	You could have created the delta field with an **Add sequence** step instead of using the **Clone num field** option in the **Clone row** step.
Number range	Creates a new field based on ranges of values. Applies to a numeric field.	You used this step for creating the performance field based on the duration of the project.
Replace in string	Replaces all occurrences of a text in a string field with another text.	The value for the `project_name` field includes the word `Project`. With this step, you could remove the word or replace it with a shorter one. The final name for `Project A` could be `Proj A` or simply `A`.
Split Fields	Splits a single field into two or more new fields. You have to specify which character acts as a separator.	Split the name of the project into two fields: the first word (that in this case is always `Project`) and the rest. The separator would be a space character.
String operations	Applies some operations on strings: trimming and removing special characters, among others.	You could convert the project name to uppercase.

Step	Description	Example
Value Mapper	Creates a correspondence between the values of a field and a new set of values.	You could define a new field based on the performance field. The value could be `Rejected` if the performance is `poor` or `unknown`, and `Approved` for the rest of the performance values.
User Defined Java Expression	Creates a new field by using a Java expression that involves one or more fields. This step may eventually replace any of the previous steps.	You used this step in the first section for creating two strings: `duration` and `message`.

Note that some of these steps can be used for generating more than one field at a time; an example of that is the **User Defined Java Expression** step (or **UDJE** for short).

Any of these steps when added to your Transformation, is executed for every row in the stream. It takes the row, identifies the fields needed to do its tasks, calculates the new field(s), and adds it (or them) to the dataset.

For more details on a particular step, don't hesitate to visit the documentation for steps at `https://help.pentaho.com/Documentation/8.0/Products/Data_Integration/Transformation_Step_Reference`. Also, for all steps, there is a handy **Help** button in their configuration window.

Explaining the PDI data types

Data types are part of the metadata and are mandatory. Every field in a PDI dataset must have a data type. You have already used some of the most common data types, namely `String`, `Date`, and `Integer`, but the full available list of supported data types is a bit longer. The following table summarizes them all:

PDI data type	Java data type	Description
`String`	`java.lang.String`	Unlimited length text
`Integer`	`java.lang.Long`	A signed long (64-bit) integer
`Number`	`java.lang.Double`	A double precision floating point value

BigNumber	java.math.BigDecimal	Unlimited precision number
Date	java.util.Date	A date-time value with millisecond precision
Timestamp	java.sql.Timestamp	A date-time value with nanosecond precision
Boolean	java.lang.Boolean	A boolean value (true/false, Y/N)
Binary	java.lang.byte[]	An array of bytes that contains any type of binary data (images, sounds, and others)
Internet Address	java.net.InetAddress	An **Internet Protocol** (**IP**) address

As you can see in the preceding table, each PDI data type has its correspondent data type in Java (recall that PDI is implemented in Java).

You don't have to worry about the Java data type unless you use the **User Defined Java Class** step or create advanced expressions in the **UDJE** step. You will learn more about this in a dedicated chapter.

Handling errors

So far, each time you got an error, you had the opportunity to discover what kind of error it was and fix it. This is quite different from real scenarios, mainly for two reasons:

- Real data has errors—a fact that cannot be avoided. If you fail to heed it, the transformations that run with test or sample data will probably crash when running with real data.
- In most cases, your final work is run by an automated process and not by a user from Spoon. Therefore, if a Transformation crashes, there will be nobody who notices and reacts to that situation.

In this section, you will learn the simplest way to trap errors that may occur, avoiding unexpected crashes. This is the first step in the creation of transformations ready to be run in a production environment.

Implementing the error handling functionality

With the error handling functionality, you can capture errors that otherwise would cause the Transformation to halt. Instead of aborting, the rows that cause the errors are sent to a different stream for further treatment.

The error handling functionality is implemented at step level. You don't need to implement error handling in every step. In fact, you cannot do that because not all steps support error handling. The objective of error handling is to implement it in the steps where it is more likely to have errors.

A typical situation where you should consider handling errors is while changing the metadata of fields. That works perfectly as long as you know that the data is good, but it might fail when executing against real data. Let's explain it with a practical example.

In this case, we will work with the original version of the `projects.txt` file. Remember that you removed an invalid row in that file. Restore it and then proceed:

1. Open the Transformation of projects and save it under a different name. You can do it from the main menu by navigating to **File** | **Save as...** or from the main toolbar.
2. Edit the **CSV file input** step and change all the data types from `Date` to `String`. Also, delete the values under the **Format** column.
3. Now add a **Select values** step and insert it into the **CSV file input** step and the **Calculator** step. We will use it to convert the strings to `Date` format.
4. Double-click on the **Select values** step and select the **Meta-data** tab. Fill the tab as follows:

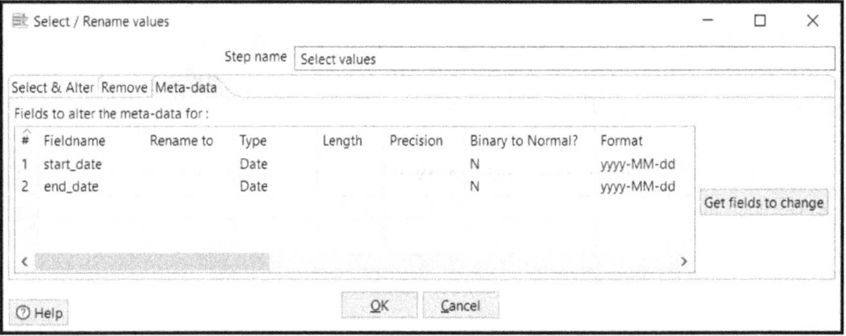

Configuring a Meta-data tab

5. Close the window and run a preview. There is an error in the **Select values** step when trying to convert the invalid value `???` to a `Date` type:

```
Select values.0 - end_date String<binary-string> : couldn't convert
string [???] to a date using format [yyyy-MM-dd] on offset location
0
```

Now let's get rid of that error by using the error handling feature:

1. Drag to the canvas the **Write to log** step. You will find it in the **Utility** category of steps.

2. Create a new hop from the **Select values** step toward the **Write to log** step. When asked for the kind of hop to create, select **Error handling of step**. Then, the following **Warning** window will appear:

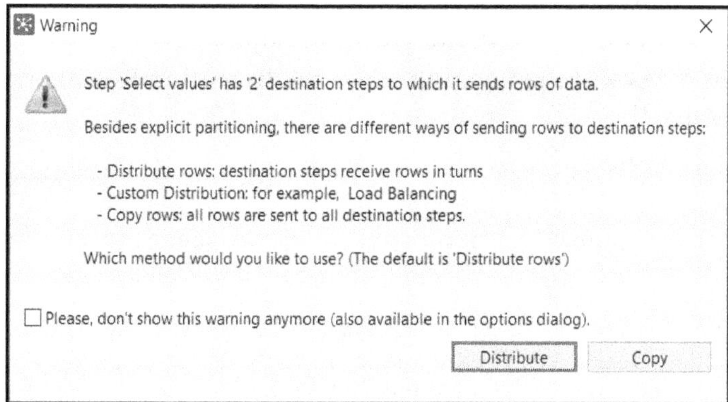

Copy or Distribute

3. Click on **Copy**.

For now, you don't have to worry about these two offered options. You will learn about them in `Chapter 6`, *Controlling the Flow of Data*.

4. Now your Transformation should look as shown in the following screenshot:

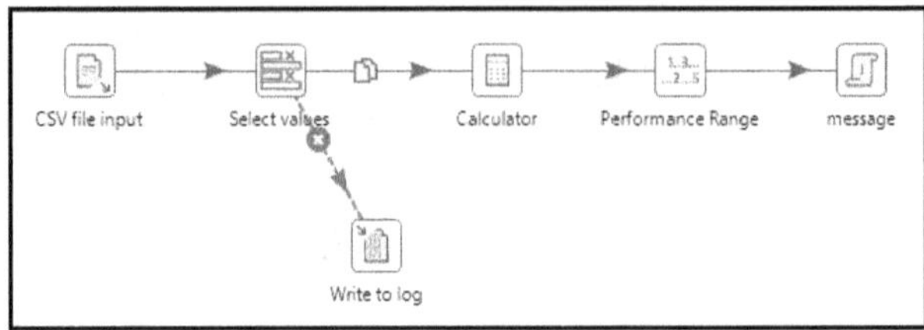

Handling errors in a select values step

5. Double-click on the **Write to log** step. In the **Write to log** textbox, type `There was an error changing the metadata of a field.`
6. Click on **Get Fields**. The grid will be populated with the names of the fields coming from the previous step.
7. Close the window and save the Transformation.
8. Now run it. Look at the **Logging** tab in the **Execution Results** window. The log will look like this:

```
- Write to log.0 - ------------> Linenr 1-------------------------
----
- Write to log.0 - There was an error changing the metadata of a
field
- Write to log.0 -
- Write to log.0 - project_name = Project C
- Write to log.0 - start_date = 2017-01-15
- Write to log.0 - end_date = ???
- Write to log.0 -
- Write to log.0 - ====================
- Write to log.0 - Finished processing (I=0, O=0, R=1, W=1, U=0,
E=0)
```

9. Run a preview of the **Calculator** step. You will see all the lines except the line containing the invalid date. This output is exactly the same as the one in the screenshot *Preview of a Transformation*.

10. Now run a preview on the **Write to log** step. You will only see the line that had the invalid `end_date` value:

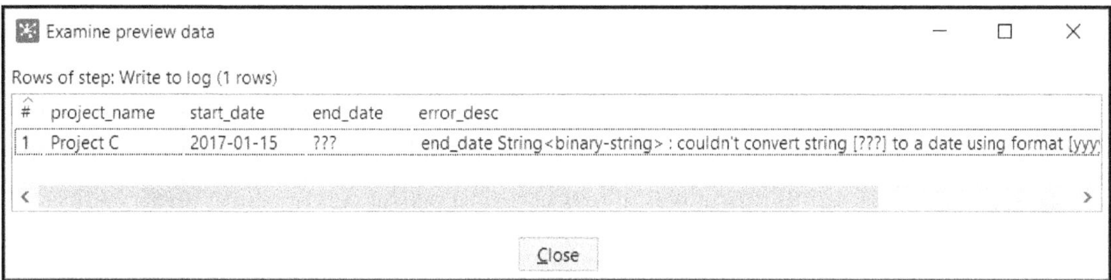

Preview of data with errors

With just a couple of clicks, you redirected the rows with errors to an alternative stream, represented by the hop in red. As you could see, both in the preview and in the **Execution Results** windows, the rows with valid values continued their way towards the **Calculator** step, while the row whose `end_date` field could not be converted to `Date` went to the **Write to log** step. In the **Write to log** step, you wrote an informative message as well as the values for all the fields, so it was easy to identify which row (or rows) caused this situation.

Note that we redirected the errors to a **Write to log** step just for demonstration purposes. You are free to use any other step for that.

As said, not all steps support error handling. It's easy to know if a step does not implement the feature.

A disabled **Error Handling ...** option in a contextual menu means that the step doesn't support Error Handling. Also, when you try to create a hop from this step toward another, the menu with the option **Error handing of step** will not show up.

Customizing the error handling

In the previous section, you handled the errors in the simplest way. There are some options that you may configure to customize the error handling.

On one hand, PDI allows you to add new fields to your dataset describing the errors, namely:

- Number of errors
- Description of the errors
- Name of the field (s) that caused the errors
- Error code

You only configure the name of the field (s) that will contain these values. The values themselves are calculated and set by the tool. You don't define error descriptions and codes; they are internal to PDI.

On the other hand, you can control the number of errors to capture, which by default is unlimited. PDI allows you to set:

- The maximum number of errors allowed. If the number of errors exceeds this value, the Transformation aborts. If this value is absent, all the errors are allowed.
- Maximum percentage of errors allowed. Same as the previous point, but the threshold for aborting is a percentage of rows instead of an absolute number. The evaluation is not done right after reading the first row. Along with this setting, you have to specify another value: the minimum number of rows to read before doing % evaluation. If this setting is absent, there is no percentage control. As an example, suppose you set a maximum percentage of `20%` and a minimum number of rows to read before doing percentage evaluation to `100`. When the number of rows with errors exceeds 20 percent of the total, PDI will stop capturing errors and will abort. However, this control is made only after having processed 100 rows.

Having said that, let's modify the previous Transformation so you can see how and where you can configure all these settings. In this case, we will add a field for the description of the error:

1. Open the Transformation from the previous section.
2. Right-click on the **Select values** step and select **Define Error handling....** The following dialog window will appear, allowing you to set all the settings described previously:

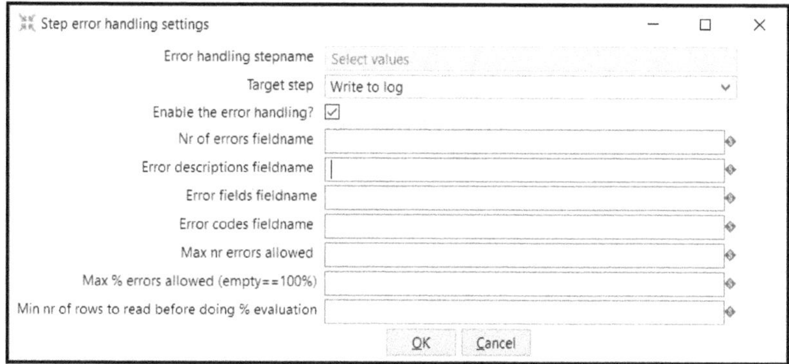

Error Handling settings

3. In the **Error descriptions fieldname** textbox, type `error_desc` and click on **OK**.
4. Double-click on the **Write to log** step and, after the last row, type or select `error_desc`.
5. Save the Transformation and run a preview on the **Write to log** step. You will see a new field named `error_desc` with the description of the error.
6. Run the Transformation. In **Execution Window**, you will see the following:

```
- There was an error changing the metadata of a field
- Write to log.0 -
- Write to log.0 - project_name = Project C
- Write to log.0 - start_date = 2017-01-15
- Write to log.0 - end_date = ???
- Write to log.0 - error_desc =
- Write to log.0 -
- Write to log.0 - end_date String<binary-string> : couldn't
convert string [???] to a date using format [yyyy-MM-dd] on offset
location 0
- Write to log.0 - ???
- Write to log.0 - ====================
```

Some final notes about the error handling setting:

- You might have noticed that the window also had an option named **Target step**. This option gives the name of the step that will receive the rows with errors. This option was automatically set when you created the hop to handle the error, but you can also set it by hand.

- Regarding the settings for describing the errors and controlling the number of errors, all of them are optional. In case of the fields, only those for which you provide a name are added to the dataset. In the Transformation you could see it when you previewed the **Write to log** step. You can also verify it by inspecting the input metadata of the **Write to log** step. Remember that you can do it by clicking on **Input Fields...** in the contextual menu of the step.

Summary

In this chapter, you created several transformations. As you did it, you got more familiar with the design process, including dealing with errors, previewing, and running Transformations. You had the opportunity of learning to use several PDI steps, and you also learned how to handle errors that may appear. At the same time, you were introduced to the basic terminology related to data, metadata, and transformations.

Now that you know the basics about data manipulation, it's time to change the focus. In the next chapter, we will introduce a very different, yet core, subject, task flows.

3
Creating Basic Task Flows

In the previous chapter, you learned how to use PDI for handling data. With PDI you can also design and run processes or task flows, which can be as simple as creating folders, or really big or complex, as, for example, loading a full data mart. In this chapter, you will learn about the PDI entities designed for handling all these task flows: jobs. These are the topics that will be covered:

- Introducing PDI jobs
- Designing and running jobs
- Executing tasks under conditions
- Managing files
- Sending emails
- Running transformations from jobs

Introducing jobs

In this section, we will introduce PDI jobs. First, we will give some basic definitions, and then we will design and run a very simple Job.

Learning the basics about jobs

A Job is an entity made of Job entries linked by hops. These entries and hops build paths, telling the engine the sequence of individual tasks to accomplish. Therefore, we say that a Job is task oriented.

Graphically, Job entries are represented with small boxes, whereas hops are represented with directional arrows, as depicted in the following sample:

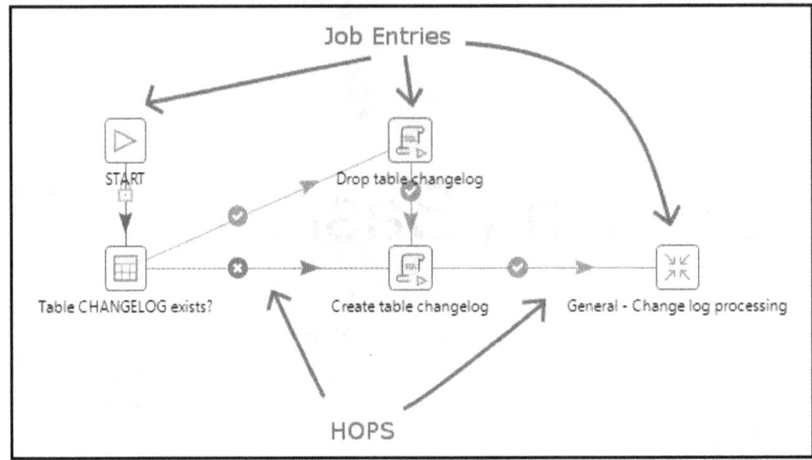

Sample Job

The unit of execution inside a Job is a Job entry. **Job Entries** are grouped into categories according to their purpose, which can be transferring files, creating folders, sending emails, running scripts, and more. There is a main category named **General**, which contains many of the most used entries. In particular, this category includes the **START** Job entry, mandatory in every Job, as you can observe in the preceding image.

A hop inside a Job is a graphical representation that links two Job entries. The direction of the hop defines the order of execution of the linked entries. The execution of a Job entry does not begin until the one that precedes it has finished. This is distinctly different from Transformation executions.

While the execution of a Transformation is parallel and synchronous in nature, a Job executes in a sequential and asynchronous way.

A hop connects only two Job entries. However, a Job entry may be reached by more than one hop. Also, more than a hop may leave a Job entry.

A Job, just as a Transformation, is neither a program nor an executable file. It is simply plain XML. The Job contains metadata which tells the PDI engine which processes to run and the order of execution of those processes. Therefore, it is said that a Job is **flow control oriented**.

Creating a Simple Job

In this tutorial, we will create a very simple Job that will create a folder. This will be enough for getting an idea of what jobs are about:

1. Open Spoon.
2. Navigate to **File** | **New** | **Job** or press *Ctrl* + *Alt* + *N*. A new Job will be created.
3. Press *Ctrl* + *J*. The **Job properties** window will appear. Give the Job a name and a description.
4. Press *Ctrl* + *S* to save the Job.
5. To the left of the screen, there is a tree with Job entries. Expand the **General** category of Job entries, select the **START** entry, and drag it to the work area, as shown next:

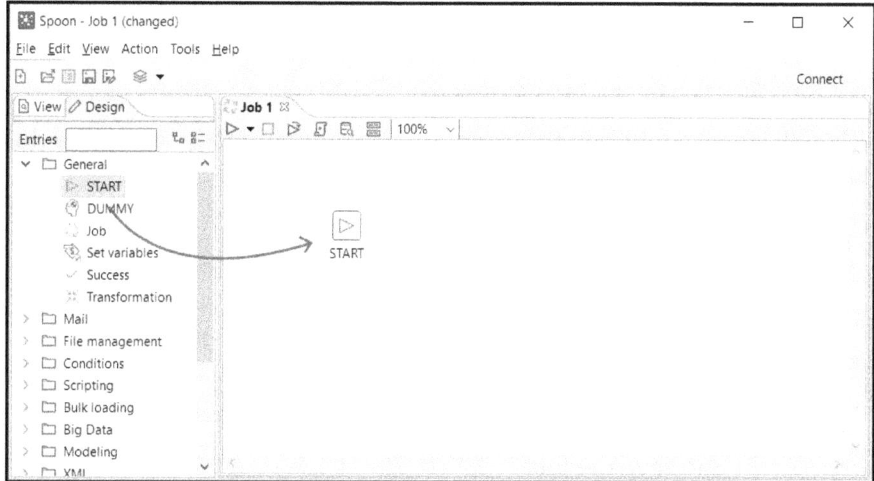

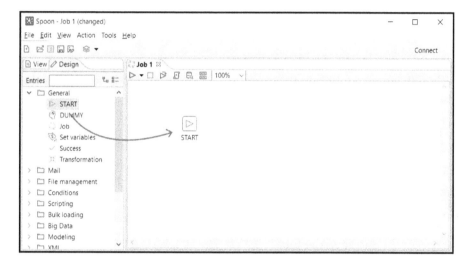

Drag and drop a Job entry

Don't forget to start your sequence of Job entries with **START**. A Job can have any mix of Job entries and hops, as long as they start with this special kind of Job entry.

6. Expand the **File management** category, select the **Create a folder** entry, and drag it to the canvas.

7. Select both entries. With the mouse cursor over the second entry, right-click and select **New hop**. A new hop will be created. Your Job should look like this:

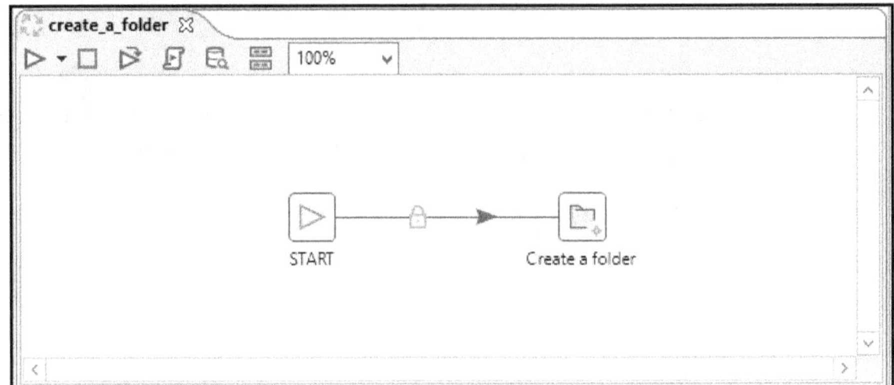

A simple Job

8. Double-click on the **Create a folder** icon.
9. We will create a folder in the same place where our Job is saved. For doing that, in the textbox next to the **Folder name** option, type `${Internal.Entry.Current.Directory}/SAMPLEFILES` and click on **OK**.

`${Internal.Entry.Current.Directory}` is an internal PDI variable, that in execution time resolves to the folder where the Job is saved.

10. Press *Ctrl* + *S* to save the Job.
11. Press *F9* to run the Job. A configuration window will appear. Click on **Launch**.

12. At the bottom of the screen, you will see the **Execution results** section. **Job metrics** will appear as follows:

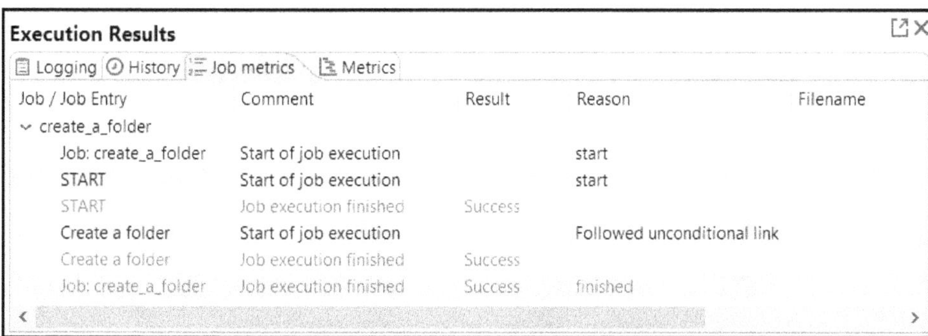

Job metrics tab

13. Select the **Logging** tab. It will appear as the following screenshot:

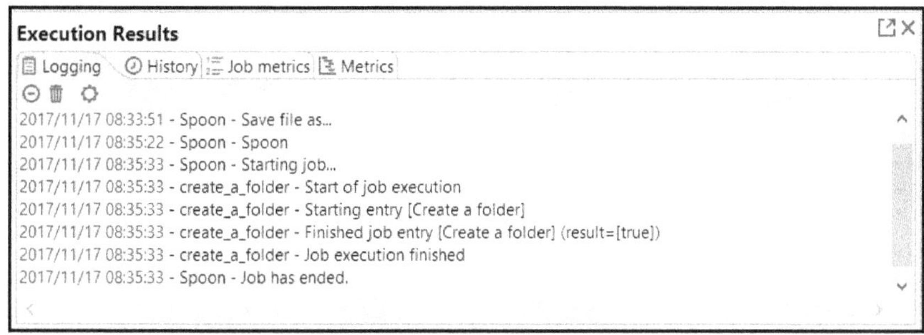

Logging tab

14. Explore your file system and go to the folder where you have saved the Job. In that folder, you should see a new folder named `SAMPLEFILES`.

Designing and running jobs

The previous section introduced you to the basics about jobs. In this section, you will have the opportunity to become more familiar with the design process of a Job.

Revisiting the Spoon interface and the editing features

You already know how to use Spoon for designing and running transformations. As you must have noticed, there are a lot of similarities when it's time to design and create a Job. Let's explain how Spoon looks like when you work with jobs:

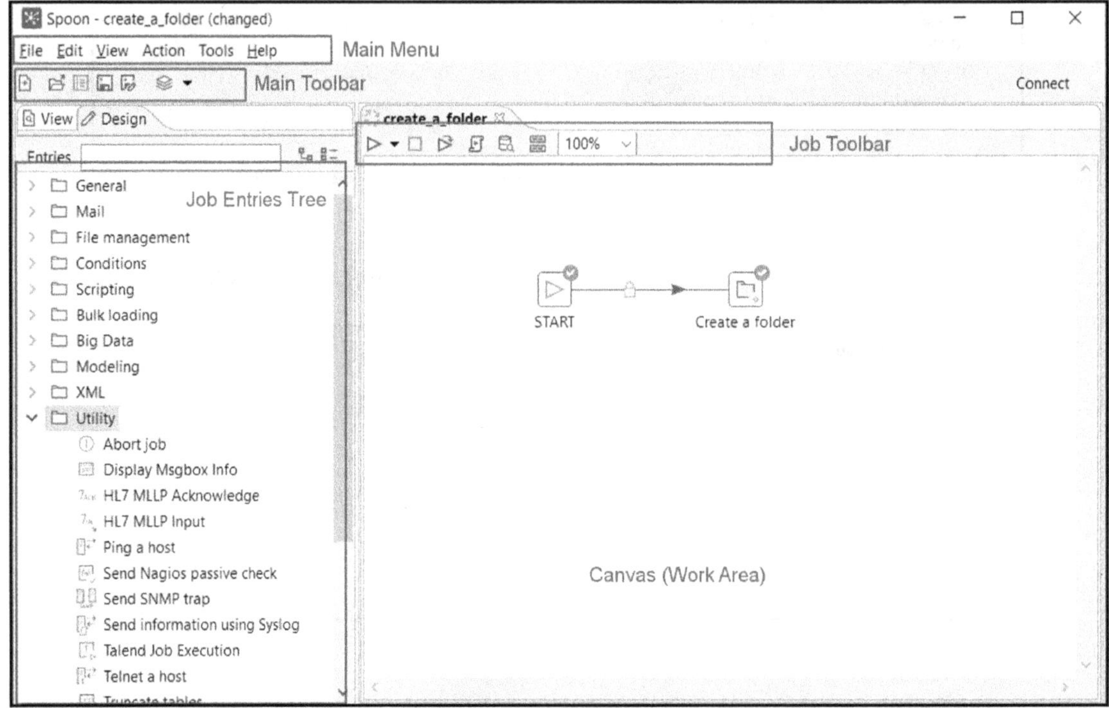

Spoon interface

The following table describes the main differences you will notice while designing a Job, as compared to designing a Transformation:

Area	Description
Design tree	You don't see a list of steps but a list of Job entries.
Job toolbar	You no longer see some options that only make sense while working with datasets. One of them is the **Preview** button. It makes no sense to preview data in jobs.
Job metrics tab (**Execution results** window)	Instead of **Step Metrics**, you have this tab. Here you can see metrics for each Job entry.

If you click on the **View** icon in the upper-left-hand corner of the screen, the tree will change to show the structure of the Job currently being edited:

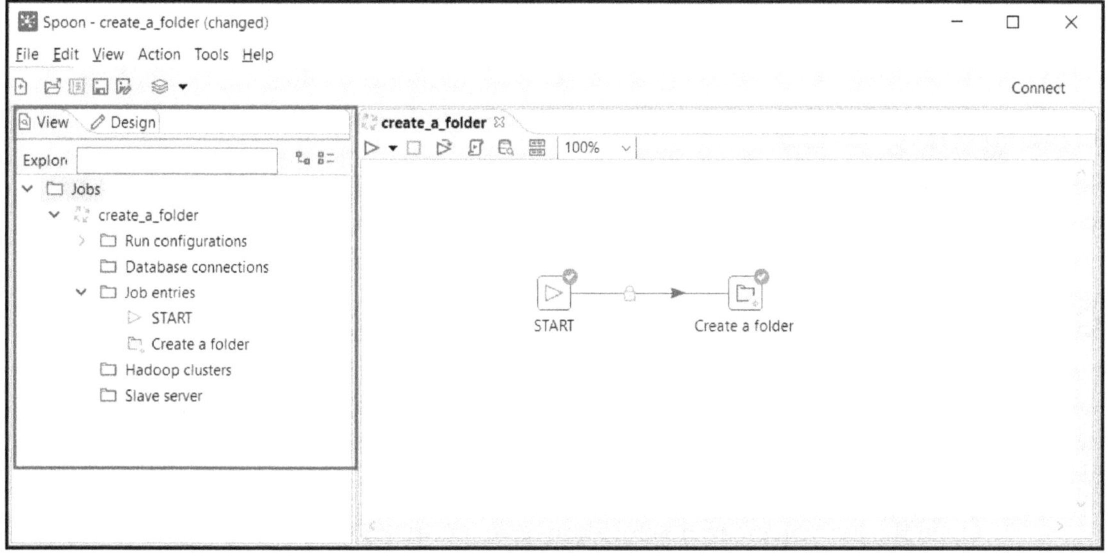

Viewing the structure of a Job

In the previous chapter, we explained some editing features which are very useful when you design a Transformation. The same features are available when you create a Job, but it's worth explaining some differences that arise:

- Using the mouseover assistance toolbar it is a tiny toolbar that is quite similar to the one you know. In this case, the toolbar appears when you position the mouse cursor over a Job entry. As we don't deal with data but with tasks, the **metadata injection** option doesn't exist in this case.
- Adding Job entries and creating hops for adding a new job entry to the work area, you can use any of the options you learned for adding a step to a Transformation. In the same way, all the options for creating a hop in a Transformation are also available for creating a hop between two Job entries.
- Working with grids contains the same kind of grids that you have in transformations are also present in some Job entries. The same shortcuts apply in this case.

For a full reference to these options, read the *Getting Familiar with Editing Features* section in `Chapter 2`, *Getting Started with Transformations*.

Designing jobs

We just described how to use Spoon when it's time to design jobs. Now it's your turn to experiment with the tool and get familiar with both Spoon and a basic set of Job entries.

Getting familiar with the job design process

Now you will create a Job similar to the one you created at the beginning of the chapter, but with the addition of some extra tasks. The new version of the Job will create a folder with a name of your choice. If an error occurs, the fact will be reported to the PDI log.
Here are the instructions:

1. Open the Job you created before and save it under a different name
2. Double-click the **Create folder** entry and replace the name of the folder with `${Internal.Entry.Current.Directory}/${MY_FOLDER}`
3. From the **Utility** category of steps, drag to the canvas a **Write To Log** entry

We want to run this last entry only when the creation of the folder fails. We do it as follows:

1. Create a new hop from the **Create folder** entry to this new entry. The hop will be green

2. Click twice on the lock of this hop so it becomes red. Leave it in this color
3. Double-click on the **Write To Log** entry and fill it as shown:

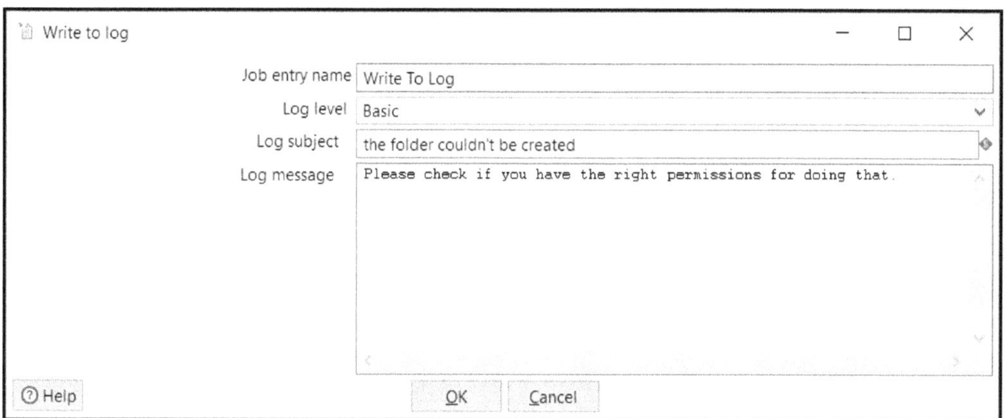

Configuring the Write To Log entry

4. Close the window. Your Job looks like this:

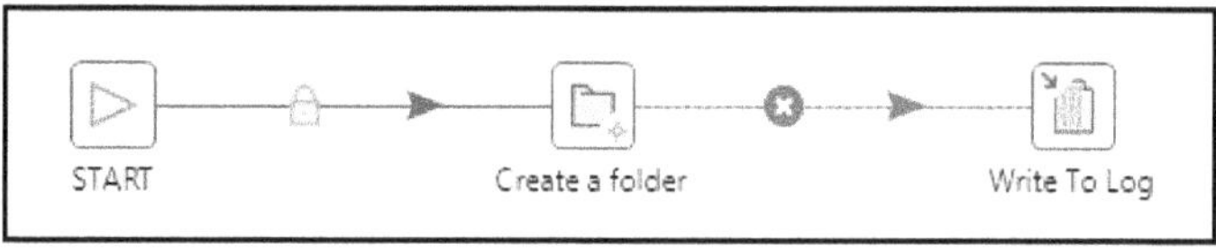

Sample job

5. Save the Job

For specifying the name of the new folder, you didn't type a fixed named but a Kettle user-defined variable named `${MY_FOLDER}`. Let's run the Job so you can see how you set this variable:

1. Click *F9* to run the Job. In the **Run Options** window, select the tab named **Variables**.

2. In the grid, you should see your variable. You should give it a value before proceeding. You do it by typing a name under the **Value** column, as shown next:

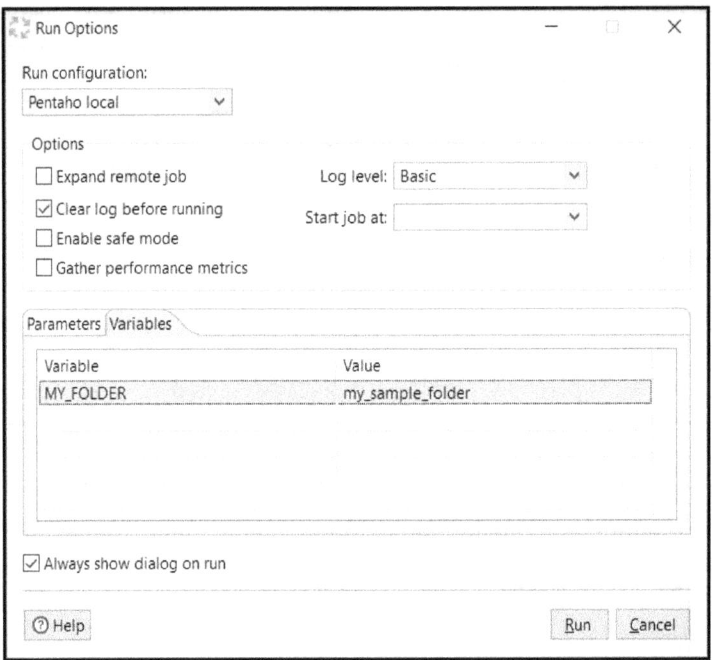

Setting variables while running a Job

3. Run the Job. A folder with the name you just typed should have been created. If you look at the work area and the result window, you should see that the **Create folder** entry succeeded; this is marked visually with a green tick on the **Create folder** icon. This is the reason why the **Write To Log** entry didn't run.
4. Run the Job again. As the new folder, type the same name as before. This time, you should see that **Create folder** failed; this is marked with a red tick on the **Create folder** icon. Because of this failure, the **Write To Log** entry runs and sends a message that you can see in the log.

Looking at the results in the Execution results window

The **Execution results** window shows you what is happening while you run a Job. As said, the difference compared to the Transformation's **Execution results** window, is that you have a **Job metrics** tab instead of the **Step Metrics** one.

The Logging tab

The **Logging** tab shows the execution of your Job. By default, the level of the logging detail is basic, but you can choose among the following options:

- **Nothing at all**
- **Error logging only**
- **Minimal logging**
- **Basic logging**
- **Detailed logging**
- **Debugging or Rowlevel (very detailed)**

The list is the same that you learned back in `Chapter 2`, *Getting Started with Transformations*, when you started working with transformations. In order to change the log level, you just select the proper option in the drop-down list available in the **Execute a Job** window. Just as you do when you run transformations, you should choose the option depending on the level of detail that you want to see.

The Job metrics tab

The **Job metrics** tab shows, for each entry of the Job, several status, and information columns. For us, the most relevant columns in this tab are:

Column	Description
Comment	Status of the execution; for example, start of Job execution
Result	Result of the execution as explained earlier; possible values are success and failure
Reason	The reason why this entry is being executed; for example, followed link after success

Note that the content of both the Logging and Job metrics tabs are color-coded:

- When there is an error, you see the lines in red
- When an entry succeeds, you can see the details in green
- If the log or metric is only informative, it is shown in a black font

Besides, the result of the execution of individual entries is represented with small ticks on top of the icons, as shown in the following screenshot:

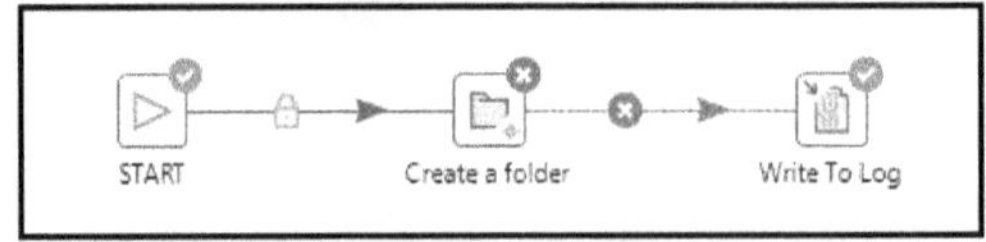

Result of the execution of a Job

Enriching your work by sending an email

When you work with ETL processes, sending emails is a very common requirement. In this section, you will learn how to send emails with PDI by enriching your previous work. In this case, the email will replace the log message.

For trying this exercise, you need access to an SMTP server. You also need at least one valid account to play with. The example uses Gmail's SMTP server (`smtp.gmail.com`), but you can use any email server, as long as you have access to the information required by PDI.

Before starting to work with Spoon, let's introduce the `kettle.properties` file. In this file, you define variables with the JVM scope. We will use it for storing the email settings:

1. Open the `kettle.properties` file located in a folder named `.kettle` inside your home directory. If you work under Windows, that folder could be `C:\Documents and Settings\<your_name>` or `C:\Users\<your_name>`, depending on the Windows version. If you work under Linux (or similar) or Mac OS, the folder will most probably be `/home/<your_name>/`.

Note that the `.kettle` folder is a system folder, and as such, may not display using the GUI file explorer on any OS. You can change the UI settings to display the folder, or use a terminal window.

2. Add the following lines, replacing the values between <> with valid information, that is, with your email and password. You may also change the values for the SMTP server as well. Then save the file as follows:

```
SMTP_SERVER=smtp.gmail.com
SMTP_PORT=465
AUTH_USER=<your email>
AUTH_PASSWORD=<your password>
```

Now we will modify the Job:

1. Restart Spoon so it can recognize the changes in the `kettle.properties` file.
2. Open the Job created in the previous exercise, and save it with a new name.
3. Delete the **Write To Log** entry and replace it with a **Mail** entry from the **Mail** category. This is how your Job will look:

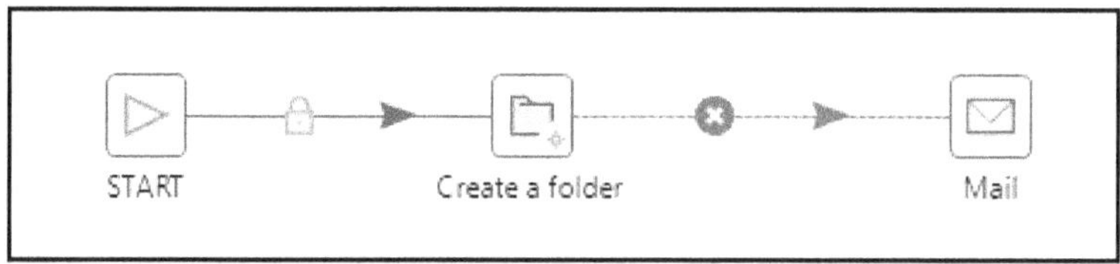

Job that sends an email

4. Double-click the **Mail** entry. Under the **Addresses** tab, fill the **Destination address** textbox with a valid email address. In addition, you need to complete the **Sender address** and the **Sender name** textboxes.

You can specify more than one destination account, using a space as a separator in the destination address of the **Mail** Job entry.

5. Complete the **Server** tab as shown in the following screenshot:

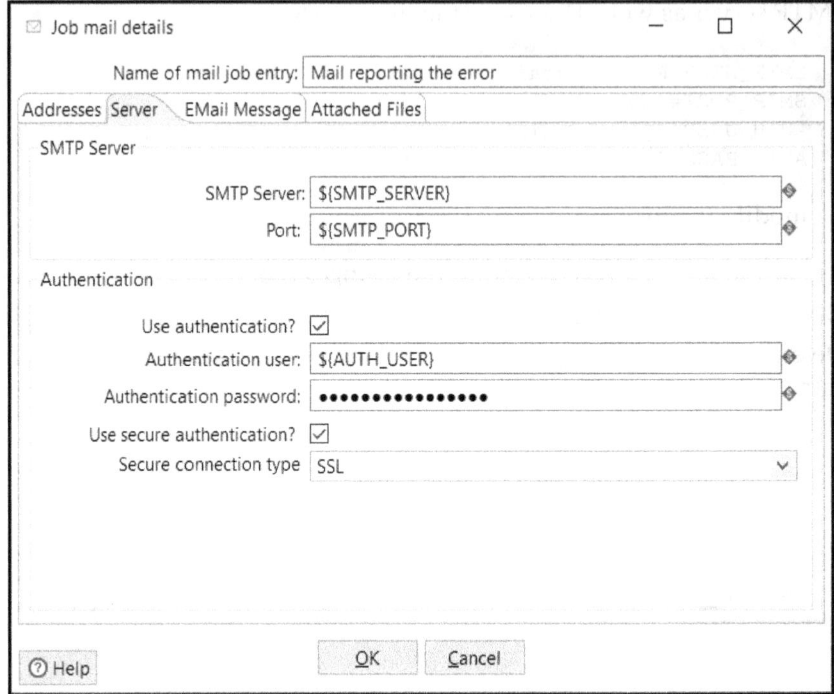

Configuring the server in a mail Job entry

The password is not visible, but it has a value: `${AUTH_PASSWORD}`. You can enter the value by hand or by pressing *Ctrl* + space and picking the value for the list of available variables.

6. Complete the **Email Message** tab, as shown next. Don't forget to check the **Only send comment in the mail body?** option:

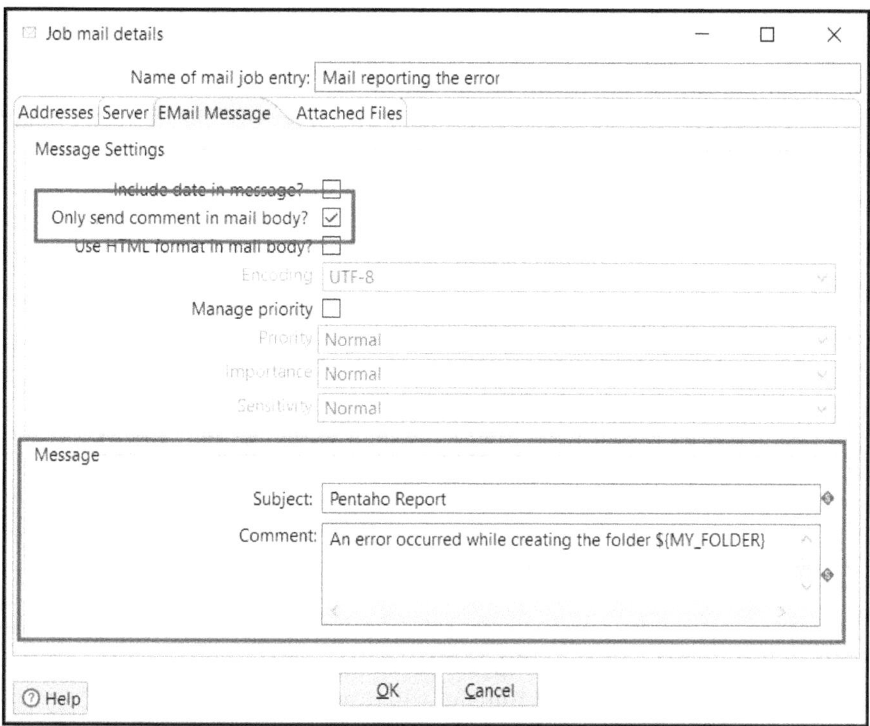

Filling the email message tab

7. Save the Job and press *F9* to run it.
8. Click on the **Variables** tab as you did before. This time you will see the list of all used variables, along with their default values set in `kettle.properties`. Among these variables, there will be one variable without a default value, `MY_FOLDER`. Provide a value, a name for the folder to be created, and click on **Run**. Supposing that the folder didn't exist, the folder will be created and the **Mail** entry will not be executed.
9. Repeat the previous step. As the value for `MY_FOLDER`, type exactly the same folder name as before. This time, the creation of the folder will fail and a mail will be sent to the destination.

As you could see, sending emails is a simple task. If you explore Spoon, you will discover that there is also a Transformation step for sending emails. In general, you could use either the step or the Job entry with similar results, but there are particular scenarios where one approach is better than the other, or where only one of the methods applies. Here you have some examples:
If your Pentaho Job failed and you want to report the status by email to an administrator, you will do it in a Job.
If you want to send several emails, with different content and to different recipients (for example, a custom welcome letter to a list of subscribers to a course), you will prefer a Transformation.
For full details about how to configure the entry, you can visit `http://wiki.pentaho.com/display/EAI/Mail`.

Running transformations from a Job

In the previous chapters, you were introduced to PDI transformations, the PDI artifacts meant to deal with data. Usually, you don't run a PDI Transformation isolated; you embed it in a bigger process. Here are some examples:

- Download a file, clean it, load the information of the file in a database, and fill an audit file with the result of the operation
- Generate a daily report and transfer the report to a shared repository
- Update a data warehouse. If something goes wrong, notify the administrator by an email

All these examples are typical processes in which a Transformation is only a part. These types of processes can be implemented by PDI jobs. In particular, one of the tasks of those jobs will be executing one or more transformations. This execution can be done with a special Job entry, the **transformation entry.**

Using the Transformation Job Entry

In this section, you will learn how to run a Transformation from a Job. For this tutorial, we will use the Transformation you created in the section *Running Transformations in an Interactive Fashion* in `Chapter 2`, *Getting Started with Transformations:*

1. Run Spoon and create a new Job.
2. Expand the **General** category of entries and drag a **START** and a **Transformation** entry to the canvas.
3. Create a hop from the **START** entry to the **Transformation** entry.
4. Save the Job.

Before continuing, look for the Transformation that generates the date range; make sure you pick the lastest version, the one that has the **Delay row** step. Copy it to a folder named `transformations` inside the folder where you just saved your Job. Rename it as `generating_date_range.ktr`.

5. Now double-click on the **Transformation** entry.
6. Position the cursor in the **Transformation:** textbox, press *Ctrl* + *Space*, and select `${Internal.Entry.Current.Directory}`.
7. Click on the icon to the left of the textbox. A window appears that lets you search for the Transformation file in your system file.

The variable `${Internal.Entry.Current.Directory}` evaluates the directory where the Job resides. As you can see, the `${Internal.Entry.Current.Directory}`variable provides a convenient starting place for looking up the Transformation file.

8. Select the Transformation **generating_date_range.ktr** and click on **OK**.

9. Now the **Transformation:** textbox has the full path to the Transformation. Replace the full Job path back to **${Internal.Entry.Current.Directory}** so the final text for the **Transformation:** field is as shown in the following screenshot:

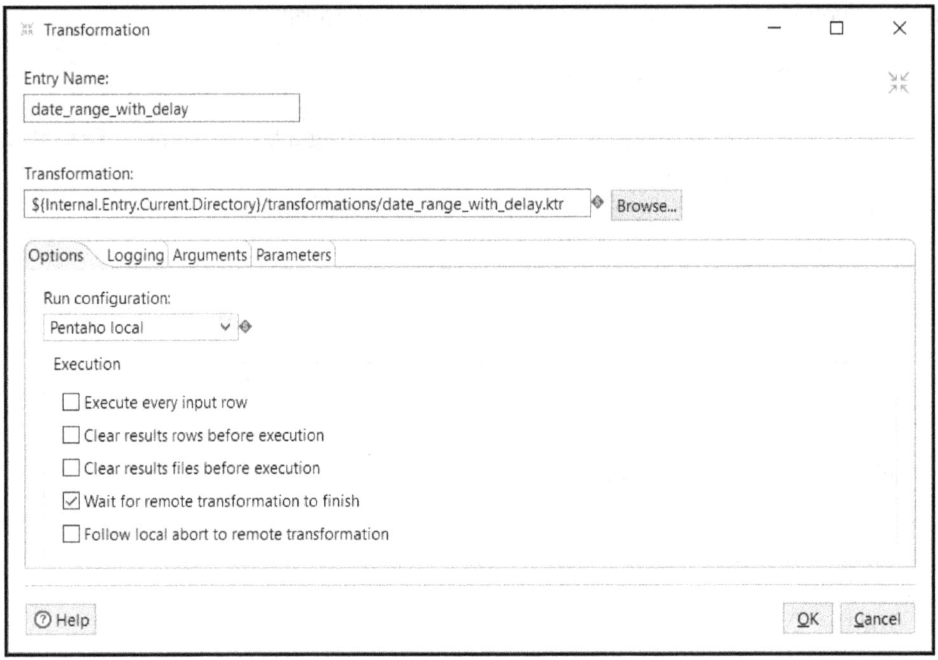

Configuring a Transformation Job entry

10. Click on **OK**.
11. Save the Job and run it.

While running, a special tick appears on top of the **Transformation** icon, meaning that the Transformation is being executed, as shown:

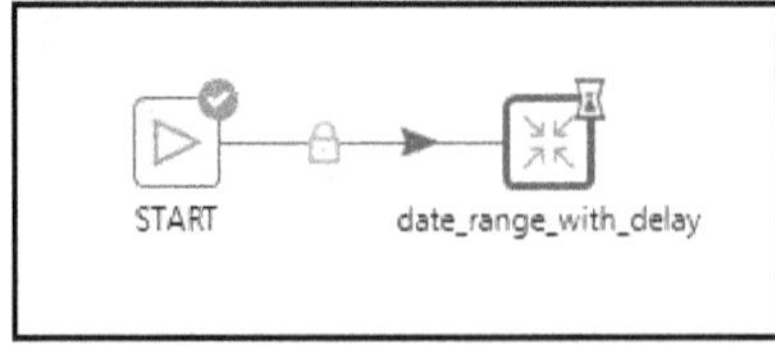

Executing a Transformation from a Job

We decided to run the Transformation with the delay row for a reason. We will show a feature named **drill-down**:

1. While running, right-click on the **Transformation** icon and select **Open Transformation**. The Transformation will be opened and you will see how it is being executed.

As usual, you could do sniff test. Remember that you do it by right-clicking on any step and selecting any of the **sniff test during execution** options in the contextual menu. For more details on this, refer to `Chapter 2`, *Getting Started with Transformations*.

2. Select the **Job** tab again. You will see that the log also displays information about the execution of the Transformation that is called by the Job.

The Job explained was just an example of how to use a **Transformation Job** entry. Note that many transformations perform their tasks by themselves. That is the case of the Transformation you ran in the tutorial.

If it makes sense to run the Transformation alone, you can do it. You are not forced to embed it into a Job.

This was just a quick view of the feature. There will be many opportunities to run transformations from jobs through the next chapters.

Understanding and changing the flow of execution

As said in the introduction, a Job must start with a **START** Job entry. All the entries that follow it are executed in a sequential way, following the direction given by the hops. Also, the execution of the destination Job entry does not begin until the Job entry that precedes it has finished.

Look at the following example:

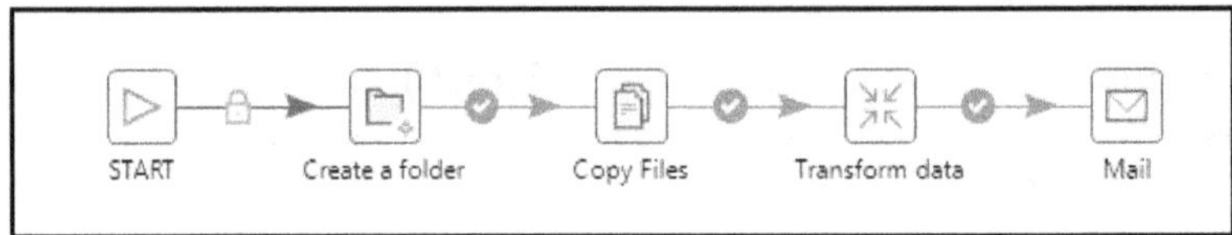

Job with a simple flow

According to what we just said, we can deduce that:

1. This Job creates a folder.
2. After the folder is created, the Job copies some files (most probably to the new folder).
3. When the files are copied, the jobs executes a Transformation. We can guess that this entry is for operating on the data in those copied files.
4. Once the Transformation finishes, the Job sends an email.

This is the simplest flow that we can find in a Job. There are, however, several ways in which we can change the flow of execution.

Changing the flow of execution based on conditions

The execution of any Job entry either succeeds or fails. For example:

- A **Mail** entry succeeds if PDI can send the message, but it fails if the specified SMTP host is unknown
- A **ZIP file** entry succeeds if PDI can zip the specified files, but will fail if the ZIP file existed and you configured the entry for failing in case PDI hits that condition
- **Create a folder** succeeds if PDI can create the folder, but fails if the folder existed or there were no permissions for creating it

Whichever the Job entry and based on the result of its execution, you decide which of the entries following the entry execute and which don't.

In particular, the Job entries under the **Conditions** category just evaluate a condition and succeed or fail upon the result of the evaluation. As an example, the **Checks if files exist** entry looks for the existence of a file. If the condition evaluates to true, that is, if the file exists, the entry succeeds. If the file doesn't exist, the entry fails.

So, when you create a Job, you not only arrange the entries and hops according to the expected order of execution, but also specify under which condition each Job entry runs.

You define the conditions in the hops. You can identify the different hops either by looking at the color of the arrow or at the small icon on it. The following table lists the possibilities:

A hop that looks...	And had the following icon...	Represents...	Which means that...
Dark gray		Unconditional execution	The destination entry executes no matter what the result of the previous entry is.
Green		Execution upon success	The destination entry executes only if the previous job entry was successful.
Red		Execution upon failure	The destination entry executes only if the previous job entry failed.

Execution conditions

At any hop, you can define the condition under which the destination Job entry will execute. In most cases, the first hop that leaves an entry is created green. The second hop leaving the entry is created red. To change the color, that is, the behavior of the hop, do any of the following:

- Right-click on the hop, select **Evaluation**, and then the condition.
- Click on the small icon on the hop. Each time you click on it, the type of hop changes.

There are two kinds of hops which you can't edit:

- The hop or hops that leave the **START** entry, mandatory in every Job
- The hop or hops that leave the **Dummy** entry, a special entry that does nothing and in general is used just as a placeholder

In both cases, the destination Job entries always execute unconditionally.

Finally, a hop can also look light grey. This means that the hop has been disabled. If you don't want an entry to be executed (mainly for testing purposes), you can disable the incoming hop or hops. You do it by right-clicking the hop and selecting **Disable**. An easier way to do it is by clicking the hop in any place but the small icon on the hop. To revert the status, you can click the hop again in the same way.

Forcing a status with an abort Job or success entry

Each Job itself ends with a status: success or failure. This status depends on the status of the last executed entry. However, you can force the final status of a Job to a fixed value.
To show this as a practical example, let's go back to the Job that created the folder; the one you created in the section *Getting Familiar with the Job Design Process*. In this Job, if the folder was not created, you wrote a message to the log. As the last entry was **Write To Log**, and PDI could successfully write to the log, the final status of the Job was a success. It makes sense, however, that the Job fails. So this is how you revert the status:

1. Open the Job.
2. Add an **Abort job** entry after **Write To Log**. You will find this entry under the **Utility** category of entries. By adding this entry, you force the Job to abort after executing **Write To Log**.
3. Save and run the Job. You will see that now the Job aborts after writing the custom message to the log.

In general, you can append an **Abort job** entry to any entry, forcing the Job to fail.

The counterpart to the **Abort job** entry is the **Success** entry, which you can find under the **General** category. If you append a **Success** entry after any entry, you are forcing a successful result, ignoring the error in case that entry fails.

Changing the execution to be synchronous

When you link two entries with a hop, you force an order of execution. Now look for the following Job:

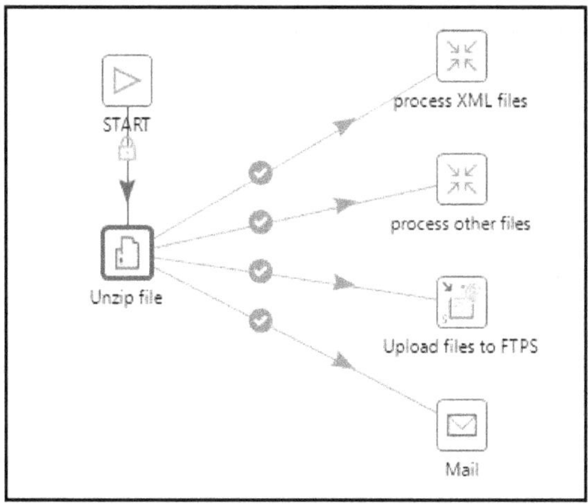

Sample Job with no predefined order of execution

Although the figure implies that the entries are run in parallel, that is not the case. On the contrary, when you create a Job like this, the entries still run in sequence, one entry after another, depending on the creation sequence.

If you really intend to run several entries in parallel, you can explicitly set that action. To do that, right-click on the entry from which the parallel task will run. Then select **Launch next entries in parallel**. Once selected, the arrows to the next Job entries will be shown in dashed lines, as shown next:

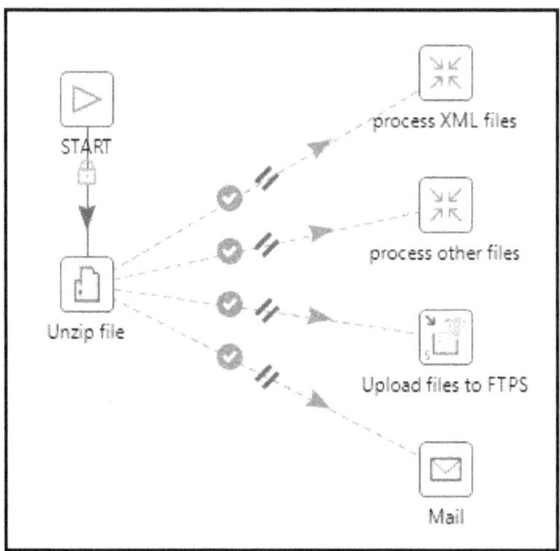

Running Job entries in parallel

Note that not only the next **job** entries are launched in parallel, but all the ones that follow them.

Managing files

One of the main tasks that you can do with PDI is to manage files: create folders, move files, unzip files, and more. Some of these tasks are very simple to implement and also quite intuitive, as, for example, creating a folder. Other tasks are a bit more elaborated and there are a couple of ways to implement them.

When we speak about performing tasks, it's highly probable that we end up creating a Job. This is true for most of the tasks related to file management. There are, however, some tasks that can also be done with transformations. In the next subsections, we will explain both cases and we will also explain when you should choose one over the other.

Creating a Job that moves some files

Now we will create a sample Job that moves some files from one folder to another. For this exercise, let's suppose that we have a folder with the following files:

```
ARTIST_1.MP3
ARTIST_2.MP3
ARTIST_3.MP3
ARTIST_4.MP3
error_2.png
error-jira.png
error-vpn.png
MySongs.mp3
SONG_2.MP3
THEBESTSONG.MP3
```

Our Job will move the `mp3` files with name starting with `ARTIST` to a new folder named `MUSIC`. If the folder doesn't exists, the Job will write a message to the log. Let's work on that:

1. Open Spoon, create a new Job, and drag the **START** entry to the work area.

2. Now add the following entries: the **Checks if files exist** entry from the **Conditions** category, the **Move Files** entry from the **File Management** category, and the **Abort** entry from the **Utility** category. Link the entries as follows:

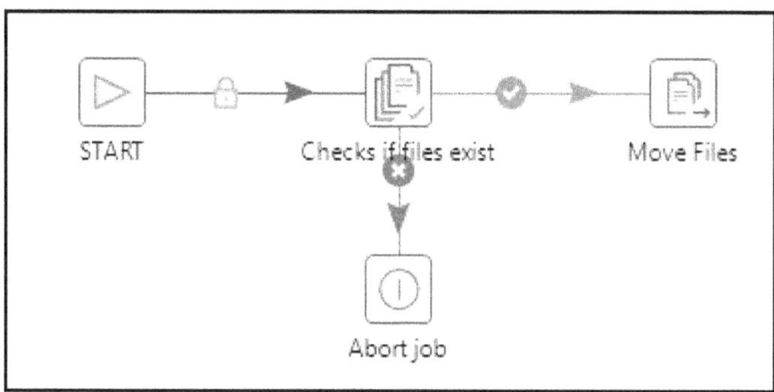

Job for moving files

3. Despite the name, the **Checks if files exist** entry serves for checking the existence of both files and folders. We will use it for verifying the existence of the `MUSIC` folder. So, double-click the entry and in the first cell of the grid, type the full path for the folder, for example, `D:/LearningPDI/MUSIC`.
4. Double-click the **Abort** entry. In the **Message:** textbox, type the following text, replacing the path with your own path: `The destination folder [D:/LearningPDI/MUSIC] doesn't exist.`

Now let's configure the core entry for this Job, the entry that will move the files:

1. Double-click the **Move Files** entry for configuring the movement of the files.
2. To the right of the **File/Folder source** label, type the full path for the source folder containing the files, for example, `D:/LearningPDI/SAMPLEFILES`. As an alternative, click on the **Folder...** button just to the right of the textbox and browse for the folder.
3. To the right of the **File/Folder destination** label, type the full path of the `MUSIC` folder. As an alternative, if the folder already exists, you could click on the **Folder...** button beside the label and browse for the folder to avoid typing.
4. Besides the label **Wildcard (RegExp)**, you will have to type a regular expression indicating which file or files you want to move. In this case, the expression is `ARTIST_.*\.MP3`, that is, all the files starting with `ARTIST_` and with extension `MP3`.

5. Click on **Add**. All the content that you just typed will be moved to the following grid. The final configuration will be like this:

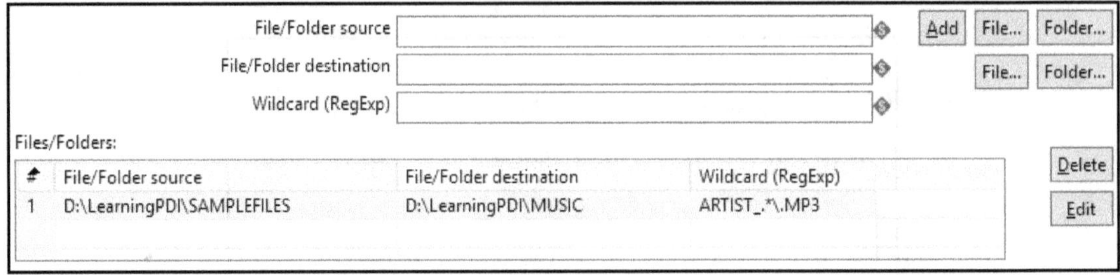

Configuring a move files entry

6. Close the window and save the Job.

Now let's see how this works:

1. Run the Job. As the folder didn't exist, the Job will fail. In the **Logging** tab, you will see the abort message.
2. Now create the `MUSIC` folder by hand.
3. Run the Job again. This time, as **Log Level:** select **Detailed**. The Job will succeed, and in the **Logging** tab, you will see the details of the moved files:

```
... - Starting job entry
... - Processing row source File/folder source : [D:/SAMPLEFILES]
... destination file/folder : [D:/LearningPDI/MUSIC]... wildcard :
[ARTIST_.*(backslash).MP3]
... -
... - Fetching folder [file:///D:/SAMPLEFILES]
... - File [file:///D:/SAMPLEFILES/ARTIST_1.MP3] was moved to
file:///D:/LearningPDI/MUSIC/ARTIST_1.MP3
... - File [file:///D:/SAMPLEFILES/ARTIST_2.MP3] was moved to
file:///D:/LearningPDI/MUSIC/ARTIST_2.MP3
... - File [file:///D:/SAMPLEFILES/ARTIST_3.MP3] was moved to
file:///D:/LearningPDI/MUSIC/ARTIST_3.MP3
... - File [file:///D:/SAMPLEFILES/ARTIST_4.MP3] was moved to
file:///D:/LearningPDI/MUSIC/ARTIST_4.MP3
... - =========================================
... - Total files in error : 0
... - Total files successfully processed : 4
... - =========================================
```

You can verify that the Job effectively moved the files by browsing your file system. You should find the new folder containing the four files:

- `ARTIST_1.MP3`
- `ARTIST_2.MP3`
- `ARTIST_3.MP3`
- `ARTIST_4.MP3`

Also, you shouldn't see these files in the source folder.

As you can see, moving some files is really a simple task. This also occurs with other operations, as, for example, copying or deleting files. Despite the simplicity, there are a couple of things that are new and deserve our attention.

Selecting files and folders

The **Move Files** entry is one of many entries that requires you to indicate files and/or folders. Let's describe the interface in detail. As shown in the screenshot *Configuring a move files entry*, you have two textboxes where you can either type or browse for the files or folders. You also have a third textbox for the wildcard. These textboxes only serve for entering the information. Unless you add them to the grid succeeding (you do this by clicking on the **Add** button), PDI will ignore them. In fact, entering the data as you did in the tutorial, or typing it by hand in the grid, is exactly the same. The advantage of the first method is that you have the **Browse** buttons to help you find the files and folders.

Note that the grid allows you to add more rows. This means that in the same entry you can move several files with different source and destination folders or file patterns. For adding more rows, the procedure is the same. You add them by hand in the grid, or with the help of the **Browse** and **Add** buttons.
No matter the purpose of the entry, the way of entering this information is the same in all cases. You will also see this kind of interface in Transformation steps.

Working with regular expressions

In this last example, you specified the files with a wildcard, which was basically a regular expression. A **regular expression** is much more than specifying the known wildcards ? or *. In the following table, you have some examples of regular expressions, which you may use to specify filenames. The **Example** column refers to the sample files in the tutorial:

The following regular expression...	**matches...**	**Example**
`.*`	Any file	Any of the sample files
`.+_2\.*`	Any file whose name ends with `_2`, no matter the extension	`ARTIST_2.MP3` and `error_2.png`
`(?i).+song.*\.mp3`	Any `mp3` file containing or ending with `song`, upper or lower case	`MySongs.mp3` and `THEBESTSONG.MP3`

Note that the * wildcard does not work the same way as it does on the command line. If you want to match any character, the * has to be preceded by a dot.

This was the first time that you faced a regular expression in PDI; however, they are used in a lot of places, both in jobs and transformations. If you are not used to them, it is highly recommended that you learn at least the basics about the subject.
Here you have some useful links in case you want to know more about regular expressions:

- Read about regular expressions at `http://www.regular-expressions.info/quickstart.html`
- Read the Java regular expression tutorial at `http://java.sun.com/docs/books/tutorial/essential/regex/`
- Read about Java regular expression pattern syntax at `https://docs.oracle.com/javase/8/docs/api/java/util/regex/Pattern.html`

Summarizing the Job entries that deal with files

In the previous subsections, you experimented with some of the many Job entries meant to deal with files. As you saw, they are mainly grouped under the **File management** and the **Conditions** categories. Most of these entries have a self-explanatory name and their use is quite intuitive. Here we have a brief summary for you to experiment with:

Purpose	Job entries
Copy/Move files and folders	**Copy Files**: Copies one or more files or folders. As an option, the source files can be removed. **Move Files**: Moves one or more files or folders. For moving files, there are more settings available here than in the **Copy Files** entry.
Delete files and folders	**Delete file**: Deletes a single file or folder with a fixed name. **Delete files**: Deletes one or more files, with a fixed name or a given pattern. **Delete folders**: Deletes one or more folders with a fixed name.
File compression	**Zip file**: Creates a zip file with the files in a given folder, with a given pattern. **Unzip file**: Unzips one or more zip files.

Note that this is not a full list of entries that deal with files. For the full list, you can explore the Spoon categories or read the documentation at `https://help.pentaho.com/Documentation/8.0/Products/Data_Integration/Job_Entry_Reference`.

There is some overlap in the purpose of some entries. This means that there is no single way to implement some tasks. As an example, the following are some other ways to move the music files, compared to what you did in the tutorial:

- Using the **Copy Files** entry. This entry has an option for removing the source files, which is equivalent to moving the files.
- Using the **Copy Files** entry followed by a **Delete files** entry.

There is no rule about when to use one or the other. You will find out by yourself which one is best for your requirements.

All the entries mentioned earlier can be used together with some **Conditions** entries, exactly as we did in the tutorial. Here are some entries that you can use:

- **File Exists**: Succeeds if a particular file or folder exists.
- **Checks if files exist**: Succeeds if all the listed files/folders exist.
- **Checks if a folder is empty**: By default, succeeds if the folder is empty. Alternatively, this entry can be configured to succeed if the folder doesn't contain files with a given pattern.
- **Evaluate file metrics**: Evaluates the number of files or the size of files in a list. There is a list of possible success criteria that can be configured in the **Advanced** tab of the entry.

For more examples of this subject, you can read *Chapter 5, File Management, Pentaho Data Integration Cookbook - Second Edition* by Packt Publishing, `https://www.packtpub.com/big-data-and-business-intelligence/pentaho-data-integration-cookbook-second-edition`

Customizing the file management

There are some cases where the options offered by these entries are not enough. Look at these following examples:

- Moving only the files created in the current month
- Copying a list of files listed in a `.csv` file
- Deleting text files that don't have a predefined header

In cases like these, you have to choose a different approach. There are basically three ways to handle this:

- Implement the operation with a PDI Transformation
- Work with result file lists
- Use arguments in the Job entries

Let's look at an example of the first approach. We will learn about the other two in `Chapter 14`, *Creating Advanced Jobs.*

The next example will recreate the Job where we copied the files to the `MUSIC` folder, but in this case, we will change the name of the files to lowercase, which is not possible to do with a Job.

In the following instructions, we assume that you have the original set of files ready to be moved:

1. Open Spoon and create a new Transformation.
2. From the **Input** category of steps, drag the **Get File Names** step to the work area. This step will allow us to specify a starting list of files to work with.
3. Double-click the step and fill the first row of the grid. Under the **File/Directory** column, type `D:/LearningPDI/SAMPLEFILES`. Under the **Wildcard (RegExp)** column, type `ARTIST_.*\.MP3`
4. Click on **Show filename(s)...** You will see the list of files that match the settings:

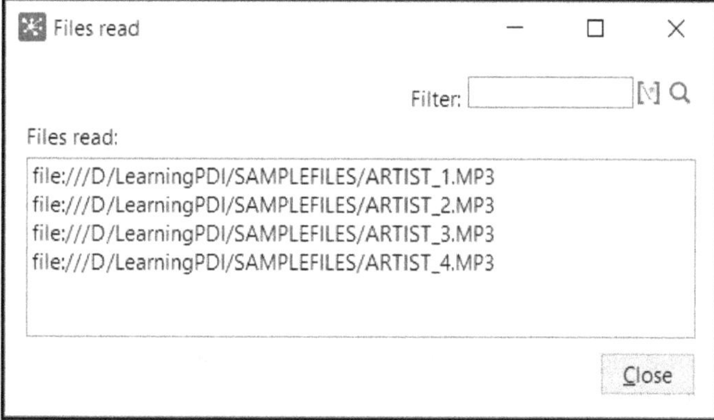

Filenames in a Get File Names step

5. Now click on **Preview rows**. You will see the output of this step, that is, information associated with the file names on the file system. This output includes filename, size, and last modified time, among others. Close the window.

Note that the output of **Get File Names** has one row per file that matches the files specified in the grid.

6. Just for simplicity and demonstration purposes, let's keep only those fields that are relevant to the exercise. After the **Get File Names** step, add the **Select Values** step and select the `filename` and `short_filename` fields.
7. We already have the source files. Now we have to build the full path for the destination files. We will do it with a **User Defined Java Expression** step from the **Scripting** category. So, after the **Select Values** step, add the **UDJE** step.

8. Double-click the step and add a new field named `destination_filename`. As **Java expression**, type `"D:/LearningPDI/MUSIC" + short_filename.toLowerCase()`. As **Value type**, select `String`.
9. Close the window and preview the Transformation. You should see this:

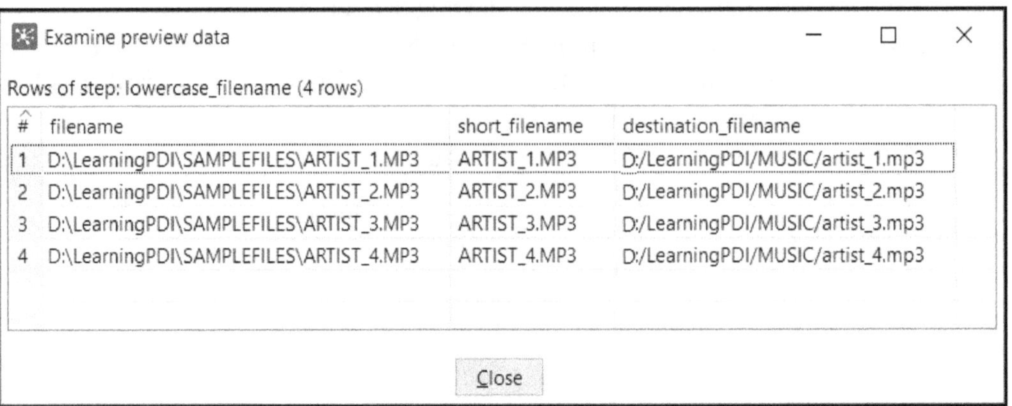

#	filename	short_filename	destination_filename
1	D:\LearningPDI\SAMPLEFILES\ARTIST_1.MP3	ARTIST_1.MP3	D:/LearningPDI/MUSIC/artist_1.mp3
2	D:\LearningPDI\SAMPLEFILES\ARTIST_2.MP3	ARTIST_2.MP3	D:/LearningPDI/MUSIC/artist_2.mp3
3	D:\LearningPDI\SAMPLEFILES\ARTIST_3.MP3	ARTIST_3.MP3	D:/LearningPDI/MUSIC/artist_3.mp3
4	D:\LearningPDI\SAMPLEFILES\ARTIST_4.MP3	ARTIST_4.MP3	D:/LearningPDI/MUSIC/artist_4.mp3

Previewing a Transformation

10. Finally, from the **Utility** category, add the **Process files** step. This is the step that will move the files. Double-click the step and configure it as follows: As **Operation**, select **Move**. As **Source filename field** and **Target filename field**, select **filename** and **destination_filename** respectively.
11. Close the window, save the Transformation, and run it. If you browse your file system, you will see that all the files matching the settings were copied, but the names were changed to lowercase.

Knowing the basics about Kettle variables

In this chapter, you used the string `${Internal.Entry.Current.Directory}` to identify the folder where the current Job was saved. You also used the string `${MY_FOLDER}` to define the name of the folder to be created. Both strings, `${Internal.Entry.Current.Directory}` and `${MY_FOLDER}`, are Kettle variables, that is, keywords linked to a value. You use the name of a variable, and when the Transformation runs, the name of the variable is replaced by its value.

The first of these two variables is an environment variable, and it is not the only one available. Other known environment variables are: `${user.home}`, `${java.io.tmpdir}`, and `${java.home}`. All these variables, whose values are auto-populated by PDI, are ready to be used any time you need, both in jobs and transformations.
The second string, `${MY_FOLDER}`, is a variable you defined in a Job directly in the entry that would use it, the **Create a folder** entry. That is not the only way to create user-defined variables. Another possibility is to use the `kettle.properties` file, as explained in the following subsection.

Understanding the kettle.properties file

The `kettle.properties` file is a file created by Spoon the first time you run the tool. The purpose of the file is to contain variable definitions with a broad scope: Java Virtual Machine.

Why should we define a variable in this file? If we want to use a variable in several jobs and/or transformations, and the values don't change from one Job/Transformation to another, then defining the variable in the `kettle.properties` file is a good idea. Now you may guess why we put the SMTP related variables in this file. It's highly probable that you reuse them in many other jobs. Also, there are low chances that the values change.
In the `kettle.properties` file, you may define as many variables as you want. The only thing you have to keep in mind is that those variables will be available inside Spoon only after you restart it.

You also have the possibility of editing the `kettle.properties` file from Spoon. You do it from the main menu, **Edit | Edit the kettle.properties file**. If you use this option to modify a variable, the value will be available immediately.

If you defined several variables in the `kettle.properties` file and you don't want your file be modified by the tool, it's not a good idea to edit it from Spoon.

When you edit the `kettle.properties` file from Spoon, PDI does not respect the order of the lines you had in the file, and it also adds to the file a lot of pre-defined variables. So, if you want to take control over the look and feel of your file, you shouldn't use this option.

How and when you can use variables

Any time you see a red dollar sign by the side of a textbox, you may use a variable. Inside the textbox, you can mix variable names with static text, as you did in the last Job when you put the name of the new folder as `${Internal.Entry.Current.Directory}/${MY_FOLDER}`.

To see all the available variables, both predefined and user-defined, you have to position the cursor in the textbox and press *Ctrl* + spacebar. A full list will be displayed, so you can select the variable of your choice. If you place the mouse cursor over any of the variables for a second, the actual value of the variable will be shown, as in the following screenshot:

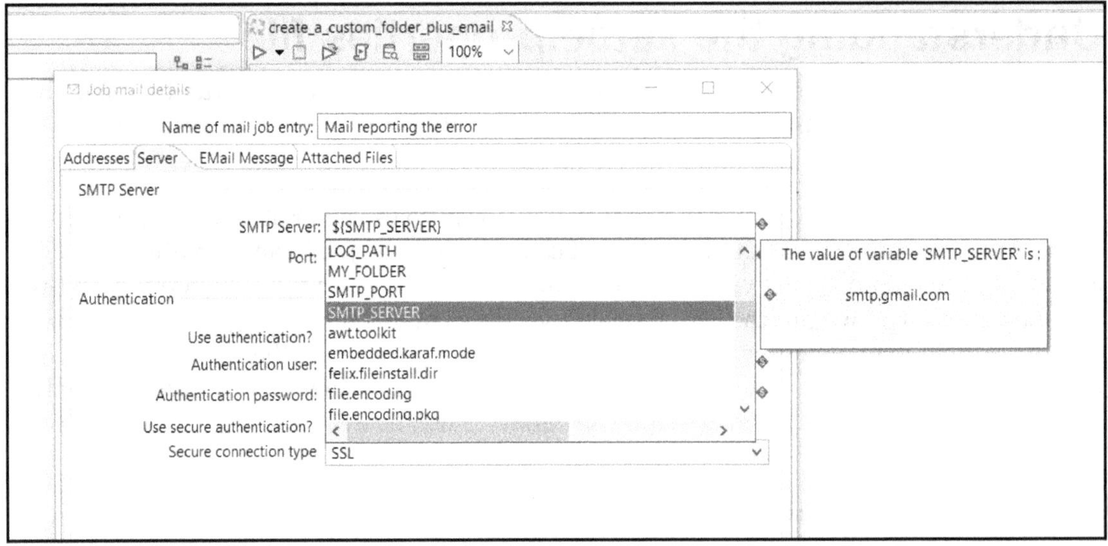

Listing the available variables

If you know the name of the variable, you don't need to select it from the list. You may type its name by using either of these notations: ${<name>} or %%<name>%%.

Summary

In this chapter, you learned the basics about PDI jobs: what a Job is, what you can do with a Job, and how jobs are different from transformations. In particular, you learned to use a Job for sending emails, working with files, and running one or more transformations.

In addition, you learned the basics about what Kettle variables are and where to use them. In the next chapter, we will switch back to the world of PDI transformations, to learn all the details about reading and writing all kinds of files.

4
Reading and Writing Files

Data is everywhere; in particular, you will find data in files. Product lists, logs, purchases details, survey results, and statistical information are just a few examples of the different kinds of information usually stored in files. This is the list of topics covered in this chapter:

- Introducing the input and output sources
- Reading data from plain files
- Different ways of building the list of input file(s) to read
- Saving data into files
- Different ways for defining where to save the data
- Working with files located in remote sites and the cloud

Reading data from files

Despite being the most primitive format used to store data, files are still broadly used and they exist in several formats, such as fixed width, comma-separated values, spreadsheets, or even free format files. **Pentaho Data Integration** (**PDI**) has the ability to read data from all kinds of files. In this section, let's see how to use PDI to get data from these files.

Reading a simple file

In this section, you will learn to read one of the most common input sources, plain files.

For demonstration purposes, we will use a simplified version of `sales_data.csv` that comes with the PDI bundle. Our sample file looks as follows:

```
ORDERDATE,ORDERNUMBER,ORDERLINENUMBER,PRODUCTCODE,PRODUCTLINE,QUANTITYORDER
ED,PRICEEACH,SALES
2/20/2004 0:00 ,10223,10,S24_4278 ,Planes ,23,74.62,1716.26
11/21/2004 0:00,10337,3,S18_4027 ,Classic Cars ,36,100 ,5679.36
6/16/2003 0:00 ,10131,2,S700_4002,Planes ,26,85.13,2213.38
7/6/2004 0:00 ,10266,5,S18_1984 ,Classic Cars ,49,100 ,6203.4
10/16/2004 0:00,10310,4,S24_2972 ,Classic Cars ,33,41.91,1383.03
12/4/2004 0:00 ,10353,4,S700_2834,Planes ,48,68.8 ,3302.4
1/20/2005 0:00 ,10370,8,S12_1666 ,Trucks and Buses,49,100 ,8470.14
3/11/2004 0:00 ,10229,6,S24_2300 ,Trucks and Buses,48,100 ,5704.32
7/19/2004 0:00 ,10270,6,S12_1666 ,Trucks and Buses,28,100 ,4094.72
8/25/2003 0:00 ,10145,4,S32_4485 ,Motorcycles ,27,100 ,3251.34
```

Before reading a file, it's important that you observe its format and content: Does the file have a header? Does it have a footer? Is this a fixed-width file? Which are the data types of the fields? Knowing these properties about your file is mandatory for reading it properly.

In our sample file, we observe that it has one row per order, there is a one-line header, and there are eight fields separated by commas. With all this information, along with the data type and format of the fields, we are ready for reading the file. Here are the instructions:

1. Start Spoon and create a new Transformation.
2. Expand the **Input** branch of the Steps tree, and drag and drop to the canvas a **Text file input** step.
3. Double-click the **Text file input** icon and give the step a name.
4. Click on the **Browse...** button and search for the `sales_data.csv` file.
5. Select the file. The textbox **File or directory** will be temporarily populated with the full path of the file, for example, `D:/LearningPDI/SAMPLEFILES/sales_data.csv`.

Note that the path contains forward slashes. If your system is Windows, you may use back or forward slashes. PDI will recognize both notations.

6. Click on the **Add** button. The full file reference will be moved from the **File or directory** textbox to the grid. The configuration window should appear as follows:

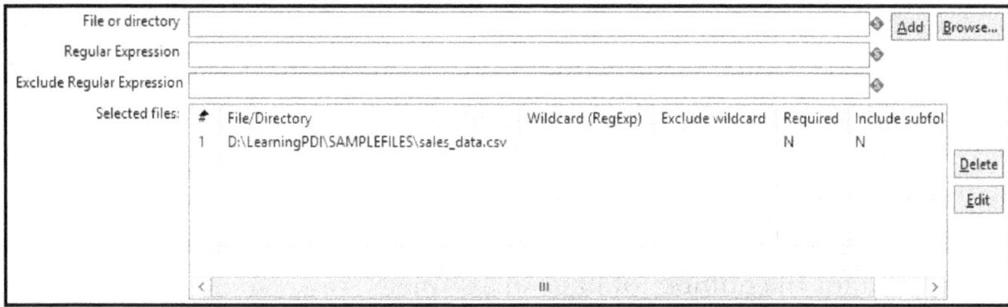

Adding a file for reading in a text file input step

7. Click on the **Content** tab, and fill it in, as shown in the following screenshot:

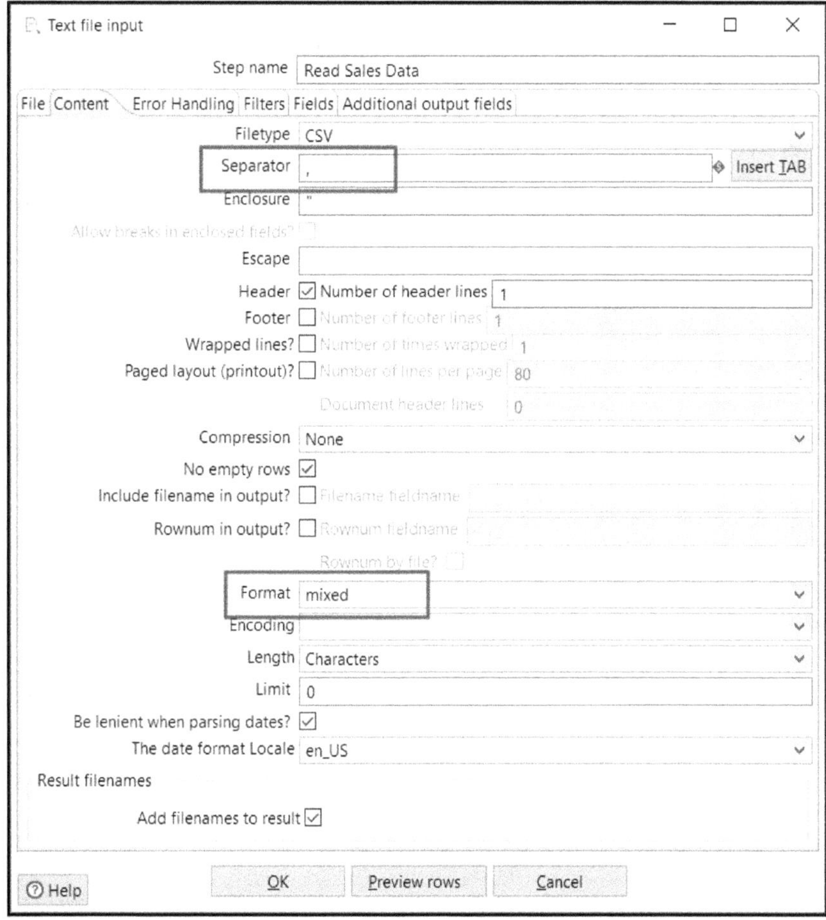

Configuring the content tab in a text file input step

By default, PDI assumes DOS format for the file. If your file has a Unix format, you will be warned that the DOS format for the file was not found. If that's the case, you can change the format in the **Content** tab. If you are not sure about the format of your file, you can safely choose **mixed**, as in the previous example, as PDI will recognize both formats.

8. Click on the **Fields** tab. Then click on the **Get Fields** button. You will be prompted for the number of lines to sample.

The **Get Fields** functionality tries to guess the metadata but might not always get it right, in which case you can manually overwrite it.

9. Click on **Cancel**. You will see that the grid was filled with the list of fields found in your file, all of the type **String**.
10. Click on the **Preview rows** button and then click on the **OK** button. The previewed data should look like the following screenshot:

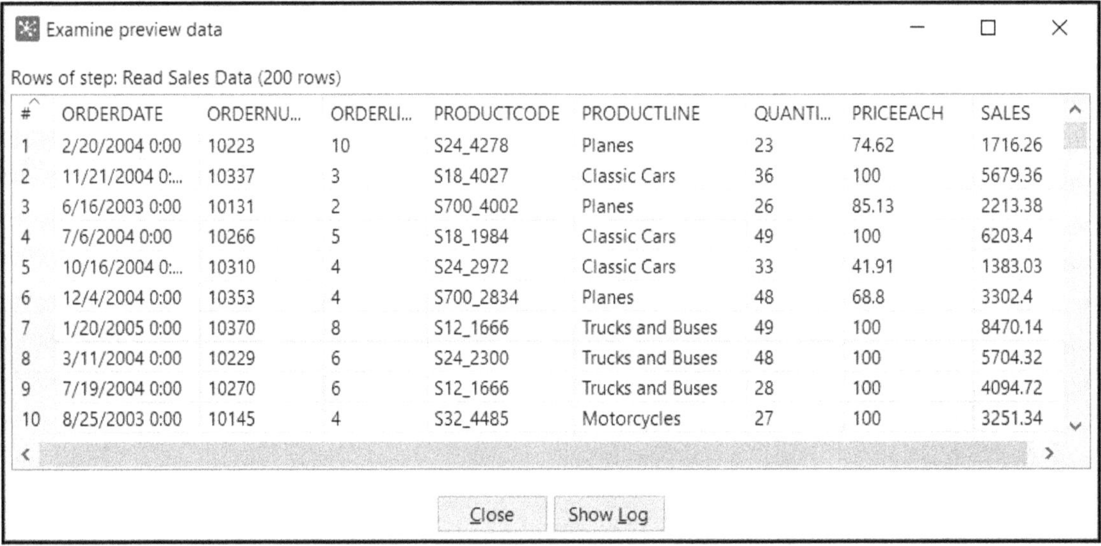

#	ORDERDATE	ORDERNU...	ORDERLI...	PRODUCTCODE	PRODUCTLINE	QUANTI...	PRICEEACH	SALES
1	2/20/2004 0:00	10223	10	S24_4278	Planes	23	74.62	1716.26
2	11/21/2004 0:...	10337	3	S18_4027	Classic Cars	36	100	5679.36
3	6/16/2003 0:00	10131	2	S700_4002	Planes	26	85.13	2213.38
4	7/6/2004 0:00	10266	5	S18_1984	Classic Cars	49	100	6203.4
5	10/16/2004 0:...	10310	4	S24_2972	Classic Cars	33	41.91	1383.03
6	12/4/2004 0:00	10353	4	S700_2834	Planes	48	68.8	3302.4
7	1/20/2005 0:00	10370	8	S12_1666	Trucks and Buses	49	100	8470.14
8	3/11/2004 0:00	10229	6	S24_2300	Trucks and Buses	48	100	5704.32
9	7/19/2004 0:00	10270	6	S12_1666	Trucks and Buses	28	100	4094.72
10	8/25/2003 0:00	10145	4	S32_4485	Motorcycles	27	100	3251.34

Previewing an input file

There is still one more thing that you should do; provide the proper metadata for the fields:

1. Change the **Fields** grid as shown in the following screenshot:

Configuring the fields tab

2. Run a new preview. You should see the same data, but with the proper format. This may not be obvious by looking at the screen but you can confirm the data types by moving the mouse cursor over each column.
3. Close the window.

This is all you have to do for reading a simple text file. Once you read it, the data is ready for further processing.

It's important to highlight that the existence of the file is not mandatory when you are creating the Transformation. It helps, however, when it's time to configure the input step.

When you don't specify the name and location of a file, or when the real file is not available at design time, you are not able to use the **Get Fields** button, nor to see if the step is well configured. The trick is to configure the step by using a real file identical to the expected one. After that, change the configuration for the name and location of the file as needed.

After configuring an input step, you can preview the data just as you did, by clicking on the **Preview rows** button. This is useful to discover if there is something wrong with the configuration. In that case, you can make the adjustments and preview again, until your data looks fine.

Troubleshooting reading files

Despite the simplicity of reading files with PDI, errors appear. Many times the solution is simple but difficult to find if you are new to PDI. The following table gives you a list of common problems and possible solutions to take into account while reading and previewing a file:

Problem	Diagnostic	Possible solutions
You get the message: **Sorry, no rows found to be previewed.**	This happens when the input file does not exist or is empty.	Check the name of the input file. Verify the syntax used and check that you didn't put spaces or any strange character as part of the name. Also, verify that you put the filename in the grid. If you just put it in the **File or directory** textbox, PDI will not read it.
When you preview the data, you see a grid with blank lines.	The file contains empty lines, or you forgot to get the fields.	Check the content of the file. Also, check that you got the fields in the **Fields** tab.
You see the whole line under the first defined field.	You didn't set the proper separator and PDI couldn't split the different fields.	Check and fix the separator in the **Content** tab.
You see strange characters.	You left the default content but your file has a different format or encoding.	Check and fix the **Format and Encoding** option in the **Content** tab. If you are not sure of the format, you can specify mixed.

You don't see all the lines you have in the file.	You are previewing just a sample (100 lines by default). Or you put a limit on the number of rows to get. Another problem may be that you set the wrong number of header or footer lines.	When you preview data, you are just seeing a sample. If you raise the previewed number of rows and still have few lines, check the **Header**, **Footer**, and **Limit** options in the **Content** tab.
Instead of rows of data, you get a window headed **ERROR** with an extract of the log.	Different errors may occur, but the most common has to do with problems in the definition of the fields.	You could try to understand the log and fix the definition accordingly. For example, suppose you see: `Couldn't parse field [Integer] with value [2014-01-15], format [null] on data row [1].` The error is that PDI found the text `2014-01-15` in a field that you defined as `Integer`. If you made a mistake, you can fix it. Or you could read all the fields as `String` and then handle the errors, as you learned to do in `Chapter 2`, *Getting Started with Transformations*.

Learning to read all kind of files

PDI can take data from several types of files, with almost no limitations. There are several steps which allow you to take a file as the input data. All those steps are in the **Input** step category; **Text file input**, **Fixed file input**, and **Microsoft Excel Input** are some of them. Despite the obvious differences that exist between these types of files, the ways to configure the correspondent steps have much in common. The next subsections explain how to proceed.

Specifying the name and location of the file

As you just learned, in order to specify the name and location of a file, you can just use a fixed value or a combination of PDI variables and fixed text. This may not suffice in all situations. There are a couple of special cases explained next.

Reading several files at the same time

In the main exercise, you used an **Input** step to read a single file. But suppose you have several files, all with the same structure. Reading those files at the same time is not much different from what you did.

For this quick tutorial, we will take as a source several files with the same structure as `sales_data.csv`, but separated by region. This is the list of files which you will find in the `SAMPLEFILES` folder:

```
sales_data_APAC.csv
sales_data_EMEA.csv
sales_data_Japan.csv
```

You have two options here. The first way for reading several files at the same time would be to provide the detailed list of filenames:

1. Open the Transformation that reads the `sales_data.csv` file.
2. Fill the grid with every filename, as shown next:

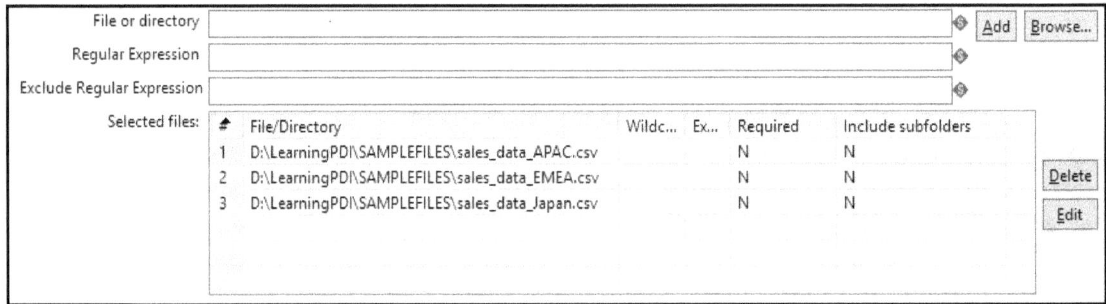

Reading several files at the same time

3. Select the **Additional output fields** tab. In the **Short filename field** textbox, type `file_name`.
4. Run a preview. You should see something like this:

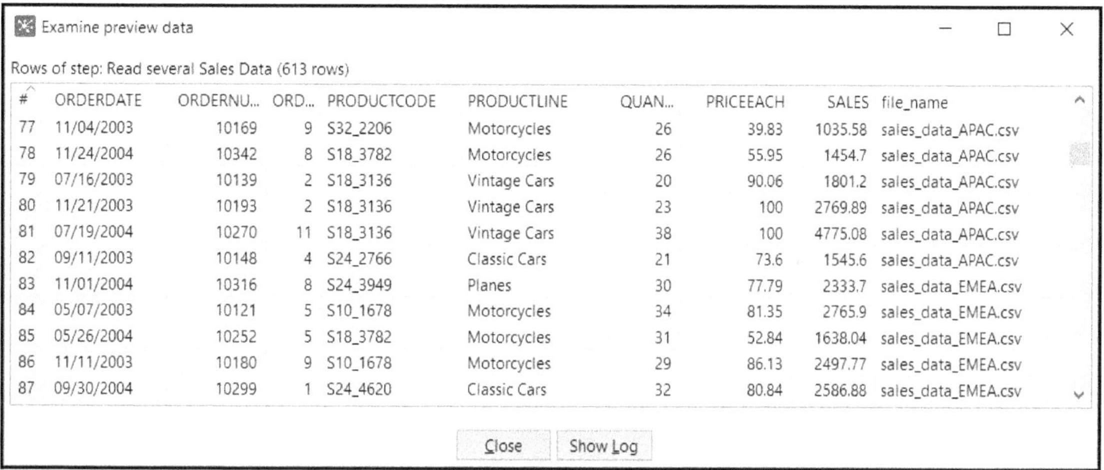

Examine preview data

Rows of step: Read several Sales Data (613 rows)

#	ORDERDATE	ORDERNU...	ORD...	PRODUCTCODE	PRODUCTLINE	QUAN...	PRICEEACH	SALES	file_name
77	11/04/2003	10169	9	S32_2206	Motorcycles	26	39.83	1035.58	sales_data_APAC.csv
78	11/24/2004	10342	8	S18_3782	Motorcycles	26	55.95	1454.7	sales_data_APAC.csv
79	07/16/2003	10139	2	S18_3136	Vintage Cars	20	90.06	1801.2	sales_data_APAC.csv
80	11/21/2003	10193	2	S18_3136	Vintage Cars	23	100	2769.89	sales_data_APAC.csv
81	07/19/2004	10270	11	S18_3136	Vintage Cars	38	100	4775.08	sales_data_APAC.csv
82	09/11/2003	10148	4	S24_2766	Classic Cars	21	73.6	1545.6	sales_data_APAC.csv
83	11/01/2004	10316	8	S24_3949	Planes	30	77.79	2333.7	sales_data_EMEA.csv
84	05/07/2003	10121	5	S10_1678	Motorcycles	34	81.35	2765.9	sales_data_EMEA.csv
85	05/26/2004	10252	5	S18_3782	Motorcycles	31	52.84	1638.04	sales_data_EMEA.csv
86	11/11/2003	10180	9	S10_1678	Motorcycles	29	86.13	2497.77	sales_data_EMEA.csv
87	09/30/2004	10299	1	S24_4620	Classic Cars	32	80.84	2586.88	sales_data_EMEA.csv

Close Show Log

Previewing the content of several files

As you can see, the preview shows data coming from all the specified files. We added the name of the file as an extra field, just for you to see where each order comes from.

When the names of the files in your list follow a pattern, then instead of a detailed list of filenames, you could use regular expressions. This option is also useful when you don't know the exact names of the files beforehand:

1. Open the Transformation that reads several files and double-click on the **Input** step.
2. Delete the lines with the names of the files.

3. In the first row of the grid, under the File/Directory column, type the full path of the input folder, for example, D:/SAMPLEFILES/. Under the Wildcard (RegExp) column, type sales_data_.+\.csv. Click on the **Show filename(s)...** button. You will see the list of files that match the expression:

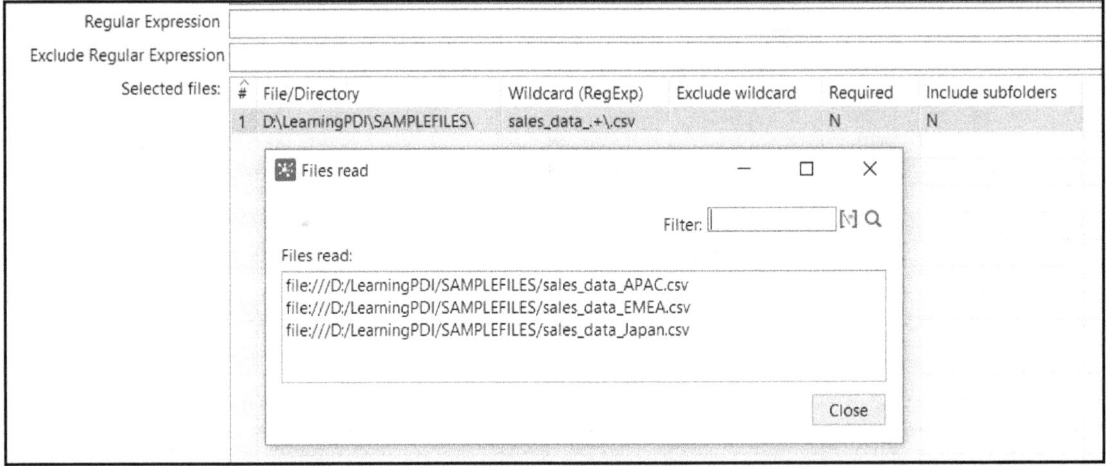

Files that match a regular expression

4. Close the tiny window and click on **Preview rows** to confirm that the file names match the expression you typed.

Reading files that are compressed or located on a remote server

In case the file you need to read is compressed or located on a remote server, you don't have to download or unzip it unless you need the file for archiving or further processing. PDI allows you to read those files by using a **Virtual File System** URL.

The syntax for reading a particular file compressed as a zip file is zip:<compressed file>!/<file name>\, where <compressed file> is the full path for the zip file and <file name> is the name of the file to read, including the path inside the zip file.

If you want to read a file over HTTP, as **File/Directory** you just use the full URL preceded by http://.

Let's explain the options with an example. Suppose you have four text files, A.txt, B.txt, C.txt, and D.txt, and you zip them as samplefiles.zip inside the D:/SAMPLEFILES folder. The following table shows some possibilities:

<table>
<tr><th>Files to read</th><th>File/Directory</th><th>Wildcard (RegExp)</th></tr>
<tr><td>The file A.txt located in D:/SAMPLEFILES/</td><td>D:/SAMPLEFILES/A.txt</td><td></td></tr>
<tr><td>The A.txt file inside the samplefiles.zip</td><td>zip:D:/SAMPLEFILES/samplefiles.zip!/A.txt</td><td></td></tr>
<tr><td>All the files in the zip file</td><td>zip:D:/SAMPLEFILES/samplefiles.zip</td><td>.*</td></tr>
<tr><td>The A.txt and B.txt files compressed as samplefiles.zip located in a remote server</td><td>zip:http://<url>/samplefiles.zip</td><td>(A|B)\.txt</td></tr>
</table>

Reading a file whose name is known at runtime

Suppose you face any of the following situations:

- The name of the file to read is specified in an XML file
- The name of the file to read is obtained as a result of a database query
- The name of the file to read is the combination of a fixed text followed by the current year and month

None of the special cases explained previously include these or similar situations. There are a couple of ways to handle this with PDI. Let's learn the simplest.

Our objective is to read one of the sales files. The exact name of the file to read is in an XML file.

In order to run this exercise, create a file named `configuration.xml` and inside the file, type the following:

```
<settings>
<my_file>sales_data_Japan</my_file>
</settings>
```

The idea is to dynamically build a string with the full filename and then pass this information to the **Text file input** step, as follows:

1. Create a new Transformation.
2. From the **Input** category of steps, drag to the canvas the **Get data from XML** step.
3. Double-click the step for editing it. In the **File** tab, browse for the `configuration.xml` file and add it to the grid.
4. Select the **Content** tab. In the **Loop XPath** textbox, type `/settings/my_file`.
5. Finally, select the **Fields** tab. Fill the first row of the grid as follows: under **Name**, type filename; under **XPath**, type a dot (`.`); and as **Type**, select or type **String**.
6. Preview the data. You should see this:

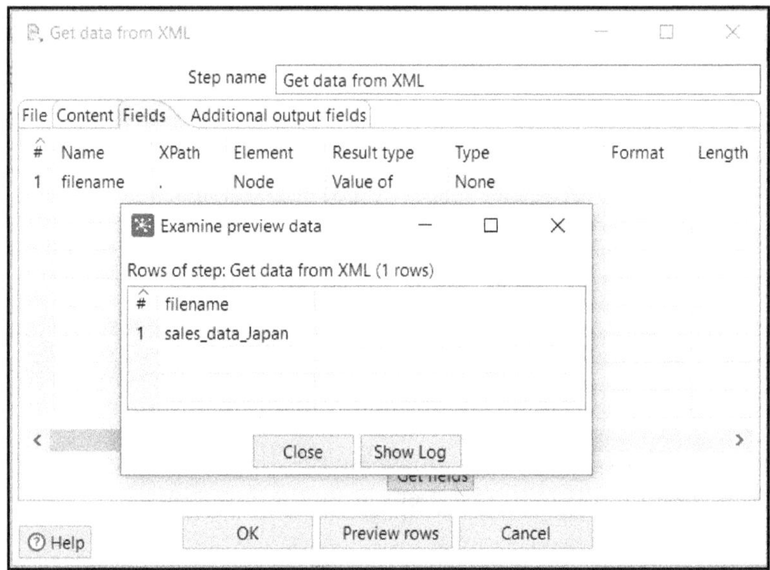

Previewing data from an XML file

7. After this step, add a **UDJE** step. Double-click it and configure it for creating the full path for the file, as in the following example:

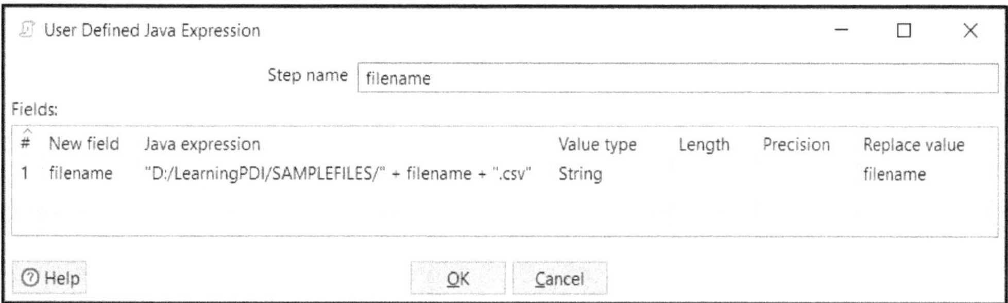

8. Configuring a **UDJE** step.
9. Close the window, select the **UDJE** step, and run a preview. You should see the full name of the file to read: `D:/LearningPDI/SAMPLEFILES/sales_data_Japan.csv`.
10. Close the preview window, add a **Text file input** step, and create a link from the **UDJE** step towards this step.
11. Double-click on the **Text file input** step and fill the lower grid as shown in the following screenshot:

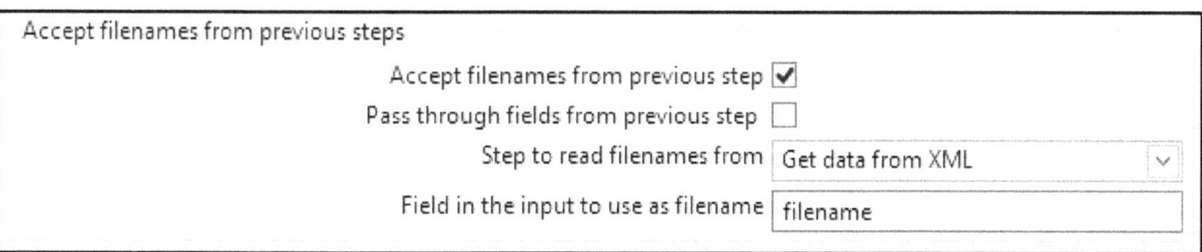

Accepting a filename for incoming steps

12. Fill in the **Content** and **Fields** tabs just like you did before. It's worth saying that the **Get Fields** button will not populate the grid as expected because the filename is not explicit in the configuration window. In order to avoid typing the fields manually, you can refer to the following tip:

Instead of configuring the tabs again, you can open any of the transformations, and copy the **Text file input** step and paste it here. Leave the **Contents** and **Fields** tabs untouched and just configure the **File** tab as explained previously.

Describing the incoming fields

When you create a new dataset taking a file as a source, you have to give PDI a proper definition of the fields so that it knows how to interpret the incoming data. In particular, the Date and Numeric fields come in several flavors and we should take some time to configure them manually so that PDI interprets the values correctly.

This also applies to the fields created from scratch; for example, with a **Data Grid** or an **Add constant** step.

If you don't specify a format when reading a Date or Numeric field, PDI will do its best to interpret the data, but this could lead to unexpected results.

Reading Date fields

Generally speaking, when a Date field is created, you have to specify the format so PDI can recognize in the values the different components of the date. There are several formats that may be defined for a date, all of the combinations of letters that represent date or time components.

These format conventions are not PDI-specific but Java standard.

The following table shows the main letters used for specifying date formats:

Letter	Meaning
y	Year
M	Month
d	Day
H	Hour (0 - 23)
m	Minutes
s	Seconds

As an example, the first field in our sales file, `ORDERDATE`, corresponds to a date. If we look at the first value, `2/20/2004`, it's clear that we have the month, then the day, and then the four digits for the year, all separated by slashes. So our mask, in this case, should be defined as `MM/dd/yyyy`.

There are more combinations to define the format for a Date field. For a complete reference, check the Java API documentation, located at `https://docs.oracle.com/javase/8/docs/api/java/text/SimpleDateFormat.html`.

Reading Numeric fields

Beside digits, Numeric fields can contain separators and dollar signs, among other characteristics. Just as it happens with dates, when you read or create Numeric fields, it's almost mandatory that you specify a format to tell PDI how to interpret the incoming number. The following are the most used symbols for numbers:

Symbol	Meaning
`#`	Digit. Leading zeros are not shown.
`0`	Digit. If the digit is not present, zero is displayed in its place.
`.`	Decimal separator.
`-`	Minus sign.
`%`	Field has to be multiplied by 100 and shown as a percentage.

In order to specify the format of your numbers, you have to combine them. As an example, in the sales file, the `SALES` field is one of the several numeric fields. As it is a number with decimal digits, the mask provided is `#.##`.

If you don't specify a format for your numbers, you may still provide a **length** and **precision**. Length is the total number of significant figures while precision is the number of floating point digits.

For a complete reference on number formats, you can check the Java API documentation at `https://docs.oracle.com/javase/8/docs/api/java/text/DecimalFormat.html`.

Continuing with our example, you can see that `ORDERNUMBER` is made of digits, but it doesn't make sense to do mathematics with it. In cases like this, you don't need to define the field as Numeric. You can, however, provide a Numeric mask like `#`, so PDI doesn't complete the field with zeros or leading blanks.

Reading only a subset of the file

In the main tutorial, we read the full file—all the rows and all the columns. What if you only need a subset of it?

If, for any reason, you don't want to read one or more of the leading fields, as, for instance, `PRICEEACH` and `SALES` in our example, you don't have to put them in the grid. In such a case, PDI will ignore them. On the other hand, even if you don't need a field in the middle, as, for example, `PRODUCTLINE`, you cannot remove it from the grid, as it would cause a bad lecture of the file. Instead, you can remove the field later by using a **Select values** step.

Regarding the rows, there is a textbox in the **Content** tab named **Limit**, that allows you to set a maximum number of lines to read. In particular, instead of reading the first N lines, you may want to read only the rows that meet some conditions. Some steps allow you to filter the data, skip blank rows, read only the first N rows, and so on.

If the criteria for keeping or discarding rows are more elaborate, most probably you will need to use some extra steps after the input step. You will learn to do this in the next chapters.

Reading the most common kinds of sources

As said, no matter the kind of source file, the **Input** steps have much in common. However, it's worth mentioning some features specific to each of them.

Reading text files

PDI offers several steps to read text files. In the tutorial, we used the most generic one, the **Text file input** step. The following table summarizes the options:

Step	Purpose	Characteristics
Text file input	This step is used to read a variety of text-files types, including CSV files and fixed-width flat files.	This is the most generic step for reading files, offering a great flexibility for configuring the lecture. As explained in the previous sections, with this step, it is possible to read several files at the same time, as soon as they share the same format.
CSV file input	This step is used to read data from a file delimited by a comma (default) or but any other separator.	Compared to **Text file input**, this step has the less flexible configuration. As a counterpart, it provides better performance. One of its advantages is the option to apply **Lazy conversion**. When checked, this flag prevents PDI from performing unnecessary data type conversions, increasing the speed for reading files. This step also offers the possibility of running in parallel. If you have multiple copies of this step running, and you check the **Running in parallel?** option, each instance reads a separate part of the file.
GZIP CSV input	This step is used to read zipped CSV files.	All the features mentioned earlier in the **CSV file input** step apply to this step.
Fixed file input	This step is used to read data from a fixed-width text file, exclusively.	It has fewer configuration options compared to the **Text file input** step but offers better performance. Just as the **CSV input** step, this step also offers the option to apply lazy conversion and to run in parallel.

Despite not having the textbox **Accept filename from previous step**, the **CSV file input** step does accept a filename. When you create a link from a step toward a **CSV file input** step, a new textbox is added to its configuration window for specifying the **filename** field. The same occurs with the **GZIP CSV input** step.

Reading spreadsheets

Spreadsheets are also very common kinds of files used in **Extract**, **Transform**, and **Load** (**ETL**) processes. The PDI step for reading spreadsheets is **Microsoft Excel Input**. Both Excel 97-2003 (XLS) and Excel 2007 (XLSX) files are allowed. Despite the name of the step, it also allows to read Open Office (`ods`) files.

The main difference between this step and the steps that read plain files is that in the **Microsoft Excel Input** step you have the possibility to specify the name of the sheet to read. For a given sheet, you will provide the name as well as the row and column to start at.

Take into account that the row and column numbers in a sheet start at 0.

You can read more than one sheet at a time, as long as all share the same format. If you want to read all sheets in the spreadsheet, or if you don't know the name of the sheet in the file, just leave the sheets grid empty.

If you don't specify any sheet name, the button for getting fields will not work. If you want to get the fields automatically, you can configure the step with a sheet name just for this purpose. Once you are ready with the fields definition, you may safely remove the sheet name from the **Sheet** configuration tab.

Reading XML files

For reading XML files, there is a step named **Get data from XML input**. In order to specify which fields to read from the file, you do two things:

1. First, select the path that will identify the current node. This is optimally the repeating node in the file. You select the path by filling in the **Loop XPath** textbox in the **Content** tab.
2. Then specify the fields to `get`. You do it by filling the grid in the **Fields** tab by using *XPath* notation. The location is relative to the path indicated in the **Content** tab.

The **Get Data from XML** step is the step that you will use for reading XML structures in most cases. However, when the data structures in your files are very big or complex, or when the file itself is very large, there is an alternative step, **XML Input Stream** (**StAX**). This step is capable of processing data very fast regardless of the file size and is also very flexible for reading complex XML structures.

Earlier in the chapter, we showed how to read a very simple XML file with the first of these two steps. In the next chapter, we will devote more time to the details about dealing with XML structures.

Reading JSON files

For reading a file with JSON structure, there is a step named **JSON Input**. For specifying the fields to read from the file, you have to use *JSONPath* notation. You do it in the **Fields** tab, in a way similar to how the *XPath* expressions are used for reading XML files.

Using this step is not the only way for reading and parsing JSON structures. In the next chapter, we will learn more about the subject.

Outputting data to files

Creating and populating files with data is another common requirement in ETL processes. This section is meant to teach you how to do this with PDI.

Creating a simple file

As well as taking data from several types of files, PDI is capable of sending data to different types of output files. All you have to do is redirect the flow of data towards the proper output step.

As a starting point, we will demonstrate how to generate a plain text file. In this case, we will generate a file with dates:

1. From the code in `Chapter 2`, *Getting Started with Transformations* open the Transformation that generates dates, `date_range.ktr`. Save it under a different name.

2. Double-click the second **Calculator** step. We will use this step for adding more fields related to each date. Fill the grid as follows:

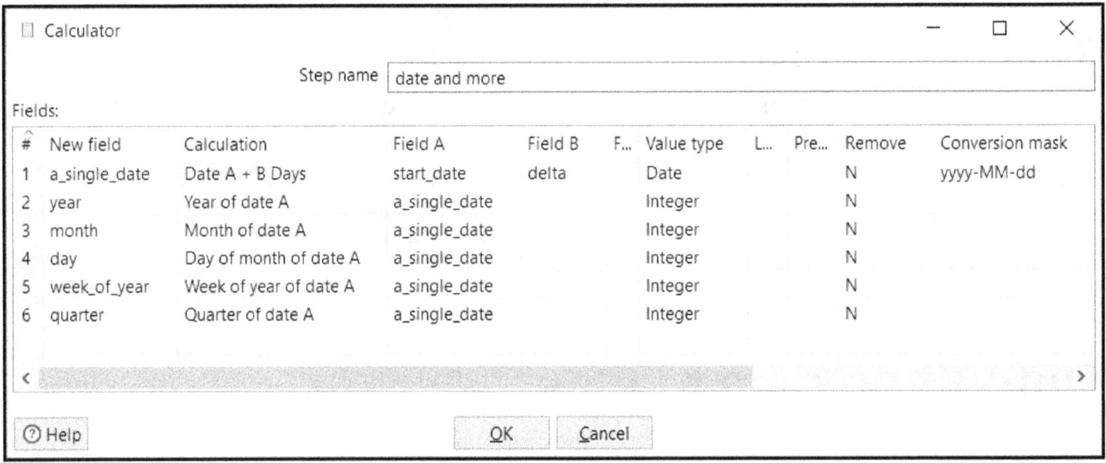

Adding fields in a Calculator step

3. Expand the **Output** branch of the **Steps** tree, look for the **Text file output** step and drag it to the work area.
4. Create a hop from the **Calculator** step to this new step.
5. Double-click on the **Text file output** step icon and give it a name. As **Filename**, type the full name for the file to generate, for example, `D:/LearningPDI/files/dates`.
6. In the **Content** tab, leave the default values.

7. Select the **Fields** tab and configure it as shown next:

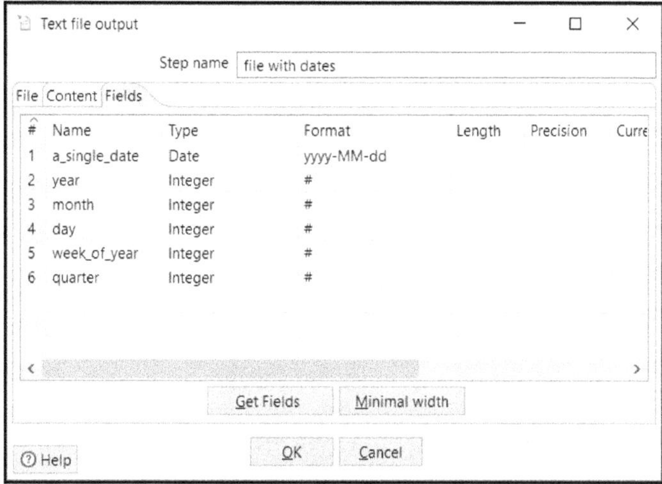

Configuring the fields grid in an output step

8. Click on **OK**.
9. Save the Transformation and run it.
10. Browse for the new file and open it. It will look as follows:

```
a_single_date;year;month;day;week_of_year;quarter
2017-01-01;2017;1;1;52;1
2017-01-02;2017;1;2;1;1
2017-01-03;2017;1;3;1;1
2017-01-04;2017;1;4;1;1
2017-01-05;2017;1;5;1;1
2017-01-06;2017;1;6;1;1
2017-01-07;2017;1;7;1;1
2017-01-08;2017;1;8;1;1
2017-01-09;2017;1;9;2;1
2017-01-10;2017;1;10;2;1
...
```

Note that if you run this Transformation more than once, PDI will overwrite the destination file. This is the default behavior. If you specify an existing file, the file will be replaced by a new one, unless you check the **Append** checkbox, present in some of the output steps. PDI will generate the output file even if there is no data to send to it. If you don't want empty files, there is a way for preventing the situation. Just check the `Do not create file at start` flag present in most output steps. If you do this, the file will not be created until the first row of data comes to it.

Learning to create all kind of files and write data into them

There are several steps which allow you to send the data to a file. All those steps are under the **Output** category; **Text file output** and **Microsoft Excel Output** being a couple of them. Just as with input files, no matter the kind of output, the configuration of the output step is similar in all of them.

Providing the name and location of an output file

In the main exercise, you specified the name of the output file as a fixed text. You can also use a PDI variable or a combination of PDI variables and fixed text. There are a couple of special cases explained next.

Creating a file whose name is known only at runtime

It is possible that a fixed name or a variable is not enough for building the name of your output file. If the filename is known only at runtime, you have to proceed differently.

Suppose you want to generate the file with dates in the same way as before, but you want to name the file as `DATES_<start date>-<end date>.txt`. For instance, for the current year, the name would be `DATES_20170101-20171231.txt`. The way to do this is similar to the way you did it for reading files. You dynamically build a string with the full filename and then pass this information to the output step:

1. Open the Transformation that generates the file with dates.
2. Delete the last hop by right-clicking it and selecting **Delete**.

3. Now add to the work area the **Select Values** step and the **UDJE** step. We will use them for generating the name of the file. Link all the steps as shown:

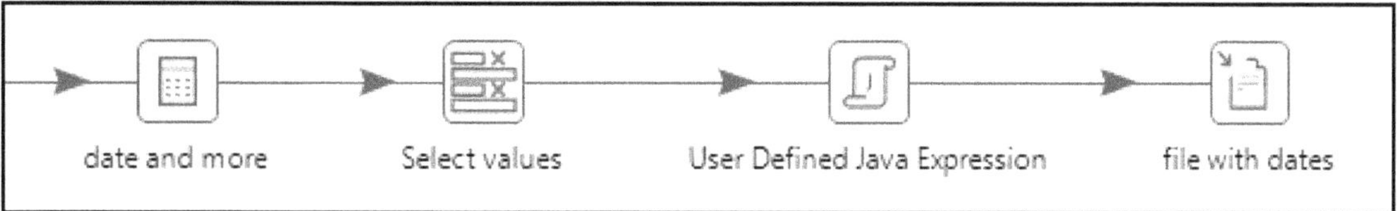

Sample Transformation

4. Double-click the **Select values** step and use it for changing the metadata of the start and end date:

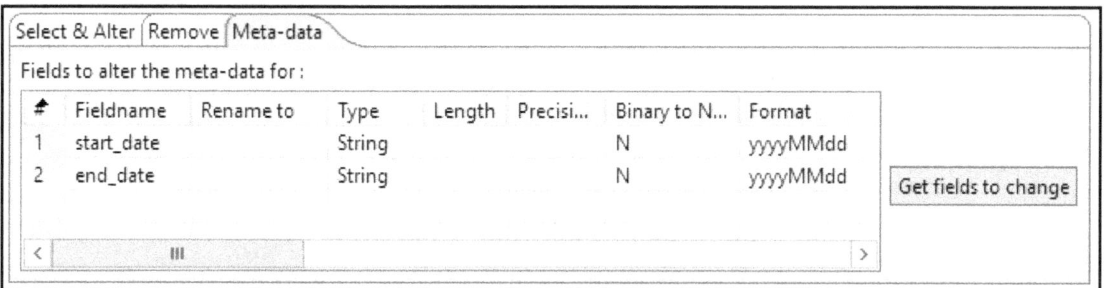

Changing the metadata from Date to String

5. Double-click **UDJE**. Add a new field named `filename`, of type `String`. As **Java expression**, type `"D:/LearningPDI/files/dates_" + start_date + "_"+ end_date + ".txt"`. If you want to generate the file in a different place, feel free to change the path. Don't forget the quotation marks!

So far, for building filenames, we've been using the **UDJE** step. This is just a choice. There are alternative steps for doing the same.

6. Double-click the **Text file output** step. Check the **Accept file name from field?** option. As **File name field**, select the field created in the previous step, `filename`.
7. Close the step, save the Transformation, and run it.

8. Browse your file system. Supposing that you left the default values for the start and end dates, namely `2017-01-01` and `2017-06-30`, you should see a new file named `dates_20170101-20170630.txt` with the same content as the file in the previous exercise.

Creating several files whose name depend on the content of the file

Similar to the previous use case, you may want to generate several files whose names will depend on the content they will have. Suppose you want to generate several sales files, one per product line. The filenames would be `sales_<product line>.txt` as in `sales_Cars.txt`. You will know the names only when you have the data ready to be sent to the output file. Doing this is really simple, as shown next:

1. Open the Transformation that reads the `sales_data.csv` file, and save it with a different name.
2. After the **Text file input** step, add the **UDJE** step. We will use this step for defining the name of the output files.
3. Double-click the **UDJE** step and add a new field named `filename`, of type `String`. As **Java expression**, type `"D:/LearningPDI/files/sales_" + PRODUCTLINE + ".txt"`. Change the path if you want to generate the file in a different folder.
4. Close the window. Make sure the **UDJE** step is selected; then run a preview. You should see this:

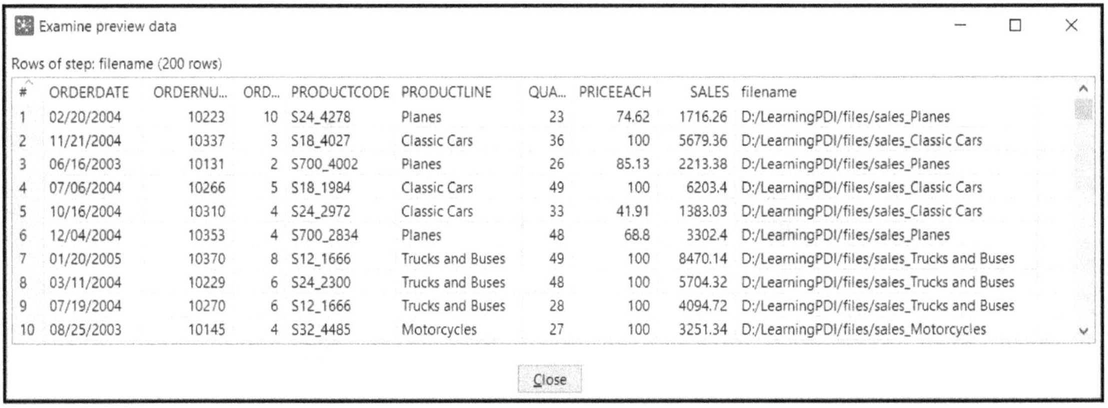

Examine preview data

Rows of step: filename (200 rows)

#	ORDERDATE	ORDERNU...	ORD...	PRODUCTCODE	PRODUCTLINE	QUA...	PRICEEACH	SALES	filename
1	02/20/2004	10223	10	S24_4278	Planes	23	74.62	1716.26	D:/LearningPDI/files/sales_Planes
2	11/21/2004	10337	3	S18_4027	Classic Cars	36	100	5679.36	D:/LearningPDI/files/sales_Classic Cars
3	06/16/2003	10131	2	S700_4002	Planes	26	85.13	2213.38	D:/LearningPDI/files/sales_Planes
4	07/06/2004	10266	5	S18_1984	Classic Cars	49	100	6203.4	D:/LearningPDI/files/sales_Classic Cars
5	10/16/2004	10310	4	S24_2972	Classic Cars	33	41.91	1383.03	D:/LearningPDI/files/sales_Classic Cars
6	12/04/2004	10353	4	S700_2834	Planes	48	68.8	3302.4	D:/LearningPDI/files/sales_Planes
7	01/20/2005	10370	8	S12_1666	Trucks and Buses	49	100	8470.14	D:/LearningPDI/files/sales_Trucks and Buses
8	03/11/2004	10229	6	S24_2300	Trucks and Buses	48	100	5704.32	D:/LearningPDI/files/sales_Trucks and Buses
9	07/19/2004	10270	6	S12_1666	Trucks and Buses	28	100	4094.72	D:/LearningPDI/files/sales_Trucks and Buses
10	08/25/2003	10145	4	S32_4485	Motorcycles	27	100	3251.34	D:/LearningPDI/files/sales_Motorcycles

Close

Previewing filenames

5. After **UDJE**, add a **Text file output** step.

6. Just as you did before, double-click the **Text file output** step. Check the **Accept file name from field?** option. As **File name field**, select the field created in the previous step, `filename`.
7. In the **Content** tab, leave the default values.
8. Select the **Fields** tab and configure it as shown next:

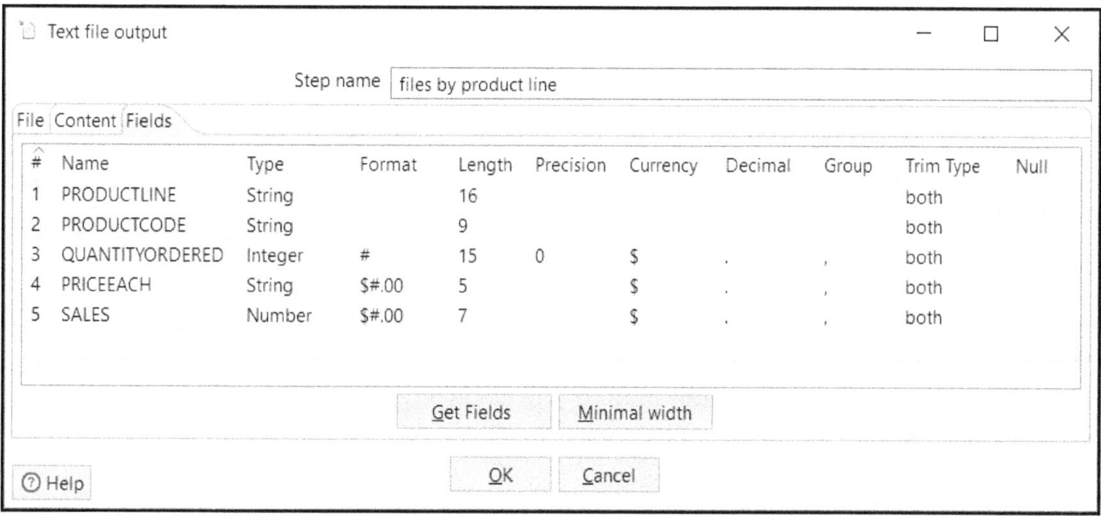

Configuring the fields grid in an output step

9. Click on **OK**, save the Transformation, and run it.
10. Browse your file system. You should see one file per product line in your `sales_data.txt` file.
11. Open the `sales_Planes.txt` file. You should see this:

```
PRODUCTLINE;PRODUCTCODE;QUANTITYORDERED;PRICEEACH;SALES
Planes ;S24_4278 ;23;$74,62;$1716.26
Planes ;S700_4002;26;$85,13;$2213.38
Planes ;S700_2834;48;$68,80;$3302.40
Planes ;S24_2841 ;43;$82,21;$3535.03
Planes ;S24_3949 ;21;$55,96;$1175.16
Planes ;S700_4002;44;$85,87;$3778.28
Planes ;S72_1253 ;45;$51,15;$2301.75
Planes ;S700_4002;35;$100,00;$4277.35
Planes ;S700_1691;39;$100,00;$5043.87
Planes ;S24_4278 ;35;$83,32;$2916.20
...
```

Describing the content of the output file

When you send data to a file, you have to provide not only the name and location but also information about the format you want for the file. This includes the delimiter character, type of encoding, and whether to use a header, among other settings.

Regarding the fields, just like in the **Input** steps, you may use the **Get Fields** button to fill the grid. In this case, the grid is filled based on the data that arrives from the previous step. You are not forced to send every piece of data coming to the **Output** step, nor to send the fields in the same order, as you can figure out from the examples.

If you leave the **Fields** tab empty, PDI will send all the fields coming from the previous step to the file.

If you check the **Header** checkbox (which is on the **Content** tab and is selected by default), the header will be built with the names of the PDI fields.

If you don't want the names of the fields as header names in your file, you may use the **Select values** step to rename those fields before they arrive at the output step.

Regarding the format of the fields, you have to give PDI a proper definition so it writes the data as you expect. There is not much to say about formatting string fields, but the Date and Numeric fields require special attention. If you don't specify a format when writing a Date or Numeric field, PDI will write the fields in a default format.

Formatting Date fields

When sending dates to a file, you have to provide a mask indicating which format to apply to the date when saving it. For formatting dates, you can use the same mask notation as explained at the beginning of the chapter.

The use of a mask to format a date in an **Output** step is analogous to the mask used when you convert a Date to a String by using a **Select values** step.

To show an example of this, let's go back to the tutorial where we wrote the dates to a file. The mask we used for the date field was `yyyy-MM-dd`. This caused the first line belonging to January 1st, 2017 to be written as `2017-01-01`. If for example, we had used the mask `yyyy-MMM-dd`, the same date would have been written as `2017-Jan-01`.

Note that the Date masks are case sensitive. While `MM` means **month in two digits**, `mm` represents minutes.

Formatting Numeric fields

In order to specify the format to apply to numbers, you can use the same notation as explained when we read files. As an example, all the currency values in the Transformation that sent sales data to a file were formatted as `$#.00`. For instance, the value `3302.4` was written as `$3302.40`.

If you neither specify the format nor the length or precision, PDI sends the data as it comes, without applying any format.

Creating the most common kinds of files

Just as it happens with input steps, there is a lot in common in output steps. Of course, there are differences depending on the output file type. The next subsections explain the main kinds of output files and how to proceed for generating them.

Creating text files

For generating plain files with PDI, there is a single step, that is the **Text file output** step that you used in the previous section. It allows you to generate all kinds of plain files: files with or without headers, unstructured files, or even fixed-width files. The configuration of the step is simple. What can be difficult, depending on your requirements, is to build the exact format of the output. In later chapters, you will learn to apply different techniques that will help you to generate any custom dataset ready for sending to an output file.

Creating spreadsheets

The classic step for generating spreadsheets with PDI is the **Microsoft Excel Output** step. The main difference compared to **Text file output** is that with this step you have to tell PDI the name of the sheet to generate. The step also has a tab for providing font names, colors, and other formatting options for header and rows.

In addition to this step, there is another one named **Microsoft Excel Writer**. The **Microsoft Excel Writer** step emerged as a PDI plugin to support features not available in the standard tool, as, for example:

- Support for templates
- Cell comments
- Hyperlinks
- Formulas, and more

With this step, you can also generate the XLSX files, which is not possible with the standard output step.

Since PDI 4.2, the **Microsoft Excel Writer** step is available in the official PDI distribution. Now both output steps coexist and you should choose the one that best fits your needs.

Creating XML files

If you want to generate an XML file with a simple structure, you can do it with an **XML output** step.

Besides the basic information you provide in any output step (as, for example, file name and location), you have to provide names for **Parent XML element** and **Row XML element**. Then the step creates the XML file as follows:

1. It encloses each row between tags with the name you provided for **Row XML element**.
2. Finally, the step encloses the whole structure between tags with the name provided for **Parent XML element**.

For more complicated structures, you should use extra steps, in particular, the **XML Join** step. The basic idea is to create partial XML structures and start merging them together until you have the final structure.

As said before, in the next chapter, we will learn to deal with these kinds of structures, so you can generate your ad hoc XML files.

Creating JSON files

For generating JSON files, you use the **JSON Output** step. Besides the basic configuration for an output step, you have to:

- Specify the name of the main JSON block
- For each field, provide the element name for the JSON structure using **JSONPath** notation

This allows generating simple JSON structures. There are alternative ways for generating JSON structures. We will look at the details later in the book.

Working with Big Data and cloud sources

While flat files and databases are the most common types of sources that you use from PDI, there are many other types of data sources available. People have started to leverage the capabilities of tools such as Hadoop, NoSQL databases, and cloud services. In this section, you will learn to connect, read data from, and load data into some of these big data sources with PDI.

Reading files from an AWS S3 instance

S3 is a scalable storage space and is a common location for files to be processed. If you have files in S3 and want to read them, you don't have to download them. PDI allows you to read those files directly from the **Amazon Web Services** (**AWS**) **Simple Storage Service** (**S3**) instance.

The step that you will use for doing this is the **S3 CSV Input** step. This step works very similarly to the **CSV Input** step. The biggest difference is that to access the file, you have to provide the bucket name where the file is located and the dual keys to access the bucket.

Before proceeding, make sure you have a file for reading on S3, as well as the access and secret key for accessing the bucket.

The steps for reading a file from S3 are simple:

1. Create a new Transformation.
2. From the **Input** category, bring over the **S3 CSV Input** step onto the canvas.
3. Open the **S3 CSV Input** step. Copy the **S3 Access key** and **S3 Secret key** into their matching fields.
4. Click on the **Select bucket** button. A listing of available buckets should appear. Select the bucket from the list.
5. Click on the **Browse...** button to find your file.
6. Make sure the **Delimiter** and **Enclosure** values are correct. Click on the **Get Fields** button. This will pull the field metadata from the file and load it into the fields grid.
7. Click on **Preview** to see the data in the file.

The **S3 CSV Input** step does not allow for compressed files or for processing multiple files. If you need to read compressed or multiple files, you can do it with the **Hadoop File Input** step, which is explained next.

Writing files to an AWS S3 instance

Exporting data to a text file on an Amazon S3 with PDI is a simple task. The step for doing this is **S3 File Output**. This is how you use it:

1. Open Spoon and create a new Transformation.
2. Create a stream of data to send to the output file.
3. From the **Output** category of steps, select and drag to the work area the **S3 File output** step.
4. Create a hop from the latest step in the stream toward this new one.
5. Double-click the new step for configuring the output file.
6. Provide values for the **Access Key:** and **Secret Key:** textboxes.
7. Under the **Filename** textbox, specify the name of the output text file.

If you leave the **Access Key:** and **Secret Key:** textboxes empty, you can include them as part of the filename by following the schema `s3://(access_key):(secret_key)@s3/(s3_bucket_name)/(absolute_path_to_file)`.

8. Configure the **Content** and **Fields** tabs just as you do in a **Text file output** step.

9. Close the window, save the Transformation, and run it.
10. Browse the S3 directory to verify that your file was generated as expected.

Getting data from HDFS

A **Hadoop Distributed File System** (**HDFS**) is a Java-based, distributed, scalable, and portable file system for the Hadoop framework. With PDI, pulling data back out from the Hadoop File System is really easy. In fact, we can treat it just like any other flat file source. Here are the steps for reading a file from Hadoop:

1. Open Spoon and create a new Transformation.
2. From the **Big Data** category, drag to the work area, the **Hadoop File Input** step.
3. Edit the **Hadoop File Input** step. This will be used to pull the input file information.
4. Under **Environment**, select **<Static>**.
5. For the **File/Folder** field, enter the connection information to get to the file. For instance, if the data is stored in a file named `samplefile.csv` under the sandbox user's `sampledata` folder, use `hdfs://<your_sandbox_ip_address>:8020/user/sandbox/sampledata/samplefile.csv`.
6. Switch to the **Content** tab and check the settings. In particular, you may have to fix **Separator**, **Format**, or **Encoding** to match the format of your file.
7. Switch to the **Fields** tab and click on **Get Fields** to get the fields metadata.
8. Click on **Preview rows** to view the data stored in the file.

If the data you have to read is across many files, you can just add a Regular Expression to bring in the files we need. The data could effectively live throughout the Hadoop cluster, but you only have to call out to the cluster with our request and the step does the rest.

In this example, you specified a Static environment and provided the exact file path to read. There are other options:

- **Local**: Choose this option if the item specified in the **File/Folder** field is in a file system that is local to Spoon. By choosing **Local**, under the **File/Folder** column, you will have a browse button for navigating to the file or folder.

- **S3**: As mentioned in the previous section, the **Hadoop File Input** step supports reading files from S3. By choosing this option, under the **File/Folder** column, you will have the opportunity to browse the S3 file system. You will have to provide the dual keys just as you do when you use an **S3 CSV Input** step.

Sending data to HDFS

Creating a file in HDFS is as easy as creating any flat file. The main difference, in this case, is that before writing to HDFS, you have to create a connection to a Hadoop cluster, by providing hostnames and ports for HDFS, Job Tracker, and other big data cluster components.

You can find detailed instructions for connecting to a Hadoop Cluster in Spoon at `https://help.pentaho.com/Documentation/8.0/Data/Hadoop/Connect_to_Cluster`.

Once you have the connection ready, you can proceed. For sending data to an HDFS system, you use a step named **Hadoop File Output**. Using this step is quite similar to using **Text file output**, but in this case, you have to tell PDI which Hadoop cluster to use. The steps to do this are as follows:

1. Open Spoon and create a new Transformation.
2. Generate the data you want to send to HDFS by using any sequence of PDI steps.
3. From the **Big Data** category, add to the canvas the **Hadoop File Output** step and put it at the end of the stream.
4. Edit the new step. Choose the Hadoop cluster to use from the **Hadoop cluster:** drop-down list, or create a new one by clicking on **New...** .
5. Under **Folder/File**, specify the location and name of the text file you want to write.
6. Configure the **Content** and **Fields** tabs as usual, and close the window.
7. Save your Transformation and run it. The file should be ready for use in the specified location.

Summary

In this chapter, you learned to get data from files and put data back into new files. Specifically, you learned how to read plain files, files with XML and JSON format, and spreadsheets. You also learned to create the same kind of files. Besides, you learned to read files located in big data sources, namely, HDFS and S3, and also write files back to the cloud.

You are now ready to continue learning to transform data and perform all kinds of useful operations, including dealing with XML and JSON structures. This will be covered in the next chapter.

5 Manipulating PDI Data and Metadata

In the previous chapters, you learned the basics of transforming data. This chapter expands your knowledge by teaching you a variety of essential features. Besides exploring new PDI steps for data manipulation, this chapter explains in detail a key resource in every process: the **Select values** step. The chapter also teaches you how to get system information and predefined variables to be used as part of the data flow. A special section is devoted to reading and writing XML and JSON structures.

In this chapter, you will learn about the following topics:

- New ways to transform data
- Understanding the **Select values** step and its different uses
- Getting system information and predefined variables
- Manipulating XML and JSON structures

Manipulating simple fields

As already said, transformations deal with the data flow. As data goes through the PDI steps of a Transformation, it is manipulated or transformed in different ways. You already experimented with some possibilities. In this section, you will learn in detail how to transform different data according to your needs.

Working with strings

For any string, there are many transformations that you can apply to it, for example:

- Extracting part of the string
- Removing leading spaces
- Converting to uppercase

PDI offers several ways to do this. It's also common to find more than one step that can be used for the same purpose. The following table summarizes the most common PDI steps used to operate on `String` fields:

PDI step	Step description
Calculator	With the **Calculator** step, it is possible to apply several transformations on strings including converting to upper and lowercase and removing special characters. You can also use the **Calculator** to concatenate two or three strings using the operations `A+B` and `A+B+C` respectively.
String Operations	This step, as its name suggests, is devoted to working exclusively on strings. It allows you to perform several operations including trimming leading blanks or removing special characters.
Replace in string	**Replace in string** is a step used to search and replace strings inside a **String** field. The searching string can be plain text or a regular expression, as explained in the next sections.
String Cut	This step allows you to cut a portion of a string.
Split Fields	You use this step to split a **String** field into two or more fields based on delimiter information.
Formula	This step allows you to define new fields based on formulas. To construct these formulas, there is a list of available functions including functions to extract parts of a string or concatenate strings, among others. Each function has correspondent documentation, so it's easy to understand how to use them.
UDJE	You already used this step for some string operations, for example, to concatenate values. The **UDJE** step is suitable to implement almost any string operation since it can be written using a single Java expression.

Besides this list of steps, the scripting steps **Modified Java Script Value** and **User Defined Java Class** allow you to implement these, and more complicated expressions, as you will learn in `Chapter 6`, *Controlling the Flow of Data.*

As inferred from the preceding table, there is no single way to operate on strings. It's up to you to choose the step that best suits the requirements in each case or the step that you feel more comfortable with.

Extracting parts of strings using regular expressions

Some of the steps in the preceding table can be used to extract static parts of a string, for example, the first N characters or the characters from position X to position Y.

Now suppose that you have a field that contains a zip code. This code can be anywhere in the field and you can recognize it because it is preceded either by `ZIP CODE:` or `ZC:`. The zip code itself has exactly five digits. There is no way to know beforehand in which position of the string the zip code is located, so none of these options serves you in this case. In order to extract the portion of the field in situations like this, you can use a **RegEx Evaluation** step. This step—classified under the **Scripting** category—verifies if a string matches a regular expression or not. Also, it allows you to extract particular substrings from an input field and use them to populate new fields.

Before implementing the solution, we have to build the regular expression that represents our field. In this case, the expression would be `.*(ZIP CODE|ZP):[0-9]{5}.*`, which means that any quantity of characters is followed by `ZIP CODE` or `ZP`, followed by a colon, then five digits (the zip code), and optionally, more characters at the end.

In order to extract the zip code, we need to capture it as a group. We do this by enclosing the zip code part of the regular expression—`[0-9]{5}`—between parentheses. Anything between parentheses will be considered as a group. As we are not interested in capturing `(ZIP CODE|ZP)` a group, we will convert that part of the expression into a non-capturing group. We do it by typing `?:` just after the opening bracket. Our final expression will be `.*(?:ZIP CODE|ZP):([0-9]{5}).*`.

Let's see how to implement the solution with a simple Transformation:

1. Create a new Transformation.
2. Create a dataset with a single field and a list of valid and invalid codes.

You could create and read a text file or simply populate a **Datagrid** with sample data.

3. At the end of the stream, add a **RegEx Evaluation** step.
4. Edit the step and fill it in as follows:

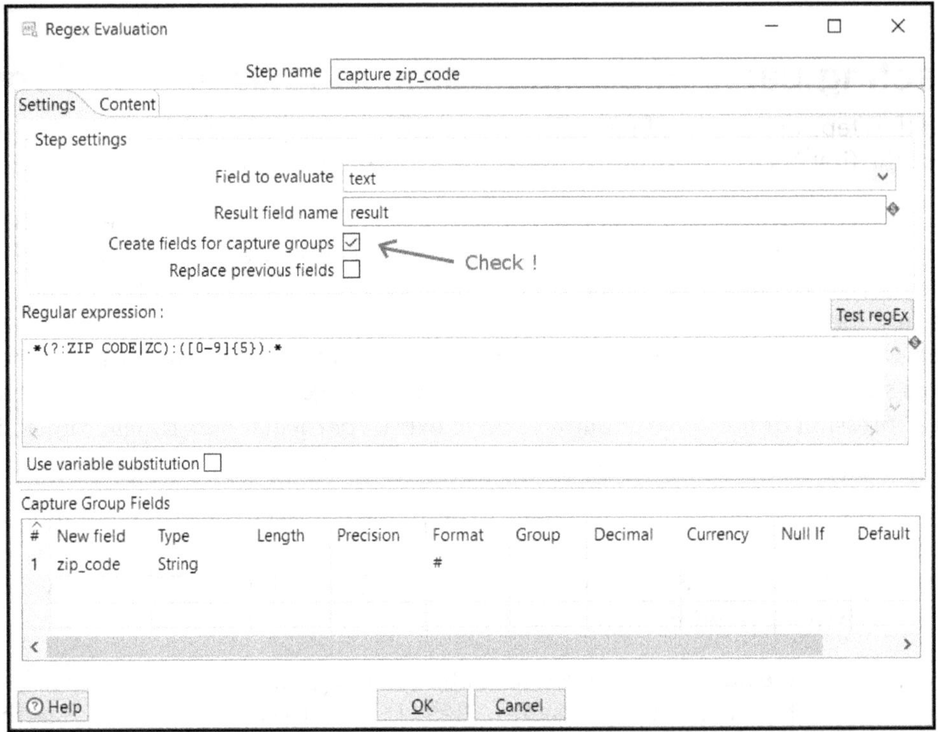

Configuring a RegEx evaluation step

5. Close the window.
6. Run a preview of this last step. You should see something similar to this (depending on your data):

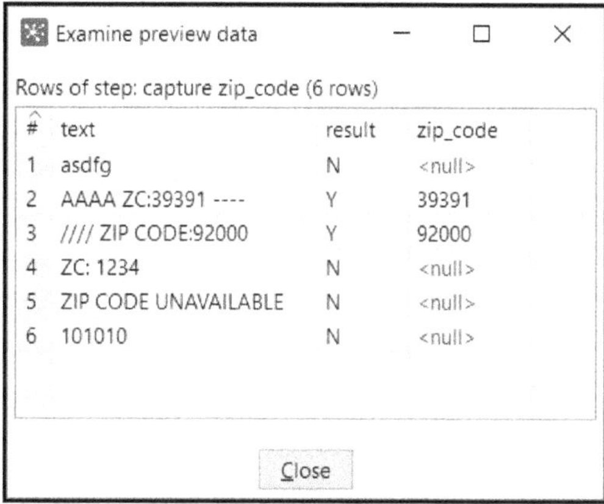

#	text	result	zip_code
1	asdfg	N	<null>
2	AAAA ZC:39391 ----	Y	39391
3	//// ZIP CODE:92000	Y	92000
4	ZC: 1234	N	<null>
5	ZIP CODE UNAVAILABLE	N	<null>
6	101010	N	<null>

Previewing the result of a RegEx evaluation step

As you can see, the step creates a flag indicating if the field matches the given expression. In the rows where the flag is `Y`, the new field `zip_code` contains the code extracted from the original field.

Searching and replacing using regular expressions

As you can deduce from the previous table, if you need to search and replace some text, one option is to use the **Replace in string** step. In the simplest scenario, you look for fixed text and replace it with other fixed text. However, this step supports more elaborate searches and replacements through the use of regular expressions and group references. Let's explain this with some examples:

1. Create a new Transformation.
2. Create a dataset with zip codes, similar to the one created in the previous example.

Alternatively, you can reuse that dataset. Open the Transformation and copy/paste into this new Transformation the step or steps that created the data.

3. At the end of the flow, add a **Replace in string** step.
4. As **In stream field**, type or select the field containing the text with the zip codes.
5. As **Out stream field**, type a name for a new field.

Now let's explore the possibilities:

- Suppose the simplest scenario where you want to replace the text `ZIP CODE` with the text `POSTAL CODE`. Under **use RegEx** type `N`, as **Search**, type `ZIP CODE` in the **Replace with** column type `POSTAL CODE`.
  The result would be like this:

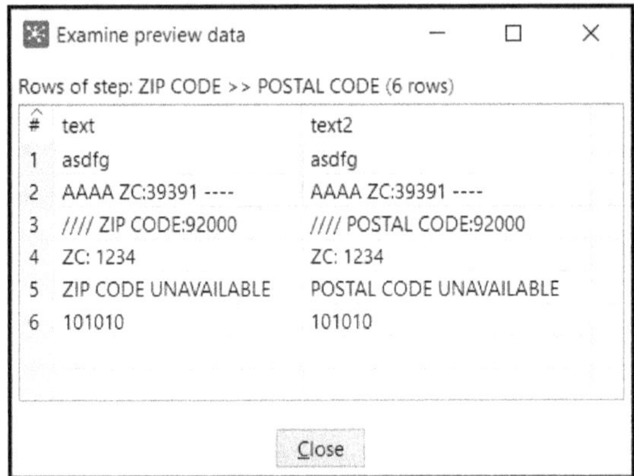

Searching and replacing fixed text

- Now you want to replace either `ZIP CODE` or `ZC` with `POSTAL CODE`. You could do this with two replacements (two lines) in the **Replace in string** step. However, a simpler way is to use a regular expression. Under **use RegEx** type `Y`, as **Search**, type `(ZIP CODE|ZC)` in the **Replace with** column type `POSTAL CODE`. Now you have the following:

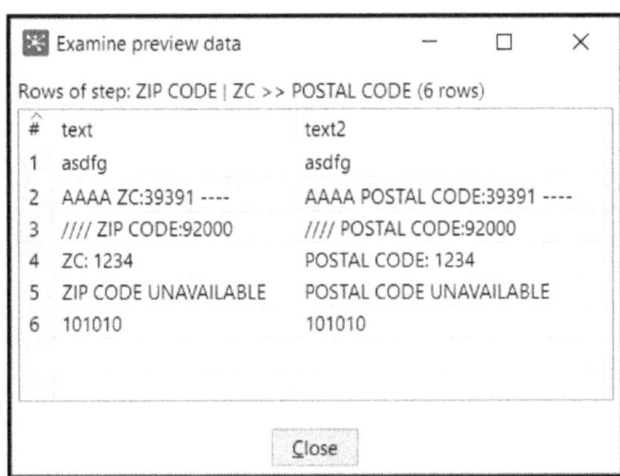

Searching and replacing regular expressions

- In this example, after replacing the text you got this: `POSTAL CODE UNAVAILABLE`. You may not want this particular text to be replaced, but only the occurrences where a zip code is present. So a new version for the same replacement could be one that uses a group reference. This time, under **use RegEx** type `Y`, as **Search**, type `(ZIP CODE|ZC):([0-9]{5})` in the **Replace with** column type `POSTAL CODE:$2`. The regular expression captures two groups: a first group with the text `ZIP CODE` or `ZC` and a second group with the zip code itself. When this pattern is found, it is replaced with the text `POSTAL CODE` followed by a semicolon and the value for the second captured group, indicated with `$2`. Now you have the following:

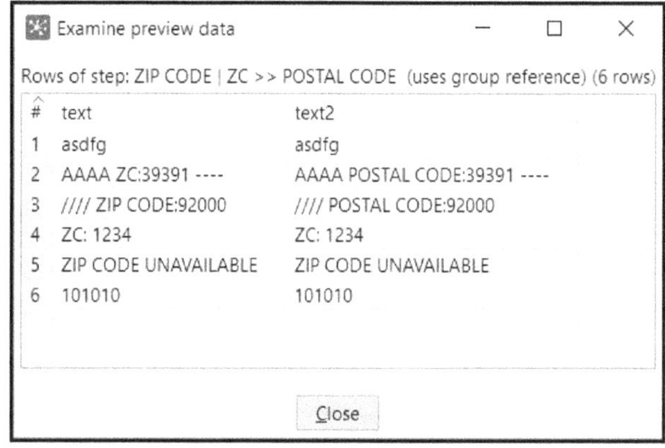

Searching and replacing regular expressions using group reference

You can also implement all these operations with a **UDJE** step using the `Replace` and `ReplaceAll` Java methods. The expressions that you should use for the preceding examples are `text.replace("ZIP CODE","POSTAL CODE")`, `text.replaceAll("(ZIP CODE|ZC)","POSTAL CODE")`, and `text.replaceAll("(ZIP CODE|ZC):([0-9]{5})","POSTAL CODE:$2")` respectively.

For details of the *Replace* and *ReplaceAll* Java methods, refer to the documentation at `https://docs.oracle.com/javase/8/docs/api/java/lang/String.html`. For more information about regular expressions, you can explore the links provided in the *Working with Regular Expressions* section in `Chapter 3`, *Creating Basic Task Flows*.

Doing some math with Numeric fields

Some of the steps presented for string operations are also suited for some math. **Calculator** is the first step you should look for if you intend to do simple operations, for example, addition, subtraction, division, percentage, among others.

For math operations, there is also the **Formula** step. The advantage of **Formula** compared to **Calculator** is that you can state more elaborated expressions that contain logical, mathematical, and relational operators. Among the available functions, there are some statistical options such as MAX, MIN, and Average.

As an example of how to use a **Formula** step, suppose that you have three Integer fields named `a`, `b`, and `c` and you want to create a new field as follows: If all the values - `a`, `b` and `c`—are positive, the new field will be the minimum value among them. In another case, the new field will be zero. The formula can be stated as `IF(AND([a]>0;[b]>0;[c]>0);Min([a];[b];[c]); 0)`.

Note that in a **Formula** step, the names of the fields are enclosed among square brackets, and the parameters of functions are separated by a semicolon.

Take into account that all of these operations work on fields in a single row. In later chapters, you will learn to perform typical operations that involve the entire dataset, for example, calculating the average of a field along with all rows.

Operating with dates

Dates are one of the most common data types and there is a vast set of operations that you may need to apply to Date fields:

- Extracting parts of a date, for example, the year
- Given a date, getting some descriptions, for example, the weekday
- Adding dates
- Comparing dates

PDI offers a lot of possibilities to manipulate Date fields. However, these features are not organized in a single place inside Spoon. There are several steps in different steps categories that allow you to manipulate dates. Also, given a particular operation, there is usually a couple of ways to perform it. This section is meant to present you the different options.

Performing simple operations on dates

The simplest way to operate with dates in PDI is a **Calculator** step. The list of operations available in a **Calculator** step is really long and it may be difficult to find a particular operation among the set. However, if you are looking for a date-related function, you can apply a filter:

1. Open the **Calculator** configuration window.
2. On top of the list of operations, you will see a search textbox. Type the word `date`, and then click on the magnifying glass. The list will be reduced to the date-related functions, as shown in the following screenshot:

Filtering Date operations in a Calculator

As you can see, most of these functions serve to extract parts of dates or add or subtract dates or parts of dates.

The **Formula** step also offers a predefined list of date-related functions, which complements the list offered by **Calculator**.

Subtracting dates with the Calculator step

Let's look at an example to demonstrate how to apply a date operation with the **Calculator** step. In this case, we have a list of dates. For each date, we want the matching date to be a week before, that is, our date minus seven days.

If you explore the **Calculator** options, there is no function to subtract dates, but there is one to add dates. So, the trick is to add a negative number. Let's proceed:

1. Create a new Transformation and add a **Data Grid** step.
2. Use the **Data Grid** to define a new field of `Date` type and populate the grid with some random values.

Alternatively, you can reuse one of the *Date Range* samples created in previous chapters.

3. After the **Data Grid**, add a **Calculator** step. We will use it for the math.
4. Fill the **Calculator** in as follows:

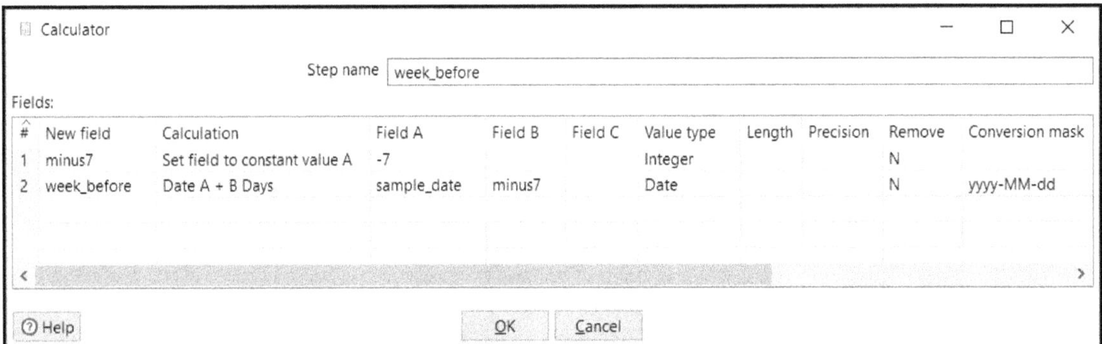

Configuring Calculator to add days

5. Close the configuration window, select the Calculator, and run a preview. You should see something like this:

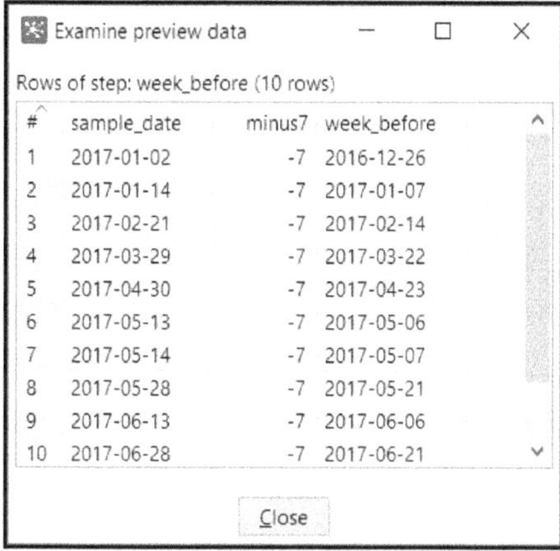
Examine preview data

Rows of step: week_before (10 rows)

#	sample_date	minus7	week_before
1	2017-01-02	-7	2016-12-26
2	2017-01-14	-7	2017-01-07
3	2017-02-21	-7	2017-02-14
4	2017-03-29	-7	2017-03-22
5	2017-04-30	-7	2017-04-23
6	2017-05-13	-7	2017-05-06
7	2017-05-14	-7	2017-05-07
8	2017-05-28	-7	2017-05-21
9	2017-06-13	-7	2017-06-06
10	2017-06-28	-7	2017-06-21

Close

Previewing some dates

In the exercise, we defined an auxiliary field—the constant `-7`—to be used in our main operation. This was a perfect example to demonstrate some characteristics of the **Calculator** step:

- The constant field had a single purpose—it helps us do the calculation. We don't need it after that. As we don't want to keep it, we have the option to select **Y** (Yes) in the **Remove** column. By doing this, the field will not be added to our dataset.
- As you saw, we defined the constant `-7` and then we used it in the same Calculator step to create another field: the new date. This shows us another feature of the step. Any field defined in a **Calculator** is immediately available to be used in the definition of other new fields.

Getting information relative to the current date

A very common requirement is to get the system date or some date or time relative to it. PDI offers a couple of ways to do this. The simplest way to get system information relative to the current date is to use the **Get System Info** step. The step offers a long list of options with most of them related to the present date. Some examples are `system date (fixed)`, `Yesterday 00:00:00`, `Last day of this month 23:59:59`, and `First day of this quarter 00:00:00`, among others.

The step doesn't provide any formatting options, so when you use this step to add date system information to your dataset, the field is added with the default date format, as you can see in the following screenshot:

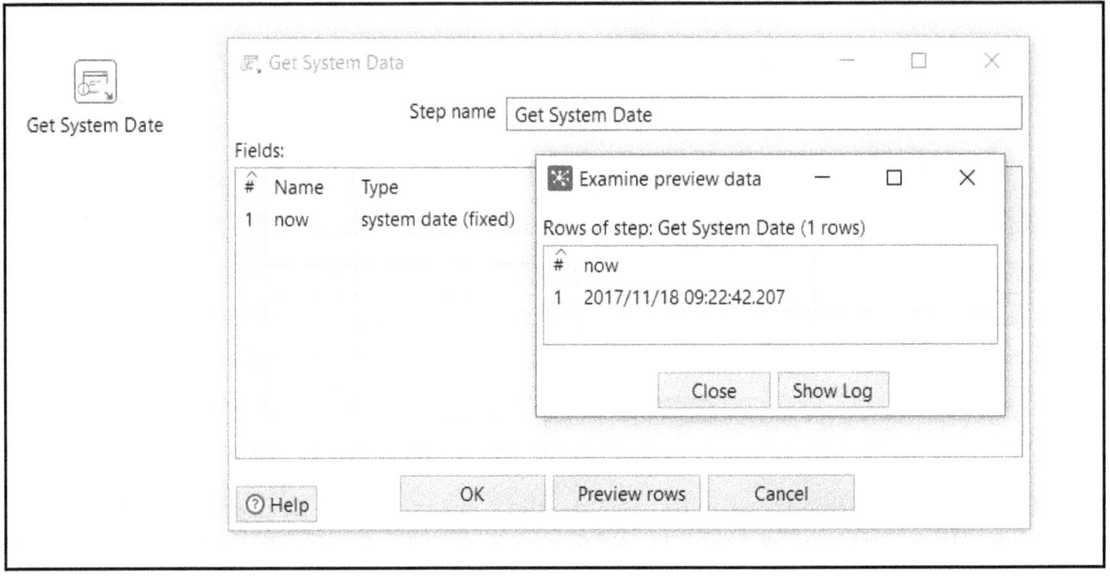

Adding the current system date

If you need the field in a different format, simply add a **Select Values** step after the **Get System Info** step to convert the field as needed.

Besides the **Get System Info** step, there is the **Formula** step that we looked at earlier, which also offers two functions relative to the current date: `TODAY()` and `NOW()`.

Using the Get System Info step

The **Get System Info** step allows you to get information from the PDI environment. As explained, the step offers a long list of options. Besides the options related to the current date, this step also presents information relating to the machine where the Transformation is running: `JVM max memory`, `Total physical memory size (bytes)`, `IP address`, and more.

In the previous example, this step was used as the first in the flow. This caused PDI to generate a dataset with a single row and one column for each defined field. In this case, there was a single field, `now`, but you could have defined more.

There is also the possibility of adding a **Get System Info** step in the middle of the flow. Suppose that in the middle of the flow, you insert a **Get System Info** step identical to the one in the example. This will cause PDI to add a new field with the current date in all rows of the dataset.

Performing other useful operations on dates

Despite the full list of options, there is a possibility that a function you are looking for is not available in any PDI step. Suppose that, among the descriptive fields for a date, you want the name of the month in your local language or the current date in a different time zone. None of the presented steps provides that information.

Fortunately, there is always the code resource. Under the **Scripting** category of steps, there are several steps that can be used for this purpose: **Modified Java Script Value**, **User Defined Java Class**, and **User Defined Java Expression**. These steps allow you to use either Java or JavaScript libraries. The next subsection gives a brief introduction to the **User Defined Java Class** so that you are ready to implement more date functions in your transformations.

Getting the month names with a User Defined Java Class step

This section will explain how to get the month description of a date in a secondary language—French in this case—with Java libraries:

1. Create a Transformation with a set of dates, just as you did before.

For this exercise, you can reuse any of the transformations used earlier.

2. From the **Scripting** category of steps, add a **User Defined Java Class** step (or **UDJC** for short) and link it to the stream of data.
3. Double-click on the step. You will be presented with a configuration window with a pane named **Class code**. Inside this pane, type the following piece of code:

```
import java.util.Calendar;
import java.util.Locale;
public boolean processRow(StepMetaInterface smi, StepDataInterface
sdi) throws KettleException
{
Object[] r = getRow();
```

```
if (r == null) {
setOutputDone();
return false;
}
Object[] outputRow = createOutputRow(r, data.outputRowMeta.size());
// HERE GOES YOUR CODE
return true;
}
```

The preceding code is just a skeleton for the main code.

Don't worry about the details; focus on the specific code for dates. You will learn to use this step in detail in `Chapter 8`, *Manipulating data by coding*.

4. In the middle of the code, where it says `// HERE GOES YOUR CODE`, insert the following:

```
Calendar cal = Calendar.getInstance();
cal.setTime(get(Fields.In, "mydate").getDate(r));
String monthName = cal.getDisplayName(cal.MONTH,Calendar.LONG, new
Locale("FR"));
get(Fields.Out, "monthName").setValue(outputRow, monthName);
putRow(data.outputRowMeta, outputRow);
```

This code will run once for every row in your dataset. The purpose of the code is to create an instance of a `Calendar`, set it with the current date field, and call the `Calendar` method `getDisplayName` to obtain the full name of the month in French. After that, it creates a new field named `monthName` and adds it to the main dataset.

For a full reference to the **Calendar** class, refer to the following link: `https://docs.oracle.com/javase/8/docs/api/java/util/Calendar.html`.

To resume the exercise, do the following:

1. In the lower grid of the **Java Class** step, fill the first row with `monthName` under the **Fieldname** column, and `String` under the **Type** column.
2. Close the window.

3. With the **Java Class** step selected, run a preview. You will see something like the following (depending on the set of dates in your Transformation):

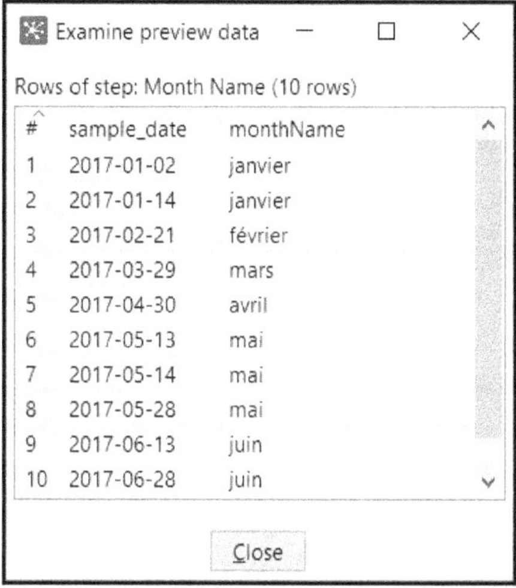

#	sample_date	monthName
1	2017-01-02	janvier
2	2017-01-14	janvier
3	2017-02-21	février
4	2017-03-29	mars
5	2017-04-30	avril
6	2017-05-13	mai
7	2017-05-14	mai
8	2017-05-28	mai
9	2017-06-13	juin
10	2017-06-28	juin

Previewing dates with month names

Modifying the metadata of streams

In the previous sections, you learned several ways to transform data using different PDI steps. There is a particular step already familiar to you, which is available across all the functionalities—the **Select values** step. Despite being classed as a **Transform** step, the **Select values** step does more than just transform data. It allows you to select, reorder, rename, and delete fields, or change the metadata of a field. The configuration window of the step has three tabs:

- **Select & Alter**
- **Remove**
- **Meta-data**

You may use only one of the **Select values** step tabs at a time. PDI will not restrain you from filling out more than one tab, but that could lead to unexpected behavior.

The **Select & Alter** tab, which appears selected by default, lets you specify the fields that you want to keep. Let's try it with a simple example:

1. Open the Transformation that generates the list of dates.
2. From the **Transform** branch of the **Steps** tree, add a **Select values** step and create a hop from the last **Calculator** step toward this one.
3. Edit the **Select values** step. In the **Select & Alter** tab (which appears selected by default), type `a_single_date` under **Fieldname**.
4. Close the window and save your work.
5. Select the **Select values** step and run a preview. You should only see the last column, `a_single_date`:

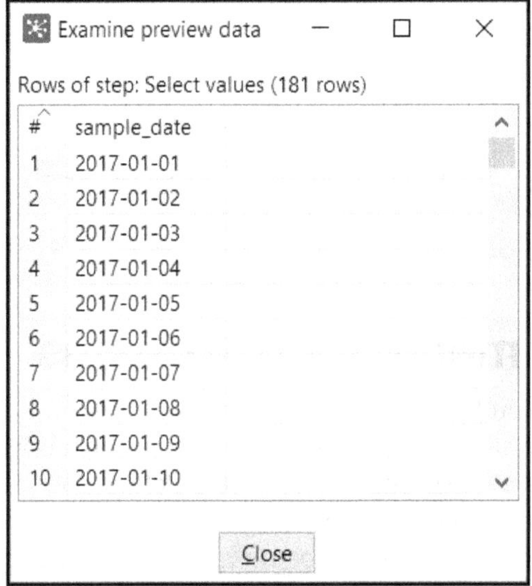

Preview after selecting a single field

You just used the first tab of the **Select values** step to keep a single field. This tab can also be used to rename the fields or reorder them. You may have noticed that each time you add a new field to a Transformation, the field is added at the end of the list of fields. If, for any reason, you want to put it in another place, you can do so with a **Select values** step.

The **Remove** tab is useful to discard unwanted fields. This tab is useful if you want to remove just a few fields. To remove many, it's easier to use the **Select & Alter** tab and specify not the fields to remove, but the fields to keep.

Removing fields using this tab is expensive from a performance point of view. Please don't use it unless needed!

Finally, the **Meta-data** tab is used when you want to change the definition of a field. You can change the type, name, or format. In the case of numbers or dates, you can apply any of the masks already explained.

The **Select values** step is just one of several steps that contain field information. In these cases, the name of the button is not necessarily **Get Fields**.

In the case of the **Select values** step, depending on the selected tab, the name of the button changes to **Get fields to select**, **Get fields to remove**, or **Get fields to change**, but the purpose of the button is the same in all cases.

Working with complex structures

The first section of the chapter explained the different ways to work with simple fields. It's common, however, to have complex structures to work with. One of the most common situations is having to parse results from a web service or a rest call, which returns data in XML or JSON format. This section explains how to parse this kind of complex data.

Working with XML

XML stands for **Extensible Markup Language**. It is basically a language designed to describe data and it's broadly used not only to store data, but also to exchange data between heterogeneous systems over the internet. In this section, we will describe what an XML structure looks like and how to parse it with PDI.

Introducing XML terminology

Before starting work with XML, let's look at a brief introduction to the structure and basic terminology. Look at this piece of XML showing information about countries:

```
<world>
...
<country>
    <name>Japan</name>
        <capital>Tokyo</capital>
        <language isofficial="T">
            <name>Japanese</name>
            <percentage>99.1</percentage>
        </language>
        <language isofficial="F">
            <name>Korean</name>
            <percentage>0.5</percentage>
        </language>
            <language isofficial="F">
            <name>Chinese</name>
            <percentage>0.2</percentage>
        </language>
        ...
</country>
...
</world>
```

This, as in any XML structure, is a set of nested elements. An element is a logical piece enclosed by a start tag and a matching end tag, for example, `<country> </country>`.

Within the start tag of an element, you may have attributes. An attribute is a markup construct consisting of a name/value pair, for example, `isofficial="F"`.

This is just the basic terminology related to XML files. For a full reference, you can visit `http://www.w3schools.com/xml/`.

Getting familiar with the XPath notation

XPath is a set of rules used to get information from an XML document. In XPath, XML documents are treated as trees of nodes. There are several kinds of nodes: elements, attributes, and texts are some of them. `world`, `country`, and `isofficial` are some of the nodes in the sample file.

Among the nodes, there are relationships. A node has a parent, zero or more children, siblings, ancestors, and descendants depending on where the other nodes are in the hierarchy.

In the sample countries file, `country` is the parent of the elements `name`, `capital`, and `language`. These three elements are the children of `country`.

To select a node in an XML document, you have to use a path expression relative to a current node.

The following table has some examples of path expressions that you may use to specify fields. The examples assume that the current node is `language`:

Path expression	Description	Sample
`node_name`	Selects all child nodes of the node `node_name`.	A sample node name for the current node `language` would be `percentage`.
`.`	Selects the current node.	`language`
`..`	Selects the parent of the current node.	`..` refers to `country`, the parent node of the current node `language`. `../capital` refers to the `capital` node inside `country`.
`@`	Selects an attribute.	`@isofficial` gets the attribute `isofficial` in the current node `language`.

Note that the expressions `name` and `../name` are not the same. The first expression selects the name of the language, while the second selects the name of the country.

This table shows only the basics of XPath.

For more information on XPath, visit `https://www.w3schools.com/xml/xpath_intro.asp`.

Parsing XML structures with PDI

With PDI, it's possible to read an XML file as well as parse an XML structure found in a field in our dataset. In both cases, to parse that structure, you use the **Get data from XML** input step. To tell PDI which information to get from the structure, it is required that you use the XPath notation explained previously.

Reading an XML file with the Get data from XML step

To demonstrate how to parse an XML structure with PDI, we will need some sample XML files.

From this book's website, download the resources folder belonging to this chapter. Inside this folder, you will see a file named `countries.xml`. Save it in a folder relative to your working directory. For example, if your transformations are in the `pdi_labs`folder, the file could be saved in `pdi_labs/resources/`.

This is how you read XML files:

1. Create a new Transformation, give it a name, and save it.
2. From the **Input** steps, drag to the canvas a **Get data from XML** step.
3. Open the configuration window for this step by double-clicking on it.

In order to specify the name and location of an XML file, you have to fill in the **File** tab just as you do in any file input step. In this case, we will read a file from a folder relative to the folder where you stored the Transformation:

1. In the **File or directory** textbox, press *Ctrl* + spacebar or *Shift* + *cmd* + space on a Mac. A drop-down list appears containing a list of defined variables:

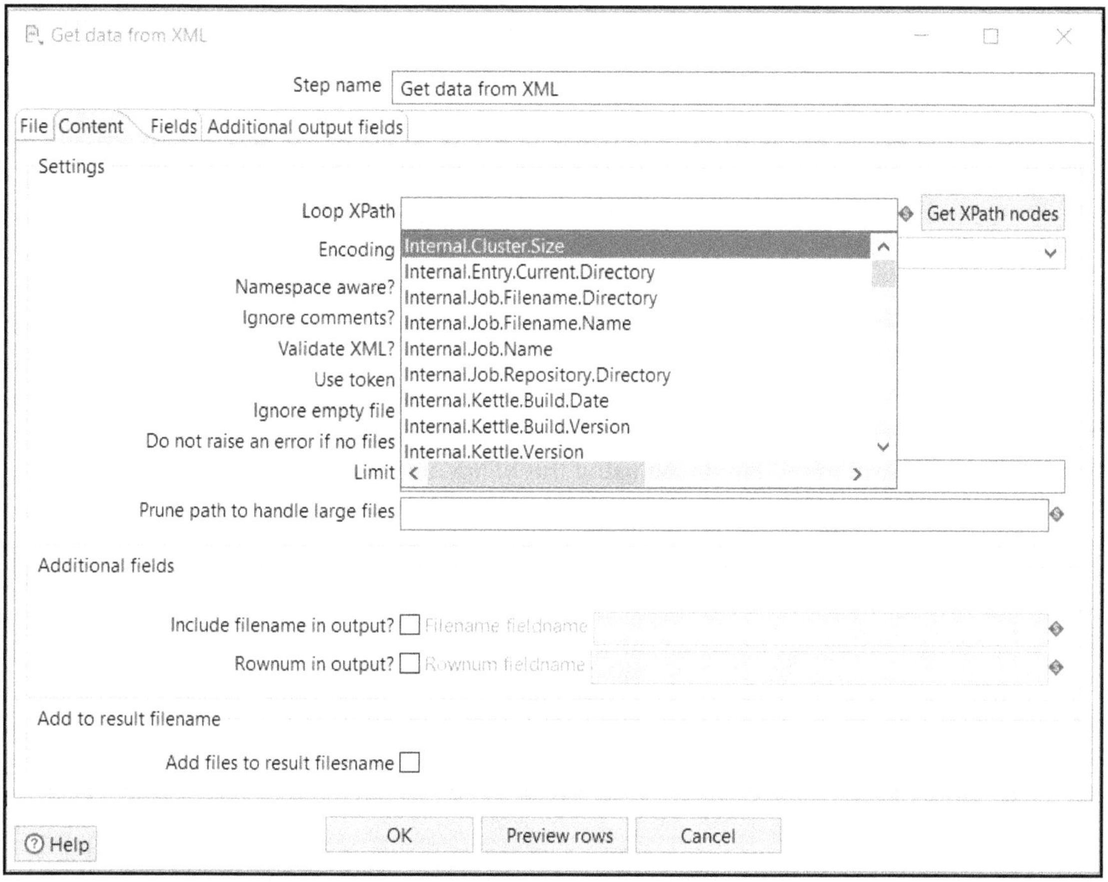

Showing predefined variables

2. Select **${Internal.Entry.Current.Directory}**. The textbox is filled with this text.
3. Complete the text so you can read this:
   `${Internal.Entry.Current.Directory}/resources/countries.xml`

When the Transformation runs, PDI replaces `${Internal.Entry.Current.Directory}` with the real path of the Transformation, for example, `D:/pdi_labs/resources/countries.xml`.

4. Click on the **Add** button. The full path is moved to the grid.

Before describing the fields to read, we have to select the path that will identify the current node. This is optimally the repeating node in the file. Once you select a path, PDI will generate one row of data for every found path:

5. Select the **Content** tab and click on **Get XPath nodes** to select the **Loop XPath**. In the list that appears, select **/world/country/language**, so PDI generates one row for each **/world/country/language** element in the file.

Alternatively, to specify the current node, you can type it by hand.

After selecting the loop XPath, you have to specify the fields to get. In order to do this, you have to fill in the grid in the **Fields** tab using the *XPath* notation.

6. Select the **Fields** tab and fill in the grid, as shown in the following screenshot:

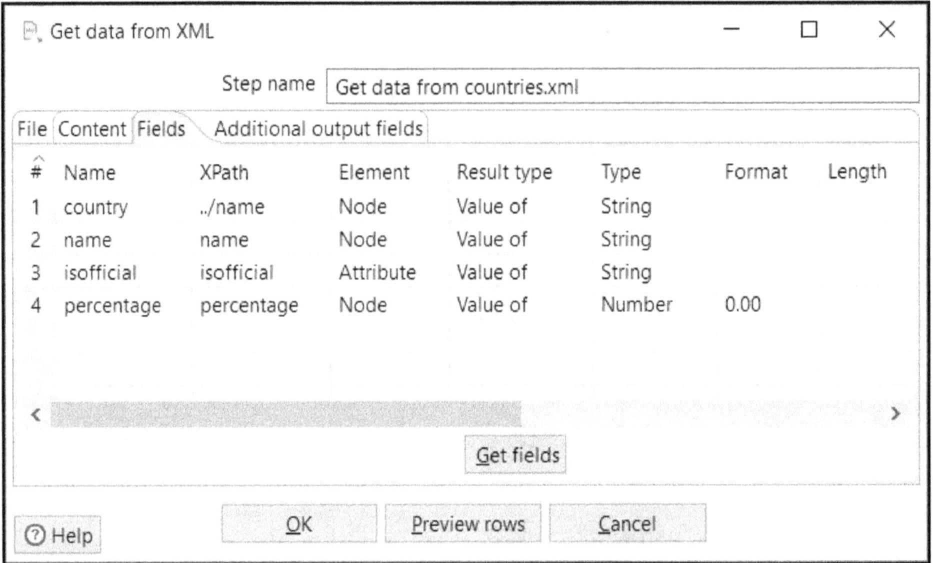

Defining fields using XPath

If you press the **Get fields** button, PDI will fill the grid with the child nodes of the current node. If you want to get some other node, you have to type its XPath by hand.

7. Click on **Preview rows**, and you should see something like the following screenshot:

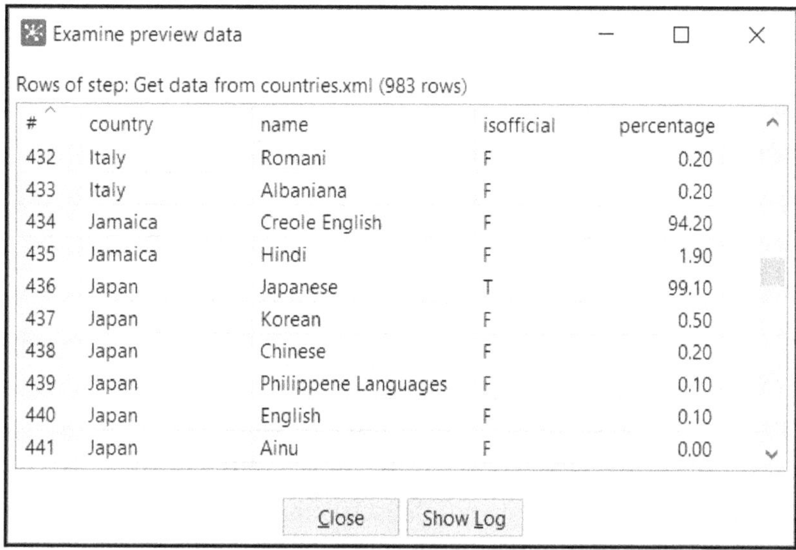

Previewing data coming from an XML file

Note the notation for the attributes. To get an attribute, you can use the `@` notation, or you can simply type the name of the attribute without `@` and select **Attribute** under the `Element` column, you did in the exercise.

If you find limitations when reading your XML files due to the size or complexity of your structure, there is an alternative step: the **XML Input Stream (StAX)** step. If you want to learn how to use it, follow this link that contains a full description of the functionality and use of the step: `https://help.pentaho.com/Documentation/8.0/Products/Data_Integration/Transformation_Step_Reference/XML_Input_Stream_(StAX)`

Parsing an XML structure stored in a field

If, as part of your dataset, you have a field containing an XML structure, you can parse it in the same way as you did before. Look at the following sample containing color palettes:

```
BlackAndWhite,<color-
palette><color>#ffffff</color><color>#b9b9b9</color><color>#8e8e8e</color><
color>#727272</color><color>#000000</color></color-palette>

primary,<color-
```

```
palette><color>#f40707</color><color>#1b00c7</color><color>#e7e035</color><
color>#17d640</color><color>#f6f3f3</color></color-palette>

Blue,<color-
palette><color>#a8cafe</color><color>#224dce</color><color>#05146e</color><
color>#0c226f</color><color>#ede7fd</color></color-palette>

Generic,<color-
palette><color>#C52F0D</color><color>#123D82</color><color>#4A0866</color><
color>#445500</color><color>#FFAA00</color></color-palette>
```

Each line contains the name of a color palette and a list of colors represented as an XML structure. Suppose that you have the previous sample in a file named `colors.txt`, and for each palette, you want to get the list of colors. You do it as follows:

1. Read the file with the **Text file input** step, setting a comma as the separator and configuring two string fields: `palette_name` and `colors`.
2. After the **Text file input** step, add a **Get data from XML** step.
3. Double-click on the step and check the option **XML source is defined in a field?**
4. Under **get XML source from a field**, select the name of the field containing the XML structure `colors`.

As with the **Get data from XML** step, you are not reading a file; PDI is not able to build the list of nodes to select, but it allows you to provide a sample XML fragment to help you configure the step:

5. Select the **Content** tab. Click on **Get XPath nodes**. A window will show up for you to provide a sample XML fragment. Copy and paste a representative XML fragment of your file into this window, for example:

```
<color-palette>
   <color>#ffffff</color>
   <color>#b9b9b9</color>
   <color>#8e8e8e</color>
   <color>#727272</color>
   <color>#000000</color>
 </color-palette>
```

6. Close the window. PDI will list the nodes found in that fragment of XML, in this case `/color-palette` and `/color-palette/color`.

7. As the current node, select `/color-palette/color`.
8. Configure the **Fields** tab. Create a field named `color`. For **XPath**, simply type a dot.

If the selected node contains more elements, you could use the **Get fields** button and PDI would fill the grid according to your selected current node and the sample XML provided.

9. Close the window and run a preview. You should see the new fields extracted from the XML structure, as well as the fields from previous steps, in this case, the name of the palette. The result will look like the following:

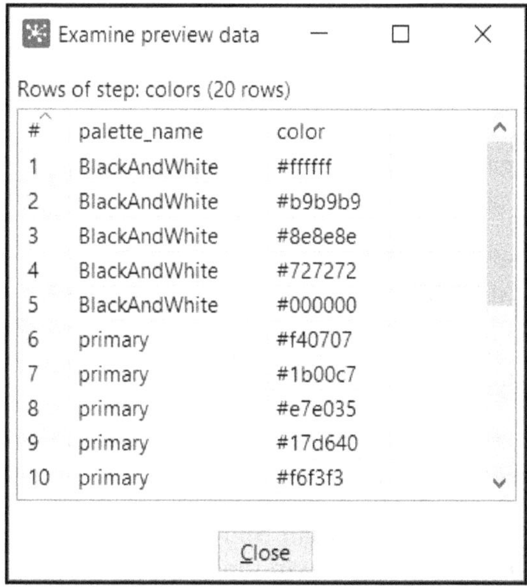

#	palette_name	color
1	BlackAndWhite	#ffffff
2	BlackAndWhite	#b9b9b9
3	BlackAndWhite	#8e8e8e
4	BlackAndWhite	#727272
5	BlackAndWhite	#000000
6	primary	#f40707
7	primary	#1b00c7
8	primary	#e7e035
9	primary	#17d640
10	primary	#f6f3f3

Previewing the result of parsing an XML structure

PDI Transformation and Job files

Despite the `ktr` and `kjb` extensions, PDI transformations and jobs are just XML files. As such, you are able to explore them and recognize different XML elements. Look at the following sample code:

```
<?xml version="1.0" encoding="UTF-8"?>
<transformation>
```

```
 <info>
 <name>hello_world</name>
 <description>My First Transformation</description>
 <extended_description>Learning Pentaho Data Integration 7
Chapter 1</extended_description>
...
</info>
</transformation>
```

This is an extract from the `hello_world.ktr` file created in `Chapter 1`, *Getting Started with Pentaho Data Integration*. Here, you can see the root element named `transformation` and some inner elements, for example, `info` and `name`. Other common nodes for transformations are `/transformation/step` and `/transformation/order/hop`, containing information about steps and hops respectively.

Analogous to transformations, a Job file contains all the details about Job entries and hops in the nodes named `/job/entries/entry` and `/job/hops/hop` respectively.

Knowing the internal format of the jobs and transformations can be useful for different purposes. By looping through `ktr` and `kjb` files, you can get specific details, as follows:

- The names of jobs that send emails
- A list of all variables that are set through a project
- A list of all the kinds of data sources used
- Which transformations use a particular step

If you want to look for a particular step inside a Transformation, you need to know the ID under which the step is saved. To access this information, do as follows:

1. Open Spoon and select the **Tools** | **Show plugin information ...** option on the main menu. A **Plugin Browser** window appears.
2. For the **Plugin type:**, select **Step**. A list of all steps will appear with information including the ID, name, description, and category to which each step belongs:

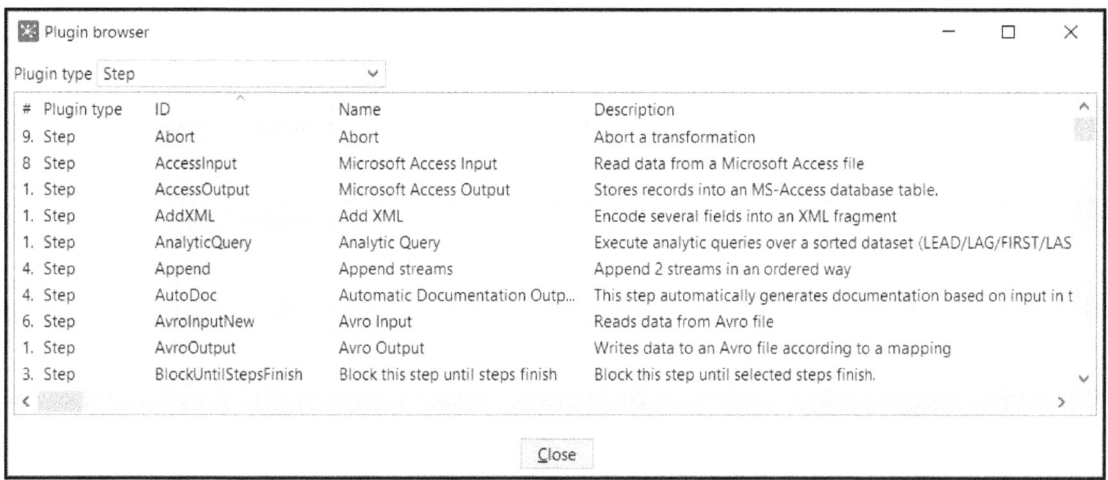

Plugin browser

Plugin type: Step

#	Plugin type	ID	Name	Description
9.	Step	Abort	Abort	Abort a transformation
8	Step	AccessInput	Microsoft Access Input	Read data from a Microsoft Access file
1.	Step	AccessOutput	Microsoft Access Output	Stores records into an MS-Access database table.
1.	Step	AddXML	Add XML	Encode several fields into an XML fragment
1.	Step	AnalyticQuery	Analytic Query	Execute analytic queries over a sorted dataset (LEAD/LAG/FIRST/LAS
4.	Step	Append	Append streams	Append 2 streams in an ordered way
4.	Step	AutoDoc	Automatic Documentation Outp...	This step automatically generates documentation based on input in t
6.	Step	AvroInputNew	Avro Input	Reads data from Avro file
1.	Step	AvroOutput	Avro Output	Writes data to an Avro file according to a mapping
3.	Step	BlockUntilStepsFinish	Block this step until steps finish	Block this step until selected steps finish.

Close

List of Transformation steps and their descriptions

3. For information about Job entries, proceed in the same way, but for the **Plugin type:**, select **Job**.

If you copy a step by selecting it in the Spoon work area and press *Ctrl* + *C*, and then paste it into a text editor, you can see its XML definition. If you copy it back to the canvas, a new identical step will be added to your Transformation.

Parsing JSON structures

JavaScript Object Notation (**JSON**) is a lightweight data interchange format and can be used to exchange or store structured information. In this section, we will describe JSON structures and how to parse them with PDI.

Introducing JSON terminology

A JSON structure can contain scalar data types such as numbers, Booleans, or strings, and also structured data as arrays or objects. In a similar way to XML, JSON can also store hierarchical data.

The objects are represented as a collection of `name_of_field:value_of_field` pairs and you can have an array of these elements represented by a list, enclosed by `[]` characters.

The following example is an extract taken from the samples that come with PDI:

```
{ "store": {
     "book": [
        { "category": "reference",
          "author": "Nigel Rees",
          "title": "Sayings of the Century",
          "price": 8.95
        },
        { "category": "fiction",
          "author": "Evelyn Waugh",
          "title": "Sword of Honour",
          "price": 12.99
        },
        { "category": "fiction",
          "author": "Herman Melville",
          "title": "Moby Dick",
          "isbn": "0-553-21311-3",
          "price": 8.99
        },
        ...
       ],
       ...
     }
}
```

You will find the original file as `samples/transformations/files/jsonfile.js` inside the PDI installation directory.

In the sample JSON structure, you can easily identify an array of books, each with some information, for example, the author and the name of the book.

Getting familiar with the JSONPath notation

In order to parse JSON structures, we use JSONPath. **JSONPath** is the XPath for JSON; it's used to refer to JSON elements in the same way as XPath is used for XML elements.

JSONPath expressions use dot notation, as in `$.store.book[0].title`.

The following table shows a basic overview of the JSONPath syntax elements. The examples refer to the book's structure presented earlier:

JSONPath expression	Description	Sample
`$`	Root object	`$` returns the whole JSON structure
`.`	Child operator; it's used to access different levels of the JSON structure	`$..title` returns the titles of the books
`*`	Wildcard for referring to all elements	`$.store.book.*` returns all books
`[]`	Array operator	`$.store.book[0]` returns the data about the first book in the array

Note the difference between `$.store.book` that returns a single element, which is an array of books, and `$.store.book.*`, which returns five elements, each corresponding to a different book.

Parsing JSON structures with PDI

With PDI, it's possible to read a file with a JSON structure as well as parse a JSON structure found in a field of our dataset. In both cases, to parse that structure, you use the **JSON input** step. To tell PDI which information to get from the structure, it is required that you use the JSONPath notation as explained previously.

Reading a JSON file with the JSON input step

Let's create a very simple Transformation to demonstrate how to read a JSON file. In this Transformation, we will read the sample file with books:

1. Create a Transformation.
2. From the **Input** category, drag to the work area a **JSON input** step.
3. Double-click on the step and configure it to read the JSON file. Add the full path of the file just as you would to read any other kind of file.

4. Once you specify the filename, click on the **Fields** tab and configure it as follows:

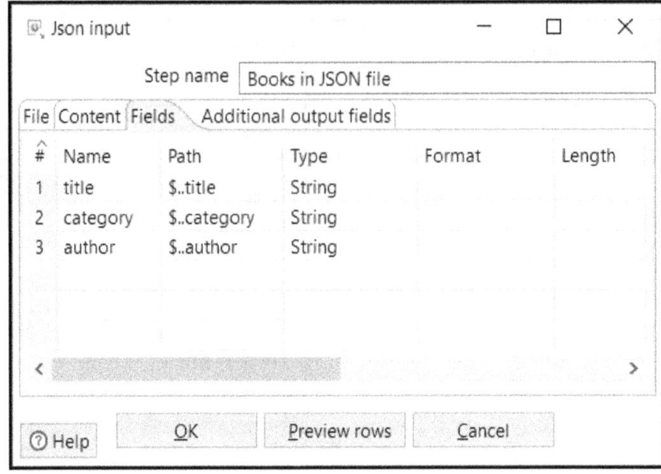

Configuring a JSON input step

5. Click on **Preview rows**. You should see the following:

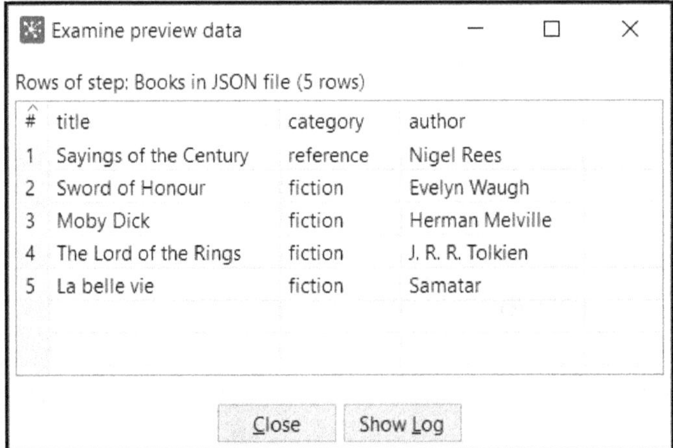

Previewing data coming from a JSON file

Parsing a JSON structure stored in a field

There is the possibility that you have a JSON structure in a field of your dataset. In this case, the way to parse the structure does not differ much from what was explained previously.

If you have a field containing a JSON structure and need to parse it in order to extract some values, proceed as follows:

1. At the end of your data stream, add a **JSON input** step.
2. Double-click on the step and check the option **Source is from a previous step**.
3. Under **Select field:**, select the name of the field that contains the JSON value.
4. Configure the **Fields** tab just as you did before.

By previewing the last step, you should see the new fields extracted from the JSON structure as well as the fields coming from previous steps.

Summary

In this chapter, you learned some of the most used and useful ways of transforming data. Specifically, you learned the most common ways to operate with different data types, and also learned to use the Select Values step to manipulate the metadata of a dataset. Besides that, you recognized and used system information and predefined PDI variables, and learned to parse XML and JSON data with dedicated PDI steps.

Even when there are a lot of steps to transform data, it may be that the Transformation you have to do is difficult or not possible to do with the available options. In that case, you have the option to write some code. This is the core subject of the next chapter.

If you have a field containing a JSON string [illegible] values, proceed as follows:

1. At the end of your stream, add a JSON Input step.
2. Double-click on the step [illegible] the [illegible] from previous step.
3. Under [illegible] fields [illegible] the name of the field [illegible]

   Configure [illegible] tab [illegible]

[illegible] from previous step [illegible]

6

Controlling the Flow of Data

In the previous chapters, you learned to transform your data in many ways. Now suppose you have to collect results from a survey. You receive several files with the data and those files have different formats. You have to merge those files somehow and generate a unified view of the information. Not only that, you want to remove the rows of data whose content is irrelevant. Finally, based on the rows that interest you, you want to create another file with some statistics. This kind of requirement is very common, but requires more background in **Pentaho Data Integration** (**PDI**).

This chapter will give you the tools for implementing flows of data similar to the samples explained atop. In particular, we will cover the following topics:

- Filtering data
- Copying, distributing, and partitioning data
- Splitting the stream based on conditions
- Merging streams
- Looking up and getting data from a secondary stream

Filtering data

By now, you have learned how to do several kinds of calculations which enrich the set of data. There is still another kind of operation that is frequently used; it does not have to do with enriching the data but with discarding or filtering unwanted information. That's the core of this section.

Filtering rows upon conditions

Suppose you have a dataset and you only want to keep the rows that match a condition. To demonstrate how to implement this kind of filtering, we will read a file, build a list of words found in the file, and then filter the nulls or unwanted words. We will split the exercise into two parts:

- In the first part, we will read the file and prepare the data for filtering
- In the second part, we will effectively filter the data

Reading a file and getting the list of words found in it

Let's start by reading a sample file.

Before starting, you'll need at least one text file to play with. The text file used in this tutorial is named `smcng10.txt`. Its content is about *Geological Observations on South America by Darwin, Charles, 1809-1882* and you can download it from `https://archive.org/details/geologicalobserv03620gut`.

The first thing we will do is to read the file and split the text into one word per row:

1. Create a new Transformation.
2. By using the **Text file input** step, read your file. The trick here is to put as a **Separator** a sign you are not expecting in the file, such as `|`. By doing so, every line will be recognized as a single field. Configure the **Fields** tab with a single `String` field named `line`.
3. This particular file has a big header describing the content and origin of the data. We are not interested in those lines, so in the **Content** tab, as **Header**, type `378`, which is the number of lines that precede the specific content we're interested in.
4. From the **Transform** category of steps, drag to the canvas the **Split field to rows** step, and create a hop from the **Text file input** step to this one.
5. Double-click the step. As **Field to split**, select `line`. As **New field name**, type `word`. Close the window.
6. With this last step selected, run a preview. Your preview window should look as follows:

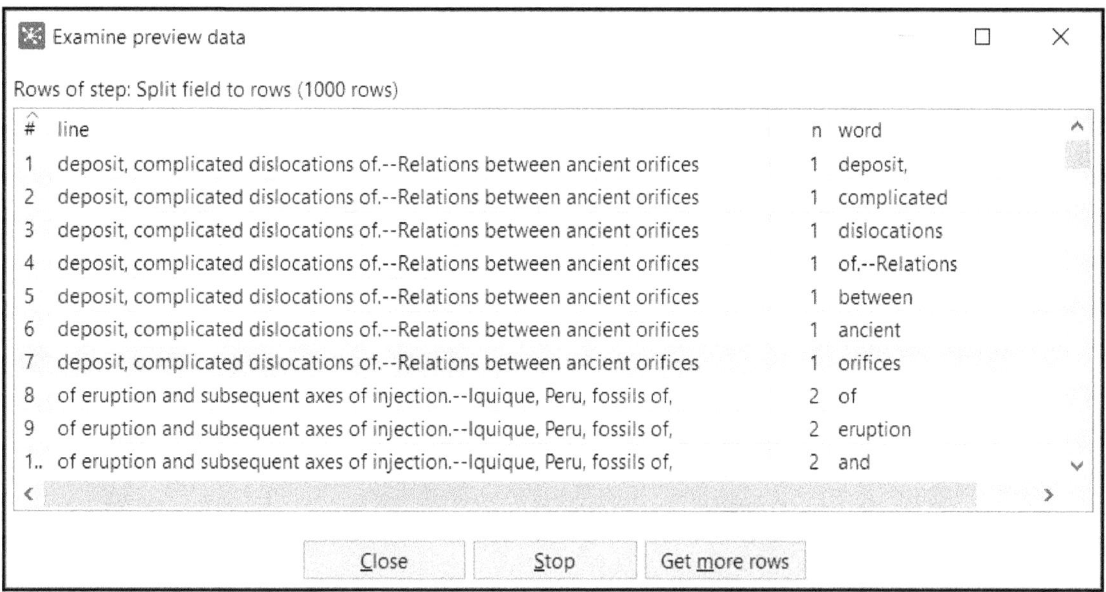

Previewing the output of Split fields to rows step

7. Close the preview window.
8. Add the **Select values** step to remove the `line` field.

It's not mandatory to remove this field, but as it will not be used any longer, removing it will make future previews clearer.

The new field named `word` is now the basis for our Transformation. As you can see in the previsualization, there are a lot of characters not relevant for us, as for example commas and quotation marks, among others. Let's get rid of those.

9. After the last step, add the **Replace in String** step. Use it to remove all characters except letters and numbers. For doing that, use the regular expression `[^A-Z0-9]`.
10. Now create a new field with the length of the word.

You can use **Formula** or the **UDJE** step, as you learned in the previous chapter.

11. Run a preview of this last step. You should see this:

Examine preview data
Rows of step: word_length (1000 rows)
n word word_length
2 1 complicated 11
3 1 dislocations 12
4 1 ofRelations 11
5 1 between 7
6 1 ancient 7
7 1 orifices 8
8 2 of 2
9 2 eruption 8
1.. 2 and 3
Close
Stop
Get more rows

Previewing a Transformation

Instead of reading the file with the regular **Text file input** file, you could have implemented a similar solution by using the **Load file content in memory** step. This step reads the whole text in memory, in a single field.

Filtering unwanted rows with a Filter rows step

You just build a list of words coming from a sample file. As you would see, there are blank rows, and also a lot of rows with pronouns, articles, and other very small words. If you want to keep only the words relevant to the subject of the text file, you will want to discard all this. For doing this, we will use the **Filter rows** step - a step dedicated to filtering rows based on conditions and comparisons. In its simplest version, for every row, the step checks a given condition and let's pass only those rows for which the condition is `true`. The other rows are lost. The following are the instructions for implementing this solution:

1. Expand the **Flow** category of steps, and drag the **Filter rows** step to the work area.
2. Create a hop from the last step to the **Filter rows** step.
3. Edit the **Filter rows** step by double-clicking on it.

4. Click on the **<field>** textbox to the left of the = sign. The list of fields appears. Select **word_length**.
5. Click on the = sign. A list of operations appears. Select **>**.
6. In the **<value>** textbox, type `4`. The window looks as follows:

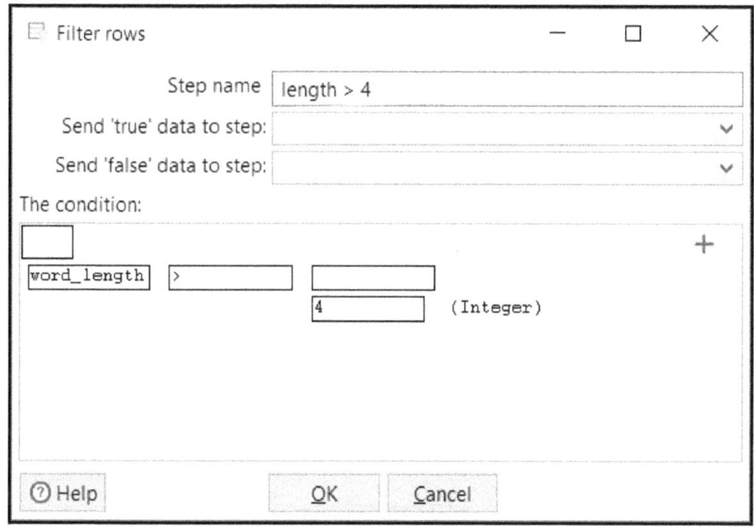

Configuring a Filter rows step

7. Click on **OK**.
8. From the **Flow** category, add the **Dummy** step.
9. Create a hop from the **Filter rows** step to the **Dummy** step. When asked for the kind of hop, select the **Main output of step**, as shown in the following screenshot:

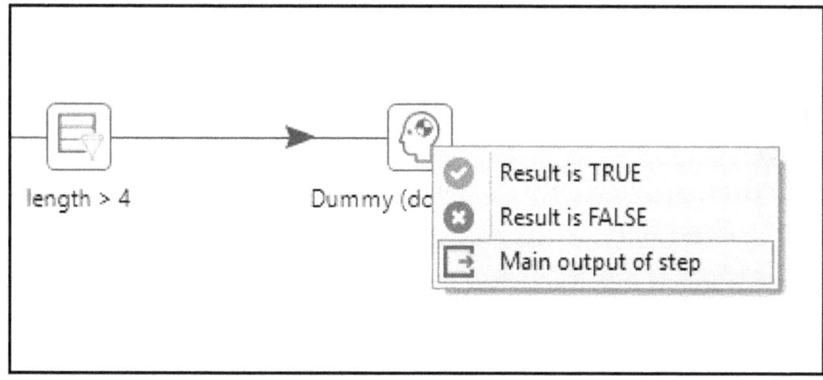

Selecting Main output of step

10. With the **Dummy** step selected, run a preview. You will see something like the following:

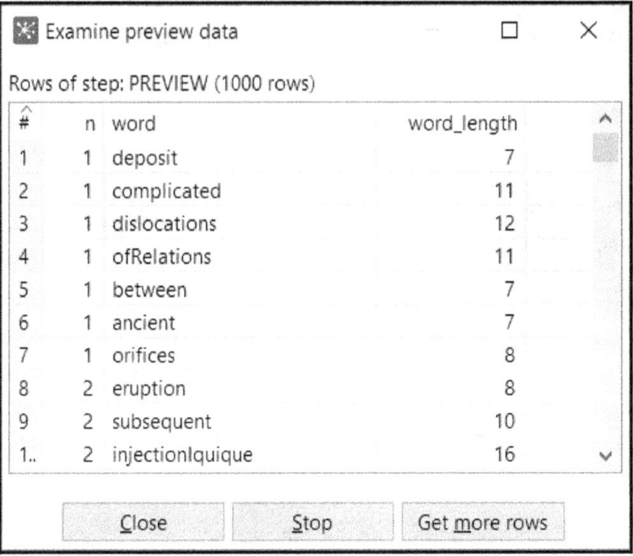

#	n	word	word_length
1	1	deposit	7
2	1	complicated	11
3	1	dislocations	12
4	1	ofRelations	11
5	1	between	7
6	1	ancient	7
7	1	orifices	8
8	2	eruption	8
9	2	subsequent	10
1..	2	injectionlquique	16

Previewing filtered data

As you can see, only the rows that matched the given condition passed the filter.

In this exercise, you entered a very simple filter, involving one field (`word_lenght`) and a constant (`4`). Following is a list of more filters we could have applied:

- `word IS NOT NULL` in this case, only the rows where the words are neither null nor with empty values pass
- `line STARTS WITH word` in this case, the row passes only if the `word` field matches the first characters in the `line` field. Note that in this example the filter involves two fields.
- `word REGEXP (g|e).+` this filter lets pass only the words starting with `g` or with `e`
- `word in list geology; sun` in this case, only the rows with words `geology` and `sun` pass the filter

When editing conditions, you always have a contextual menu, which allows you to combine conditions, as, for example:

```
word CONTAINS geo
AND
len_word>8
```

You also have the option to create sub-conditions, such as:

```
   (
   word CONTAINS geo
AND
   len_word>8
   )
OR
   (word in list earth; rocks)
```

In this example, the condition lets pass all words with length greater than `8` containing the string `geo` and also the words `earth` and `rocks`.

Filtering rows by using the Java Filter step

As an alternative to the **Filter rows** step, there is another step for the same purpose: the **Java Filter** step. This step is useful when your conditions are too complicated and it becomes difficult or impossible to create them in a regular **Filter rows** step.

With the **Java Filter** step, instead of creating the condition interactively, you write a **Java expression** that evaluates to `true` or `false`. Look at the last example in the previous section:

```
  (
   word CONTAINS geo
AND
   len_word>8
   )
OR
   (word in list earth; rocks)
```

The same condition can be expressed with a Java expression as `(word.matches(".*geo.*") && word_length>8) || word.equals("earth") || word.equals("rocks")`.

Following is how you implement this alternative way of filtering:

1. Open the Transformation created in the previous exercise and save it under a different name.
2. Remove the **Filter** rows and the **Dummy** step.
3. From the **Flow** category, add the **Java Filter** step.
4. Double-click the **Java Filter** step.
5. In the **Condition (Java expression)** textbox, type `(word.matches(".*geo.*") && word_length>8) || word.equals("earth") || word.equals("rocks")`.
6. Close the window.
7. With **Java Filter** selected, run a preview. You will see the following:

Examine preview data

Rows of step: combined condition (393 rows)

#	n	word	word_length
26	161	geographical	12
27	164	geological	10
28	168	geological	10
29	173	rocks	5
30	176	rocks	5
31	177	geological	10
32	179	geologists	10
33	182	rocks	5
34	191	geologistsand	13
35	192	rocks	5

Close

Previewing data filtered with a Java Filter step

When you run a preview, you see the rows coming out of a step. As such, a preview of the **Java Filter** step only shows rows that match the condition. This is also true for the **Filter row** step.

Filtering data based on row numbers

Until now you've been filtering upon conditions on the values of the fields. You could also filter rows based on the row numbers. There are a couple of steps that allow us to do that. Here is a brief summary of them:

Step	Description
Sample rows (**Statistics** category)	This step samples the rows based on a list of row numbers or row number ranges. For example, `1,5,10..20` will filter row `1`, row `5`, and all the rows from `10` up to `20` (`10` and `20` included).
Reservoir Sampling (**Statistics** category)	This step allows you to sample a fixed number of rows. The step uses uniform sampling, which means that all incoming rows have an equal chance of being selected.
Top / Bottom / First / Last filter (**Transform** category)	This plugin allows you to filter the first `N` rows or the last `N` rows of your dataset.
Filter rows / Java Filter steps (**Flow** category)	These steps offer a general alternative for filtering one or more rows based on their numbers. The only precondition for doing that is to have a field in your dataset containing the row number.
Identify last row in a stream + Filter rows or Java Filter	The **Identify last row in a stream** step generates a Boolean field which is true only for the last row in the dataset. Based on that field, you could filter the last row either with the **Filter row** or the **Java Filter** step.

The **Top / Bottom / First / Last filter** step is a plugin that you can install through the Marketplace. For more information about the installation of plugins, refer to *Extending the PDI functionality through the Marketplace* section of `Chapter 1`, *Getting Started with Pentaho Data Integration.*

Splitting streams unconditionally

Until now, you have been working with simple and straight flows of data. However, often the rows of your dataset have to take different paths and those simple flows are not enough. This situation can be handled very easily, and you will learn how to do it in this section.

For the exercises about splitting streams, we will use information from the Pentaho BI Platform Tracking site. So, before starting with the PDI subject, let's introduce the Tracking site. On this site, you can see the current Pentaho roadmap and browse its issue-tracking system.

The following instructions are for exporting the list of proposed new features for PDI from the site:

1. Access the main Pentaho Tracking site page at `http://jira.pentaho.com`.

At this point, you may want to create a user ID. Logging is not mandatory, but it is beneficial if you want to create new issues or vote or comment on existing ones.

2. In the menu at the top of the screen, select **Issues** | **Search for issues**. A list of issues will be displayed.
3. At the top of the list, you will have several drop-down list boxes for filtering. Use them to select the following:
    - **Project: Pentaho Data Integration - Kettle**
    - **Issue Type: New Feature**
    - **Status: Open, In Progress**

As you select the filters, they are automatically applied and you can see the list of issues that match the filters:

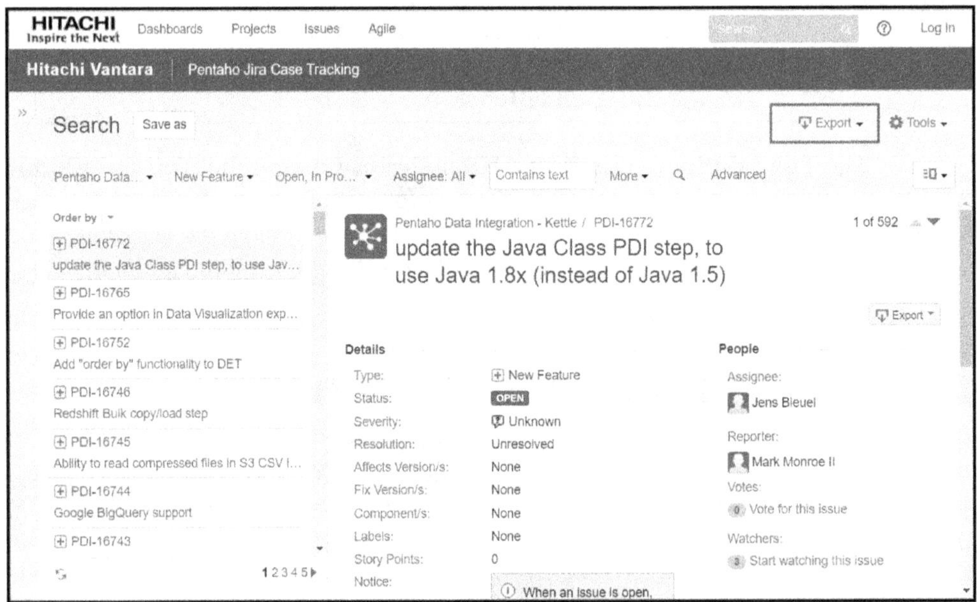

Issues in the Pentaho Tracking site

4. Preceding the list of search criteria, click on **Export** and a list of options will be displayed. Among the options, select **Excel (Current fields)** to export the list to an Excel file.
5. Save the file to the folder of your choice.

Currently, PDI does not recognize the Excel file exported from the JIRA website. It throws the following exception: `jxl.read.biff.BiffException: Unable to recognize OLE stream`. To solve this issue, simply open the file and save it to a version previous to MS Office 2010.

Copying rows

At any place in a Transformation, you may decide to split the main stream into two or more streams. When you do so, you have to decide what to do with the data that leaves the last step: **copy** or **distribute**.

To copy means that the whole dataset is copied to each of the destination steps. Why would you copy the whole dataset? Mainly because you want to apply different treatments to the same set of data. For example, with our Excel file exported from the JIRA platform, we may want to generate two different outputs:

- A detailed file with the issues
- A spreadsheet with some statistics, as, for example, quantity of issues per severity per status

This is a typical situation where we want to copy the dataset. Copying rows is a very straightforward task. Let's see how you do it with a very simple example:

1. Create a Transformation.

2. Read the file exported from JIRA by using the **Microsoft Excel Input** step. After providing the filename, click on the **Sheets** tab and fill it as shown in the following screenshot, so it skips the header rows and the first column:

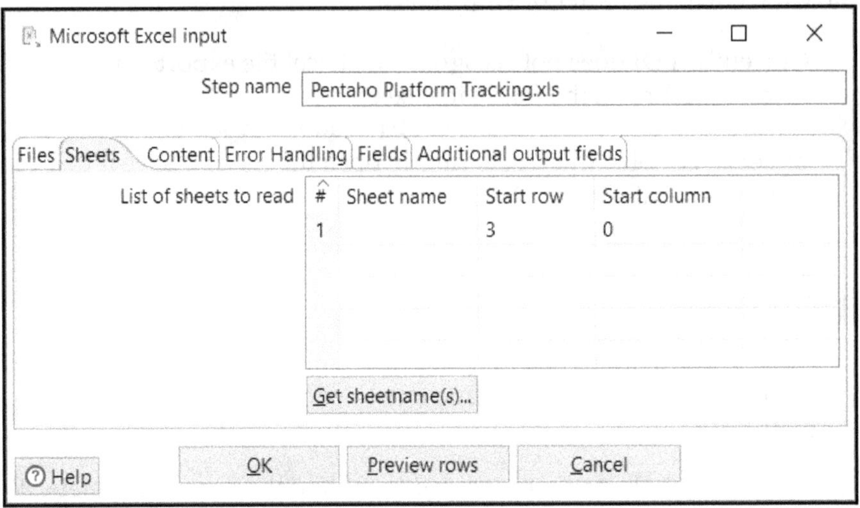

Configuring the sheets when reading an Excel file

3. Click on the **Fields** tab and fill in the grid by clicking on the **Get fields from header row...** button.
4. Click on **Preview rows** just to be sure that you are reading the file properly. You should see all the contents of the Excel file except the first column and the three heading lines.
5. Click on **OK**.
6. From the **Flow** category, add two **Dummy** steps.
7. Create a hop from the **Excel Input** step toward one of the **Dummy** steps.
8. Now create a second hop from the **Excel Input** step toward the second **Dummy** step.

A warning window will appear, asking you to decide whether to copy or distribute rows. Click on **Copy**....You will have the following:

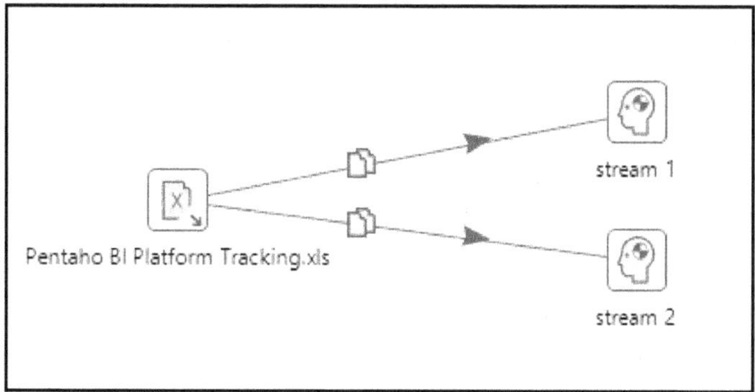

Copying rows

Note that when you copy, the hops that leave the step from which you are copying change visually to indicate the copy action.

9. Save the Transformation and run it.

Look at the **Step Metrics** tab in the **Execution** window:

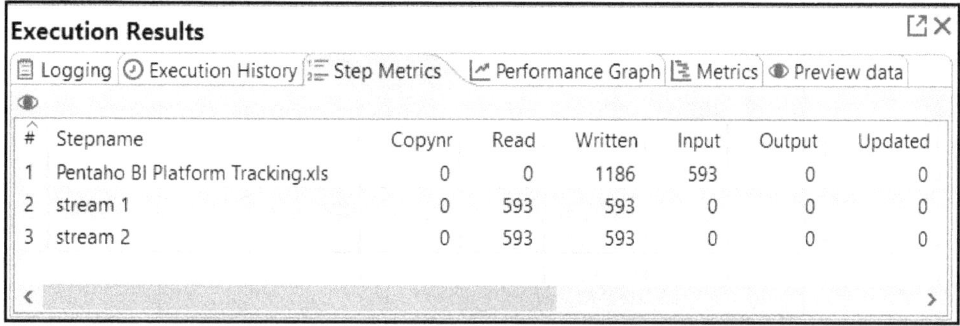

Execution Results

Logging | Execution History | Step Metrics | Performance Graph | Metrics | Preview data

#	Stepname	Copynr	Read	Written	Input	Output	Updated
1	Pentaho BI Platform Tracking.xls	0	0	1186	593	0	0
2	stream 1	0	593	593	0	0	0
3	stream 2	0	593	593	0	0	0

Step Metrics after copying rows

Take into account that the number of rows you see may not match the ones shown here, as you derived your own source data from the JIRA system and it changes all the time.

As you can see in the **Step Metrics** tab, the number of written rows in the Excel input step (`1188`) double of the number of input rows (`594`). This is because all the rows were copied to each **Dummy** step, as you can also see in the **Input** columns correspondent to the **Dummy** steps in the same grid. Another way to verify this is to run a preview of each **Dummy** step to see that the rows are the same in both.

From the moment you copy the dataset, the copies become independent. So in this example, you could put any sequence of steps after any of the **Dummy** steps and each stream will follow its own way without modifying the data in the other stream.

You should not assume a particular order in the execution of steps due to its asynchronous nature. As the steps are executed in parallel and all the output streams receive the rows in sync, you don't have control over the order in which they are executed.

In this example, we used **Dummy** steps just for simplicity. Any step would have served the same purpose of copying the rows generating separate streams.

Also, in the example, you created only two streams, but it's possible to create any number of streams, like in the following example:

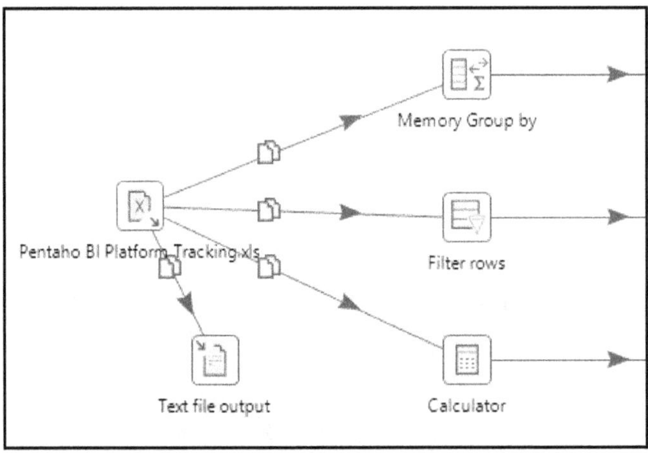

Copying the dataset to several streams of data

Distributing rows

As said, when you split a stream, you can either copy or distribute the rows. **Copying** is about creating copies of the whole dataset and sending each of them to each output stream. **Distributing** means that the rows of the dataset are distributed among the destination steps. Those steps run in separate threads, so distribution is a way to implement **parallel processing**.

When you distribute, the destination steps receive the rows in a round-robin fashion. For example, if you have three target steps, as for example, the three calculators in the following screenshot the first row of data goes to the first target step, the second row goes to the second step, the third row goes to the third step, the fourth row goes to the fourth step, and so on.

Visually, when the rows are distributed, the hops leaving the steps from which you distribute are plain; they don't change their look and feel, as shown next:

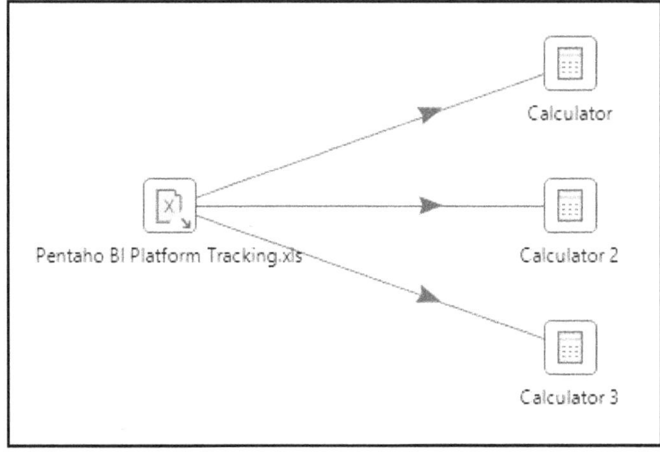

Distributing rows

Throughout the book, we will always use the **Copy** option. To avoid being asked for the action to take every time you create more than one hop leaving a step, you can set the **Copy** option by default. You do it by opening the **PDI options** window (**Tools** | **Options...** from the main menu) and unchecking the option **Show Copy or Distribute dialog:**. Remember that to see the change applied, you will have to restart Spoon.

Once you have changed this option, the default method is `Copy rows`. If you want to distribute rows, you can change the action by right-clicking on the step from which you want to copy or distribute, selecting **Data Movement...** in the contextual menu that appears, and then selecting the desired option.

Another way to distribute is to change the number of copies of a step. The following step-by-step instructions create three copies of the **Calculator** step. The result is technically equivalent to the previous example:

1. Right-click a step.
2. From the contextual menu, select **Change Number of Copies to Start...** .
3. As **Number of copies**, specify `3`. Close the window. The look and feel change as follows:

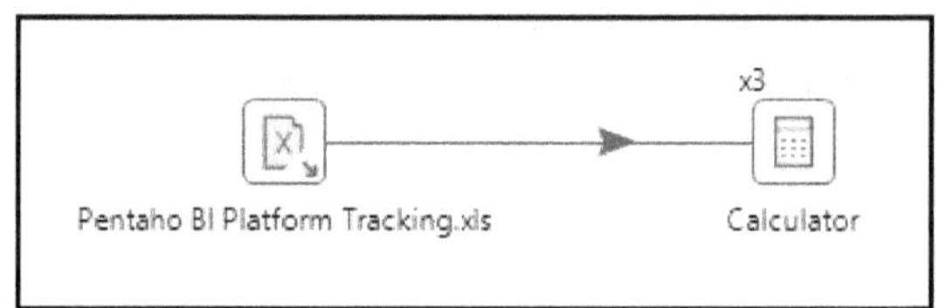

Changing the number of copies of a step

Introducing partitioning and clustering

For taking advantage of processing power, distributing rows is a good option. It gives you a better performance, which is critical if you have a heavy processing work or your dataset is huge.

A step further in the distribution of rows is the concept of **partitioning**. Partitioning is about splitting the dataset into several smaller datasets, but the distribution is made according to a rule that is applied to the rows.

The standard `partitioning` method offered by PDI is **Remainder of division**. You choose a partitioning field, and PDI divides its value by the number of predefined partitions.

As an example, in our sample Transformation, we can create a partitioning schema with three partitions and choose `Severity` as the partitioning field. Then, PDI will calculate the remaining of the dividing the value of our partitioning field by three, which is the number of partitions. Actually, as our partitioning field is a non-integer value, PDI will do the calculation on a checksum created from the `Severity` value.

At runtime, each row goes to a different partition, depending on the calculated value. This way, all the rows for which the partition field has the same value, go to the same partition.

In our example, all rows with the same `Severity` will go to the same partition. The following screenshot shows how the partition is shown graphically in Spoon:

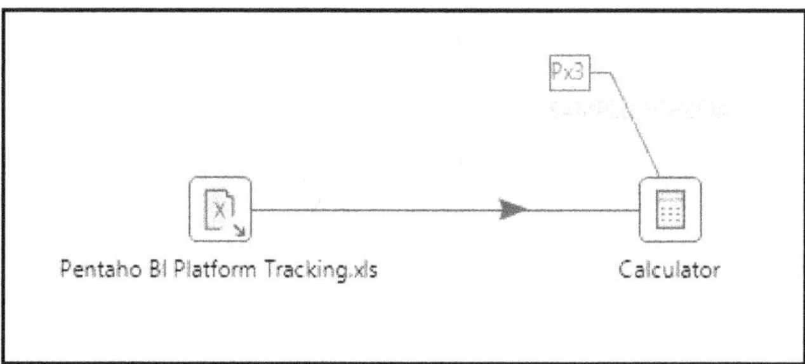

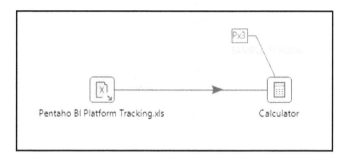

Transformation with partitioning

Also, in the **Step metrics** tab, you can see how the rows are distributed among the partitions. This is clearly different from the standard round-robin method of distribution explained before:

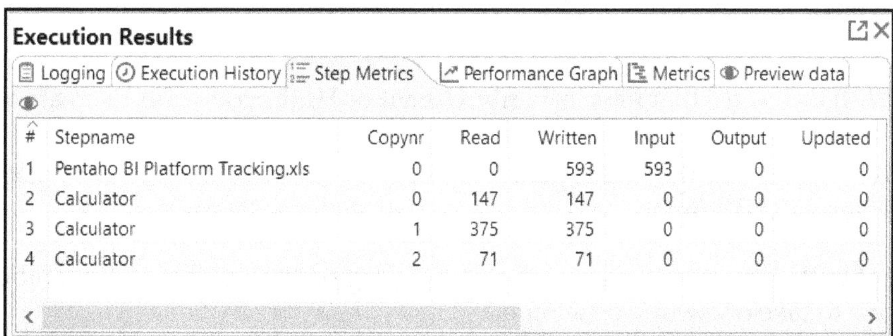

#	Stepname	Copynr	Read	Written	Input	Output	Updated
1	Pentaho BI Platform Tracking.xls	0	0	593	593	0	0
2	Calculator	0	147	147	0	0	0
3	Calculator	1	375	375	0	0	0
4	Calculator	2	71	71	0	0	0

Step Metrics after partitioning

To scale out, there is one more step, the **clustering** feature, which allows you to distribute the ETL tasks on several machines. When you run a Transformation on a cluster, you may also want to partition the dataset in a particular way. So you may also use partitioning in conjunction with clustering.

For a very instructive article about partitioning and clustering, you can read the blog entry by Diethard Steiner at `http://diethardsteiner.github.io/pdi/2015/04/28/PDI-Parallelism-and-Partitioning.html`. Also, for an advanced and complete material about the subject, you can read *Chapter 16: Parallelization, Clustering, and Partitioning* of the book *Pentaho Kettle Solutions: Building Open Source ETL Solutions with Pentaho Data Integration* by Matt Caster, the creator of PDI.

Splitting the stream based on conditions

In the previous section, you learned to split the main stream of data into two or more streams. Now you will learn how to put conditions, so the rows take one way or another depending on the results of evaluating those conditions.

Splitting a stream based on a simple condition

For this subsection, we will work one more time with the Excel file exported from JIRA, containing all the new features proposed for next releases of PDI. This time, suppose that you want to implement different treatments to the data, depending on the `Severity` of the issues. For example:

- With the issues that have severity **Urgent** or **High**, you want to create a list and send it by email
- With the rest of the issues, you want to create an Excel file order by status and severity, and copy this output to a shared folder to be revised

The source of both outputs is the same, but depending on the characteristics of the issues, the rows have to take one way or the other.

Following is how you implement the flow:

1. Create a new Transformation.
2. Read the Excel file just as you did in the previous section.
3. Add the **Filter rows** step and create a hop from the Excel input step toward this one.

Now we will configure the **Filter rows** step as follows, where we will put a condition just as we did in the first part of this chapter. The main difference here is that we will not discard the rows that don't meet the condition. We will split the stream in two:

- One stream with the rows for which the condition is true
- A second stream with the rows that don't meet the condition

For doing that, proceed as follows:

1. Add two **Dummy** steps. We will use them as the destination of the rows coming from the **Filter rows** step.
2. Create a hop from **Filter row** to one of those steps. As the type of the hop, select **Result is TRUE**.
3. Create a hop from the **Filter row** step to the other **Dummy** step. This time, as the type of the hop, select **Result is FALSE**. The Transformation looks as follows:

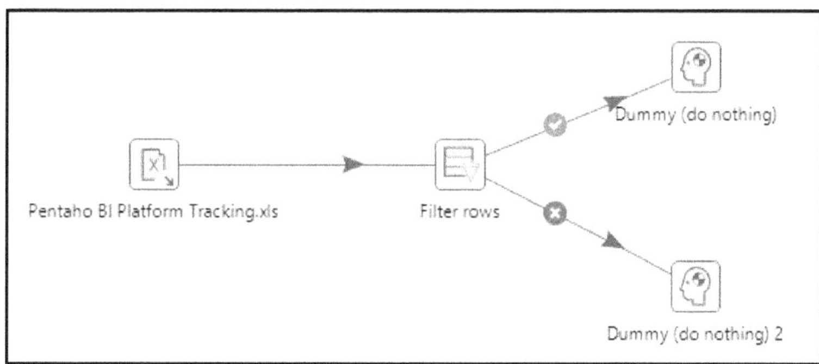

Transformation with a Filter row

4. Double-click on the **Filter rows** step to edit it.

Note that the content of the textboxes **Send true data to step** and S**end false data to step** should be the names of the destination steps—the two **Dummy** steps.

5. Enter the condition `Severity = [High] OR Severity = [Urgent]`. Then close the window.

Alternatively, you can use a single condition: `Severity IN LIST High;Urgent`.

One way to verify the behavior of the filter is to run a preview of the **Dummy** steps:

1. Select the **Dummy** step coming out from the `True` condition, the one after the arrow with the green mark. You will only see issues with severity `High` or `Urgent`:

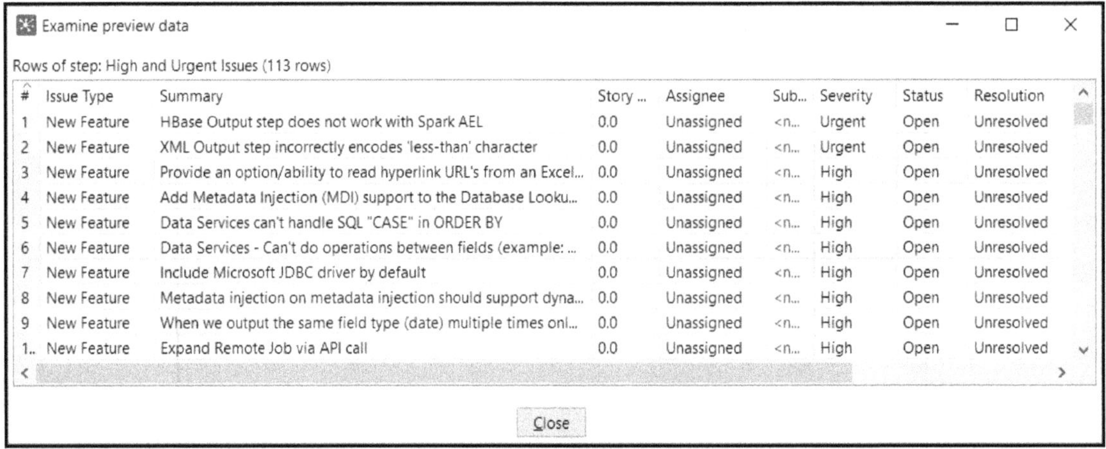

Examine preview data

Rows of step: High and Urgent Issues (113 rows)

#	Issue Type	Summary	Story ...	Assignee	Sub...	Severity	Status	Resolution
1	New Feature	HBase Output step does not work with Spark AEL	0.0	Unassigned	<n...	Urgent	Open	Unresolved
2	New Feature	XML Output step incorrectly encodes 'less-than' character	0.0	Unassigned	<n...	Urgent	Open	Unresolved
3	New Feature	Provide an option/ability to read hyperlink URL's from an Excel...	0.0	Unassigned	<n...	High	Open	Unresolved
4	New Feature	Add Metadata Injection (MDI) support to the Database Looku...	0.0	Unassigned	<n...	High	Open	Unresolved
5	New Feature	Data Services can't handle SQL "CASE" in ORDER BY	0.0	Unassigned	<n...	High	Open	Unresolved
6	New Feature	Data Services - Can't do operations between fields (example: ...	0.0	Unassigned	<n...	High	Open	Unresolved
7	New Feature	Include Microsoft JDBC driver by default	0.0	Unassigned	<n...	High	Open	Unresolved
8	New Feature	Metadata injection on metadata injection should support dyna...	0.0	Unassigned	<n...	High	Open	Unresolved
9	New Feature	When we output the same field type (date) multiple times onl...	0.0	Unassigned	<n...	High	Open	Unresolved
1..	New Feature	Expand Remote Job via API call	0.0	Unassigned	<n...	High	Open	Unresolved

Close

Previewing the output of a Filter rows step

2. Now run a preview of the other **Dummy** step. You should see the rest of the issues.

Another visual indicator that you can see to verify that the rows are going to one or the other stream is **Execution** window. In the **Step Metrics** tab, you will see how many rows are going to each stream:

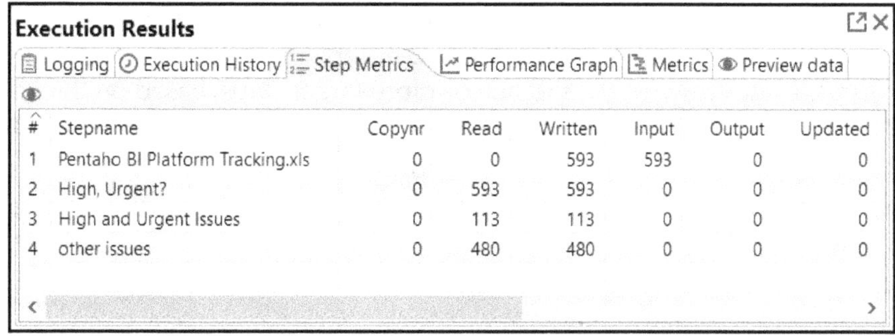

Execution Results

Logging | Execution History | Step Metrics | Performance Graph | Metrics | Preview data

#	Stepname	Copynr	Read	Written	Input	Output	Updated
1	Pentaho BI Platform Tracking.xls	0	0	593	593	0	0
2	High, Urgent?	0	593	593	0	0	0
3	High and Urgent Issues	0	113	113	0	0	0
4	other issues	0	480	480	0	0	0

Sample Step Metrics tab after running a transformation with the Filter rows step

In this example, we used **Dummy** steps just to demonstrate how you redirect the rows. In your Transformations, you can use any step as the destination of the `True` or the `False` condition.

Exploring PDI steps for splitting a stream based on conditions

When you have to make a decision, and upon that decision split the stream into two, you can use the **Filter rows** step, as you did in this last exercise. Alternatively, you can use the **Java Filter** step. As said in `Chapter 5`, *Manipulating PDI Data and Metadata* the purpose of both the steps, **Filter rows** and **Java Filter**, is the same; the main difference is the way in which you type or enter the conditions.

For details about the use and the differences between both the **Filter rows** and the **Java Filter** steps, you can go back to the *Filtering* section of this chapter.

Sometimes you have to make nested decisions; for example:

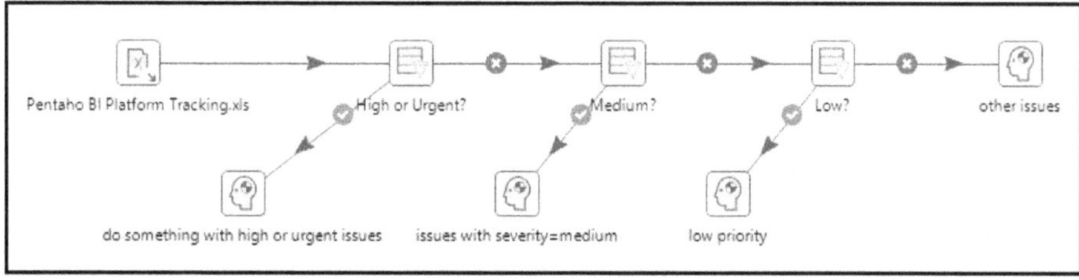

Sample Transformation with nested conditions

When the conditions are as simple as testing whether a field is equal to a value, you have a simpler alternative solution using the **Switch / case** step. This step, grouped under the **Flow** category of steps, routes rows of data to one or more target steps, based on the value encountered in a given field. If we take the preceding example and replace the filters with the **Switch / case** step, we would have something like the following:

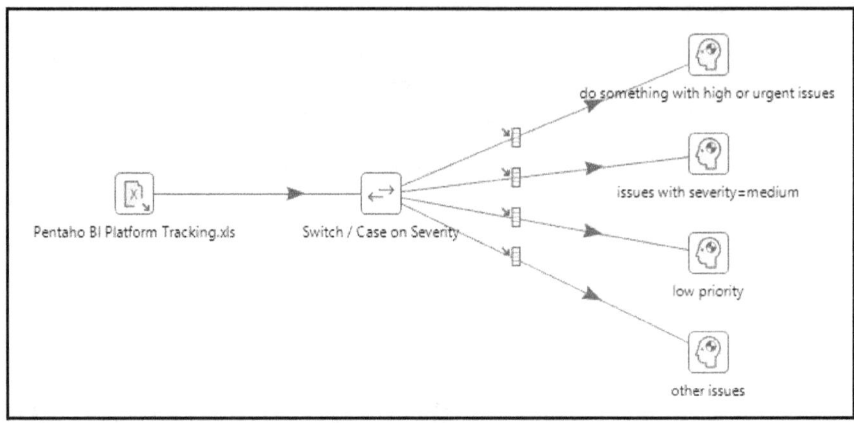

Using the Switch / case step

The configuration for the **Switch / case** step would look as follows:

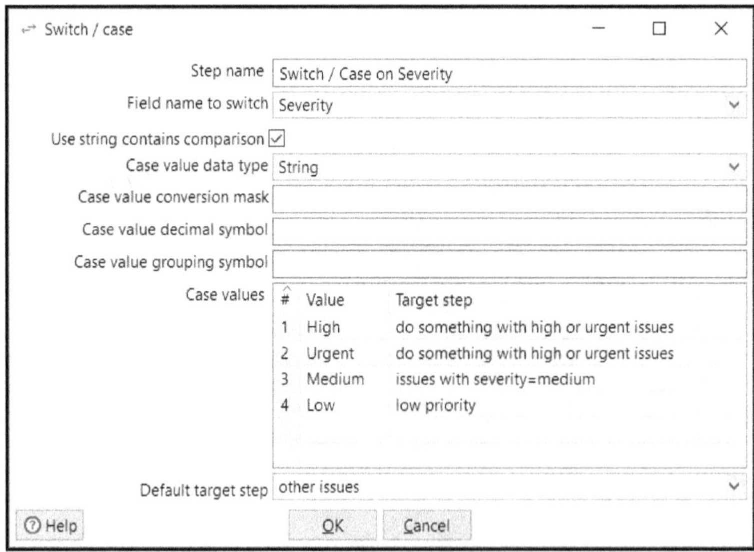

Configuring the Switch / case step

With this solution, the field to use for comparisons is `Severity`, and the values against which we compare are `Urgent`, `High`, `Medium`, and `Low`. Depending on the values of the `Severity` field, the rows will be sent to any of the target steps.

Note that in the configuration grid of the **Switch / case** step, it's possible to specify the same target step more than once.

The **Default target** step represents the step where the rows which don't match any of the case values are sent. In this example, the rows with a priority not present in the list will be sent to the step **other issues**.

Merging streams in several ways

You have just seen how the rows of a dataset can take different paths. Here you will learn the opposite, how data coming from different places are merged into a single stream. We will break this section into two parts:

- Merging two or more streams
- Customizing the way of merging streams

Merging two or more streams

For demonstrating how to merge streams, let's export a new file from the JIRA website. Following the same instructions as before, we will export the issues with a different set of filters:

- **Project: Pentaho Data Integration - Kettle**
- **Issue Type: Bugs**
- **Status: All excepting CLOSED and RESOLVED**

This time, instead of exporting the current fields, we will select the option **Excel (All fields)**.

If you open the Excel file, you will note that this version contains much more information as compared to the previous version.

Now we have:

- One Excel file containing new features for PDI.
- A second Excel file containing the list of unresolved bugs of PDI. This file has many more fields than the other. To be exact, there are 104 columns in this one, versus just ten columns in the simplest version.

The idea is to read both the files and generate a single dataset. Among all the fields available, we will only keep the following:

- Issue type
- Summary
- Severity
- Status
- Affects version/s

The most important concept you have to know before merging two or more streams is that the datasets have to share the same metadata. So in our example, besides reading both the Excel files, we have to transform the datasets in a way that both look the same. Follow these steps:

1. Create a new Transformation.
2. Drag to the canvas the **Microsoft Excel Input** step and read the Excel file with the new features.

For saving time, you can copy and paste the step from the Transformations created earlier.

3. As the file doesn't have the `Affects Version/s` field, we will create it with a default value. So, from the **Transform** category of steps, add the **Add constants** step and create a hop from the first **Excel input** step toward this step.
4. Use the **Add constants** step to add a field of type `String`, with name `Affects Version/s` and value `N/A`.
5. Finally, add the **Select values** step to keep only the proposed fields: `Issue Type`, `Summary`, `Severity`, `Status`, and `Affects Version/s`.
6. Add another **Microsoft Excel Input** step and use it to read the new file.
7. After the **Filter rows** step, add another **Select values** step and configure it to keep the same list of fields that you kept with the other **Select values** step.

8. From the **Flow** category, add the **Filter rows** step.
9. Create a hop from each **Select values** toward this step. When asked for the kind of hop, select the **Main output of step**. Your Transformation should look like the following:

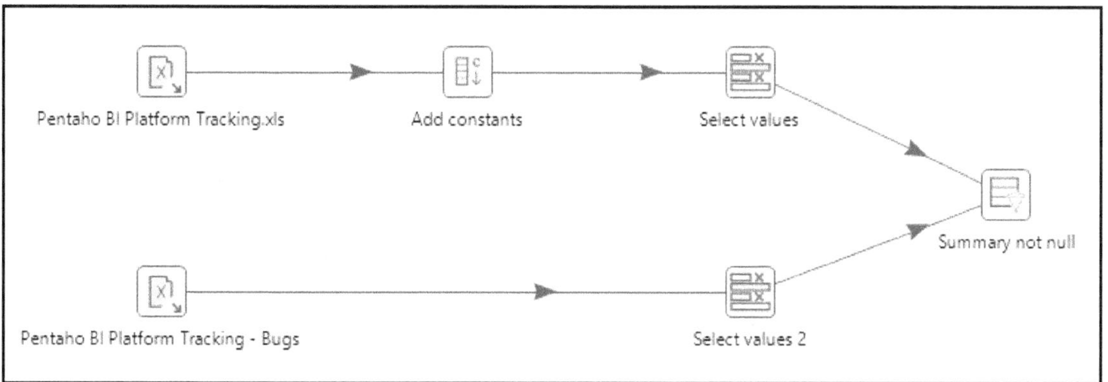

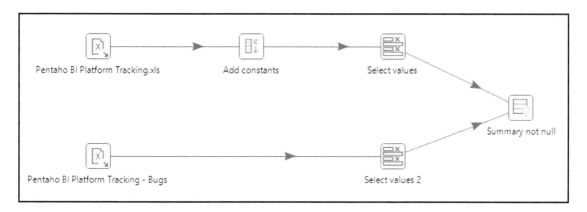

Transformation for merging streams

10. Use the **Filter rows** step to filter the rows with `Summary` null.
11. With the **Filter rows** step selected, run a preview. You will see the following:

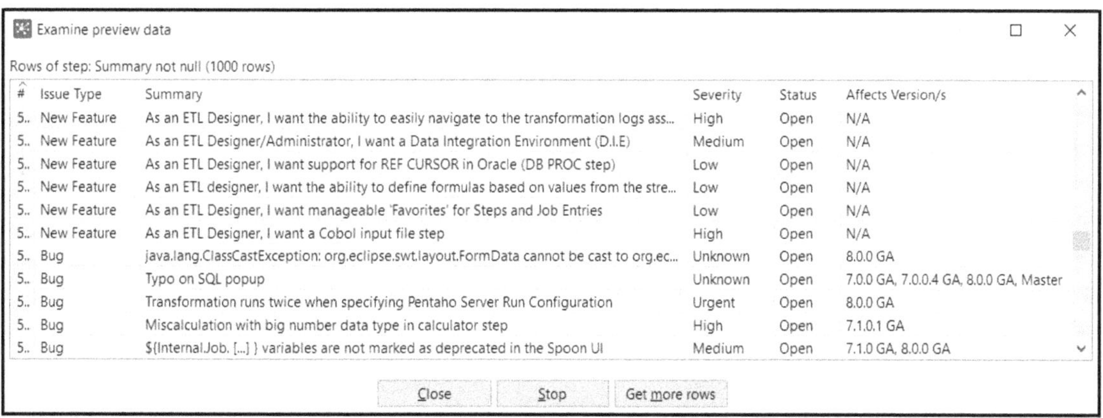
Examine preview data

Rows of step: Summary not null (1000 rows)

#	Issue Type	Summary	Severity	Status	Affects Version/s
5..	New Feature	As an ETL Designer, I want the ability to easily navigate to the transformation logs ass...	High	Open	N/A
5..	New Feature	As an ETL Designer/Administrator, I want a Data Integration Environment (D.I.E)	Medium	Open	N/A
5..	New Feature	As an ETL Designer, I want support for REF CURSOR in Oracle (DB PROC step)	Low	Open	N/A
5..	New Feature	As an ETL designer, I want the ability to define formulas based on values from the stre...	Low	Open	N/A
5..	New Feature	As an ETL Designer, I want manageable 'Favorites' for Steps and Job Entries	Low	Open	N/A
5..	New Feature	As an ETL Designer, I want a Cobol input file step	High	Open	N/A
5..	Bug	java.lang.ClassCastException: org.eclipse.swt.layout.FormData cannot be cast to org.ec...	Unknown	Open	8.0.0 GA
5..	Bug	Typo on SQL popup	Unknown	Open	7.0.0 GA, 7.0.0.4 GA, 8.0.0 GA, Master
5..	Bug	Transformation runs twice when specifying Pentaho Server Run Configuration	Urgent	Open	8.0.0 GA
5..	Bug	Miscalculation with big number data type in calculator step	High	Open	7.1.0.1 GA
5..	Bug	${Internal.Job. [...] } variables are not marked as deprecated in the Spoon UI	Medium	Open	7.1.0 GA, 8.0.0 GA

Close Stop Get more rows

Previewing merged streams

As you can deduce from the values in the `Issue Type` and the `Affects Version/s` columns, the step unifies the data from both incoming streams.

In the example, the step used for joining the streams was the **Filter rows** step, but any step can be used for that purpose. Whichever the step, the most important thing you need to have in mind is that you cannot mix rows that have different layouts. The rows must have the same metadata, that is, same length, same data type, same fields names, and the same order of all the fields. Fortunately, there is a **trap detector** that provides warnings at design time if a step receives mixed layouts.

Try this:

1. Delete the first **Select values** step.
2. Create a hop from the **Add constants** step to the **Filter rows** step. A warning message appears:

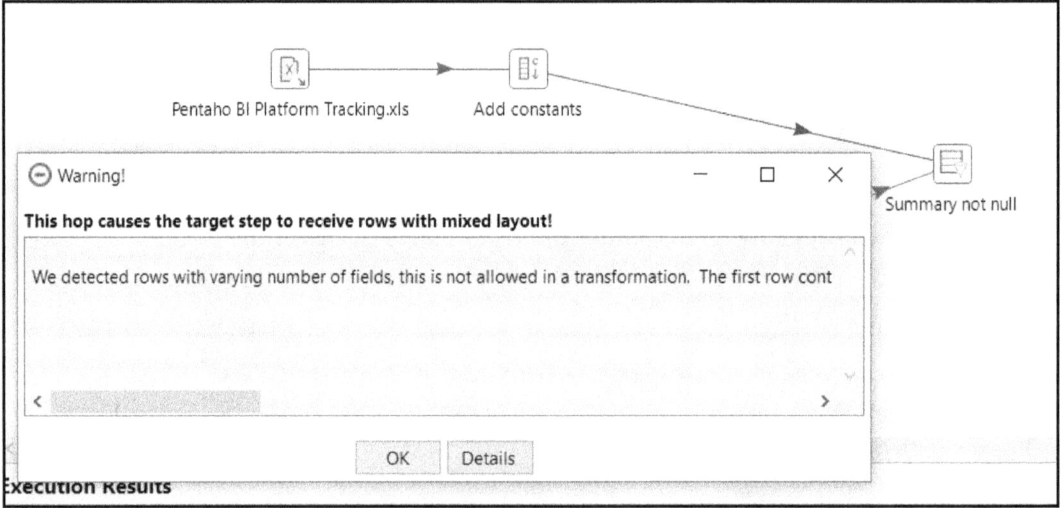

Trap detector

In this case, the message says that the rows contained a varying number of fields, which is not allowed in a transformation.

Note that PDI warns you but doesn't prevent you from mixing row layouts when creating the Transformation. If you want PDI to prevent you from running Transformations with mixed row layouts, you can check the option **Enable safe mode** in the window that shows up when you dispatch the transformation. Keep in mind that doing this will cause a performance drop.

Customizing the way of merging streams

When you use an arbitrary step to unify streams, the rows remain in the same order as they were in their original stream, but the streams are joined in any order. Take a look at the example's preview, the rows with new features and the rows with bugs remained sorted within their original group. However, you did not tell PDI to put the new features before or after the rows of the other stream. If you care about the order in which the union is made, there are some steps that can help you. Here are the options you have:

If you want to ...	**You can do this ...**
Append two or more streams and don't care about the order	Use any step. The selected step will take all the incoming streams in any order and then will proceed with the specific task.
Append two or more streams in a given order	For two streams, use the **Append streams** step from the **Flow** category. It allows you to decide which stream goes first. For two or more, use the **Prioritize streams** step from the **Flow** category. It allows you to decide the order of all the incoming streams.
Merge two streams ordered by one or more fields	Use the **Sorted Merge** step from the **Joins** category. This step allows you to decide on which field(s) to order the incoming rows before sending them to the destination step(s). Both input streams must be sorted on that field(s).

Merge two streams keeping the newest when there are duplicates	Use the **Merge Rows (diff)** step from the **Joins** category. You tell PDI the key fields, that is, the fields that tell you that a row is the same in both streams. You also give PDI the fields to compare when the row is found in both the streams. PDI tries to match rows of both streams based on the key fields. Then it creates a field that will act as a flag and fills it as follows: • If a row was only found in the first stream, the flag is set to `deleted` • If a row was only found in the second stream, the flag is set to `new` • If the row was found in both streams, and the fields to compare are the same, the flag is set to `identical` • If the row was found in both streams, and at least one of the fields to compare is different, the flag is set to `changed`

Whether you use arbitrary steps or some of the special steps mentioned here to merge streams, don't forget to verify the layout of the streams you are merging. Pay attention to the warnings of the trap detector and avoid mixing row layouts.

Looking up data

Until now, you worked with a single stream of data. When you did calculations or created conditions to compare fields, you only involved fields of your stream. Usually, this is not enough, and you need data from other sources. In this section, you will learn how to look up data outside your stream.

Looking up data with a Stream lookup step

Suppose that you have a list of people along with their nationalities, and you want to find out the language that they speak. This is a typical case where you have to look for information in another source of data, your main stream is the dataset with people information, and you need a secondary stream with information about the languages. This secondary stream is where we will look for new information. In PDI, we do that with the **Stream lookup** step.

To explain how to use this step, we will implement the proposed exercise where we will read a list of people and find out the languages that people on the list speak:

1. Create a new Transformation.
2. By using the **Get data from XML** step, read the file with information about the countries that you used in `Chapter 5`, *Manipulating PDI Data and Metadata*, `countries.xml`.

To avoid configuring the step again, you can open the Transformation that reads this file, copy the **Get data from XML** step, and paste it here.

3. Drag to the canvas the **Filter rows** step.
4. Create a hop from the **Get data from XML** step to the **Filter rows** step.
5. Edit the **Filter rows** step and create the condition `isofficial= T`.

6. Click on the **Filter rows** step and run a preview. The list of previewed rows will show the countries along with the official languages, as shown in the following screenshot:

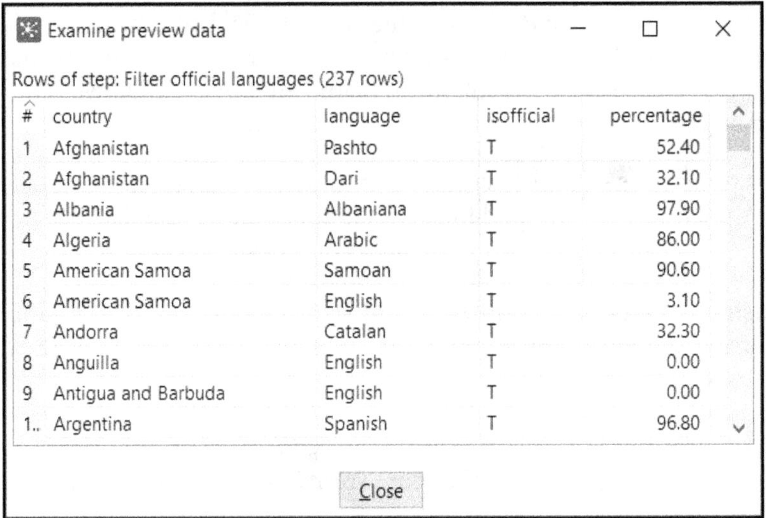

Previewing data coming from an XML file

Now that we have the stream where we will look for data, let's create the main flow of data:

1. From the Packt Publishing website, `www.packtpub.com`, download the file with the list of people. It looks like this:

```
ID;Country Name;Name
1;Russia;Mikhail Davydova
2;;Anastasia Davydova
3;Spain;Carmen Rodriguez
4;;Francisco Delgado
5;Japan;Natsuki Harada
6;;Emiko Suzuki
7;China;Lin Jiang
8;;Wei Chiu
9;United States;Chelsea Thompson
10;;Cassandra Sullivan
11;Canada;Mackenzie Martin
12;;Nathan Gauthier
13;Italy;Giovanni Lombardi
14;;Federica Lombardi
```

2. In the same Transformation, drag to the canvas the **Text file input** step and read the downloaded file.

For this exercise, feel free to create your own file with data about people.

We have two streams, the main one with the list of people, and a second one with the list of countries and their official languages. Now we will do the main task of this tutorial:

1. Expand the **Lookup** category of steps and drag to the canvas the **Stream lookup** step.
2. Create a hop from the **Text file input** step you just created, to the **Stream lookup** step.
3. Create another hop from the **Filter rows** step to the **Stream lookup** step. When asked for the kind of hop, choose **Main output of step**. So far, you have the following:

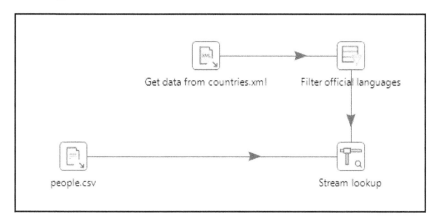

Adding a Stream lookup step to a Transformation

4. Edit the **Stream lookup** step by double-clicking on it.
5. In the **Lookup step** drop-down list, select **Filter official languages**. This selection is for telling PDI which of the incoming streams is the stream used to look up.

6. Now we will fill the upper grid in the configuration window. This grid allows you to specify the names of the fields that are used to look up. In the left column, **Field**, you indicate the field of your main stream: `Country Name`. In the right column, **LookupField**, you indicate the field of the secondary stream: `language`. The configured grid looks as follows:

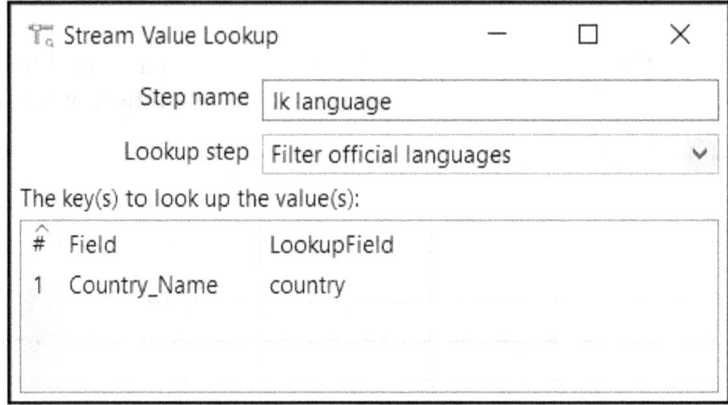

Configuring the keys to lookup in a Stream lookup step

You can fill in the first column in the upper grid by using the Get Fields button and deleting all the fields that you don't want to use.

7. In the lower grid, you specify the names of the fields that you want back as result of the lookup. Those fields will come from the secondary stream. In this case, we want the field `language`. Fill the grid as shown:

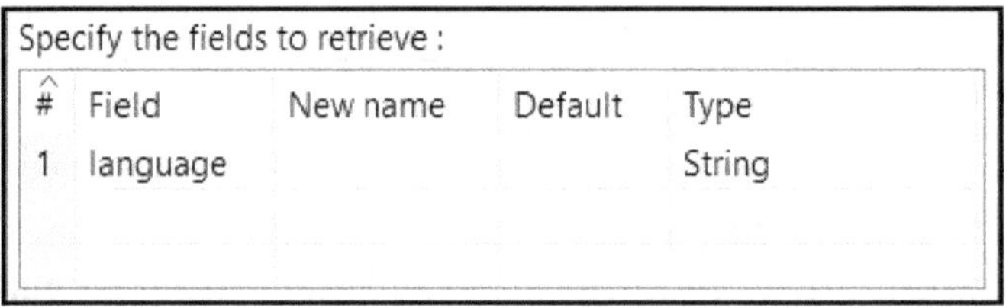

Configuring the fields to retrieve in a Stream lookup step

You can fill in this column by using the **Get lookup fields** button and deleting all the fields that you don't want to retrieve.

8. Click on OK.
9. The hop that goes from the **Filter rows** step to the **Stream lookup** step changes its look and feel. The icon that appears over the hop shows that this is the stream where the **Stream lookup** step is going to look up, as shown in the following screenshot:

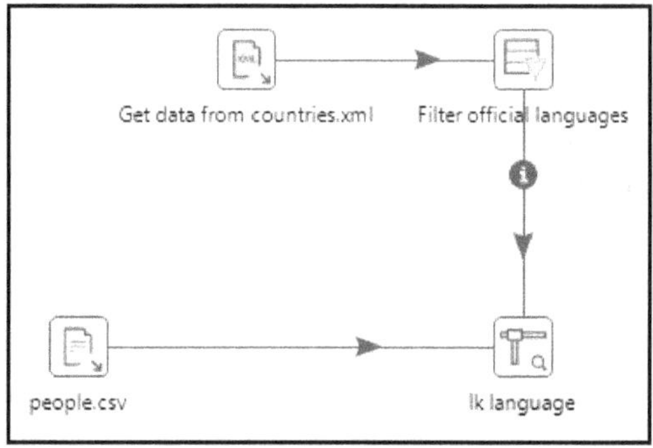

L&F of a Stream lookup

10. Run a preview of the **Stream lookup** step. You will see the following:

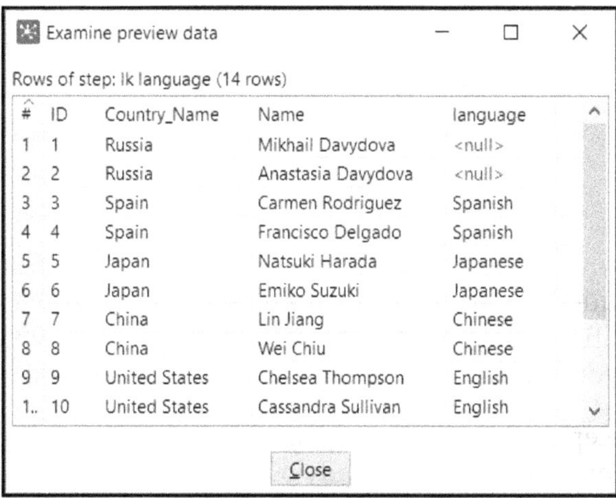

Examine preview data

Rows of step: lk language (14 rows)

#	ID	Country_Name	Name	language
1	1	Russia	Mikhail Davydova	<null>
2	2	Russia	Anastasia Davydova	<null>
3	3	Spain	Carmen Rodriguez	Spanish
4	4	Spain	Francisco Delgado	Spanish
5	5	Japan	Natsuki Harada	Japanese
6	6	Japan	Emiko Suzuki	Japanese
7	7	China	Lin Jiang	Chinese
8	8	China	Wei Chiu	Chinese
9	9	United States	Chelsea Thompson	English
1..	10	United States	Cassandra Sullivan	English

Close

Previewing the result after looking up for data

How does the **Stream lookup** step work? When a row of data comes to the step, a lookup is made in the secondary stream: For every pair in the upper grid, the step looks for a row where the value of **Field** is equal to the value of **LookupField**. If there is one, the lookup will be successful. In our Transformation, we entered a single pair of the field for comparison, but it's possible to do the lookup by comparing more fields.

After the lookup, new fields are added to your dataset, one for every row of the lower grid:

- For the rows for which the lookup is successful, the values for the new fields will be taken from the lookup stream
- For the others, the fields will remain null, unless you set a default value

Let's explain it with a sample row, the row for `Francisco Delgado` from `Spain`. When this row gets to the **Stream lookup** step, PDI looks in the list of countries for a row with country `Spain`, that is, a row where the value of the field `country` (**Lookup Field** in the upper grid) is equal to the field `Country Name` (**Field** in the upper stream). It finds it. Then, it returns the value of the column `language`, which is `Spanish`.

Now take another sample row, the row with the country `Russia`. When the row gets to the **Stream lookup** step, PDI looks for it in the list of countries but it does not find it. So, what you get as language is a null string.

Whether the country is found or not, one new field is added to your stream, the field `language`.

Note that when using the **Stream lookup** step, you get only one row per key. If the key you are looking for appears more than once in the lookup stream, only one will be returned. In our example, when there is more than one official language spoken in a country, only one is returned.

Summary

In this chapter, you learned different options for combining or splitting flows of data. The topics we covered included copying and distributing rows, partitioning data, and splitting streams based on conditions. You also learned how to filter rows, which is a very useful functionality. Finally, you saw different ways to merge independent streams.

With all these new concepts, plus all the material you learned in the previous chapters, the kind of tasks you are able to do now is already broad. You are now ready to apply your knowledge in the validation and cleansing of data in the next chapter.

7
Cleansing, Validating, and Fixing Data

You already have a set of tools to manipulate data. This chapter offers different ways of applying the learned concepts to cleanse data and also deal with invalid data, either by discarding it or fixing it.

We will cover the following topics in this chapter:

- Standardizing information and improving the quality of data
- Introducing some steps useful for data cleansing
- Dealing with non-exact matches
- Validating data
- Treating invalid data by splitting and merging streams

Cleansing data

Data from the real world is not always as perfect as we would like it to be. On one hand, there are cases where the errors in data are so critical that the only solution is to report them or even abort a process.

There is, however, a different kind of issue with data: minor problems that can be fixed somehow, as in the following examples:

- You have a field that contains years. Among the values, you see 2912. This can be considered a typo; assume that the proper value is 2012.

- You have a string that represents the name of a country, and it is supposed that the names belong to a predefined list of valid countries. You, however, see the values as USA, U.S.A., or United States. On your list, you have only USA as valid, but it is clear that all of these values belong to the same country and should be easy to unify.
- You have a field that should contain integer numbers between one and five. Among these values, you have numbers such as 3.01 or 4.99. It should not be a problem to round these numbers so that the final values are all in the expected range of values.

All these examples are about data cleansing. The objective of **data cleansing** is to reduce errors in data, improve the quality of data, and standardize the information. While validation means mainly rejecting data, data cleansing detects and tries to fix not only invalid data but also data that is considered illegal or inaccurate in a specific domain. In this section, you will implement some of these cleansing tasks, and we will give you all the tools so that you can clean your own data.

Cleansing data by example

Let's put into practice a bit of what we said in the introduction of this section. Here, you have two simple examples where some data cleansing is needed, along with a proposed solution implemented with **Pentaho Data Integration** (**PDI**).

Standardizing information

In the *Looking up data* section in `Chapter 6`, *Controlling the Flow of Data,* there were missing countries in the `countries.xml` file. In fact, the countries were there, but with different names. For example, `Russia` in our file is `Russian Federation` in the XML file. What we should do to enhance the solution is standardize the information, sticking to a unique naming for the countries.

Modify the Transformation that looks for the language in the following way:

1. Open the Transformation created in `Chapter 6`, *Controlling the Flow of Data,* and save it with a new name.
2. Delete the hop that links your main stream with the **Lookup Stream** step.

3. After reading your data, add a **Value Mapper** step and use it to get the standard name for the countries. Only the countries for which you know different notations will be here. Look at the following example:

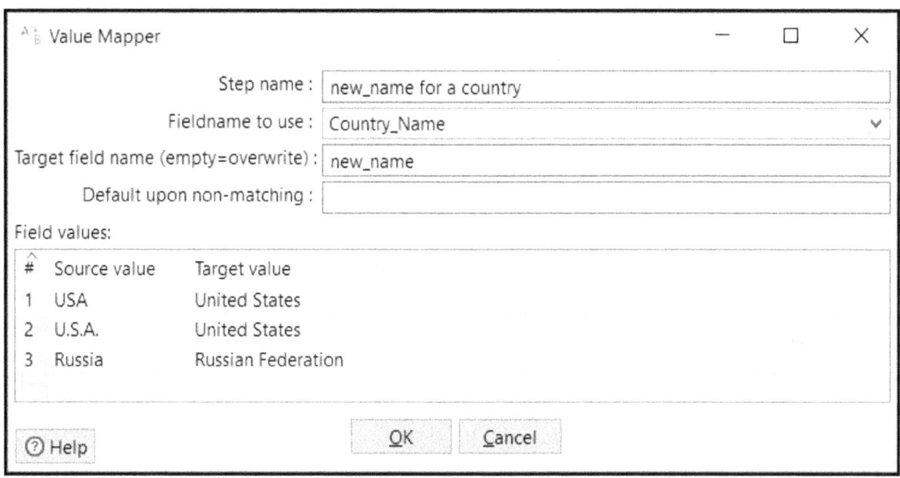

Configuring a Value Mapper

4. With a **User Defined Java Expression** (**UDJE**) step, overwrite the country names that didn't have the standard value. In our example, the `Russia` value will be replaced with `Russian Federation`. This is how you configure the step:

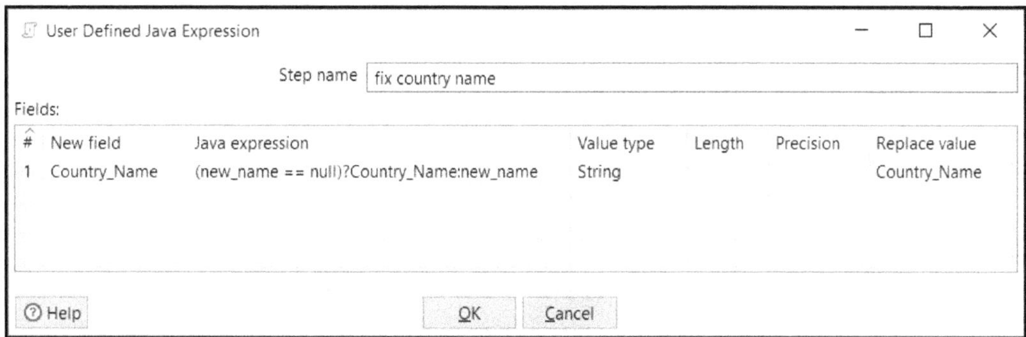

Configuring a UDJE step

5. Create a hop from this last step toward the **Lookup Stream** step.
6. Run a preview of this step. Now you will see that you have a successful search for all rows.

Improving the quality of data

In the *Filtering Data* section in `Chapter 6`, *Controlling the Flow of Data,* you identified words found in a text file. On that occasion, you already did some cleaning by eliminating from the text all the characters that weren't part of legal words, for example, parentheses, hyphens, and so on. Recall that you used the **Replace in String** step for this.

There is more cleansing that we can do in this text. For example, if your intention is to calculate some statistics with geological-related words, you might prefer to discard a lot of words that are valid in the English language but useless for your work. Let's look at a way to get rid of these:

1. Open the Transformation from `Chapter 6`, *Controlling the Flow of Data,* and save it under a different name.
2. Remove all the steps after the **Replace in String** step.
3. Run a preview of this last step. You will see words that you are not interested in, for example, the ones highlighted in the following screenshot:

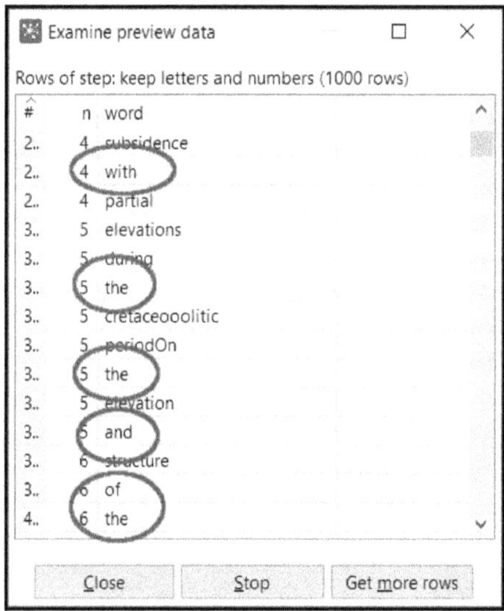

List of words

4. Create a new stream of data that contains words that you want to exclude. You should have one word per row. Some candidate words are `a`, `and`, `as`, `at`, `by`, `from`, `it`, `in`, `of`, `on`, `that`, `the`, `this`, `to`, `which`, `with`, `is`, `are`, `have`, and `been`.

You can build the list of words in a **Data Grid**, or you can read the list from a plain file.

5. Use a **Stream Lookup** to look up words from your main stream in this new list. Your Transformation will look as follows:

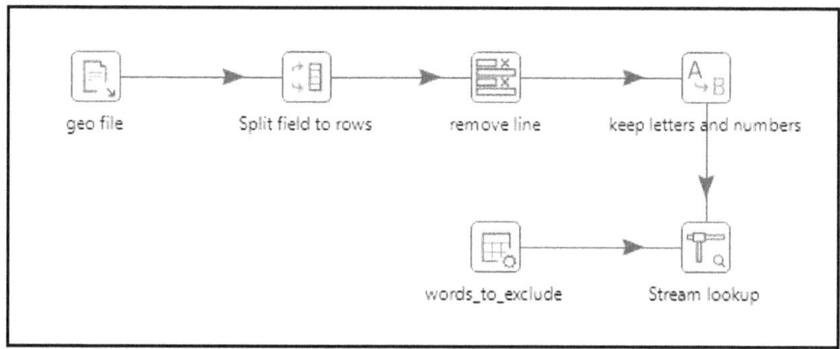

Looking up words to discard

6. Configure the **Stream Value Lookup** as follows:

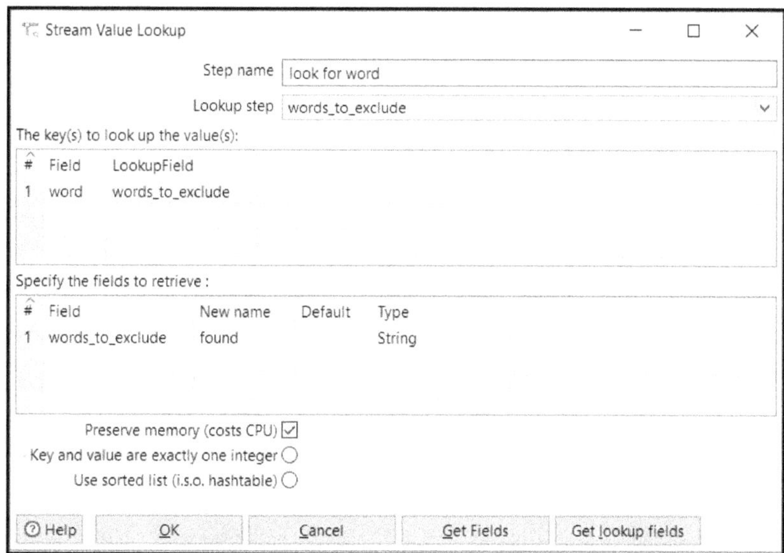

Configuring a Stream Value Lookup step

7. After this step, add a **Filter rows** step and use it to discard the common words, that is, the words not found. As a filter, use `found_word IS NULL`.
8. Run a preview of the **Filter rows** step. You will see that the unwanted words have been discarded.

Introducing PDI steps useful for cleansing data

Data cleansing, also known as **data cleaning** or **data scrubbing**, may be done manually or automatically, depending on the complexity of the cleansing. Knowing in advance the rules that apply, you can do automatic cleaning using any PDI step that suits you.

The following are some steps particularly useful, including the ones that we used in the previous examples:

Step	**Purpose**
If field value is null	If a field is `null`, it changes its value to a constant. It can be applied to all fields of the same data type, for example, to all `Integer` fields or to particular fields.
Null if...	Sets a field value to `null` if it is equal to a given constant value.
Number range	Creates ranges based on a numeric field. An example of its use is converting floating numbers to a discrete scale, as `0`, `0.25`, `0.50`, and so on.
Value Mapper	Maps values of a field from one value to another. For example, you can use this step to convert `yes/no`, `true/false`, or `1/0` values to a unique notation as `Y/N`.
Replace in string	Replaces all occurrences of a string inside a field with a different string. It allows the use of regular expressions as explained in `Chapter 5`, *Manipulating PDI Data and Metadata*.
String operations	Useful for the trimming and removing of special characters and more.
Calculator	Allows you to remove special characters, convert to upper and lowercase, and retrieve only digits from a string, among other operations.
Stream lookup	Looks up values coming from another stream. In data cleansing, you can use it to set a default value if your field is not in a given list.
Database lookup	The same as **Stream Value Lookup**, but looks in a database table.

Step	Purpose
Unique rows	Removes double consecutive rows and leaves only unique occurrences.

For examples that use these steps or for more information about them, refer to `Chapter 5`, *Manipulating PDI Data and Metadata*, or to the PDI steps reference at `https://help.pentaho.com/Documentation/8.0/Products/Data_Integration/Transformation_Step_Reference`.

Note that we could combine the steps. For example, before doing a lookup in an external list, we could convert both our data and the data in the reference list to uppercase, remove special characters such as quotation marks, and so on. By doing this, we would have improved the chances of a successful lookup task.

Dealing with non-exact matches

A common situation, in particular when the values were entered manually, is as follows:

- Data with typographical errors
- Mix of upper and lowercase letters

In some languages different from English, it's common to have the following:

- Missing accent marks
- Words with special characters such as `tradução` or `niño` are typed as `traducao` or `ninio`

As an example, suppose that we have a field containing the names of states in the USA. Among the values, we could have `Hawaii`, `Hawai`, and `Howaii`. Despite being simple typos, none of the steps mentioned earlier would help clean the wrong values so you end up with the proper value, `Hawaii`. Here comes an alternative technique to fix the issue: **fuzzy string searching**, a technique of finding a pattern by proximity. In the next subsections, we will implement this technique both to cleanse and deduplicate data.

Cleansing by doing a fuzzy search

With a fuzzy search, we don't look for exact matches but for similar values. PDI allows you to perform fuzzy searches with the special step **Fuzzy match**. With this step, you can find approximate matches to a string using matching algorithms.

In order to see how to use this step, let's go back to our example. Suppose that we have a list of valid states along with their codes, as follows:

```
State;Abbreviation
Alabama;AL
Alaska;AK
Arizona;AZ
...
West Virginia;WV
Wisconsin;WI
Wyoming;WY
```

On the other hand, we have a stream of data and, among the fields, one field representing states. The problem is that not all values are correct.

The following could be a list of incoming values:

```
Califronia
Calorado
Washington
Masachusetts
Alsaka
Conneticut
Road Island
Hawai
Ohio
Kentuky
```

Some of the values are correct, others are wrong. The idea is, for each state on our list, to look at the correct list for the value that most resembles our value. This is how we do it:

1. Create a Transformation.
2. Create a stream of data with the list of states in the USA.

You could use a **Data Grid** and type them, or read the file included in the bundle material for this chapter.

3. Use a **Data Grid** to create a list of proper and incorrect values for states. You could type the ones listed earlier or create your own list.
4. From the **Lookup** category, drag a **Fuzzy match** step to the work area.

5. Link the steps as shown:

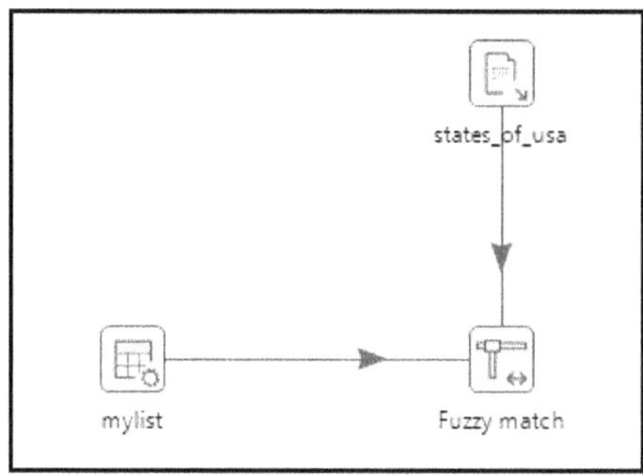

Adding a Fuzzy match step to a Transformation

6. Now we will configure the step, whose configuration windows looks as follows:

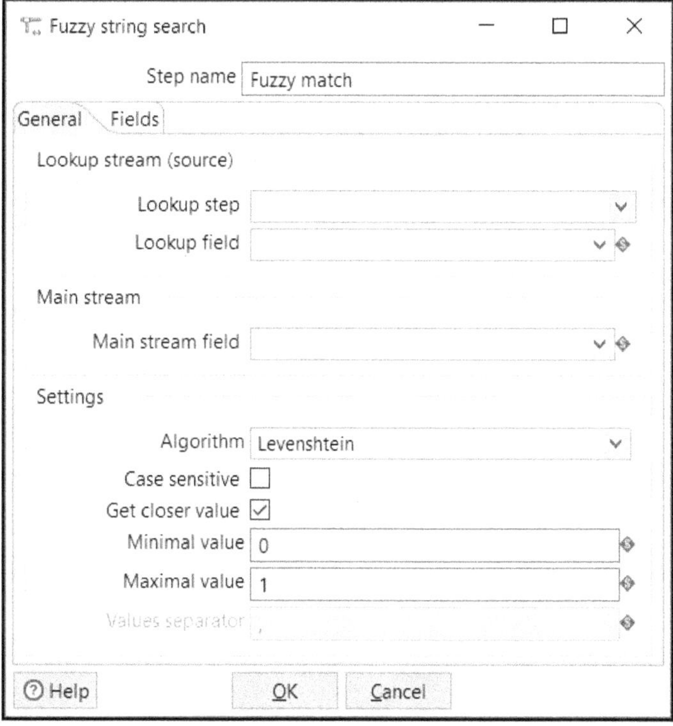

Fuzzy match configuration window

In the upper area, you indicate which stream is the one where you will look, and we also indicate which fields to compare: one from the **Main stream** and the other from the **Lookup stream (source)**. This is quite the same as configuring a regular **Stream lookup** step.

For details about the use of a **Stream lookup**, you can refer to `Chapter 6`, *Controlling the Flow of Data*.

In the lower part of the configuration window, we specify the details of the fuzzy search. First of all, we should decide which matching algorithm to use. A **fuzzy match** algorithm compares two strings—in this case, one coming from **Main stream**, the other coming from the **Lookup stream (source)—**and calculates a similarity index. The row with the lowest index is returned as long as it is between a minimum and a maximum value. The **Fuzzy match** step allows you to choose among several matching algorithms that fall into one of the following groups:

- Algorithms based on a metric distance, the comparison is based on how the terms are spelt
- Phonetic algorithms, the comparison is based on how the terms sound when read in English

For this exercise, we will choose the first algorithm in the list, the **Levenshtein** algorithm, which belongs to the first of the two groups. This algorithm calculates the distance between two strings as the number of edit steps needed to get from one string to another. These edits can be character insertion or deletion, or replacements of a single character. For example, to go from `Hawai` to `Hawaii`, we need to insert one character: an `i`. Then the distance between these words is `1`.

Now that you understand the idea, you are ready to configure the steps:

1. Double-click on the **Fuzzy match** step

2. Fill in the configuration window as follows:

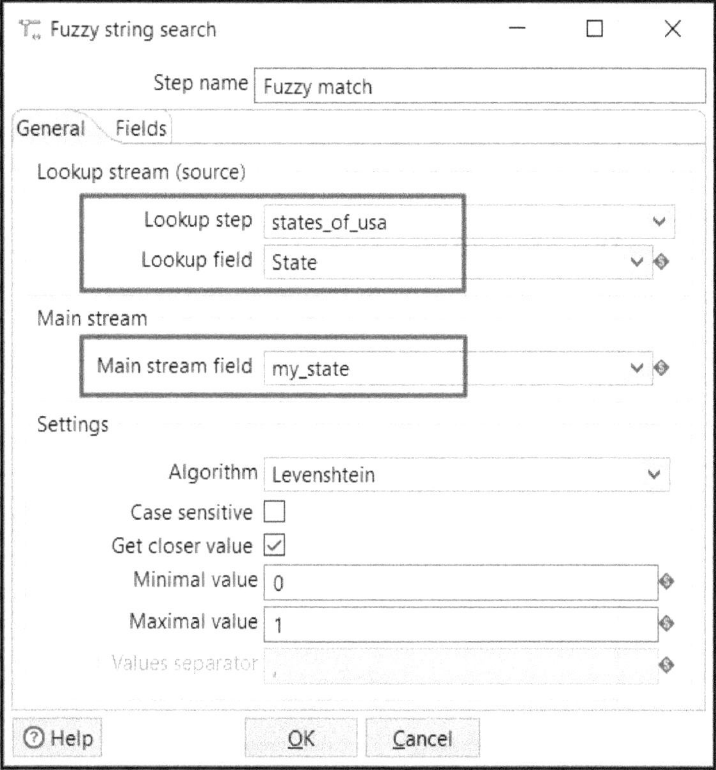

Configuring a Fuzzy match step

3. Close the window.

4. With this step selected, run a preview. You should see this:

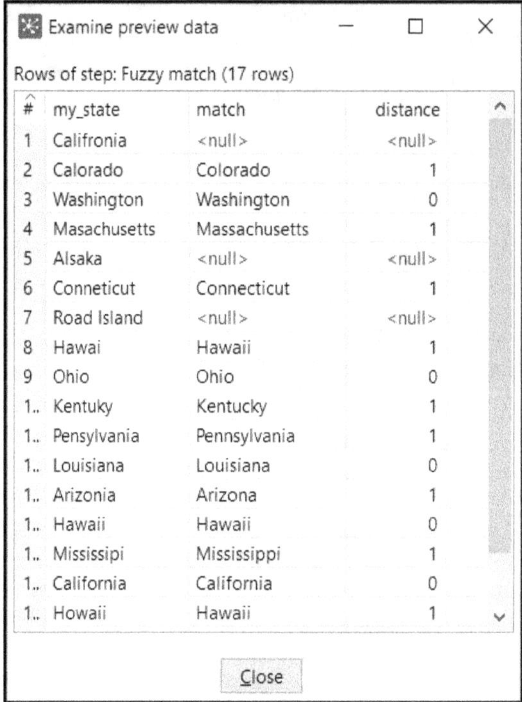

#	my_state	match	distance
1	Califronia	<null>	<null>
2	Calorado	Colorado	1
3	Washington	Washington	0
4	Masachusetts	Massachusetts	1
5	Alsaka	<null>	<null>
6	Conneticut	Connecticut	1
7	Road Island	<null>	<null>
8	Hawai	Hawaii	1
9	Ohio	Ohio	0
1..	Kentuky	Kentucky	1
1..	Pensylvania	Pennsylvania	1
1..	Louisiana	Louisiana	0
1..	Arizonia	Arizona	1
1..	Hawaii	Hawaii	0
1..	Missisipi	Mississippi	1
1..	California	California	0
1..	Howaii	Hawaii	1

Previewing the results of a fuzzy search

As you can see, in almost all cases, there was a short distance between the wrong and the matched states.

If you are satisfied with the result, you can replace the old value with the value found by the algorithm. If you don't like how the algorithm behaves with your data, you have other options: either you change the configuration, for instance, you can change the maximum allowed distance, or you can choose an algorithm that fits better.

For example, you could try the next in the list: the **Damerau-Levenshtein** algorithm, which is similar to Levenshtein but adds the transposition operation. If you try this one, you will see that this time the result is better. You will have more matches.

Deduplicating non-exact matches

In addition, suppose that we have the same data as before and want to create a list of the states that appear in our dataset. Among the values, we have `Hawaii`, `Hawai`, and `Howaii`. We don't want the three values on our final list. We only want a single state: `Hawaii`. If we try to deduplicate the data with the **Unique rows** step, we will still have three values. The only solution is trying to fix the values with a fuzzy search algorithm, and only after that doing the deduplication. This doesn't differ much from the previous solution:

1. Open the transformation you just created and save it under a different name.
2. Run a preview of the **Fuzzy match** step. In the preview window, click on the title of the **match** column to sort the rows by that field. You will see that there are duplicated values:

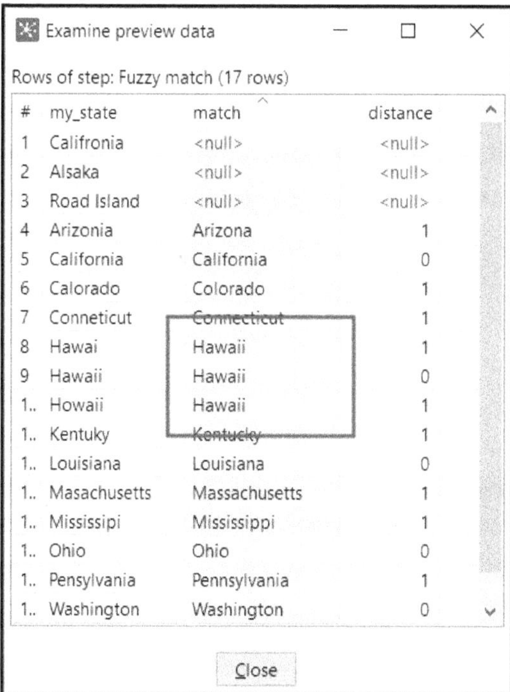

#	my_state	match	distance
1	Califronia	<null>	<null>
2	Alsaka	<null>	<null>
3	Road Island	<null>	<null>
4	Arizonia	Arizona	1
5	California	California	0
6	Calorado	Colorado	1
7	Conneticut	Connecticut	1
8	Hawai	Hawaii	1
9	Hawaii	Hawaii	0
1..	Howaii	Hawaii	1
1..	Kentuky	Kentucky	1
1..	Louisiana	Louisiana	0
1..	Masachusetts	Massachusetts	1
1..	Missisipi	Mississippi	1
1..	Ohio	Ohio	0
1..	Pensylvania	Pennsylvania	1
1..	Washington	Washington	0

Duplicate values in a list

The sorting function you just applied has effect only in the preview window. The rows in your dataset remain in the original order.

3. After the **Fuzzy match** step, add a UDJE step and configure it to keep the correct state:

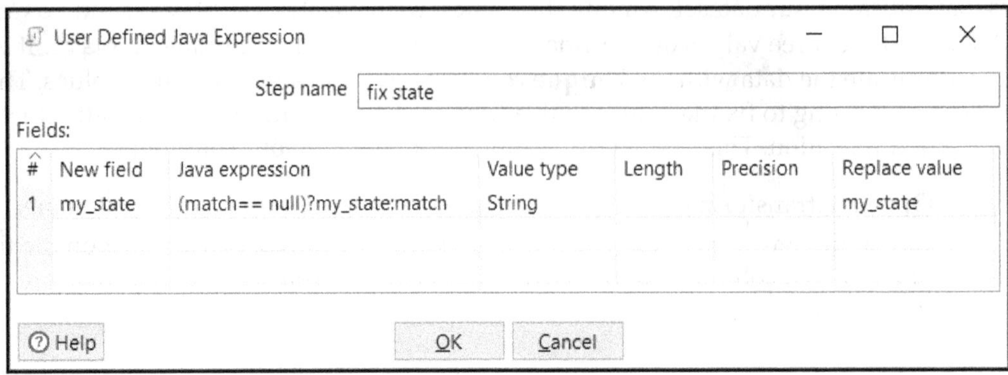

Configuring a UDJE

4. Use the **Select values** step to keep only the column with the state.
5. From the **Transform** category, select and drag a **Sort rows** step and create a hop from the **Select Values** step toward this one.
6. Double-click on the **Sort rows** step. In the grid, add a row and select the only field available: `my_state`. Also, check the option **Only pass unique rows?**.

Don't worry about all the configuration settings of this step. We will explain them in detail in `Chapter 9`, *Transforming the Dataset*.

7. With the **Sort rows** step selected, run a preview. You will see the following list, where there is only one occurrence of `Hawaii` and it is correctly spelt. Also, the `Hawaii` state, which was also a duplicated value, appears once:

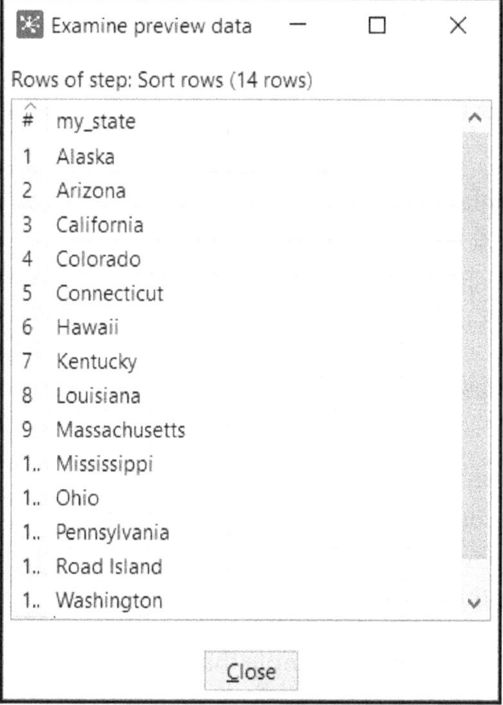

Deduplicating non-exact matches

In this exercise, we eliminated duplicated rows with the **Sort rows** step. If the data were sorted by state, we could have used a **Unique rows** step instead.

Validating data

It's a fact that data from the real world has errors. In `Chapter 2`, *Getting Started with Transformations,* we saw that errors in data can cause a Transformation to crash, and we learned to deal with them. There are other kinds of issues that don't cause the Transformation to abort but don't respect business rules. This section is about detecting these kinds of issues and reporting them.

Validating data with PDI

Validating data is about ensuring that incoming data contains expected values. There are several kinds of constraints that we may need to impose on our data. The following are just some examples:

- A field must contain only digits
- A date field must be formatted as `MM-dd-yyyyy`
- A field must be either `YES` or `NO`
- The value of a field must exist in a reference table

If a field doesn't respect theses rules or constraints, we have to proceed somehow. Some options are as follows:

- Reporting the error to the log
- Inserting the inconsistency into a dedicated table
- Writing the line with the error in a file for further revision
- Discarding just the row of data containing the error

The following section shows a simple example that demonstrates how to validate a field and report the error to the log.

Validating and reporting errors to the log

For this tutorial, we will use the `sales_data.csv` file that we used in `Chapter 4`, *Reading and Writing Files*. This is a simplified version of the file with the same name that comes with the PDI bundle.

The following are sample lines of our file:

```
ORDERDATE,ORDERNUMBER,ORDERLINENUMBER,PRODUCTCODE,PRODUCTLINE,QUANTITYORDER
ED,PRICEEACH,SALES
2/20/2004 0:00 ,10223,10,S24_4278 ,Planes ,23,74.62,1716.26
11/21/2004 0:00,10337,3,S18_4027 ,Classic Cars ,36,100 ,5679.36
6/16/2003 0:00 ,10131,2,S700_4002,Planes ,26,85.13,2213.38
7/6/2004 0:00 ,10266,5,S18_1984 ,Classic Cars ,49,100 ,6203.4
10/16/2004 0:00,10310,4,S24_2972 ,Classic Cars ,33,41.91,1383.03
12/4/2004 0:00 ,10353,4,S700_2834,Planes ,48,68.8 ,3302.4
1/20/2005 0:00 ,10370,8,S12_1666 ,Trucks and Buses,49,100 ,8470.14
```

Among the columns, there is a product code made up of two parts: a prefix and a number. We expect that the prefix be one of the following: `S10`, `S12`, `S18`, `S24`, `S32`, `S50`, `S70`, or `S72`. We will implement this validation. If the value doesn't belong to this list, the row will be reported as an error and the row of data will be discarded:

1. Create a new Transformation and read the `sales_data.csv` file.
2. After the step that reads the file, add a **Filter rows** step, a **Dummy** step, and a **Write to log** step. Link the steps as follows:

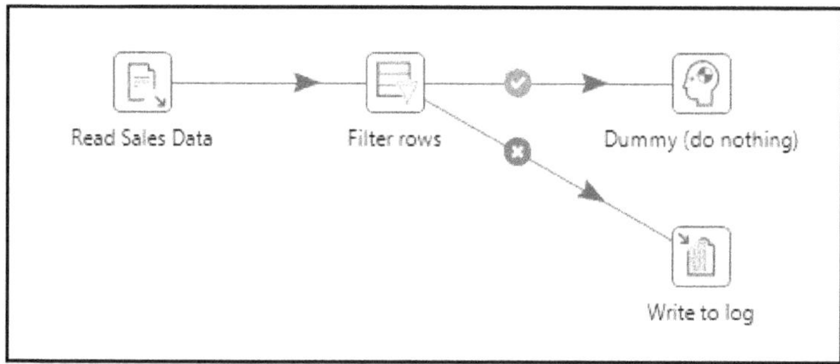

Designing a Transformation

3. Double-click on the **Filter rows** step and configure it with the following condition:

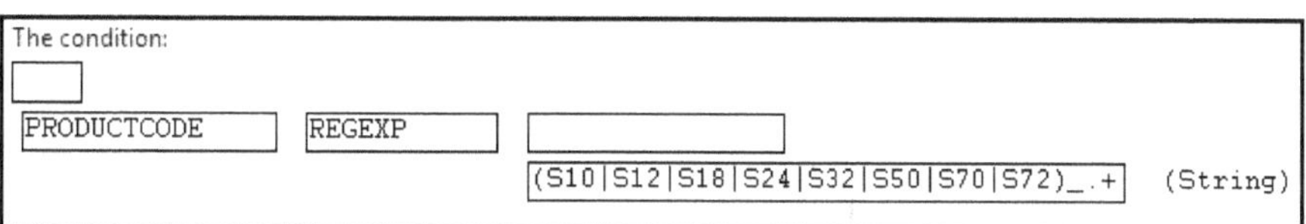

Configuring a Filter rows step

4. Double-click on the **Write to log** step and configure it as follows:

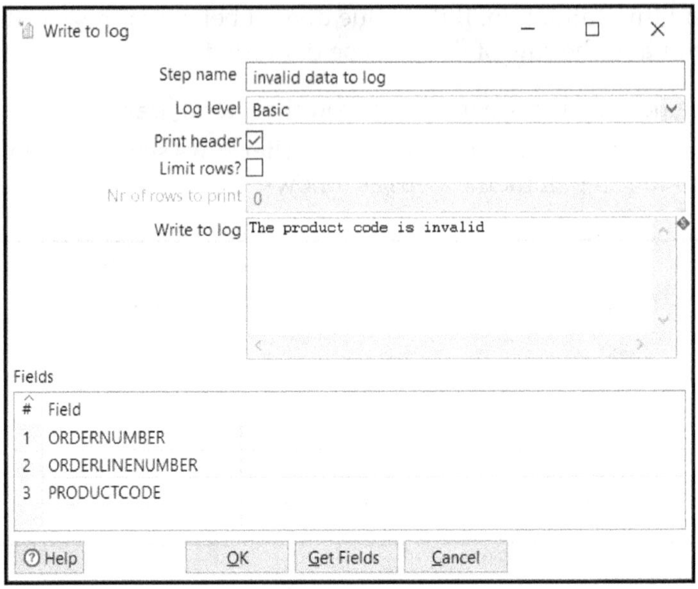

Configuring a Write to log step

5. Close the window.
6. Run the Transformation. You will see that all the rows for which the product code is invalid are reported to the log, as in the following sample lines of the log:

```
... - invalid data to log.0 - ------------> Linenr 1---------------
--------------
... - invalid data to log.0 - The product code is invalid
... - invalid data to log.0 -
... - invalid data to log.0 - ORDERNUMBER = 10131
... - invalid data to log.0 - ORDERLINENUMBER = 2
... - invalid data to log.0 - PRODUCTCODE = S700_4002
... - invalid data to log.0 -
... - invalid data to log.0 - ====================
... - invalid data to log.0 -
```

The rows that contain errors are redirected to the **Write to log** step and then they are lost. Only the correct data follows the true stream coming out of the **Filter rows** step and are available for further processing.

In this case, we reported the error to the log, but you can choose any other option, for example, the ones mentioned in the introduction.

Introducing common validations and their implementation with PDI

The validation in the preceding example was very simple. Depending on the kind of constraint, we may need a single PDI step as in this case, or a combination of steps. For example, if we want to verify that the length of a string value is less than 50, first of all, we should calculate the length and then we will compare it against the limit of 50 characters.

The following table describes the most common kinds of constraints and the PDI steps that we can use to evaluate the expected rules:

Constraint	**Implementation**
Value must have a given data type such as `String` or `Date`	You can read the field as `String` and use the **Select Values** to convert to the expected data type. Implement error handling to identify data that cannot be converted.
Value must have a given length	Use any of the known steps to calculate the length plus a filter step such as the **Filter rows** or the **Java Filter**.
Value cannot be null	Use a **Filter rows** (`IS NULL` function) or a **Java Filter** step
Numbers or dates should fall inside an expected range	Use a **Filter rows** (>, <, or = functions) or a **Java Filter** step
Values must belong to a known discrete list	Use a **Filter rows** (`IN LIST`, or `REGEXP` functions), a **Java Filter** step, or a **RegExp Evaluation** step, plus a filter step.
Values must belong to list found in an external source such as a file or a database	Use a **Stream lookup** step or a **Database lookup** step depending on the kind of source, then a filter to determine whether the value was found or not.
A field or a combination of fields must be unique across the dataset	Use a **Group by** or a **Memory Group by** step to count the occurrences, then use a filter to determine if there are duplicates.
Values must adhere to a required pattern or mask	For generic fields, use **Filter rows** (`LIKE`, `CONTAINS`, `STARTS WITH`, `ENDS WITH`, or `REGEXP` functions), a **Java Filter** step, or a **RegExp Evaluation** step, plus a filter step. For specific kind of data such as credit card numbers or email addresses, you can use the **Credit card validator** or the **Mail validator**, respectively.

Regarding the **Filter rows**, all of the mentioned operations are available to compare not only a field against a fixed value, but to compare two fields among them. For example, you could evaluate if a field in your stream is lower, higher, or equal than another field in your stream.

Some of the steps mentioned in the preceding table, namely, the **Group by** and the **Database lookup** steps, haven't been covered yet. Their use will be explained in `Chapter 9`, *Transforming the Dataset* and `Chapter 10`, *Performing Basic Operations with Databases* respectively.

As an alternative for several of the cases explained in the table, you can also use any of the **Scripting** steps you know from earlier chapters. Besides all these options, there is a special step named **Data Validator**. This step allows you to define several validation rules in a single step.

The constraints listed in the previous table refer to single fields. There are other kinds of constraints not included in the list, which involves more than one field. As an example, you need to verify that a field is not null, but only when another field equals Y. Using the steps mentioned previously plus all the knowledge you already have, it shouldn't be difficult to implement more elaborate validations like this one.

Treating invalid data by splitting and merging streams

When you are transforming data, it is not uncommon that you detect inaccuracies or errors. Sometimes the issues you find may not be severe enough to discard the rows. Maybe you can somehow guess what data was supposed to be there instead of the current values, or it can happen that you have default values for the invalid values. Let's see some examples:

- You have a field defined as a string, and this field represents the date of birth of a person. As values, you have, besides valid dates, other strings, for example `N/A`, `-`, `???`, and so on. Any attempt to run a calculation with these values would lead to an error.

- You have two dates representing the start date and end date of the execution of a task. Suppose that you have `2018-01-05` and `2017-10-31` as the start date and end date respectively. They are well-formatted dates, but if you try to calculate the time that it took to execute the task, you will get a negative value, which is clearly wrong.
- You have a field representing the nationality of a person. The field is mandatory but there are some null values.

In these cases and many more like these, the problem is not so critical and you can do some work to avoid aborting or discarding data because of these anomalies:

- In the first example, you could delete the invalid year and leave the field empty.
- In the second example, you could interchange the values assuming that the user that typed the dates switched the dates unintentionally
- Finally, in the last example, you could set a predefined default value.

In general, in any situation, you can do your best to fix the issues and send the rows back to the main stream. This is valid both for regular streams and streams that are a result of error handling.

In this section, you will see an example of fixing these kinds of issues and avoiding having to discard the rows that cause errors or are considered invalid. You will do it using the concepts learned in the last chapter: splitting and merging streams.

Fixing data that doesn't match the rules

At the beginning of the *Validating Data* section in this chapter, you learned to validate a field discarding the rows with invalid values. Now you will learn how to avoid discarding the row. You will fix the issue by proposing a product code equal to `<invalid>`. After doing so, you will send the rows with invalid values back to the main stream:

1. Open the Transformation you created in the *Validating Data* section and save it with a different name.

2. After the **Write to log** step, add a **UDJE** step. Use the step to replace the invalid product code with the text `<invalid>` and also to add two strings—a flag to indicate that there is an error and a new field named `ERR_DESC` with the description of the problem:

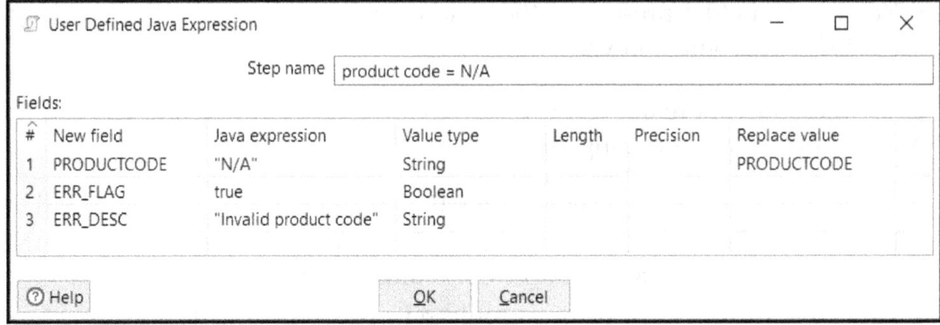

Fixing data

3. As you want to merge the wrong rows with the good ones, you have to add the fields in the other stream as well. So as the true stream of the **Filter rows** step, add an **Add constant** step to add the same fields, but with different values: `ERR_FLAG` = false and `ERR_DESC` empty.
4. Use a **Dummy** step to join the streams, as follows:

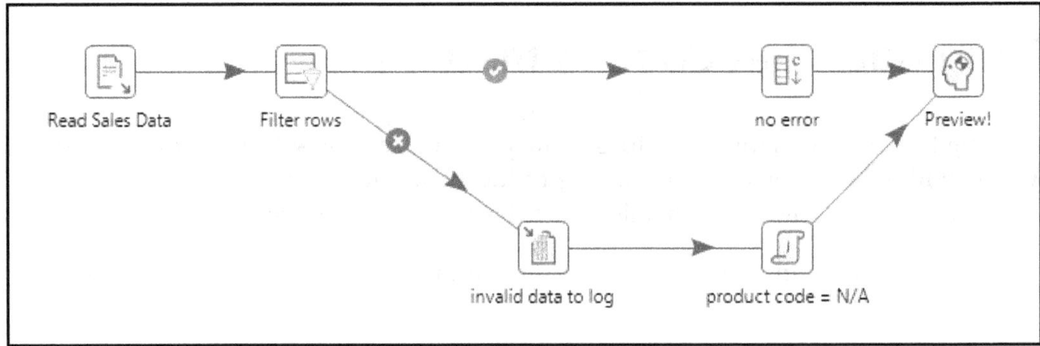

Transformation that fixes an error

5. Run a preview on this last step. You will see all the rows--the rows with correct product codes and the rows with the fixed values:

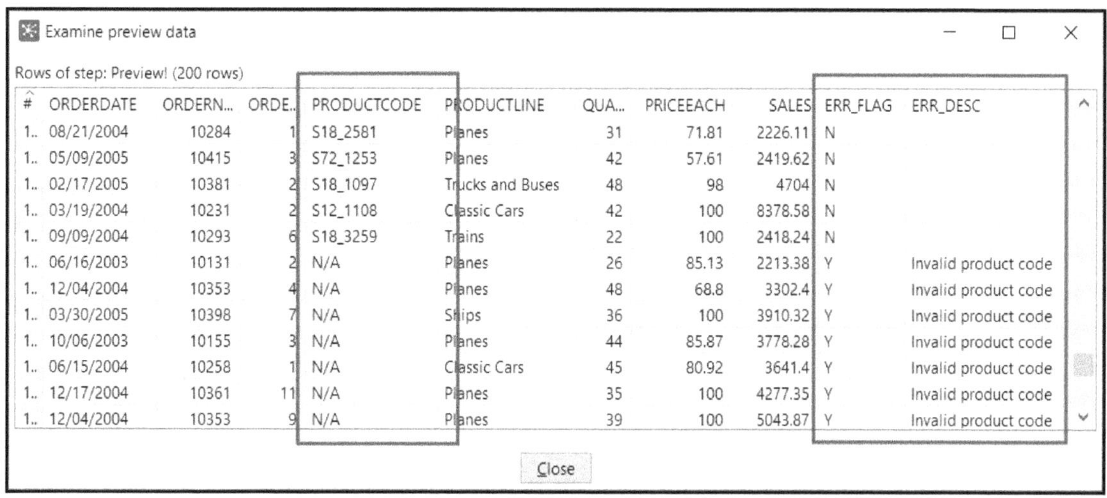

#	ORDERDATE	ORDERN...	ORDE..	PRODUCTCODE	PRODUCTLINE	QUA...	PRICEEACH	SALES	ERR_FLAG	ERR_DESC
1..	08/21/2004	10284	1	S18_2581	Planes	31	71.81	2226.11	N	
1..	05/09/2005	10415	3	S72_1253	Planes	42	57.61	2419.62	N	
1..	02/17/2005	10381	2	S18_1097	Trucks and Buses	48	98	4704	N	
1..	03/19/2004	10231	2	S12_1108	Classic Cars	42	100	8378.58	N	
1..	09/09/2004	10293	6	S18_3259	Trains	22	100	2418.24	N	
1..	06/16/2003	10131	2	N/A	Planes	26	85.13	2213.38	Y	Invalid product code
1..	12/04/2004	10353	4	N/A	Planes	48	68.8	3302.4	Y	Invalid product code
1..	03/30/2005	10398	7	N/A	Ships	36	100	3910.32	Y	Invalid product code
1..	10/06/2003	10155	3	N/A	Planes	44	85.87	3778.28	Y	Invalid product code
1..	06/15/2004	10258	1	N/A	Classic Cars	45	80.92	3641.4	Y	Invalid product code
1..	12/17/2004	10361	11	N/A	Planes	35	100	4277.35	Y	Invalid product code
1..	12/04/2004	10353	9	N/A	Planes	39	100	5043.87	Y	Invalid product code

Previewing fixed data

By running the Transformation instead of just previewing the data, you can observe in the **Logging** tab of the **Execution Results** window that there were many rows with wrong product codes. However, in the **Step Metrics** tab, you can see that the **Dummy** step receives the total of rows coming out of the first step.

There are no rules for what to do with bad rows where you detect invalid or improper data. You always have the option to discard the bad rows or try to fix them. Sometimes you can fix only a few and discard the rest of them. It always depends on your particular data or business rules. In any case, it's a common behavior to log erroneous rows for manual inspection at a later date.

Summary

In this chapter, you learned what cleansing is about. You were introduced to the different options that PDI offers for accomplishing that task including standardizing, improving quality and deduplicating. In particular you learned to deal with non-exact matching by applying fuzzy search. Then you learned how PDI can be used for validating data. You were presented a set of common validations and the way you can implement them with PDI. You also learned how to report or fix errors that happen.

In the next chapter, you will enhance your PDI knowledge by learning how to insert code into your transformations. This will bring you an alternative to do some tasks, but mainly a way to accomplish other tasks that are complicated or even not possible of doing with the regular PDI steps.

8
Manipulating Data by Coding

Whatever Transformation you need to do on your data, you have a good chance of finding **Pentaho Data Integration** (**PDI**) steps able to do the Job. Despite that, it may be that there are no proper steps that serve your requirements or that an apparently minor Transformation consumes a lot of steps linked in a very confusing arrangement that is difficult to test or understand. Dropping colorful icons here and there and making notes to clarify a Transformation can be practical to a point, but there are some situations like the ones described here where you inevitably will have to code.

This chapter explains how to insert code into your transformations. Specifically, you will learn the following topics:

- Doing simple tasks with the JavaScript step
- Parsing unstructured files with JavaScript
- Doing simple tasks with the JavaScript step
- Avoiding coding using purpose-built steps

Doing simple tasks with the JavaScript step

In the first versions of PDI, coding in JavaScript was the only way users had to perform many tasks. In the latest versions, there are many other ways for these tasks but JavaScript is still an option. There is the JavaScript step that allows you to insert code into a PDI Transformation.

Using the JavaScript language in PDI

JavaScript is a scripting language primarily used in website development. However, inside PDI, you use just the core language—you don't run a web browser and you don't care about HTML. There are many available JavaScript engines. PDI uses the **Rhino** engine from **Mozilla**. Rhino is an open source implementation of the core JavaScript language; it doesn't contain objects or methods related to the manipulation of web pages.

If you are interested in getting to know more about Rhino, follow this link: `https://developer.mozilla.org/en/Rhino_Overview`

The core language is not too different from other languages that you might know. It has basic statements, block statements (statements enclosed by curly brackets), conditional statements (`if-else` and `switch-case`), and loop statements (`for`, `do-while`, and `while`).

If you are interested in the language itself, you can access a good *JavaScript Guide* at `https://developer.mozilla.org/en-US/docs/Web/JavaScript/Guide`. There is also a complete tutorial and reference guide at `http://www.w3schools.com/js/`. Despite being quite oriented to web development, which is not your concern here, it is clear, complete, and has plenty of examples.

Besides the basics, you can use JavaScript to parse XML as well as generate XML. Rhino 1.6 and greater implement **ECMAScript for XML (E4X)**, designed to make XML data easier to work with. As explained in previous chapters, there are dedicated PDI steps for this, but when the structure of those objects is too complex, you may prefer to do the task by coding.

Inserting JavaScript code using the JavaScript step

The **Modified JavaScript Value** step—**JavaScript** step for short—allows you to insert JavaScript code inside your Transformation. The code that you type in the main script area is executed once per row coming to the step.

Let's explore its dialog window:

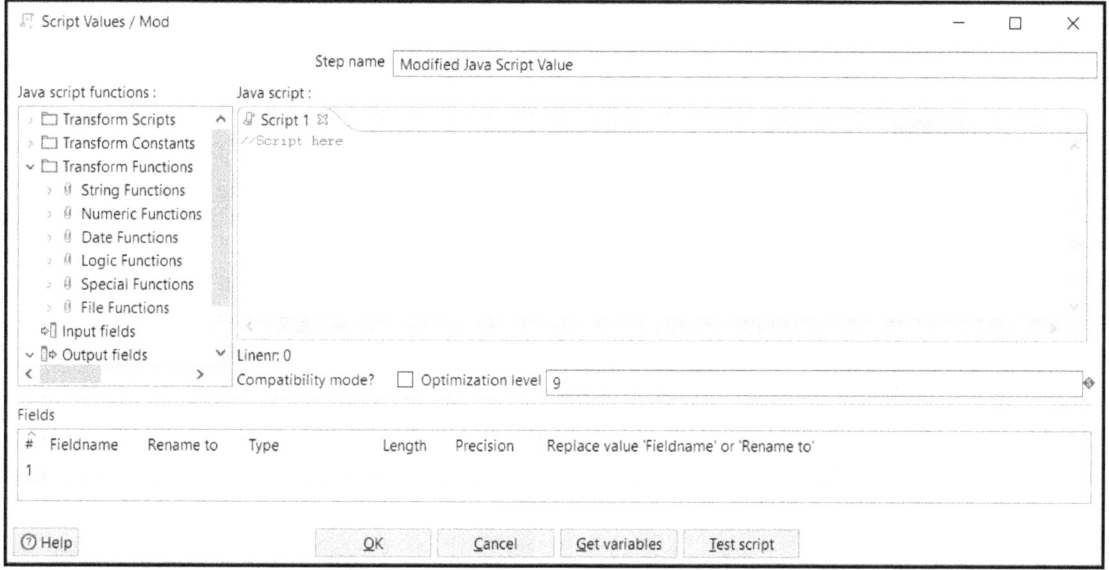

JavaScript dialog window

Most of the window is occupied by the editing area. It's there where you write JavaScript code using the standard syntax of the language and the functions and fields from the tree on the left side of the window.

The **Transform Functions** branch of the tree contains a rich list of functions that are ready to use. The functions are grouped by category:

- The **String**, **Numeric**, **Date**, and **Logic** categories contain usual JavaScript functions.

This is not a full list of JavaScript functions. You are allowed to use JavaScript functions even if they are not in this list.

- The **Special** category contains a mix of utility functions. Most of them are not JavaScript functions but PDI functions. One of these functions is `writeToLog()`, very useful to display data in the PDI log.
- Finally, the **File** category, as its name suggests, contains a list of functions that do simple verification or actions related to files and folders, for example, `fileExist()` or `createFolder()`.

To add a function to your script, simply double-click on it, or drag it to the location in your script where you wish to use it, or just type it.

If you are not sure about how to use a particular function or what a function does, just right-click on the function and select **Sample**. A new script window appears with a description of the function and sample code showing you how to use it.

The **Input fields** branch contains the list of the fields coming from previous steps. To see and use the value of a field for the current row, you double-click on it or drag it to the code area. You can also type it by hand.

When you use one of the input fields in the code, it is treated as a JavaScript variable. As such, the name of the field has to follow the conventions for a variable name, for instance, it cannot contain dots or start with non-character symbols. As PDI is quite permissive with names, you can have fields in your stream whose names are not valid for use inside JavaScript code.

If you intend to use a field with a name that does not follow the name rules, rename it just before the JavaScript step with a **Select Values** step. If you use that field without renaming it, you will not be warned when coding, but you'll get an error or unexpected results when you execute the Transformation.

Finally, **Output fields** is a list of the fields that will leave the step.

In the following subsections, you will recreate a Transformation from `Chapter 6`, *Controlling the Flow of Data*, by replacing part of its functionality with JavaScript. So before continuing, perform the following:

1. Open the Transformation that read a file and filtered words from `Chapter 6`, *Controlling the Flow of Data*.
2. Select the first two steps—the **Text file input** and the **Split field to rows** steps—and copy them to a new Transformation.

3. From the **Scripting** category of steps, select and drag a **Modified Java Script Value** step to the work area. Create a hop from the **Split field to rows** step toward this.

This new Transformation will be the base for the examples that you will build.

Adding fields

The simplest task you can do with JavaScript adds a field. Let's see how to create a simple field that contains the length of the `word` field:

1. Double-click on the **Modified Java Script Value** step—**JavaScript** step from now on and under the text `//Script here`, type the following:

```
var len_word = word.length;
```

2. Click on the **Get variables** button. The lower grid will be filled with the defined variable, `len_word`.
3. Close the configuration window and save the Transformation.
4. Make sure the **JavaScript** step is selected and do a preview. You should see the following:

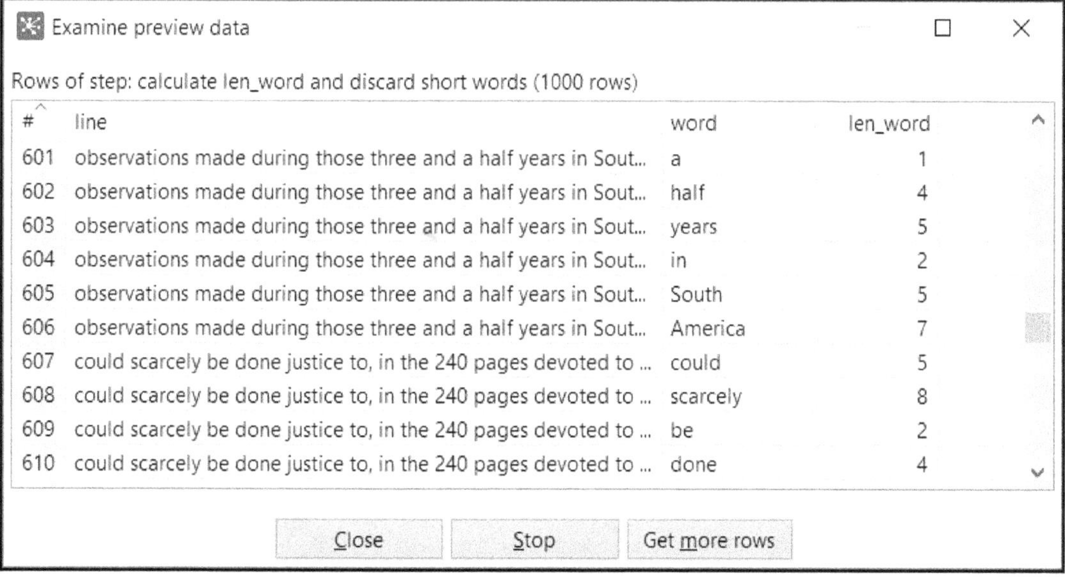

Examine preview data
Rows of step: calculate len_word and discard short words (1000 rows)
line word len_word
601 observations made during those three and a half years in Sout... a 1
602 observations made during those three and a half years in Sout... half 4
603 observations made during those three and a half years in Sout... years 5
604 observations made during those three and a half years in Sout... in 2
605 observations made during those three and a half years in Sout... South 5
606 observations made during those three and a half years in Sout... America 7
607 could scarcely be done justice to, in the 240 pages devoted to ... could 5
608 could scarcely be done justice to, in the 240 pages devoted to ... scarcely 8
609 could scarcely be done justice to, in the 240 pages devoted to ... be 2
610 could scarcely be done justice to, in the 240 pages devoted to ... done 4
Close
Stop
Get more rows

Previewing a Transformation

Note that you see the first 1000 rows. If you want to see more, just click on **Get more rows**.

As you can deduce from the preview window, the code you typed was executed for every row in your dataset. In this simple code, you declared a variable named `len_word`, gave it a value, and then added it to the lower grid. By doing so, the variable was added to a new field in your dataset.

In this example, you typed a single line of code. In general, you can write all the code you need to create the output fields. In your code, you can use the **Input fields** just by double-clicking on them in the left tree or by typing them as you did in the example with the `word` field. Also, in a single **JavaScript** step, you can add as many fields as you want. Note that in order to add a new field, the declaration of the `var` sentence is mandatory.

The variables you define in the JavaScript code are not Kettle variables. Recall that you learned about Kettle variables in `Chapter 3`, *Creating Basic Tasks Flows*. JavaScript variables are local to the step and have nothing to do with Kettle variables.

Modifying fields

With the **JavaScript** step, you can also modify an existing field. This doesn't differ much from the way you add new fields. In this exercise, we will modify the `word` field by converting it to uppercase:

1. Double-click on the **JavaScript** step and after the code, you typed in the previous exercise, type the following:

```
var u_word = upper(word);
```

2. In the lower grid, add the new variable `u_word`, which will substitute the `word` field as follows:

Fields

#	Fieldname	Rename to	Type	Length	Precision	Replace value 'Fieldname' or 'Rename to'
1	len_word		Integer		0	N
2	u_word	word	String			Y

Replacing fields in a JavaScript step

3. Close the window and run a preview. You will see this:

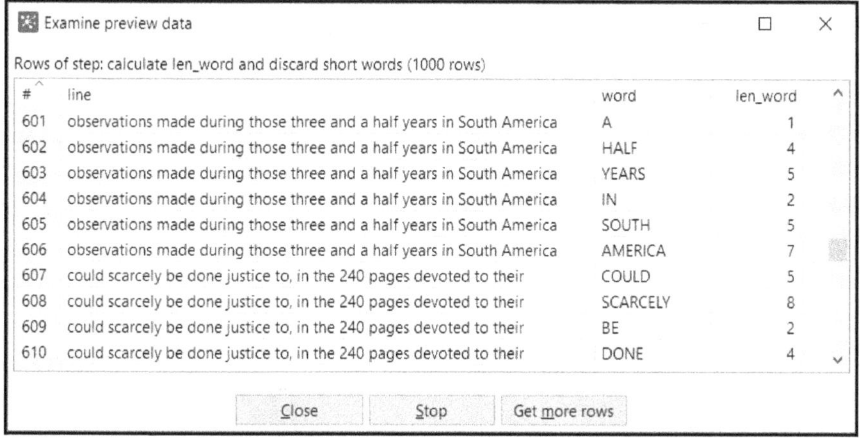

Examine preview data

Rows of step: calculate len_word and discard short words (1000 rows)

#	line	word	len_word
601	observations made during those three and a half years in South America	A	1
602	observations made during those three and a half years in South America	HALF	4
603	observations made during those three and a half years in South America	YEARS	5
604	observations made during those three and a half years in South America	IN	2
605	observations made during those three and a half years in South America	SOUTH	5
606	observations made during those three and a half years in South America	AMERICA	7
607	could scarcely be done justice to, in the 240 pages devoted to their	COULD	5
608	could scarcely be done justice to, in the 240 pages devoted to their	SCARCELY	8
609	could scarcely be done justice to, in the 240 pages devoted to their	BE	2
610	could scarcely be done justice to, in the 240 pages devoted to their	DONE	4

Close Stop Get more rows

Previewing a Transformation

As you can see, the difference between adding a field and modifying a field is the setting in the lower grid. To replace a field, you just set the **Replace value 'Fieldname' or 'Rename to'** value to `Y`.

Organizing your code

As said, the code you type in the script area is executed for every incoming row. If it happens that you need to initialize values that apply to all the rows, you can and should do it in a separate script. If you don't, all the initialization code will be executed for every row in your dataset. This is how you create a new start script:

1. Right-click on top of the code area and select **Add new**:

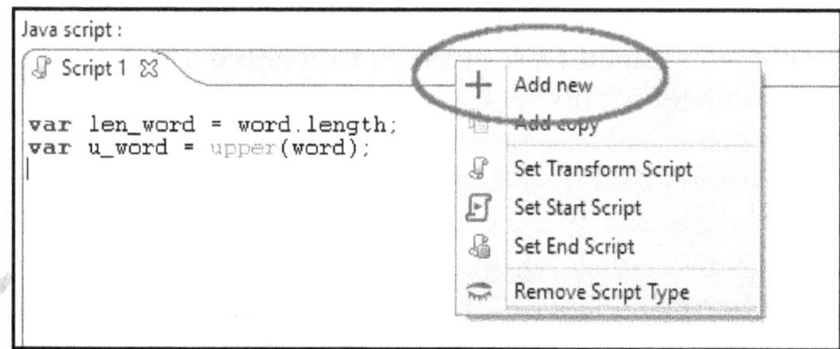

Adding a new script

2. A new **Script** tab will appear both in the main area and in the list of scripts to the left:

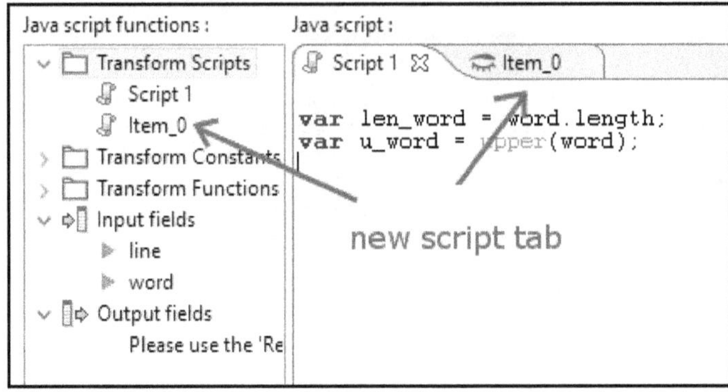

Scripts in a Javascript step

3. In the **Transform Scripts** tree, right-click on the name of the new script and select **Rename** to give it a meaningful name.
4. Right-click on top of the **Script** tab and select **Set Start Script**. The icon beside the title will change so you can recognize this script as the starting one. This action will cause that all the script was written here be executed before any row comes into the step.

All the variables inside JavaScript keep their values between rows. In particular, all the variables that you define in the start script will keep their values.

In the same way that you create a *Start Script*, you can create an *End Script* to be executed after the last row leaves the step. In this case, you select **Set End Script** instead.

Besides these particular scripts, you can add more tabs in order to have your code organized. For example, you can add a script with function definitions. Then in the main **Script** tab, just call the functions. This is how you do it:

1. Right-click on top of the code area and select **Add new**. By default, the script hasn't a script type associated. Leave it like that.
2. Give the **Script** tab a meaningful name and type all the code you need.
3. In your **Start Scripting** tab, call the LoadScriptFromTab(<your script>); function. This will load the code from the recently created tab.

Note that if you load a script in the main script, the code will be loaded on each processing row.

Controlling the flow using predefined constants

JavaScript has a way of controlling the flow of data, that is, deciding which rows follow the normal flow and which ones are discarded. It acts as a filter. To control the flow, you play with a special variable named `trans_Status`. This variable is evaluated for each row in your dataset and depending on the value, the result is different, as shown in the following table:

If the `trans_Status` value is set to ...	**The current row ...**
`SKIP_TRANSFORMATION`	is removed from the dataset.
`CONTINUE_TRANSFORMATION`	is kept. Nothing happens to it.
`ERROR_TRANSFORMATION`	causes the abortion of the Transformation.

The way you set the values is as simple as the following:

```
trans_Status = SKIP_TRANSFORMATION
```

The three possible values are predefined constants that you can find in the tree at the left side of the JavaScript window under **Transformation Constants**. You can type the values by hand or you can double-click on them in the tree to the left.

To demonstrate the use of these concepts, we will add more functionality to our example. Now we will keep only the words with length greater than 3:

1. Double-click on the **JavaScript** step and succeeding your code, add the following:

```
if (len_word > 3)
    trans_Status = CONTINUE_TRANSFORMATION;
else
    trans_Status = SKIP_TRANSFORMATION;
```

2. Close the window and run a preview. You will see this:

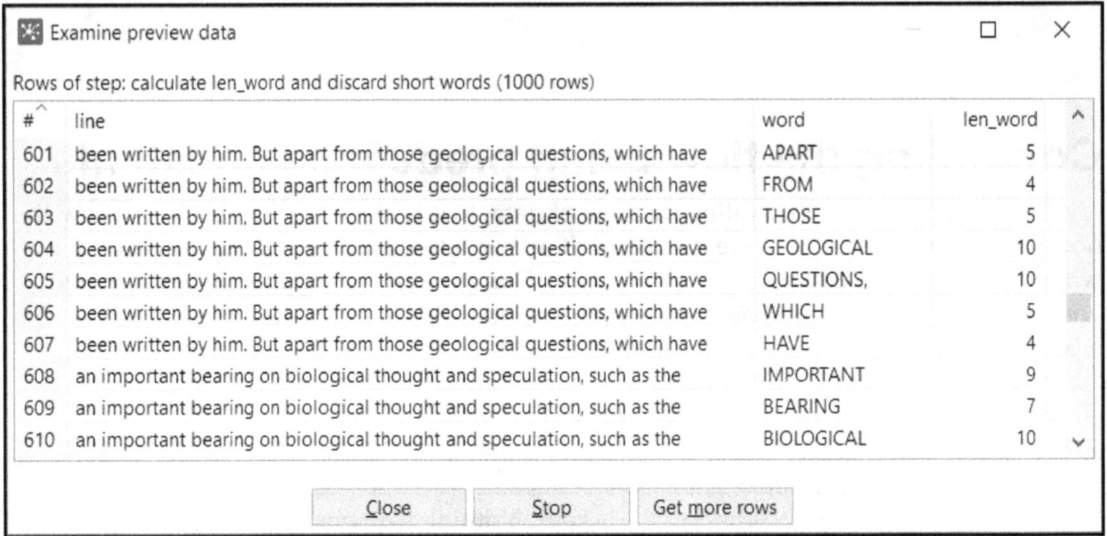

#	line	word	len_word
601	been written by him. But apart from those geological questions, which have	APART	5
602	been written by him. But apart from those geological questions, which have	FROM	4
603	been written by him. But apart from those geological questions, which have	THOSE	5
604	been written by him. But apart from those geological questions, which have	GEOLOGICAL	10
605	been written by him. But apart from those geological questions, which have	QUESTIONS,	10
606	been written by him. But apart from those geological questions, which have	WHICH	5
607	been written by him. But apart from those geological questions, which have	HAVE	4
608	an important bearing on biological thought and speculation, such as the	IMPORTANT	9
609	an important bearing on biological thought and speculation, such as the	BEARING	7
610	an important bearing on biological thought and speculation, such as the	BIOLOGICAL	10

Previewing data

This piece of code is meant to keep only the words whose length is greater than `3`. You accomplish it by setting the value of the predefined PDI variable `trans_Status` to `CONTINUE_TRANSFORMATION` for the rows you want to keep and to `SKIP_TRANSFORMATION` for the rows you want to discard. If you pay attention to the last preview, you will notice that all the words have at least a length of three characters.

If you run the Transformation, you will see that there is a big difference between the number of rows entering the **JavaScript** step and the rows that come out of the step. This is clearly because of the filter that has been applied.

You can see the number of read and written rows in the **Execution Results** window under the **Read** column and **Written** column respectively.

Testing the script using the Test script button

In the example that we just built, the code was very simple and didn't require much attention. However, when you have more code or maybe a complicated algorithm to run on your data, testing the code effectively before running it with your data could be a great idea. The **Test script** button allows you to do this: checking whether the script does what it is intended to do. It actually generates a Transformation in the back with two steps: a **Generate Rows** step with sample data and a copy of the **JavaScript** step that works on that sample.

This is how you test your JavaScript code:

1. Click on the **Test script** button and a window will appear to create a set of rows to test. Fill it as shown in the following screenshot:

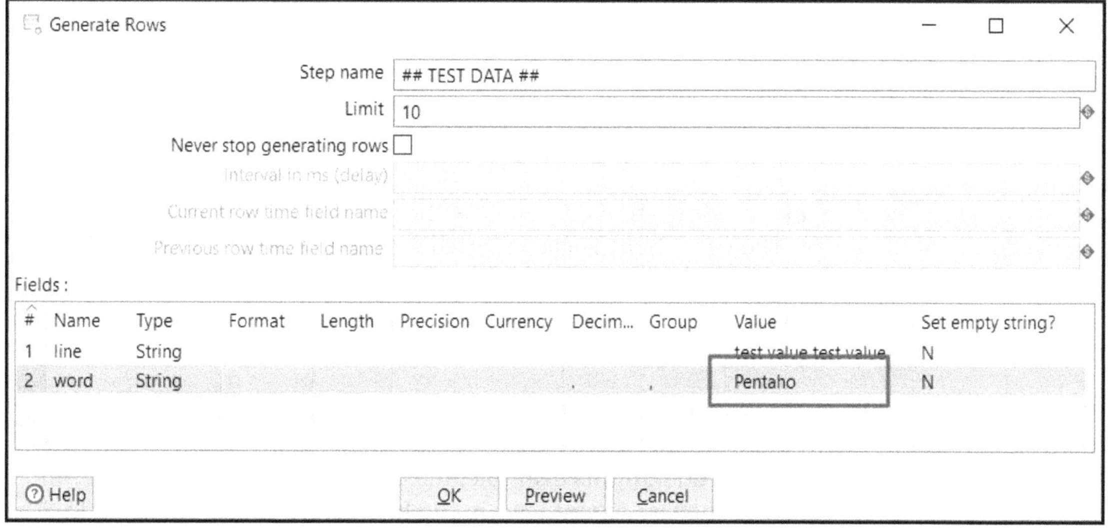

Creating sample data

2. Click on **Preview** and a window appears showing ten identical rows with the provided sample values.

3. Close the **Preview** window and click on **OK** to test the code. A window appears with the result of having executed the script on the test data:

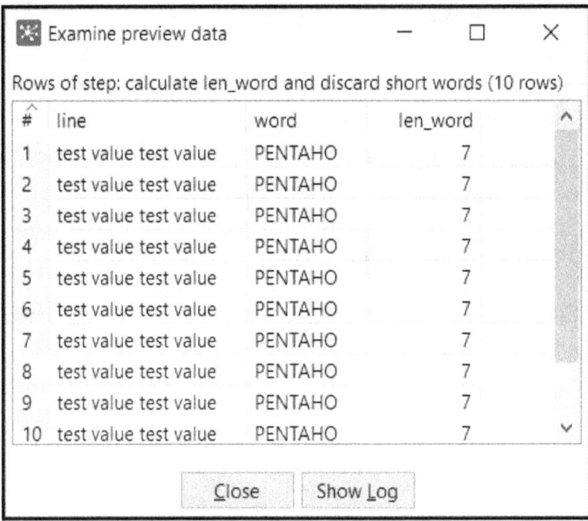

Testing JavaScript code

As you can see, the **Preview** window showed you how the sample dataset looks like after the execution of the script. The `word` field was converted to uppercase, and a new field named `len_word` was added to the length of the sample word. Also, the words with length lower than three were excluded. If you run a new test and type a word with three or less characters, nothing will appear, as expected.

Once you click on **OK** in the **Generate Rows** window to effectively run the test, the first thing that the `test` function does is to verify that the code is properly written, that is, that there are no syntax errors in the code. In this example, the code hadn't any errors and ran without problems. Try deleting the last parenthesis in the **JavaScript** code you wrote in the previous section and click on the **Test script** button. When you click on **OK** to see the result of the execution, instead of a dataset, you will see an **ERROR** window. Among the lines, you will see something like this:

```
...
Unexpected error
org.pentaho.di.core.exception.KettleValueException:
Couldn't compile javascript:
missing ) after condition (script#6)
...
```

If you hit a situation like this, you can check the code, fix it, and test it again until you see that everything works properly.

Parsing unstructured files with JavaScript

It's ideal to have input files where the information is well-formed, that is, the number of columns and the type of its data is precise, all rows follow the same pattern, and so on. However, it is very common to find input files where the information has little or no structure or the structure doesn't follow the matrix (n rows by m columns) you expect. This is one of the situations where JavaScript can help.

Suppose that you have a file with a description of houses, which looks like the following:

```
...
Property Code: MCX-011
Status: Active
5 bedrooms
5 baths
Style: Contemporary
Basement
Laundry room
Fireplace
2 car garage
Central air conditioning
More Features: Attic, Clothes dryer, Clothes washer, Dishwasher

Property Code: MCX-012
4 bedrooms
3 baths
Fireplace
Attached parking
More Features: Alarm System, Eat-in Kitchen, Powder Room

Property Code: MCX-013
3 bedrooms
...
```

You want to compare the properties among them but it would be easier if the file had a precise structure. The **JavaScript** step can help you with this.

The first attempt to give structure to the data will be to add to every row the code of the house to which that row belongs. The purpose is to have the following:

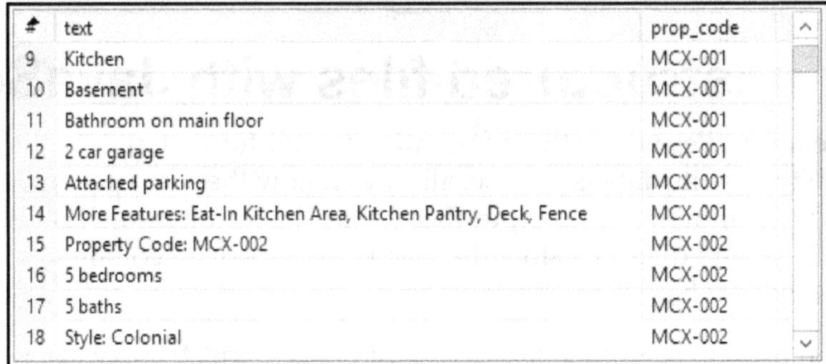

#	text	prop_code
9	Kitchen	MCX-001
10	Basement	MCX-001
11	Bathroom on main floor	MCX-001
12	2 car garage	MCX-001
13	Attached parking	MCX-001
14	More Features: Eat-In Kitchen Area, Kitchen Pantry, Deck, Fence	MCX-001
15	Property Code: MCX-002	MCX-002
16	5 bedrooms	MCX-002
17	5 baths	MCX-002
18	Style: Colonial	MCX-002

Previewing some data

1. Create a new Transformation.
2. Get the sample file from the book site and read it with a **Text file input** step. Uncheck the **Header** checkbox and create a single field named `text`.
3. Run a preview. You should see the content of the file under a single column named `text`.
4. After the input step, add a **JavaScript** step and double-click on it to edit it.
5. In the editing area, type the following JavaScript code to create a field with the code of the property:

```
var prop_code;
posCod = indexOf(text,'Property Code:');
if (posCod>=0)
   prop_code = trim(substr(text,posCod+15));
```

The `indexOf` function identifies the column where the property code is in the text. The `substr` function cuts the `Property Code:`, `text`, keeping only the code itself.

6. Click on **Get variables** to add the `prop_code` variable to the grid under the code. The variable will contain for every row, the code for the house to which it belongs.
7. Click on **OK** and with the JavaScript step selected, run a preview. You should see the data transformed as expected.

The code you wrote may seem a little strange at the beginning, but it is not really so complex. The general idea is to simulate a loop over the dataset rows.

The code creates a variable named `prod_code`, which will be used to create a new field to identify the houses. When the JavaScript code detects a property header row as for example:

```
Property Code: MCX-002
```

It sets the `prop_code` variable to the code it finds in that line, in this case, `MCX-002`.

Here comes the trick: until a new header row appears, the `prop_code` variable keeps that value. Thus, all the rows following a row like the one shown previously will have the same value for the `prop_code` variable.

This is an example where you can keep values from the previous rows in the dataset to be used in the current row.

Note that here you use JavaScript to see and use values from previous rows, but you can't modify them! JavaScript always works on the current row.

Doing simple tasks with the Java Class step

Just as the JavaScript step, the **User Defined Java Class** step is also meant to insert code into your transformations but in this case, it's Java code. Whether you need to implement a functionality not provided in built-in steps or want to reuse some external Java code, or to access Java libraries, or to increase performance, this step is what you need. In this section, you will learn how to use it.

Using the Java language in PDI

Java—originally developed at Sun Microsystems, which then merged into Oracle Corporation—is one of the most popular programming languages in use, particularly for client-server web applications. In particular, PDI and the whole Pentaho platform have been developed using Java as the core language.

It was to be expected that eventually, a step would appear that allows you to code Java inside PDI. This step is **User Defined Java Class**, which we will call **UDJC** or **Java Class** step for short. The goal of this step is to allow you to define methods and logic using Java but also to provide a way of executing pieces of code as fast as possible. Also, one of the purposes of this step, when it was created, was to overcome performance issues—one of the main drawbacks of JavaScript.

For allowing Java programming inside PDI, the tool uses the Janino project libraries. **Janino** is a super-small, super-fast, embedded compiler that compiles Java code at runtime.

To see a full list of *Janino* features and limitations, you can follow this link: `http://janino-compiler.github.io/janino/`

As previously said, the goal of the UDJC is not to do full-scale Java development but to allow you to execute pieces of Java code. If you need to do a lot of Java development, you should think of doing it in a Java IDE, exposing your code in a `jar` file, and placing that library in the Kettle classpath, namely, the `libext` folder inside the PDI installation directory. Then you can include the library at the top of the step code using the regular Java syntax, for example:

```
import my_library.util.*;
```

Also, a good choice, if you find yourself writing extensive amounts of Java code, is to create a new step, which is a drop-in **Plug and Play** (**PnP**) operation.

The creation of plugins is outside the scope of this book. If you are interested in this subject, a good starting point is the Pentaho article, *Create Step Plugins*. You can find this entry at `https://help.pentaho.com/Documentation/8.0/Developer_Center/PDI/Extend/000`. If you are not familiar with the Java language and think that your requirement could be implemented with JavaScript, you could use the **Modified Java Script Value** step instead. Take into account that the code in the **JavaScript** step is interpreted, whereas the code in UDJC is compiled. This means that a Transformation that uses the UDJC step will have a much better performance.

Inserting Java code using the Java Class step

The **User Defined Java Class** step allows you to insert Java code inside your Transformation. The code you type here is executed once per row coming to the step.

The UI for the **UDJC** step is very similar to the UI for the **JavaScript** step, as shown in the following screenshot:

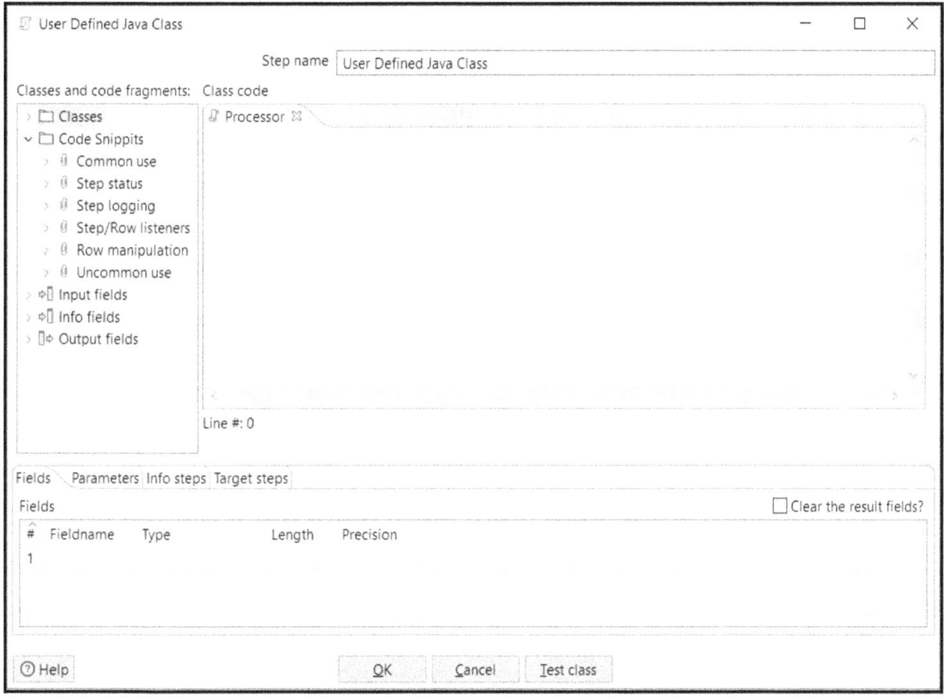

UI for the Java Class step

Most of the window is occupied by the editing area. Here, you write the Java code using the standard syntax of the language. On the left, there is a panel with a lot of fragments of code ready to use (**Code Snippits**) and a section with sets and gets for the input and output fields. To add one of the provided pieces of code to your script, either double-click on it and drag it to the location in your script where you wish to use it, or just type it in the editing area.

The code you see in the **Code Snippits** is not pure Java. It has a lot of PDI predefined functions to manipulate rows, look at the status of steps, and more.

The input and outputs fields appear automatically in the tree when the Java code compiles correctly.

Then you have some tabs at the bottom. The next table summarizes their functions:

Tab	Function
Fields	To declare the new fields added by the step
Parameters	To add parameters to your code along with their values
Info steps	To declare additional PDI steps in your Transformation that provide information to be read inside your Java code
Target steps	To declare the PDI steps where the rows will be redirected, in case you want to redirect rows to more than one destination

In the next subsections, we will give more details and examples for each of these features.

Learning to insert java code in a Java Class step

Just as we did in the JavaScript section, in order to show you how to use the Java Class step, we will implement the same Transformation from `Chapter 6`, *Controlling the Flow of Data*, this time using Java code:

1. Open the Transformation created earlier and save it with a different name.
2. Delete the **JavaScript** step.
3. From the **Scripting** category of steps, select and drag a **User Defined Java Class** step to the work area. Create a hop from the **Split field to rows** step toward this.

This new Transformation will be the base for the examples that you will build.

Before introducing your own code, PDI requires that you enter a basic skeleton. This is the minimal piece of code that you have to write and it is mandatory no matter how simple your code is. So, first of all, you have to do the following:

1. Double-click on the **User Defined Java Class** step—**UDJC** from now on—and in the **Processor** tab, type the following:

```
public boolean processRow(StepMetaInterface smi, StepDataInterface
sdi) throws KettleException {
   Object[] r = getRow();
   if (r == null) {
      setOutputDone();
```

```
        return false;
    }

    if (first) {
        first = false;
    }

    Object[] outputRow = createOutputRow(r,
data.outputRowMeta.size());

// HERE GOES YOUR CODE

    putRow(data.outputRowMeta, outputRow);

    return true;
}
```

You can save time by expanding the **Code Snippits** tree to the left of the window and double-clicking on the option **Main** after expanding **Common use**. This action will populate the **Processor** tab with a template and you just need to modify the code so it looks like the one shown previously.

Here, you have a brief explanation of what this code does:

- The `processRow()` function at the beginning of the code is a predefined PDI function that processes a new row.
- The `getRow()` function, another predefined PDI function, gets the next row from the input steps. It returns an `Object` array with the incoming row. A `null` value means that there are no more rows to process.

The following code only executes for the `first` row:

```
if (first) {
        first = false;
    }
```

You can use the `first` flag to prepare a proper environment for processing the rows. If you don't need to do anything special for the `first` row, you can just set the `first` flag to `false`.

The next line ensures that your output row's `Object` array is large enough to handle any new fields created in this step:

```
Object[] outputRow = createOutputRow(r, data.outputRowMeta.size());
```

After this line, there is a call to `putRow()`, a function that sends the row on to the next step:

```
putRow(data.outputRowMeta, outputRow);
```

This very first code simply receives the rows and sends them to the output step without applying any Transformation. If you run a preview of this step, you should see exactly the same data that came into the step.

Data types equivalence

The code you type inside the **UDJC** step is pure Java. Therefore, the fields of your Transformation will be seen as Java objects according to the following equivalence table:

Data type in PDI	Java Class
`String`	`Java.lang.String`
`Integer`	`Java.lang.Long`
`Number`	`Java.lang.Double`
`Date`	`Java.util.Date`
`BigNumber`	`BigDecimal`
`Binary`	`byte[]`

The opposite occurs when you create an object inside the Java code and want to expose it as a new field of your Transformation. For example, in the Java code, if you define a `long` variable in the **Fields** tab, you have to define the correspondent output field as `Integer`.

Adding fields

Adding new fields to the dataset is really simple. This is how you do it:

1. In the code, you define the field as an internal variable and calculate its value.
2. Then you have to update the output row. Supposing that the name for the new field is `my_new_field` and the name of the internal variable is `my_var`, you update the output row as follows:

   ```
   get(Fields.Out, "my_new_field").setValue(outputRow, my_var);
   ```

3. Finally, you have to add the field to the lower grid. You just add a new line of each new field. You have to provide at least the **Fieldname** and **Type**.

To know exactly which type to put in there, refer to the *Data types equivalence* section of this chapter.

In our example, we want to add a field to the length of the `word` field. We do it with the following simple steps:

1. Type the following lines in the Java code, replacing the line `// HERE GOES YOUR CODE`:

```
String word = get(Fields.In, "word").getString(r);
long len_word = word.length();
get(Fields.Out, "len_word").setValue(outputRow, len_word);
```

The first line uses the `get()` method to set the internal variable `word` with the value of the `word` field. In the second line, we calculate the length of the word and save it in an internal variable named `len_word`. In the third line, we create a new output field named `len_word` with the calculated value.

2. Fill in the **Fields** tab in the lower grid as follows:

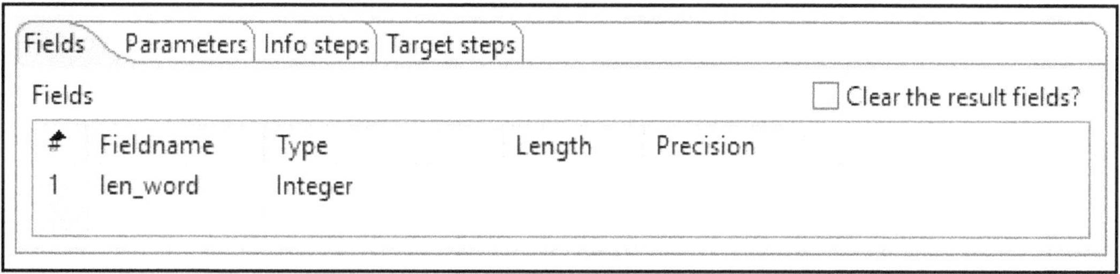

Configuring the Fields tab in a Java Class step

3. Click on **OK** to close the window and save the Transformation.

4. Double-click on the **Java Class** step again. This time, you will see that the **Input fields** and **Output fields** branches of the tree on the left have been populated with the name of the fields coming in and out of the step:

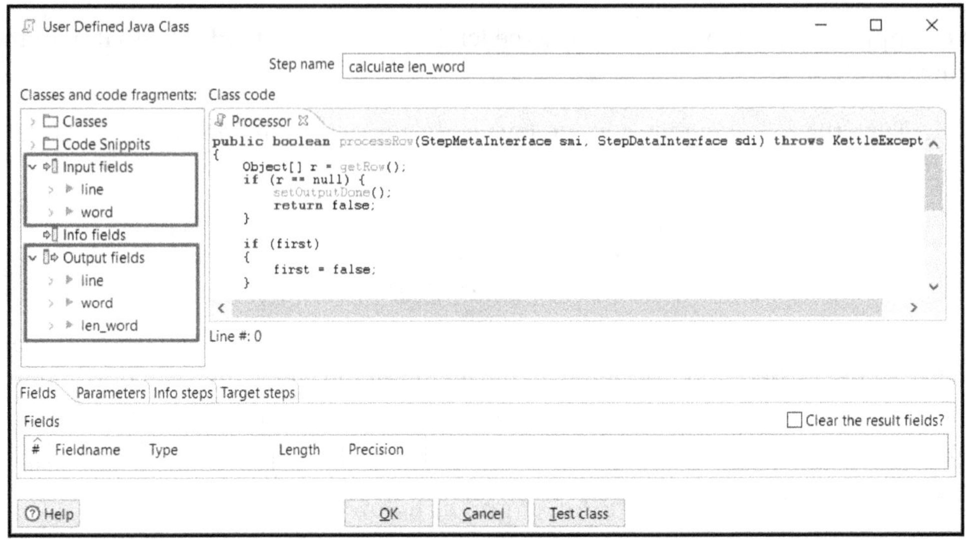

Input and Output fields in a Java Class step

5. One more time, close the window. This time, with the step selected, run a preview. You will see the old fields plus the new field `len_word`:

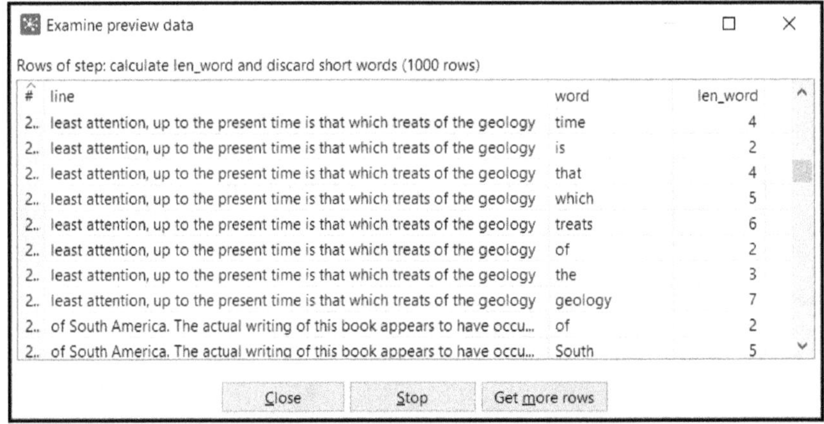

Previewing the output of a Java Class step

Modifying fields

Modifying a field instead of adding a new one is even easier. Supposing that the name of your field is `my_field` and the value you want to set is stored in a variable named `my_var`; you just set the field to the new value using the following syntax:

```
get(Fields.Out, "my_field").setValue(r, my_var);
```

By doing it this way, you are modifying the output row. When you send the row to the next step using the `putRow()` method, the field already has its new value.

In our sample Transformation, we want to convert the word to uppercase. For this, you have to add the following line to your code that converts the word to uppercase:

```
get(Fields.Out, "word").setValue(outputRow, word.toUpperCase());
```

This line takes the uppercase value of the `word` variable and uses that string to set the value of the output field `word`.

If you run a preview of the **Java Class** step, you will see all the words converted to uppercase.

It is irrelevant for our example if you put this line before or after the lines that calculate the length of the word—the lines that we added before—as long as you put this before the `putRow()` function.

Controlling the flow with the putRow() function

With the **Java Class** step, you control which rows go to the next step using the `putRow()` method. With this method selectively, you decide which rows to send and which rows to discard.

As an example, if we want to apply a filter and keep only the words with length greater than three, we could move the `putRow()` function inside an `if` clause, as shown in the following sample:

```
if (len_word > 3) {
   putRow(data.outputRowMeta, outputRow);
   }
```

Your final code should look as follows:

```
public boolean processRow(StepMetaInterface smi, StepDataInterface sdi)
throws KettleException {
 Object[] r = getRow();
 if (r == null) {
     setOutputDone();
     return false;
    }
 if (first) { first = false;}
 Object[] outputRow = createOutputRow(r, data.outputRowMeta.size());

 String word = get(Fields.In, "word").getString(r);
 get(Fields.Out, "word").setValue(outputRow, word.toUpperCase());
 long len_word = word.length();
 get(Fields.Out, "len_word").setValue(outputRow, len_word);
 if (len_word > 3) {
    putRow(data.outputRowMeta, outputRow);
    }

return true;
 }
```

If you run a preview, you will see something like this:

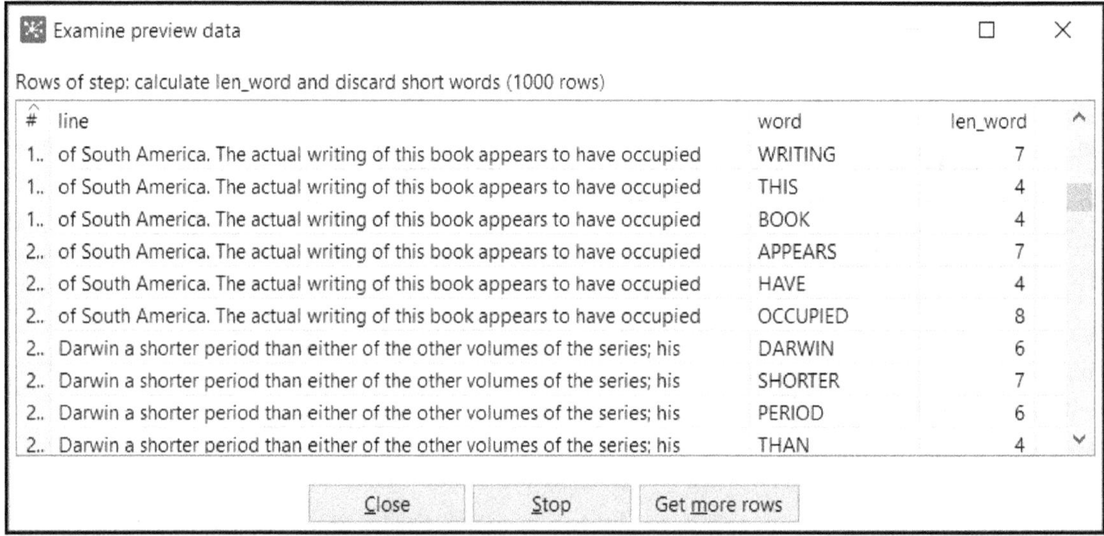
Examine preview data

Rows of step: calculate len_word and discard short words (1000 rows)

#	line	word	len_word
1..	of South America. The actual writing of this book appears to have occupied	WRITING	7
1..	of South America. The actual writing of this book appears to have occupied	THIS	4
1..	of South America. The actual writing of this book appears to have occupied	BOOK	4
2..	of South America. The actual writing of this book appears to have occupied	APPEARS	7
2..	of South America. The actual writing of this book appears to have occupied	HAVE	4
2..	of South America. The actual writing of this book appears to have occupied	OCCUPIED	8
2..	Darwin a shorter period than either of the other volumes of the series; his	DARWIN	6
2..	Darwin a shorter period than either of the other volumes of the series; his	SHORTER	7
2..	Darwin a shorter period than either of the other volumes of the series; his	PERIOD	6
2..	Darwin a shorter period than either of the other volumes of the series; his	THAN	4

Close Stop Get more rows

Previewing the output of a Java Class step

In summary, the output dataset differs from the original in that it has a new field named `len_word`, but only contains the rows where the length of the `word` field is greater than `3`. Also, the `word` field has been converted to uppercase.

Testing the Java Class using the Test class button

The method to test the code in a **Java Class** step is similar to the one that you saw in the *JavaScript* section:

1. Click on the **Test class** button at the bottom of the window.
2. A window appears to create a set of rows for the testing. Fill it in as shown in the screenshot:

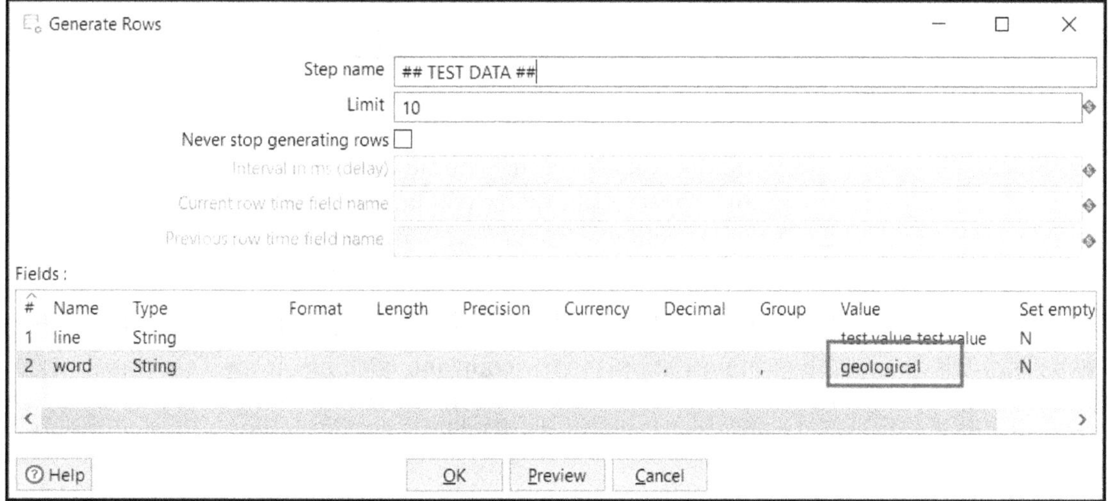

Sample data

3. Click on **Preview** and a window appears showing ten identical rows with the provided sample values.
4. Click on **OK** in the preview window to test the code.

5. A window appears with the result of having executed the code on the test data:

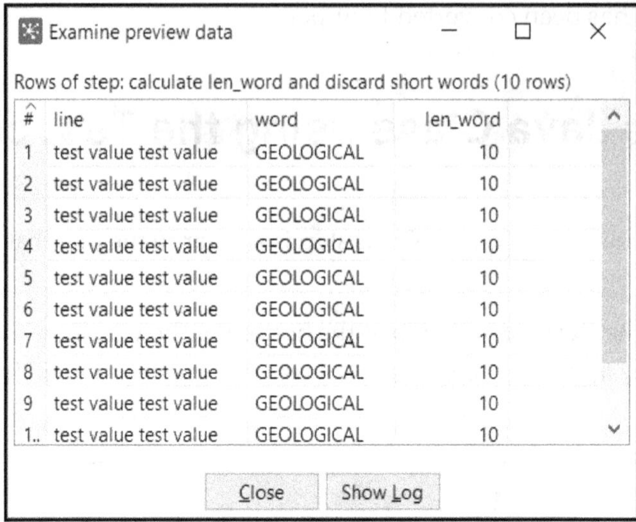

Previewing the result of a Java Class code

As you can see, after confirming the creation of the sample data—the data created with **Generate Rows**—a new window appeared showing you how the created dataset looks after the execution of the code: the `word` field was converted to uppercase and a new field named `len_word` was added, containing as value the length of the sample word.

When you effectively run the test, the first thing that the test function does is compile the Java class. Try deleting the last parenthesis in the code and clicking on the **Test class** button. When you click on **OK** to see the result of the execution, instead of a dataset, you will see an **Error during class compilation** window. If you are lucky, you will clearly see the cause of the error as in this case:

```
Line 24, Column 3: Operator ")" expected
```

It may be that the error is much more complicated to understand or, on the contrary, does not give you enough details. You will have to be patient, comment the parts that you suspect are causing the problem, review the code, fix the errors, and so on, until your code compiles successfully. After that, what follows is the preview of the result of the **Java Class** step for the Transformation in the back, that is, the Java code applied to the test dataset.

If the previewed data shows the expected results, you are done. If not, you can check the code and modify or fix it until the results are as expected.

Getting the most out of the Java Class step

In the previous sections, you learned how to use the **Java Class** step to accomplish basic tasks. The step has a few more characteristics that allow you to create a rich code. The following subsections summarize some of them.

Receiving parameters

To write a more flexible code, you can add parameters. You can do it by configuring the **Parameters** tab in the lower grid of the Java Class configuration window. For each new parameter, you have to provide a name under the **Tag** column and a value under the **Value** column as follows:

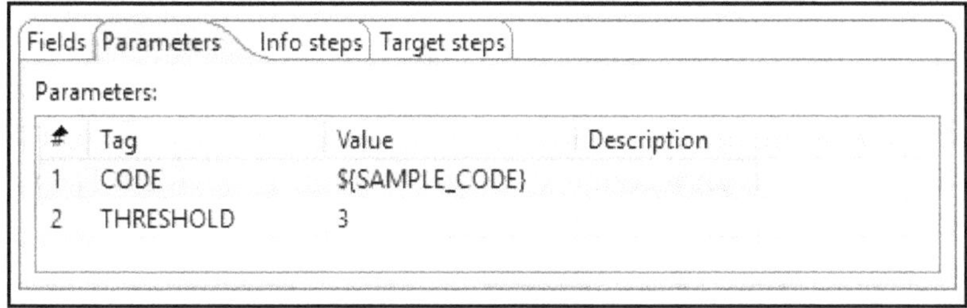

Adding parameters

Note that the value for a **Java Class** parameter can be a fixed value as well as a PDI variable.

In your code, you read a parameter using the `getParameter()` function, as follows:

```
String code = getParameter("CODE");
```

Note that the parameters don't have a data type and they are read as string values. In case you need to use them in a different format, you should cast the values to the proper data type, as shown in the following example:

```
long threshold = Integer.parseInt(getParameter("THRESHOLD"));
```

Reading data from additional steps

The **Java Class** step allows you to read data from one or more secondary streams. In order to do this, the first thing you have to do is connect the steps to your **Java Class** step icon as follows:

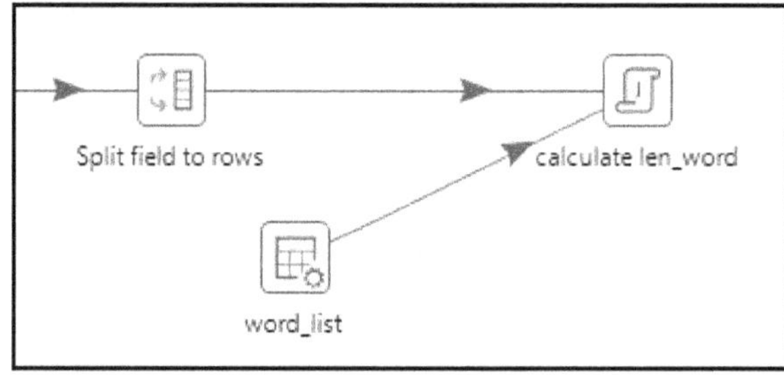

Sample Transformation with Info steps

Then, you have to configure the **Info steps** tab in the lower grid of the **Java Class** configuration window. For each secondary stream, you must provide a **Tag** name and select the name of the incoming step, as shown in the following screenshot:

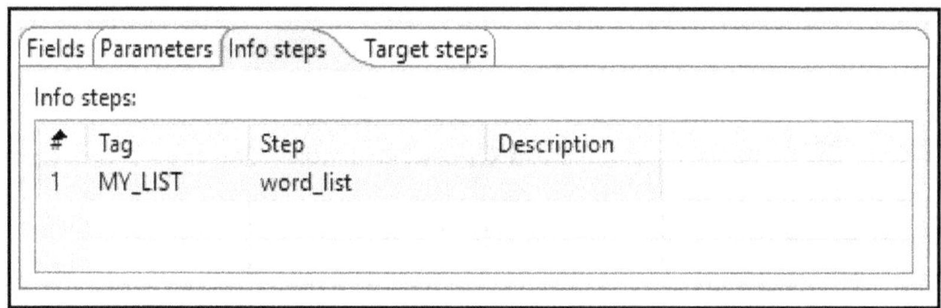

Configuring the Info steps tab

Once you do this, the hops from the **Info steps** toward the **Java Class** step change its look and feel:

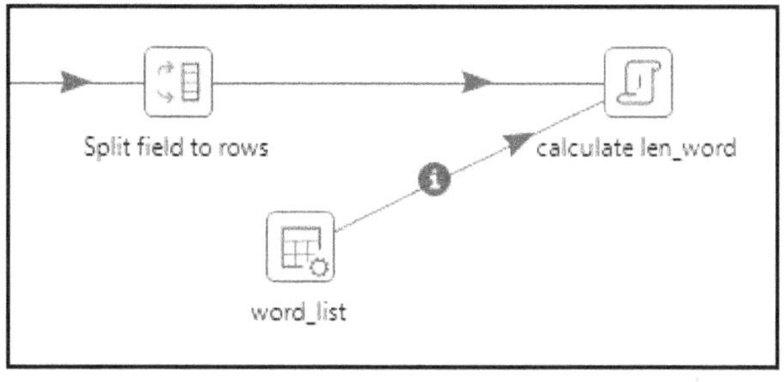

Info steps

In the Java code, you can use the `findInfoRowSet()` method to reference the **Info step**, and the `getRowFrom()` method to read the rows in a cycle, as shown in the following sample code:

```
RowSet infoStream = findInfoRowSet("my_list");
Object[] infoRow = null;
while((infoRow = getRowFrom(infoStream)) != null){
    < your code here >
 }
```

Redirecting data to different target steps

In the same way, as you can receive data from more than one incoming stream, you can redirect rows to different target steps. After creating the hops from the **Java Class** toward each target step, you have to configure the **Output steps** tab in the lower grid of the **Java Class** configuration window.

In the Java code, you use the `findTargetRowSet()` method to identify the target rowset, and the `putRowTo()` method to specify to which target step you want to redirect each row:

```
private RowSet targetStreamA = null;
private RowSet targetStreamB= null;

public boolean processRow( ...) {

if (first){
    first = false;
    targetStreamA = findTargetRowSet("target1");
    targetStreamB = findTargetRowSet("target2");
```

```
    }

if (<condition>)
    putRowTo(data.outputRowMeta, r, targetStreamA);
else
    putRowTo(data.outputRowMeta, r, targetStreamB);

...
}
```

Parsing JSON structures

If you need to parse complex JSON structures and the **JSON Input** step doesn't meet your needs, you can resolve the task with a **Java Class** step. A simple way for this is with the `org.json.simple` package. Among the classes found in this package, you will mainly use the following:

`org.json.simple` **Class**	**Description**
`JSONParser`	This class parses JSON text
`JSONValue`	This class has methods to parse JSON string into Java objects
`JSONObject`	It's an unordered collection of name/value pairs
`JSONArray`	It's an ordered sequence of values

To use this package in a **Java Class** step, you just import the needed libraries at the beginning of the code, as follows:

```
import org.json.simple.JSONArray;
import org.json.simple.JSONObject;
import org.json.simple.JSONValue;
```

Once you import the libraries, you can use them in your code. For example, in your dataset, if you have a field named `content` that contains a JSON structure, you can parse it with the following lines of code:

```
String contentStr = get(Fields.In, "content").getString(r);
JSONObject data = (JSONObject) JSONValue.parse(contentStr);
```

Then you can get the values in your object just by calling the `get()` function:

```
String name = (String) data.get("title");
```

Avoiding coding using purpose-built steps

You saw through the exercises how powerful the JavaScript and **Java Class** steps are to help you in your transformations. In older versions of PDI, coding JavaScript was the only means you had for specific tasks. In the latest releases of PDI, actual steps appeared that eliminate the need to code in many cases. Here you have some examples of these steps:

- **Formula step**: Before the appearance of this step, there were a lot of functions, such as the right or left text function, that you could solve only with JavaScript
- **Analytic Query**: This step offers a way to retrieve information from rows before or after the current row
- **Split field into rows**: This step is used to create several rows from a single string value
- **Add value fields changing sequence**: Similar to the **Add sequence** step, but the sequence value resets each time a value in the list of specified fields changes

Other steps have enhanced their capabilities. For example, the number of available calculations in the **Calculator** step increases with every new release.

Despite the appearance of new steps, you still have the choice to do the tasks using code.

In fact, quite a lot of tasks you do with regular PDI steps may also be done with code using the JavaScript or the **Java Class** step, as you saw in the sections of this chapter. This is a temptation to programmers who end up with transformations with plenty of code in them.

Whenever there is a step that does what you want to do, you should prefer to use that step rather than coding.

Why should you prefer to use a specific step rather than code? There are some reasons:

- Coding takes more development time. You don't have to waste your time coding if there are steps that solve your problem.
- The code is hard to maintain. If you have to modify or fix a Transformation, it will be much easier to attack the change if the Transformation is made of plenty of colorful steps with meaningful names, rather than if the Transformation is made of just a couple of JavaScript or Java Class icons.
- A bunch of icons is self-documented. JavaScript or **Java Class** steps are like Pandora's box. Until you open them, you don't know exactly what they do and whether they contain just a line of code or thousands.

- In the case of JavaScript, you should know that it is inherently slow. Faster alternatives for simple expressions are the **User Defined Java Expression** (also in the **Scripting** category of steps) and **Calculator** (in the **Transform** category) steps. They are typically more than twice as fast.

The **User Defined Java Expression** (or **UDJE**) step allows you to create new fields in an easy way by typing Java expressions. You already saw several examples of its use throughout the chapters. The step doesn't replace the functionality of the **UDJC** step, but it is more practical when the task to accomplish is simple.

On the contrary, there are situations where you may prefer or have to code. Let's enumerate some of them:

- To handle unstructured input data
- To manipulate complicated XML or JSON objects
- To access Java libraries
- When you need to use a function provided by the JavaScript or Java language and it is not provided by any of the regular PDI steps
- In the case of JavaScript, when the code saves a lot of regular PDI steps (as well as screen space), and you think it is not worth showing the details of what those steps do
- In the case of Java, for performance reasons, if you have to deal with millions of rows and very complicated operations, a Java class may be all you need to end up with a Transformation that performs very well

When you have doubts about the proper solution—to code or not to code—keep the following points in mind:

- Time to develop, will you save time if you choose to implement the solution with the code?
- Maintenance, will it be easier to maintain the code or to maintain the solution with specific PDI steps?
- Documentation, will you have to spend extra time in documenting the solution?
- Ability to handle unstructured data, do PDI steps allow you to handle the structures of your data?
- Number of needed steps, do you need few or a lot of PDI steps for implementing the solution?
- Performance, is the chosen solution performant?

Doing it this way, you will have arguments to help you decide which option is preferable. At the end, it is up to you to choose one or the other.

Summary

In this chapter, you learned how to insert code into your PDI transformations.

In the first place, you learned how to insert Javascript code. You used this option both to modify and to add new fields to your dataset. You also used Javascript code for filtering data, and for dealing with unstructured input data.

After that, you learned to use the UDJC step for inserting Java code. You used this option to insert and modify fields, and also to control the flow of data.

Besides, you received tips and directions to parse XML and JSON structures by coding. You also saw a list of the pros and cons of coding inside your Transformations, as well as alternative ways to do things, such as avoiding writing code when possible.

If you feel confident with all you have learned until now, you are certainly ready to move on to the next chapter. There, you will learn how to solve more advanced problems such as aggregating data or normalizing data from pivoted tables in a simple fashion.

[illegible] this way, you will have arguments to help you choose which option is preferable. At the end, it is up to you to choose one or the other.

Summary

[illegible] how to [illegible] (TDL [illegible]

[illegible] first place [illegible] learned how to insert Jav[illegible] [illegible] both to [illegible] [illegible] databases [illegible] [illegible] [illegible] input [illegible]

[illegible] TD[illegible] [illegible]

[illegible]

9
Transforming the Dataset

There are occasions when your dataset does not have the structure you like or the structure you need. The solution is not always about changing or adding fields or about filtering rows. The solution has to do with looking around (rows preceding or succeeding the current one) or altering the whole dataset. This chapter explains techniques to implement this behavior and transform the dataset as a whole, for example, aggregating data or normalizing pivoted tables.

The topics covered will be as follows:

- Sorting data
- Working on groups of rows
- Converting rows to columns called denormalizing
- Converting columns to rows called normalizing

Sorting data

To have the data sorted, something that we haven't cared about until now, is a very common requirement in real use cases. It can be a purpose by itself, but it's also a prerequisite for many of the operations that we will discuss in this chapter.

Sorting a dataset with the sort rows step

Sorting with PDI is really easy to implement but there are a couple of settings that you have to consider when doing it. Learning to do that is the objective of this quick tutorial.

For this exercise, we will use, one more time, the `sales_data.csv` file that we used in `Chapter 4`, *Reading and Writing Files*. Here, you have sample lines of the file:

```
ORDERDATE,ORDERNUMBER,ORDERLINENUMBER,PRODUCTCODE,PRODUCTLINE,QUANTITYORDER
ED,PRICEEACH,SALES
2/20/2004 0:00 ,10223,10,S24_4278 ,Planes ,23,74.62,1716.26
11/21/2004 0:00,10337,3,S18_4027 ,Classic Cars ,36,100 ,5679.36
6/16/2003 0:00 ,10131,2,S700_4002,Planes ,26,85.13,2213.38
7/6/2004 0:00 ,10266,5,S18_1984 ,Classic Cars ,49,100 ,6203.4
10/16/2004 0:00,10310,4,S24_2972 ,Classic Cars ,33,41.91,1383.03
12/4/2004 0:00 ,10353,4,S700_2834,Planes ,48,68.8 ,3302.4
1/20/2005 0:00 ,10370,8,S12_1666 ,Trucks and Buses,49,100 ,8470.14
```

Our purpose is to sort the rows by product code, and then by sales, in descending order:

1. Create a Transformation, give it a name and description, and save it in a folder of your choice.
2. Using a **Text file input** step, read the file.

To save time, you can copy and paste the step from the original Transformation.

3. Run a preview just to confirm that the step is well configured.
4. Just for simplicity, we will keep only a subset of the fields. So add a **Select values** step to select and reorder the columns as follows: `ORDERDATE`, `PRODUCTLINE`, `PRODUCTCODE`, `QUANTITYORDERED`, `SALES`.
5. From the **Transform** category of steps, add a **Sort rows** step and create a link from the **Select values** step toward this new step.

6. Double-click on the **Sort rows** step and configure it, as shown in the following screenshot:

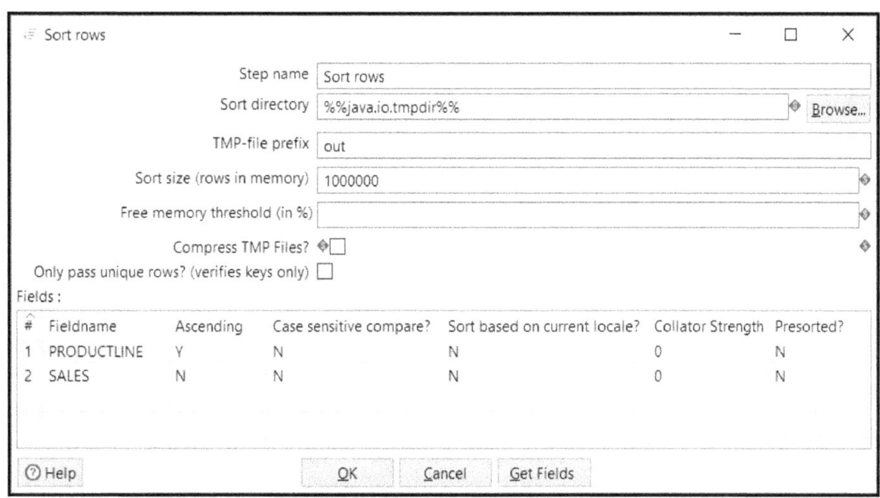

Configuring a Sort rows step

7. Click on **OK**.
8. With the **Sort rows** step selected, run a preview. You should see the rows sorted as expected:

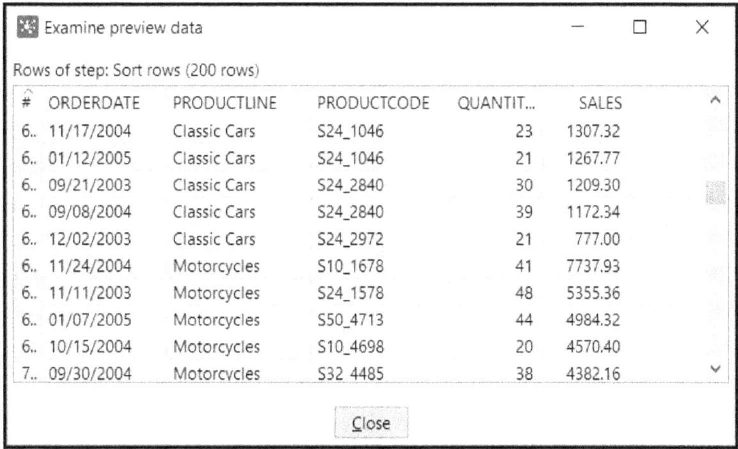

Sorted dataset

Sorting rows is as easy as this. The focus has to be put on the sort settings, which depend both on the size of your dataset and the hardware on which the process will run. For small datasets, the sorting algorithm runs mainly using the JVM memory. When the number of rows exceeds the specified sort size, it works differently. Suppose that you put `5000` as the value of the **Sort size** field. Every 5,000 rows, the process sorts the rows and writes them to a temporary file. When there are no more rows, it does a merge sort on all of those files and gives you back the sorted dataset. You can conclude that for huge datasets, a lot of reading and writing operations are done on your disk, which slows down the whole Transformation.

To avoid this, you can change the number of rows in memory (one million by default) by setting a new value in the **Sort size (rows in memory)** textbox. The bigger this number, the faster the sorting process. In summary, the amount of memory allocated to the process will offset the speed gained, and as soon as the JVM starts using swap space, the performance will degrade.

Note that a **Sort size** that works in your system may not work on a machine with a different configuration. To avoid this risk, you can use a different approach. In the **Sort rows** configuration window, you can set a **Free memory threshold (in %)** value. The process begins to use temporary files when the percentage of available memory drops succeeding the indicated threshold. The lower the percentage, the faster the process.

You cannot, however, just set a small free memory threshold and expect that everything runs fine.

As it is not possible to know the exact amount of free memory, it's not recommended to set a very small free memory threshold. You definitely should not use that option in complex transformation, or when there is more than one sort going on, as you could still run out of memory.

Finally, and before changing the subject, let's briefly explain the **Only pass unique rows? (verifies keys only)** switch. We already experimented with it in `Chapter 7`, *Cleansing, Validating, and Fixing Data*. On that occasion, you had a single field and used the switch to deduplicate. In general, the uniqueness in this step is forced only on a specific list of fields: the fields by which you are sorting. To see it in practice, do the following:

1. In the Transformation, double-click on the **Sort rows** step.
2. Remove the field, `SALES`.
3. Click on the **Only pass unique rows? (verifies keys only)** switch and close the window.
4. Run a preview on the **Sort rows** step. You will see one line per `PRODUCTCODE`.

Note that when there are two or more rows that have identical values for the fields by which you are sorting, only the first is passed to the next step (s).

To remove an entire duplicated line, you should either select all the fields in the **Sort rows** grid or use a **Unique rows** step, as you already learned in `Chapter 7`, *Cleansing, Validating, and Fixing Data.*

Working on groups of rows

Until now, you have been working on individual rows. There are a lot of operations that work on the dataset as a whole. You just learned to sort the dataset, which is a starting point to implement a list of many other operations. The first and one of the most used in this category is the aggregation of data.

Aggregating data

Suppose that you have a list of daily temperatures in a given country over a year. You may want to know the overall average temperature, the average temperature by region, or the coldest day in the year. In this section, you will learn how to solve these calculations with PDI, specifically with the **Group by** step.

The **Group by** step allows you to create groups of rows and calculate new fields over these groups. To understand how to do the aggregations, let's explain it by example. We will continue using the sales Transformation from the first section of the chapter. Now the objective will be as follows—for each pair product line/product code, perform the following:

- Calculate the total sales amount for each product
- Calculate the average sales amount per row (that is, per orderline)
- Count the number of dates in which the product was sold

The first thing that we have to do is decide which field or fields are the keys for the operations. For every combination of values for those fields, PDI will build a new group. Then for each group, it will calculate the aggregations.

Recall that we have (among others) the following fields: `PRODUCTLINE`, `PRODUCTCODE`, `ORDERDATE`, and `SALES`.

In our example, the keys will be the `PRODUCTLINE` and `PRODUCTCODE` fields. Each time the value for any of these fields changes, PDI creates a new group.

After defining the groups, we can define all the aggregations. An aggregation is a new field defined as a function over some of the existent fields. In our example, the aggregations can be defined as follows:

- The total sales amount for each product is the result of applying the `Sum` function over the field, `SALES`
- The average sales amount per row is the result of applying the `Average` function over the field, `SALES`
- The number of dates in which the product was sold is the result of applying the `Number of Distinct Values (N)` function over the field, `ORDERDATE`

In this last example, we cannot use the `Number of Values (N)` function because, if there is more than one sale for the same product on a given date, we would count the same date several times, which is clearly wrong.

Now that we have in mind what we want as a final result, we can translate that into a Transformation. The following step-by-step instructions show you how to do it:

1. Create a new Transformation and read the sale data. Either start from scratch or copy/paste the **Text file input** step from any of the transformations where you used it.
2. Do a preview just to confirm that the step is well configured.
3. In order to calculate the aggregations correctly, we also need to sort the data by those keys. After the input step, add a **Sort rows** step and use it to sort the dataset by the key fields, `PRODUCTLINE` and `PRODUCTCODE`, in ascending order.
4. Expand the **Statistics** category of steps and drag a **Group by** step to the work area. Create a hop from the **Sort rows** step to this new step.
5. Double-click on the **Group by** step and fill in the configuration window, as shown in the following screenshot:

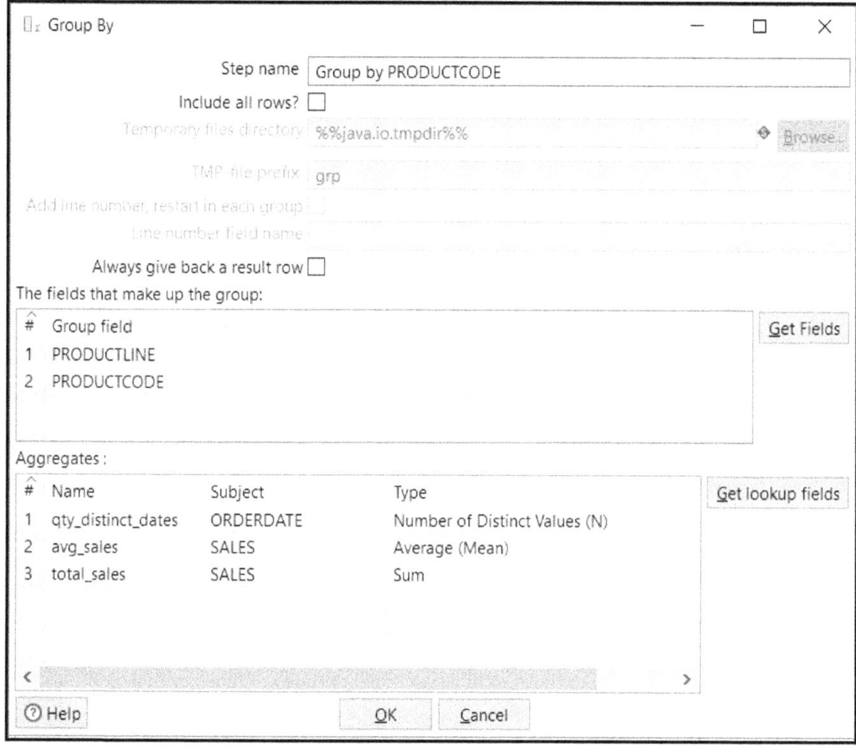

Configuring a Group by step

6. When you click on the **OK** button, a window appears to warn you that this step needs the input to be sorted on the specified keys. Click on **I understand**.
7. Select the **Group by** and the **Sort rows** steps. We will preview the output of both steps.
8. Click the **Preview** button, and then click on **Quick Launch**. The following window appears:

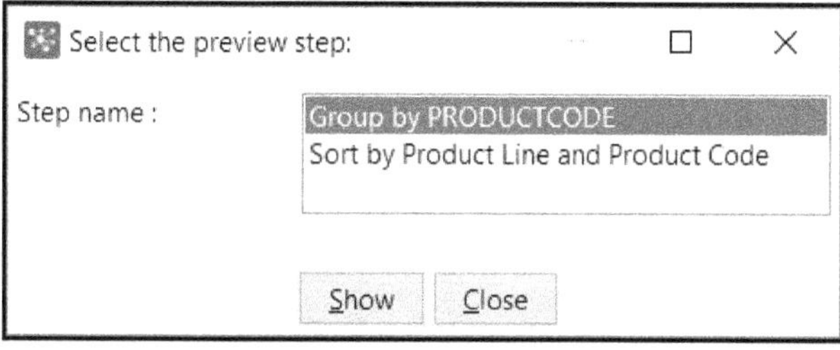

Previewing more than one step output

9. Double-click on the **Sort rows** option. A window appears with the data coming out of the **Sort rows** step:

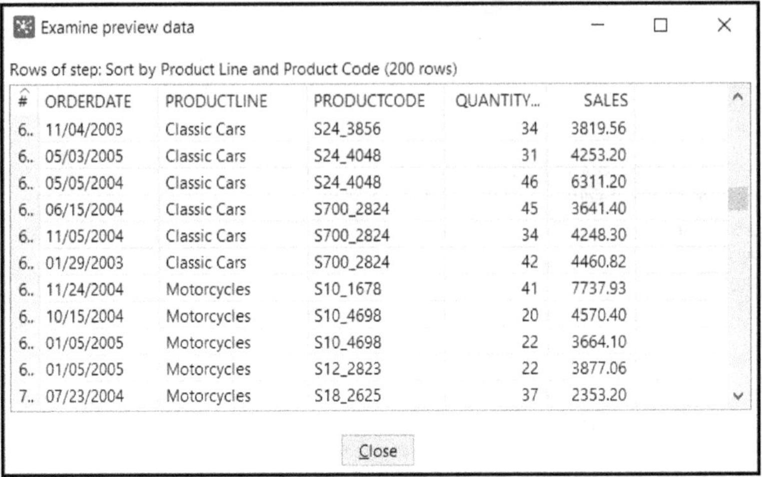

Examine preview data

Rows of step: Sort by Product Line and Product Code (200 rows)

#	ORDERDATE	PRODUCTLINE	PRODUCTCODE	QUANTITY...	SALES
6..	11/04/2003	Classic Cars	S24_3856	34	3819.56
6..	05/03/2005	Classic Cars	S24_4048	31	4253.20
6..	05/05/2004	Classic Cars	S24_4048	46	6311.20
6..	06/15/2004	Classic Cars	S700_2824	45	3641.40
6..	11/05/2004	Classic Cars	S700_2824	34	4248.30
6..	01/29/2003	Classic Cars	S700_2824	42	4460.82
6..	11/24/2004	Motorcycles	S10_1678	41	7737.93
6..	10/15/2004	Motorcycles	S10_4698	20	4570.40
6..	01/05/2005	Motorcycles	S10_4698	22	3664.10
6..	01/05/2005	Motorcycles	S12_2823	22	3877.06
7..	07/23/2004	Motorcycles	S18_2625	37	2353.20

Close

Sort rows output

10. Double-click on the **Group by** option. A window appears with the data coming out of the **Group by** step:

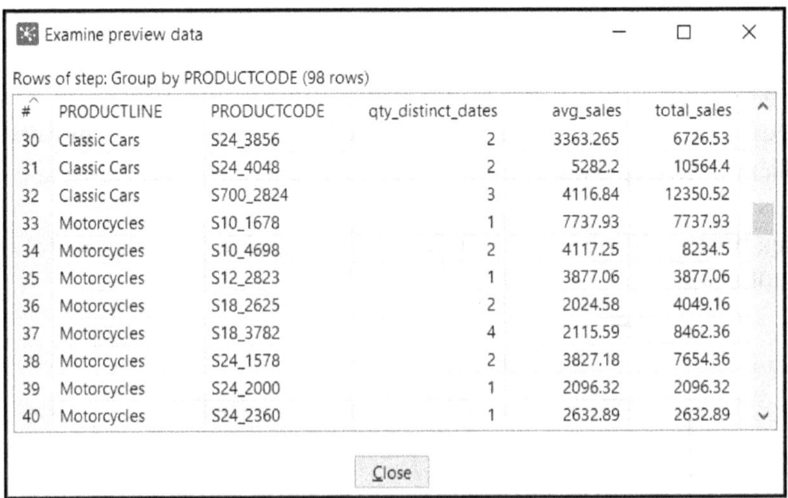

Examine preview data

Rows of step: Group by PRODUCTCODE (98 rows)

#	PRODUCTLINE	PRODUCTCODE	qty_distinct_dates	avg_sales	total_sales
30	Classic Cars	S24_3856	2	3363.265	6726.53
31	Classic Cars	S24_4048	2	5282.2	10564.4
32	Classic Cars	S700_2824	3	4116.84	12350.52
33	Motorcycles	S10_1678	1	7737.93	7737.93
34	Motorcycles	S10_4698	2	4117.25	8234.5
35	Motorcycles	S12_2823	1	3877.06	3877.06
36	Motorcycles	S18_2625	2	2024.58	4049.16
37	Motorcycles	S18_3782	4	2115.59	8462.36
38	Motorcycles	S24_1578	2	3827.18	7654.36
39	Motorcycles	S24_2000	1	2096.32	2096.32
40	Motorcycles	S24_2360	1	2632.89	2632.89

Close

Group by output

11. If you rearrange the preview windows, you can see both preview windows at a time and understand better how the calculations were done.

As you can see in the final preview, the output of the **Group by** step has the new fields with the expected aggregated values. Let's summarize the way in which the **Group by** step works.

The step operates on consecutive rows. It traverses the dataset and each time the value for any of the grouping field changes, it creates a new group. The step works in this way even if the data is not sorted by the grouping field.

As you probably don't know how the data is ordered, it is safer and recommended that you sort the data using a **Sort rows** step just before using a **Group by** step.

There is an alternative for small datasets.

In case you have a small dataset, you can replace the **Group by** step with a **Memory Group by** step. This step processes all rows in memory and doesn't require a sorted dataset.

Regarding the **Aggregates** grid, this is how you interpret its columns:

- **Name** designates the name of the new field, for example, `avg_sales`
- **Subject** is the name of the field that is the base for the aggregation, for example, `SALES`
- **Type** is the kind of aggregate to apply, for example, `Average (Mean)`

Now let's check how the aggregations were calculated for the product line, `Classic Cars`, and product code, `S10_4962`, just to pick an example. There are four rows in this group. For these rows, PDI calculated the following:

- `avg_sales`: The average amount of sales: `(3347.74 + 5362.83 + 4033.38 + 6678.00) / 4` = `4855.5`
- `total_sales`: The total amount of sales: `3347.74 + 5362.83 + 4033.38 + 6678.00` = `19422`
- `qty_distinct_dates`: The quantity of distinct dates in which this product was sold: There were `4` (`05/28/2003`, `11/06/2003`, `06/15/2004`, `10/22/2004`)

The same calculations were made for every group. You can verify the details by looking at the preview windows shown earlier.

In this example, we just used three of the available functions. If you look at the drop-down list in the **Group by** configuration window, you will see many more options. Among these, there are a couple that deserve a particular explanation:

- **Concatenate strings separated by** concatenates the values of the **Subject** field and separates them by a comma. If you want to do the same but use a different separator, you can select **Concatenate strings separated by** (the option without the comma) and under the **Value** column, type the separator of your choice.
- **Number of rows (without field argument)** returns the number of rows in the group. There is no need to put anything under the **Subject** column when you use this function.

Finally, you have the option to calculate aggregate functions over the whole dataset. You do this by leaving the upper grid blank. Following with the same example, you could calculate the same aggregations over all the rows. Just leave the upper grid empty and run a preview; you get the following:

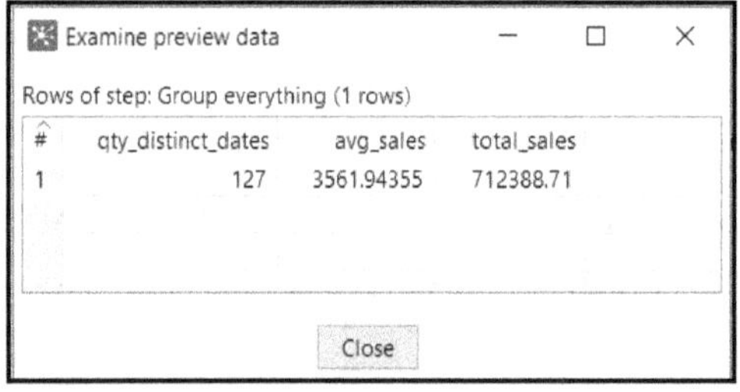

Aggregating without defining groups

Now go back to the original example with the aggregations by `PRODUCTLINE` and `PRODUCTCODE`. Look at the **Step Metrics** tab in the **Execution Results** window:

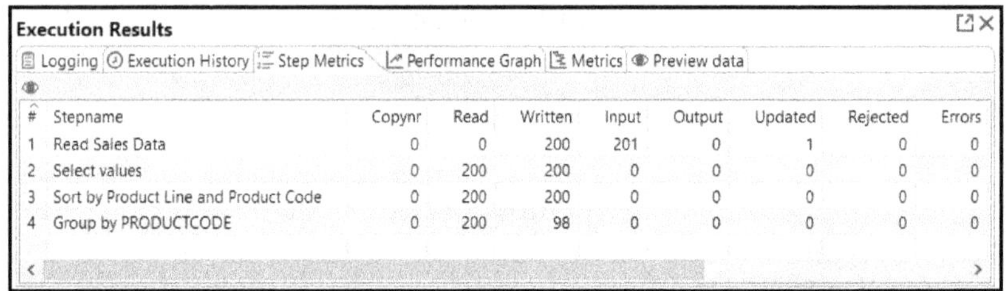

Step Metrics after grouping rows

Note that **200** rows came into the **Group by** step and only **98** came out of that step. This is because after the grouping, you no longer have the details of the sales but the aggregated information. The output of the **Group by** step is your new data now: one row for every group.

In general, as a result of the **Group by** step, you will no longer have the detailed rows unless you check the **Include all rows?** checkbox. The following screenshot shows a sample preview of the data after selecting this checkbox:

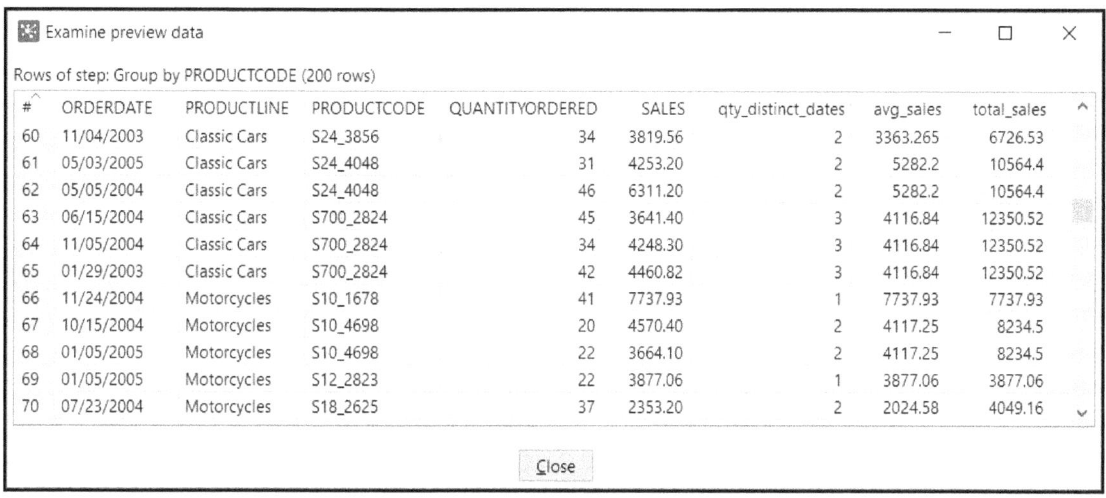

Examine preview data

Rows of step: Group by PRODUCTCODE (200 rows)

#	ORDERDATE	PRODUCTLINE	PRODUCTCODE	QUANTITYORDERED	SALES	qty_distinct_dates	avg_sales	total_sales
60	11/04/2003	Classic Cars	S24_3856	34	3819.56	2	3363.265	6726.53
61	05/03/2005	Classic Cars	S24_4048	31	4253.20	2	5282.2	10564.4
62	05/05/2004	Classic Cars	S24_4048	46	6311.20	2	5282.2	10564.4
63	06/15/2004	Classic Cars	S700_2824	45	3641.40	3	4116.84	12350.52
64	11/05/2004	Classic Cars	S700_2824	34	4248.30	3	4116.84	12350.52
65	01/29/2003	Classic Cars	S700_2824	42	4460.82	3	4116.84	12350.52
66	11/24/2004	Motorcycles	S10_1678	41	7737.93	1	7737.93	7737.93
67	10/15/2004	Motorcycles	S10_4698	20	4570.40	2	4117.25	8234.5
68	01/05/2005	Motorcycles	S10_4698	22	3664.10	2	4117.25	8234.5
69	01/05/2005	Motorcycles	S12_2823	22	3877.06	1	3877.06	3877.06
70	07/23/2004	Motorcycles	S18_2625	37	2353.20	2	2024.58	4049.16

Close

Previewing the result of a Group by step including all rows

Summarizing the PDI steps that operate on sets of rows

Sorting and grouping a dataset are just two of several operations that you can apply to the set of rows as a whole, rather than to single rows. The following table gives you an overview of the main PDI steps that fall into this particular group of steps:

Step	Purpose
Group by	Builds aggregates as `Sum`, `Maximum`, and so on, on groups of rows.
Memory Group by	Same as **Group by**, but doesn't require sorted input.
Analytic Query	Computes lead, lag, first, and last fields over a sorted dataset.

Univariate Statistics	Computes some simple statistics. It complements the **Group by** step. It is much simpler to configure, but has less capabilities than that step.
Split Fields	Splits a single field into more than one. Actually, it doesn't operate on a set of rows, but it's common to use it combined with some of the steps in this table. For example, you could use a **Group by** step to concatenate a field, followed by a **Split Fields** step that splits that concatenated field into several columns.
Row Normaliser	Transforms columns into rows making the dataset more suitable to process.
Row denormaliser	Moves information from rows to columns according to the values of a key field.
Row flattener	Flattens consecutive rows. You could achieve the same using a **Group by** to concatenate the field to flatten, followed by a **Split Field** step.
Sort rows	Sorts rows based upon field values. Alternatively, it can keep only unique rows.
Split field to rows	Splits a single string field and creates a new row for each split term.
Unique rows	Removes double consecutive rows and leaves only unique occurrences.

Many of the steps in the table have a clear purpose and are very easy to use. There are, however, a couple of steps that require an extra explanation. The rest of the chapter is meant to give you more details about them. In particular, you will learn all about the **Row Normalizer**, the **Row denormaliser**, and the **Analytic Query** steps.

For examples that use the steps in the previous table or for more information about them, refer to the PDI steps reference at `https://help.pentaho.com/Documentation/8.0/Products/Data_Integration/Transformation_Step_Reference`.

Converting rows to columns

In most datasets, each row belongs to a different element such as a different sale or a different customer. However, there are datasets where a single row doesn't completely describe one element. Take, for example, the file from `Chapter 8`, *Manipulating Data by Coding*, containing information about houses. Every house was described through several rows. A single row gave incomplete information about the house. The ideal situation would be one in which all the attributes for the house were in a single row. With PDI, you can convert the data to this alternative format.

Converting row data to column data using the Row denormaliser step

The **Row denormaliser** step converts the incoming dataset to a new dataset by moving information from rows to columns according to the values of a key field.

To understand how the **Row denormaliser** works, let's introduce an example. We will work with a file containing a list of French movies of all times. This is how it looks:

```
...
Caché
Year: 2005
Director: Michael Haneke
Cast: Daniel Auteuil, Juliette Binoche, Maurice Bénichou

Jean de Florette
Year: 1986
Genre: Historical drama
Director: Claude Berri
Produced by: Pierre Grunstein
Cast: Yves Montand, Gérard Depardieu, Daniel Auteuil

Le Ballon rouge
Year: 1956
Genre: Fantasy | Comedy | Drama
...
```

In the file, each movie is described through several rows. Our purpose is to have all rows belonging to each movie merged into a single row, that is, we want the information denormalized. This is what we are looking for:

#	film	Year	Genres	Director	Actors
1	Persepolis	2007	Animation | Comedy | Drama | History	Marjane Satrapi	Chiara Mastroianni, Catherine Deneuve, Danielle D
2	Trois couleurs - Rouge	1994	Drama	Krzysztof Kieslowski	Irène Jacob, Jean-Louis Trintignant, Frédérique Fed
3	Les Misérables	1933	Drama | History	Raymond Bernard	
4	Au revoir, les enfants	1987	Drama	Louis Malle	
5	La France	2007	Drama | Musical | Romance | War	Serge Bozon	Sylvie Testud, Pascal Greggory, Guillaume Verdier
6	L'Atalante	1934	Drama | Romance	n/a	Michel Simon, Dita Parlo, Jean Dasté
7	La môme	2007	Biography | Drama | Music	Olivier Dahan	Marion Cotillard, Sylvie Testud, Pascal Greggory, E
8	MR 73	2008	Crime | Drama	n/a	Daniel Auteuil, Olivia Bonamy, Catherine Marchal,
9	Manon Des Sources		Drama | Romance	Claude Berri	Yves Montand, Daniel Auteuil, Emmanuelle Béart
10	Un Coeur en Hiver	1992	Drama | Romance | Music	Claude Sautet	Daniel Auteuil, Emmanuelle Béart, André Dussollie

Denormalized data

Before explaining how to denormalize, let's read the file into a new Transformation:

1. Download the `movies.txt` file from the book's website.
2. Create a Transformation and read the file with a **Text file input** step.
3. In the **Content** tab of the **Text file input** configuration step, put : as a separator. Also, uncheck the **Header** and **No empty rows** options.
4. In the **Fields** tab, enter two string fields: `feature` and `description`. Preview the input file to see if it is well configured. You should see two columns: `feature` with the text to the left of the semicolons and `description` with the text to the right.
5. Now we will create a field to identify the films. Add a **JavaScript** step, create a hop from the **Text file input** step toward this, and edit this new step. Type the following code:

```
var film;

if (getProcessCount('r') == 1) film = '';

if (feature == null)
    film = '';
else if (film == '')
    film = feature;
```

The previous code is similar to the one we created for the file about houses in the previous chapter. To understand how it works, refer to `Chapter 8`, *Manipulating Data by Coding*.

6. Click on the **Get Variables** button to add the `film` field to the dataset.
7. Close the window.
8. After the **Javascript** step, add a **Filter rows** step with the condition, `description IS NOT NULL`.
9. With the **Filter rows** selected, run a preview. This is what you should see:

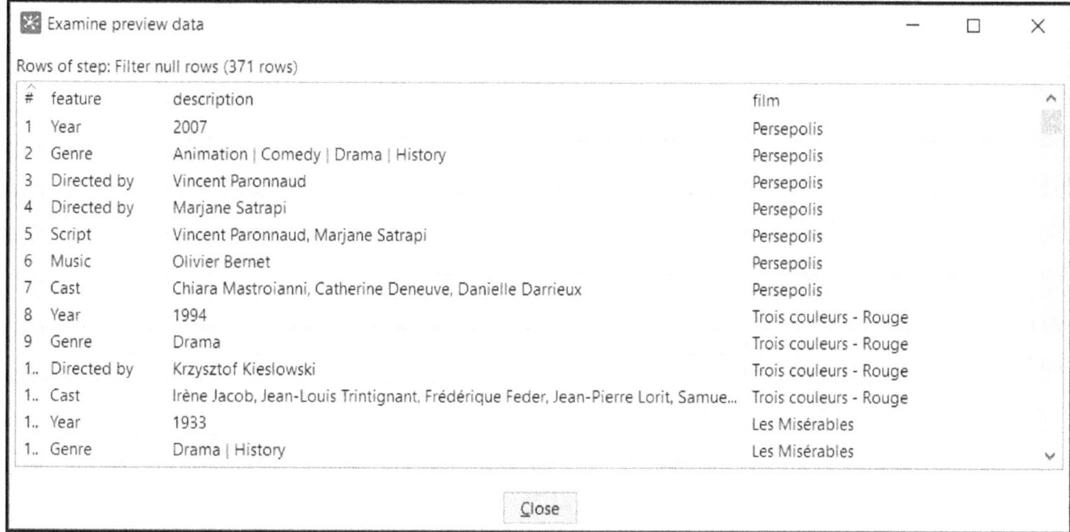

Reading information about films

Now that you have read the file, you can start thinking of denormalizing. To tell PDI how to combine a group of rows into a single one, there are three things you have to think about. They are as follows:

- Among the input fields, there must be a **key field**. Depending on the value of this key field, you decide how the new fields will be filled. In your example, the key field is `feature`. Depending on the value of the `feature` column, you will send the value of the `description` field to some of the new fields: `Year`, `Genres`, `Director`, or `Actors`.

- You have to group the rows together to form a related set of data. Each set of related data will eventually become a single row. The way you group will depend on the value of one or more fields. In our example, that field is `film`. All rows with the same value for the `film` field will become a single row.
- Decide the rules that have to be applied in order to fill in the new target fields. All rules follow this pattern: If the value for the key field is equal to A, put the value of the field B into the new field C. A sample rule could be: if the value for the field feature (our key field) is equal to Directed by, put the value of the field description into the new field Director.

Once you have these three things clear, all you have to do is fill in the **Row Denormaliser** configuration window to tell PDI how to do this task. This is the purpose of the next steps:

1. After the **Filter rows** step, add a **Row Denormaliser** step. You can find it under the **Transform** category. When asked for the kind of hop leaving the **Filter row** step, choose **Main output of step**.
2. Double-click on the step and fill in its fields, as shown in the following screenshot:

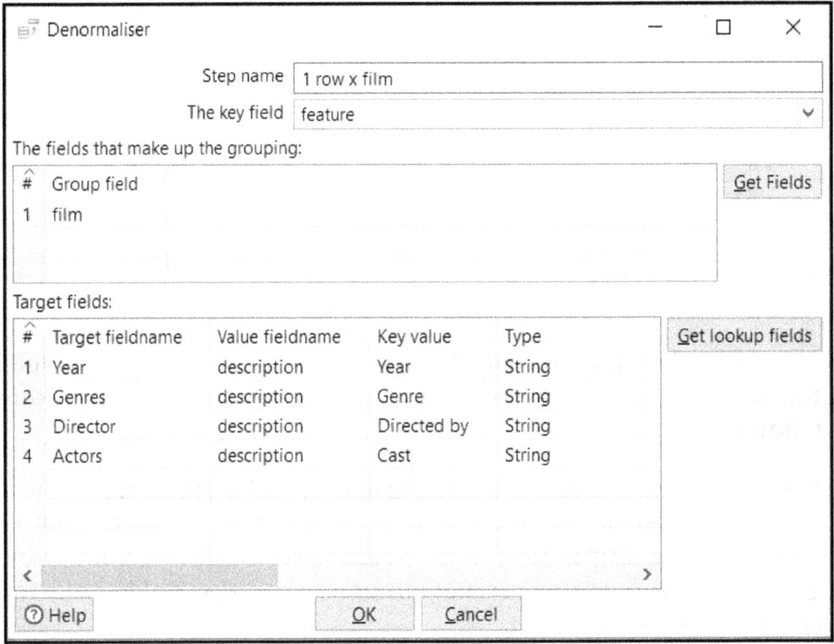

Configuring a Row Nenormaliser step

When closing the window, a warning window appears telling that the rows must be sorted. Our data is already sorted by the key field. If it wasn't, we should have sorted the rows before denormalizing.

3. With this last step selected, run a preview. The result is like the following, as expected:

#	film	Year	Genres	Director	Actors
1	Persepolis	2007	Animation | Comedy | Drama | History	Marjane Satrapi	Chiara Mastroianni, Catherine Deneuve, [
2	Trois couleurs - Rouge	1994	Drama	Krzysztof Kieslowski	Irène Jacob, Jean-Louis Trintignant, Frédé
3	Les Misérables	1933	Drama | History	Raymond Bernard	<null>
4	Au revoir, les enfants	1987	Drama	Louis Malle	<null>
5	La France	2007	Drama | Musical | Romance | War	Serge Bozon	Sylvie Testud, Pascal Greggory, Guillaume
6	L'Atalante	1934	Drama | Romance	<null>	Michel Simon, Dita Parlo, Jean Dasté
7	La môme	2007	Biography | Drama | Music	Olivier Dahan	Marion Cotillard, Sylvie Testud, Pascal Gr
8	MR 73	2008	Crime | Drama	<null>	Daniel Auteuil, Olivia Bonamy, Catherine
9	Manon Des Sources	<null>	Drama | Romance	Claude Berri	Yves Montand, Daniel Auteuil, Emmanue
1..	Un Coeur en Hiver	1992	Drama | Romance | Music	Claude Sautet	Daniel Auteuil, Emmanuelle Béart, André

Denormalized data

After denormalizing, some of the new fields remain with null values. You could replace the nulls with a default value using an **If field value is null** step from the **Utility** category of steps.

The configuration of the **Row denormaliser** step may seem a bit confusing at the beginning, so let's explain it by example. The selection of a key field is simple. As explained earlier, depending on the value of the key field (`feature` in our case), we will decide how to fill in the new fields. Then you have the group field (s). These fields (in our example, just `film`) define the group of rows that will be converted to a single row.

Once we have the key field and the group field (s) defined, the trick here is to define the new fields correctly. Suppose that you want a new field with the director of the film. Technically speaking, you want to implement the following rule:

> *If the value for the field feature (our key field) is equal to Directed by, put the value of the field description into the new field Director.*

To put this rule in the lower grid of the **Row denormaliser** window, you have to fill in the fields as follows:

- **Key value**: `Directed by`
- **Value fieldname**: `description`
- **Target fieldname**: `Director`

For every rule, you must fill in a different row in the target fields' grid.

Let's see how the row denormaliser works for the following sample rows:

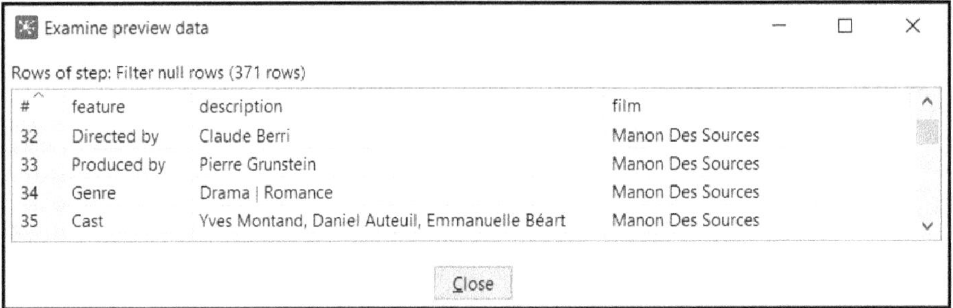

Examine preview data

Rows of step: Filter null rows (371 rows)

#	feature	description	film
32	Directed by	Claude Berri	Manon Des Sources
33	Produced by	Pierre Grunstein	Manon Des Sources
34	Genre	Drama | Romance	Manon Des Sources
35	Cast	Yves Montand, Daniel Auteuil, Emmanuelle Béart	Manon Des Sources

Close

Sample data for denormalizing

First of all, PDI creates an output row for the film, `Manon Des Sources` (which is the key value). Then, it processes every row looking for values to fill the new fields: `Year`, `Genres`, `Director`, and `Actors`.

If we look at the first row of data, we see that the value for the key field `feature` is `Directed by`. In the **Target fields** grid, PDI looks for an entry where `Key value` is `Directed by`:

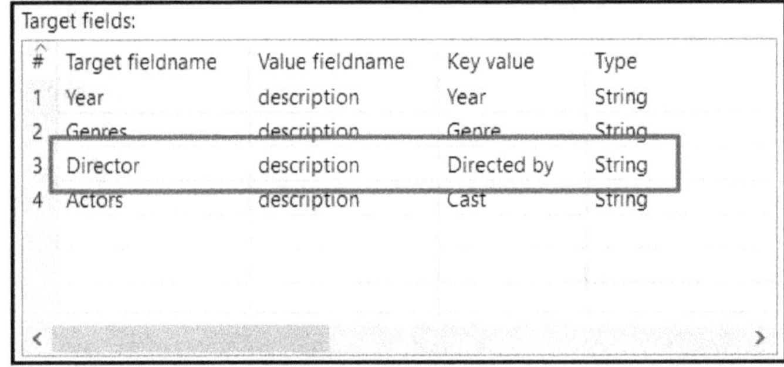

Target fields:

#	Target fieldname	Value fieldname	Key value	Type
1	Year	description	Year	String
2	Genres	description	Genre	String
3	Director	description	Directed by	String
4	Actors	description	Cast	String

Looking for a Key value

Then, it puts the value of the `description` field as the content for the target field `Director`. The output row is now as follows:

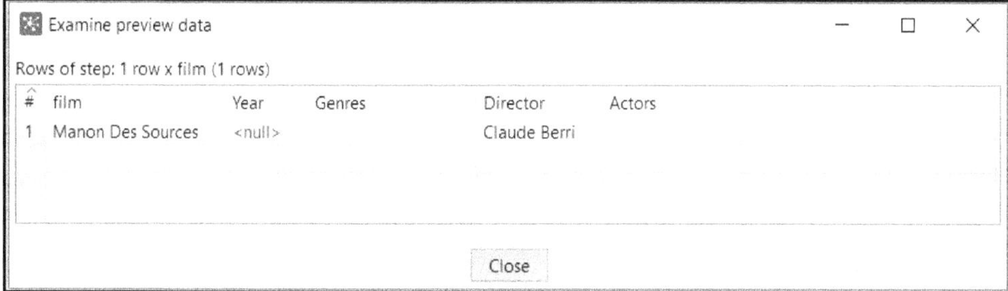

Denormalized field

Now, take the second row. The value for the key field `feature` is `Produced by`.

PDI searches in the **Target fields** grid to see if there is an entry where `Key value` is `Produced by`. It doesn't find this and the information for this source row is discarded.

The following screenshot shows the rule applied to the third sample row. It also shows how the final output row looks:

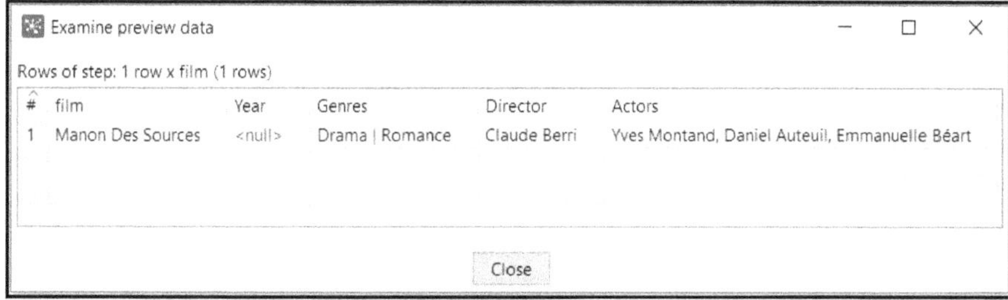

Sample denormalized data

Note that it is not mandatory that the rows will be present for every key value entered in the target fields' grid. If an entry in the grid is not used, the target field is created anyway, but it remains empty. In this sample film, the year was not present, hence the `Year` field remained empty.

If you want to practice more, you can take the file with data about houses and create a Transformation that denormalizes the data, generating one row per house. As examples for the new fields, you could have: `style_of_house`, `fireplace`(yes/no), `qty_bathrooms`, or `qty_bedrooms`.

Aggregating data with a Row Denormaliser step

In the previous section, you learned how to use the **Row Denormaliser** step to combine several rows into one. This step can also be used to generate a new dataset with aggregated or consolidated data. If you take a look at the file with films, you will notice that the first of the films has two directors. However, when we denormalized the data, PDI picked only the first one to fill in the `Directed by` field. By aggregating fields, we can easily fix this situation. Let's modify the Transformation that you created earlier and do a couple of modifications: we will fill in the `Directed by` field with the list of directors and we will create a new field with the number of directors for each film:

1. Open the Transformation created before and save it with a different name.
2. Double-click on the **Row Denormaliser** step and modify its content as follows:

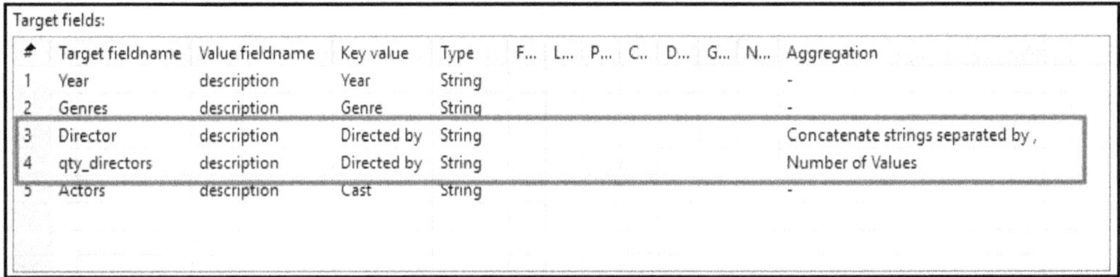

Target fields:

#	Target fieldname	Value fieldname	Key value	Type	F...	L...	P...	C..	D...	G...	N...	Aggregation
1	Year	description	Year	String								-
2	Genres	description	Genre	String								-
3	Director	description	Directed by	String								Concatenate strings separated by ,
4	qty_directors	description	Directed by	String								Number of Values
5	Actors	description	Cast	String								-

Aggregating data while denormalizing

3. Close the window and run a preview. You will see this:

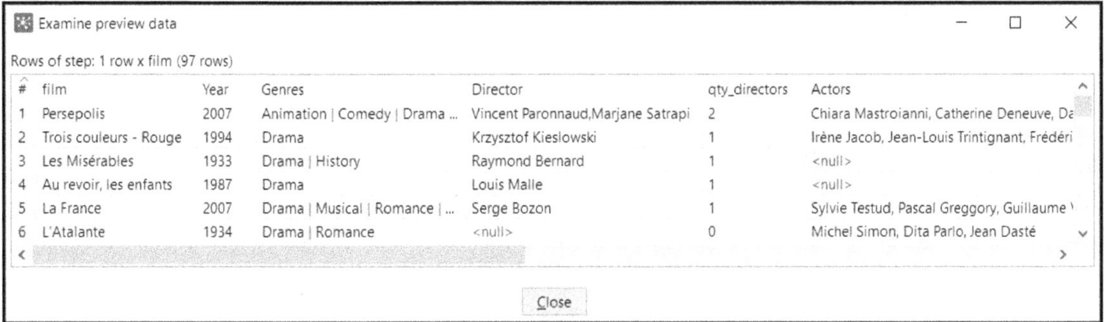

#	film	Year	Genres	Director	qty_directors	Actors
1	Persepolis	2007	Animation | Comedy | Drama ...	Vincent Paronnaud,Marjane Satrapi	2	Chiara Mastroianni, Catherine Deneuve, Da
2	Trois couleurs - Rouge	1994	Drama	Krzysztof Kieslowski	1	Irène Jacob, Jean-Louis Trintignant, Frédéri
3	Les Misérables	1933	Drama | History	Raymond Bernard	1	<null>
4	Au revoir, les enfants	1987	Drama	Louis Malle	1	<null>
5	La France	2007	Drama | Musical | Romance | ...	Serge Bozon	1	Sylvie Testud, Pascal Greggory, Guillaume
6	L'Atalante	1934	Drama | Romance	<null>	0	Michel Simon, Dita Parlo, Jean Dasté

Denormalizing using aggregate functions

The novelty here compared with the previous version is the **aggregation** of values, that is, the combination of measures using different operations. In this case, you grouped the directors using the aggregation, **Concatenate strings separated by,** and calculated the number of directors using the aggregation, **Number of Values**. As you can see, these are just two of several possible aggregate functions. When you define aggregations, PDI works like this: if more than one row in the group matches the value for the key field, the new output field is calculated as the result of applying the aggregate function to all the values. Note that the aggregate functions available are a subset of those in the **Group by** step.

Normalizing data

Some datasets are nice to view but complicated for further processing. Take a look at the following information about product sales, aggregated by year and product line:

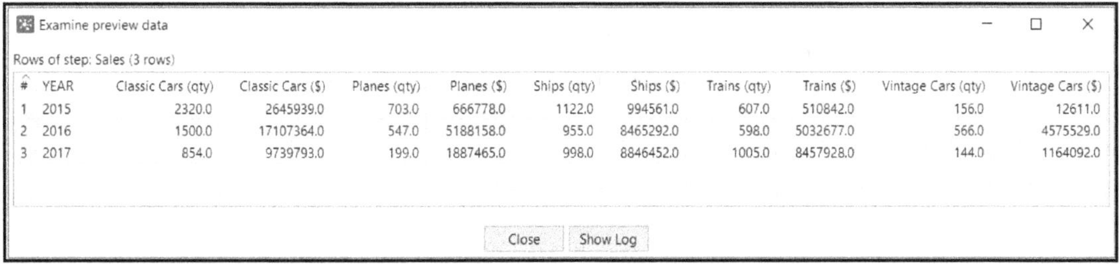

#	YEAR	Classic Cars (qty)	Classic Cars ($)	Planes (qty)	Planes ($)	Ships (qty)	Ships ($)	Trains (qty)	Trains ($)	Vintage Cars (qty)	Vintage Cars ($)
1	2015	2320.0	2645939.0	703.0	666778.0	1122.0	994561.0	607.0	510842.0	156.0	12611.0
2	2016	1500.0	17107364.0	547.0	5188158.0	955.0	8465292.0	598.0	5032677.0	566.0	4575529.0
3	2017	854.0	9739793.0	199.0	1887465.0	998.0	8846452.0	1005.0	8457928.0	144.0	1164092.0

Product sales

Suppose that you want to answer the following questions:

- Which product line was the best sold?
- How many cars did you sell (including Classic and Vintage)?
- Which is the average price per product sold?

The dataset is not prepared to answer these questions, at least in an easy way. In order to simplify the task, you will have to normalize the data first, that is, convert it to a suitable format before proceeding. The next subsection explains how to do that.

Modifying the dataset with a Row Normaliser step

The **Row Normaliser** step takes a pivoted dataset and normalizes the data. In simple words, it converts columns to rows. In order to explain how to use and configure the step, we will normalize the data shown earlier. Our purpose, in this case, will be to have something like this:

#	YEAR	product_line	qty	amount
1	2015	Cars	2320,0	264593,9
2	2015	Planes	703,0	66677,8
3	2015	Ships	1122,0	99456,1
4	2015	Trains	607,0	51084,2
5	2016	Cars	1500,0	171073,64
6	2016	Planes	547,0	51881,58
7	2016	Ships	955,0	84652,92
8	2016	Trains	598,0	50326,77
9	2017	Cars	854,0	97397,93
10	2017	Planes	199,0	18874,65
11	2017	Ships	998,0	88464,52
12	2017	Trains	1005,0	84579,28

Product sales normalized

First of all, let's prepare the source data:

1. Create a Transformation and use a **Data Grid** to enter the data as shown in the example.

You can save time by downloading the sample Transformation from the book's site.

2. Run a preview to make sure the input is well configured.

Taking into account the final result, configuring the step it is just a matter of creating a correspondence between the old columns and rows, and the new ones. This is how we do it:

1. First of all, we should identify the desired new fields. In our example, the new fields are `qty` and `amount`.
2. We should also define a classification that will allow us to map the old columns into the new rows. In our example, we will classify the data into `Cars`, `Planes`, `Ships`, and `Trains`. Each of these elements (that PDI calls *Types*) will group one or more of the old columns. As an example, the `Plane` type will group the values for `Planes (qty)` and `Planes ($)`. The `Cars` type will group the values for `Classic Cars (qty)`, `Classic Cars ($)`, `Vintage Cars (qty)`, and `Vintage Cars ($)`.
3. Now we have to define the correspondence between the old fields and the new ones. For example, the old value or `Classic Cars (qty)` will be stored under the new `qty` column in a row with the `Cars` type.

With all these concepts clear, we are now able to configure the **Row Normaliser** step, whose configuration window looks as follows:

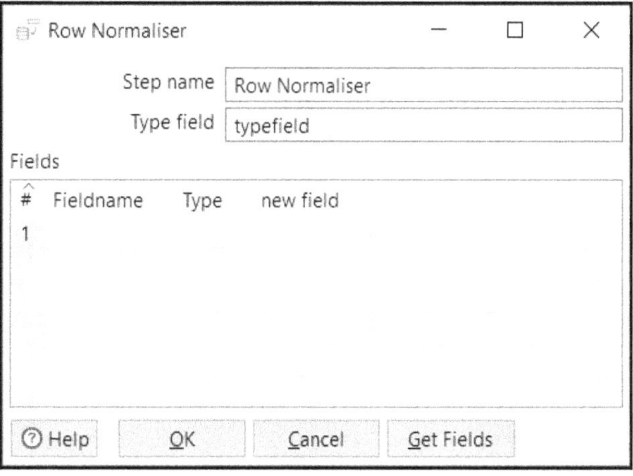

Row Normaliser configuration window

As **Type field**, you type the name of the field that will contain the type; in our example, the name of the **Type field** will be `product_line` and will contain the values Cars, Planes, and so on.

To fill in the grid, think of how you want to create the new dataset, for example, as you want the `Classic Cars (qty)` value to be classified as `Cars` and stored in a column named `qty`, you will fill in a row with the following:

- **Fieldname**: `Classic Cars (qty)`
- **Type**: `Cars`
- **new field**: `qty`

In general, for each column to be normalized, you add one row to the grid and fill the row as follows:

- **Fieldname**: The name of the old column that contains the value mentioned
- **Type**: The category under which you will classify the value
- **new field**: The name of the field that will contain the value

Now you are ready to complete the work:

1. From the **Transform** category of steps, drag a **Row Normaliser** step to the work area.
2. Create a hop from the last step to this new one.
3. Double-click on the **Row Normaliser** step to edit it and fill in the window as follows:

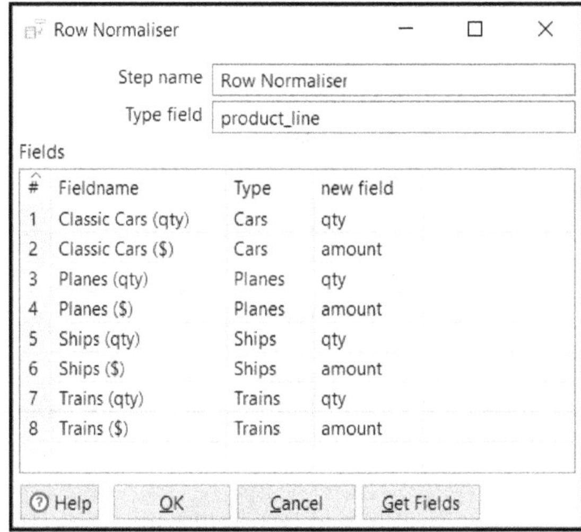

Configuring a Row Normaliser step

4. Close the window and, with the step selected, run a preview. You should see this:

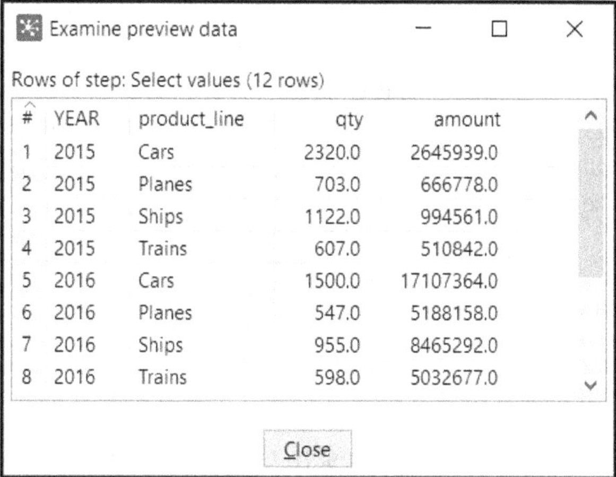
Examine preview data

Rows of step: Select values (12 rows)

#	YEAR	product_line	qty	amount
1	2015	Cars	2320.0	2645939.0
2	2015	Planes	703.0	666778.0
3	2015	Ships	1122.0	994561.0
4	2015	Trains	607.0	510842.0
5	2016	Cars	1500.0	17107364.0
6	2016	Planes	547.0	5188158.0
7	2016	Ships	955.0	8465292.0
8	2016	Trains	598.0	5032677.0

Close

Normalized data

As you saw, the configuration of the **Row Normaliser** step is quite simple. With the final dataset, it is easy now to answer the questions proposed at the beginning of the section.

There are just a couple of observations about the use and result of using the step:

- The fields not mentioned in the configuration of the **Row Normaliser** (the `YEAR` field in the example) are kept without changes. They are simply duplicated for each new row.
- As shown in the tutorial, there are no restrictions on how many columns are mapped to new types or categories. For example, four columns were mapped to the Cars category, while only two were mapped to the Planes category.

Going forward and backward across rows

Besides the common use cases explained in the previous sections, there are other use cases that work with groups of rows, looking for rows before or after the current one within each group.

Some examples of this are as follows:

- You have a dataset with monthly sales, group by product line. For each product line, you want to calculate the variation of sales from one month to the next.
- You have daily sales and want to infer the number of days without sales. (This is the gap in days between a date and the next in your dataset.)
- You have a dataset with a list of sales amounts and sales commissions. The fields in your dataset are `sales_amount_from`, `sales_amount_to`, and `commission_%`. You detected that there are overlaps in the data:

```
sales_amount_from, sales_amount_to, commission_%
0, 1000, %5
1001, 5000, %15
4500, 9999, %15
```

You want to automatically fix these overlaps. In this case, you want to change the second row to the following:

```
1001, 4499, %15
```

In all these examples, in order to calculate the necessary information, you need the values in rows different from the current one:

- In the first case, in order to calculate the variation in sales for each month, you need the sales value from the previous row (within the same product line)
- In the second example, to calculate the number of days without sales, you need the sales date from either the previous or next row. With that date and the current, you will be able to calculate the days in between them
- In the last example, to fix one row, you need to know the value of the next one

All these examples and many others like these can be solved using the **Analytic Query** step, which is explained in the following sections.

Picking rows backward and forward with the Analytic Query step

The **Analytic Query** step allows us to pick data from different rows in order to combine their values with the values in the current row. To demonstrate how to use this step, we will implement the first of the examples mentioned in the introduction. We have a list of sales by product line and date and want to see how sales evolve through months.

First of all, we will prepare the dataset:

1. Create a new Transformation
2. One more time, we will use our sample file with sales. So read the sample file with a **Text file input** step or copy and paste the step from another Transformation that reads it
3. We have the date on which a product was sold. As we need the month, use a **Select values** step to change the metadata of the date field from **Date** to **String**. As **Format**, type `yyyy-MM`
4. Use another **Select values** step to keep just the fields relevant to this exercise: `PRODUCTLINE`, `MONTH`, and `SALES`
5. With the last step selected, run a preview. You should see this:

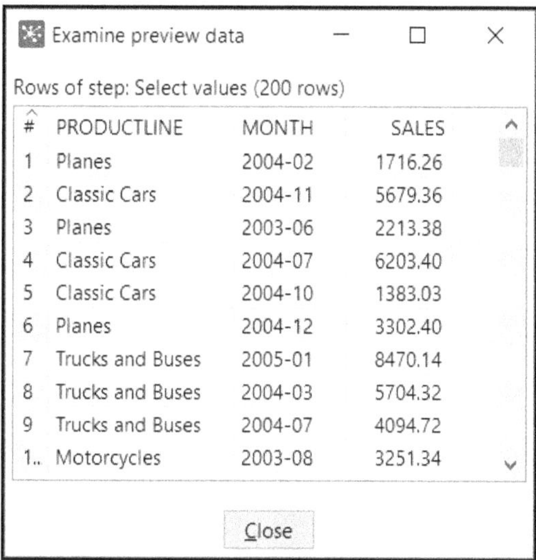

#	PRODUCTLINE	MONTH	SALES
1	Planes	2004-02	1716.26
2	Classic Cars	2004-11	5679.36
3	Planes	2003-06	2213.38
4	Classic Cars	2004-07	6203.40
5	Classic Cars	2004-10	1383.03
6	Planes	2004-12	3302.40
7	Trucks and Buses	2005-01	8470.14
8	Trucks and Buses	2004-03	5704.32
9	Trucks and Buses	2004-07	4094.72
1..	Motorcycles	2003-08	3251.34

Previewing data by product line and month

To compare monthly sales, we need the data already aggregated by month. So we still have one more step to do: grouping and aggregating the information by product line and month.

6. After the last step, add a **Sort rows** step and use it to sort by `PRODUCTLINE` and `MONTH`.

7. After the **Sort rows** step, add a **Group by** step and use it to aggregate the sales. The next screenshot shows you how to fill in the grids in the configuration window:

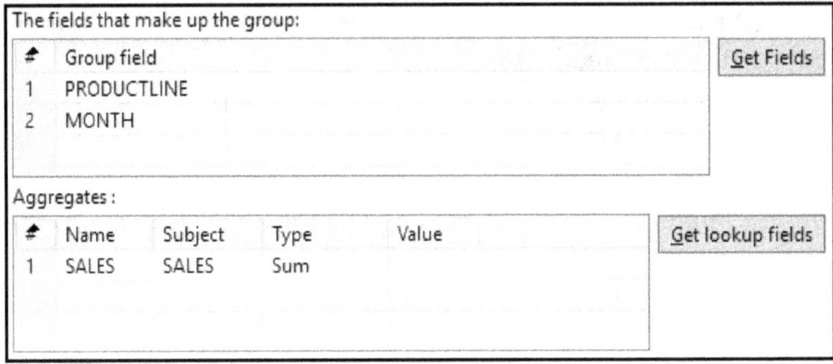

Configuring a Group by step

8. Run a preview of this last step. As you can see in the next screenshot, the data is now suitable to run our calculations:

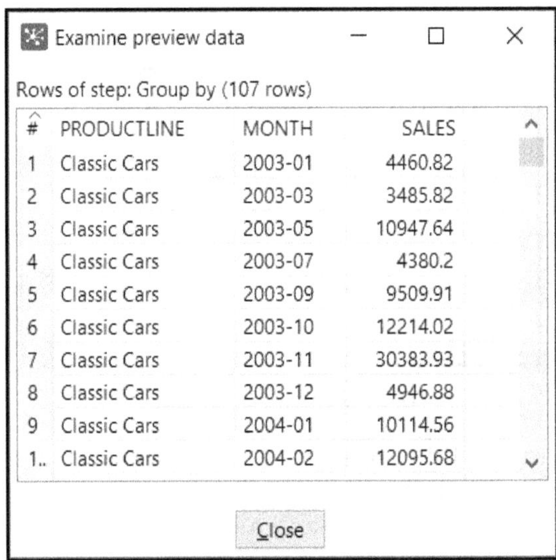

Previewing aggregated data

9. From the **Statistics** category, add an **Analytic Query** step and create a hop from the **Sort rows** step toward this one.

10. Double-click on the step and configure it as follows:

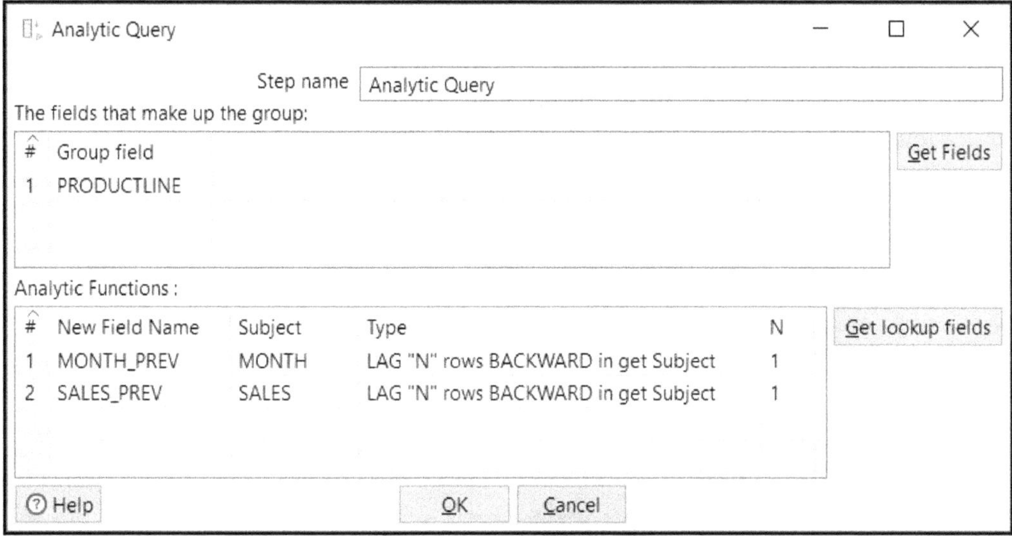

Configuring an Analytic Query step

11. Close the window and run a preview. You will see the following:

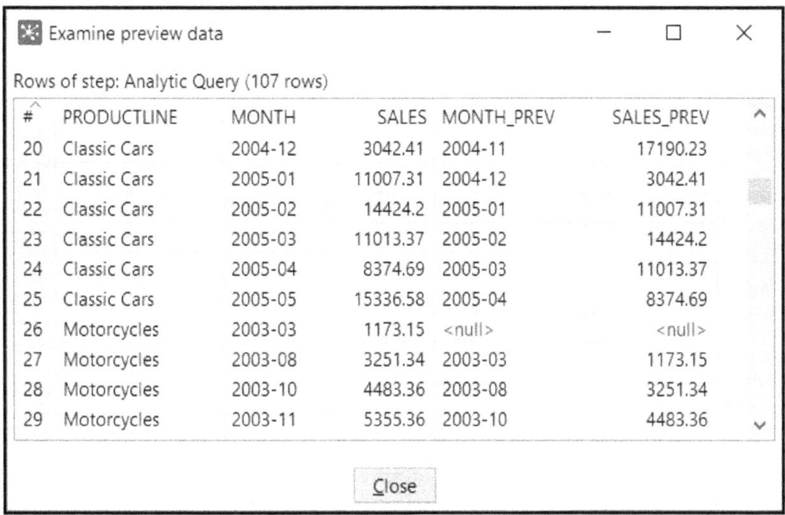

Previewing the result of an Analytic Query step

Now in every row, you have the sales for the current month (`SALES` field) and the sales for the previous one (`SALES_PREV` field). You have all you need to calculate the variation from the sales in the previous month and the current one.

12. As the final step, add a **Calculator** step. Use it to calculate the variation. The following screenshot shows you how to do it:

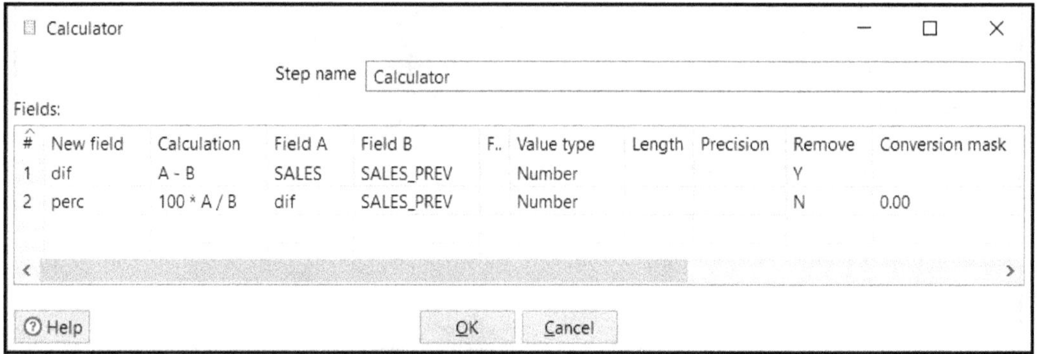

Calculating a variation in sales

13. Run a preview on the **Calculator** to see the final results:

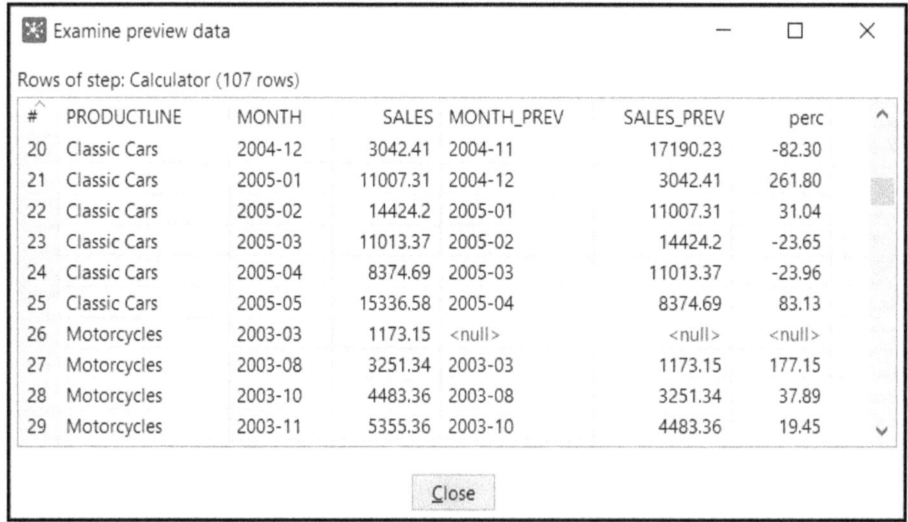

#	PRODUCTLINE	MONTH	SALES	MONTH_PREV	SALES_PREV	perc
20	Classic Cars	2004-12	3042.41	2004-11	17190.23	-82.30
21	Classic Cars	2005-01	11007.31	2004-12	3042.41	261.80
22	Classic Cars	2005-02	14424.2	2005-01	11007.31	31.04
23	Classic Cars	2005-03	11013.37	2005-02	14424.2	-23.65
24	Classic Cars	2005-04	8374.69	2005-03	11013.37	-23.96
25	Classic Cars	2005-05	15336.58	2005-04	8374.69	83.13
26	Motorcycles	2003-03	1173.15	<null>	<null>	<null>
27	Motorcycles	2003-08	3251.34	2003-03	1173.15	177.15
28	Motorcycles	2003-10	4483.36	2003-08	3251.34	37.89
29	Motorcycles	2003-11	5355.36	2003-10	4483.36	19.45

Previewing final data

Now that you saw how the **Analytic Query** step works, let's explain its configuration in detail so that you can adapt it for your own use cases.

In the first grid of the configuration window, you put the fields by which you want to group the data. In this case, the field is `PRODUCTLINE`.

In the second grid, you create the new fields. Each row you add to this grid will contain a value that you get from another row. The rows are defined as follows:

- In the **Type** column, you put one of these two options:
    - **LAG N rows BACKWARD in get Subject** to get a value from `N` rows backward
    - **LAG N rows FORWARD in get Subject** to get a value from `N` rows forward
- In the **Subject** column, you indicate the value to get
- In the column **N,** you tell PDI how many rows to move backward or forward to get the value
- Finally, the **New Field Name** column will give a name to the new fields

A couple of remarks about the step:

- You can leave the first grid empty. This means that you don't want to group the rows. The step will always go backward or forward and bring the asked values without caring about groups.
- When you use the **BACKWARD** option, in the first row or rows within a group, the new fields will have null values. The number of rows with null values will depend on **N**. The same will occur in the last row or rows when you use the **FORWARD** option.

Just a note about our particular example:

In our Transformation, we get the previous row and name it `PREV_MONTH`. Note that if there are months without sales, this will not be strictly the previous month. It's just the previous line in the dataset.

Summary

In this chapter, you learned how to work on groups of rows in very different ways. First of all, you learned to sort, a very simple but useful task. Then you learned to aggregate data obtaining statistics such as sum, count, average, and so on, and also calculating other useful numbers as for example the first or last value in a dataset. After that, you learned to transform your dataset by applying two very useful steps: Row Normaliser and Row denormaliser. They do a great task in quite a simple way. Finally, you used the Analytic Query step to grab and use values in rows different than the current one.

So far, you have been transforming data stored mainly in files. In the next chapter, we will start learning to work with databases, which will enrich a lot of your possibilities in the creation of **Extract**, **Transform**, and **Load** (**ETL**) processes.

10
Performing Basic Operations with Databases

Database systems are the main mechanisms used by most organizations to store and administer organizational data. Online sales, bank-related operations, customer service history, and credit card transactions are some examples of data stored in databases.

This is the first of two chapters fully dedicated to working with databases. Here is a list of the topics that will be covered in this chapter:

- Connecting to a database and exploring its content
- Previewing and getting data from a database
- Inserting, updating, and deleting data
- Verifying a connection, running **Data Definition Language** (DDL) scripts, and other useful tasks
- Looking up data in different ways

Connecting to a database and exploring its content

Before interacting with a database in PDI, you need to prepare the environment. In the next sections, you will learn to create a connection to a database and explore the database from within Spoon.

For demonstration purposes, we will work with PostgreSQL, but with minor changes, you should be able to reproduce the same exercises with any other RDBMS engine. Also, the examples will be based on Pagila. **Pagila** is the PostgreSQL version of the **Sakila** database and represents the business processes of a DVD rental store.

Connecting with Relational Database Management Systems

PDI has the ability to connect to both commercial RDBMS such as Oracle or MS SQL Server, and free RDBMS such as MySQL or PostgreSQL. In order to interact with a particular database, you have to define a connection to it. A PDI database connection describes all the parameters needed to connect PDI to a database. To create a connection, you must give the connection a name and at least fill in the general settings as follows:

Setting	Description
Connection Type	Type of database system: HSQLDB, Oracle, MySQL, Firebird, and so on.
Method of access	Native (JDBC), ODBC, JNDI, or OCI. The available options depend on the type of database.
Host name	Name or IP address for the host where the database is located.
Database name	Identifies the database to which you want to connect.
Port number	PDI sets as default the most usual port number for the selected type of DB. You can change it, of course.
User Name/Password	Name of the user and password to connect to the database.

Besides, PDI also needs the correspondent JDBC driver. As Pentaho cannot redistribute some third-party database drivers due to licensing restrictions, you may have to execute some manual installation:

1. Open the `lib` directory inside the PDI installation folder and verify if a driver—a JAR file—for your database engine is already present. If there is one, skip the following instructions unless you want to replace it with a newer version.
2. Download a JDBC driver from your database vendor or a third-party driver developer.
3. Copy the JDBC driver to the `lib` directory.
4. Restart Spoon.

Once you have the driver installed, you will be able to create the connection. As an example, the following instructions explain how to connect to the Pagila database installed on a local server:

1. Open Spoon and create a new Transformation.
2. In the upper-left corner of the screen, click on **View**.
3. Right-click on the **Database connections** option and click on **New**.
4. Fill in the **Database Connection** dialog window with the proper settings. The following screenshot shows the settings for the sample database:

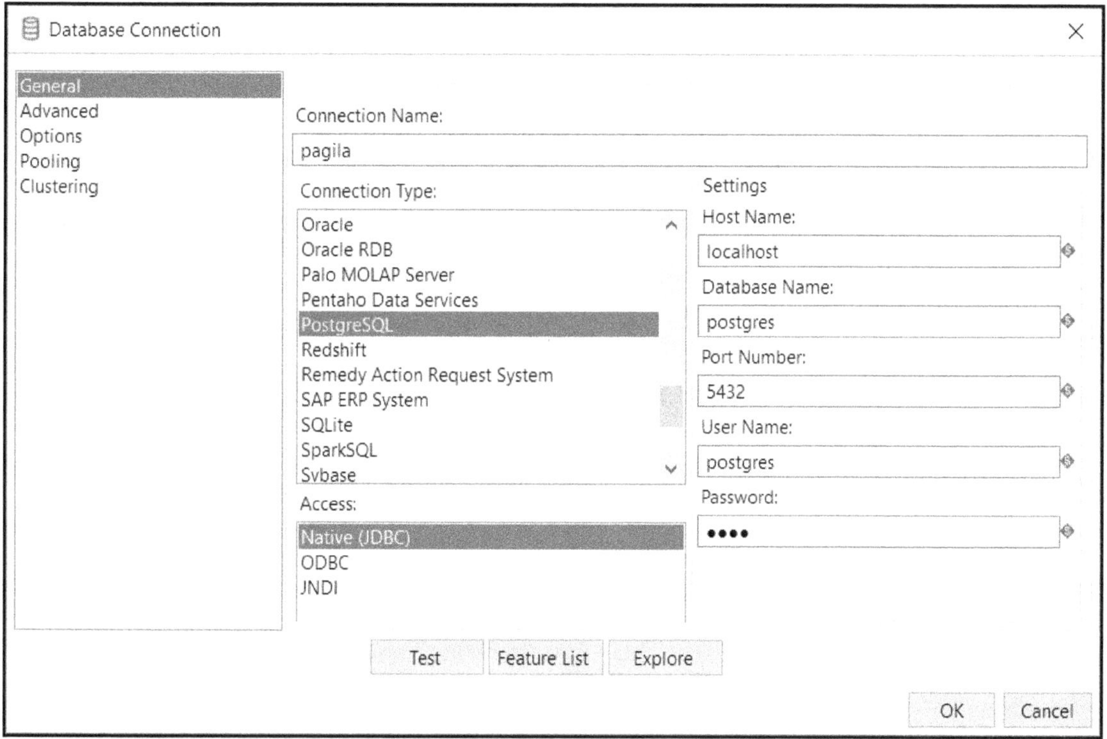

Configuring a database connection

5. Click on the **Test** button. If everything was correct, the following window will show up:

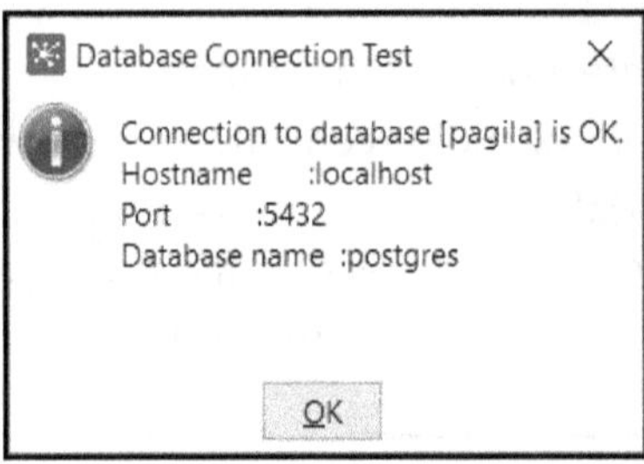

Database connected

If you get an error message instead of this, recheck the data that you entered in the connection window. Also, verify that the database is running.

6. Click on **OK** to close the **Test** window, and click on **OK** again to close the database definition window. A new database connection named `pagila` is added to the tree.
7. Right-click on the created database connection and click on **Share** so that the connection is available in all transformations or jobs you create from now on. The shared connections are shown in bold letters:

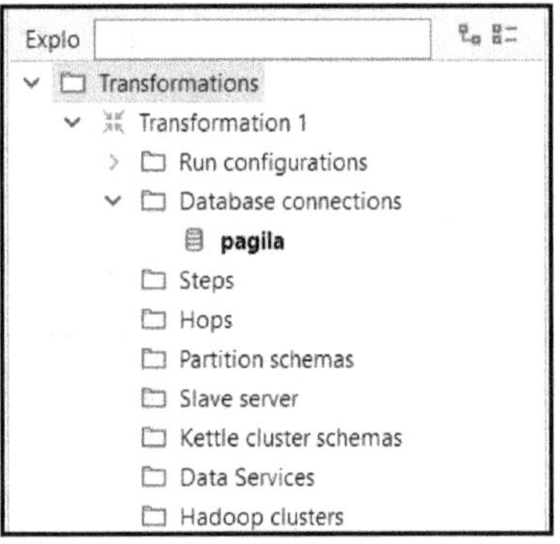

Shared connections

8. Save the Transformation.

In general, to connect to any database, simply follow the preceding instructions—just replace the sample settings with your own settings.

As you can see in the **Database Connection** window, there are more tabs with additional configuration settings. These tabs are useful, for example, to set a preferred schema or a charset to use. Filling these tabs is optional and it depends on your particular database and preferences.

It may happen that the database engine to which you want to connect is not in the list.

If you don't find your database engine in the list, you can still connect to it by specifying the **Generic database** option as a **Connection Type**. In that case, you have to provide a connection URL and the driver class name. If you need more help on this, check out the official website for your database engine.

The database connections will only be available in the Transformation where you defined them unless you shared them for reuse as you did previously. Normally, you share connections because you know that you will use them later in many transformations. You can also stop sharing the connection: just right-click on the database connection and select **Stop sharing**.

The information about shared connections is stored in a file named `shared.xml` located in the same folder as the `kettle.properties` file.

When you use a shared connection and you save the Transformation, the connection information is saved in the Transformation itself.

If there is more than one shared connection, all of them will be saved along with the Transformation, even if the Transformation doesn't use them all. To avoid this, go to the editing options and check the **Only save used connections to XML?** option. This option limits the XML content of a Transformation just to the used connections.

Exploring a database with the Database Explorer

You just learned how to connect to an RDBMS from PDI. Before beginning to work with the data stored in a database, it would be useful to be familiar with that database or to verify if the database contains all the data that you need. For this, Spoon offers a **Database Explorer**. There are several ways to access the explorer:

- Right-click on the connection in the **Database connections** list and select **Explore** in the contextual menu.
- Click on **Explore** in the **Database Connection** window.
- Go to the menu option, **Tools** | **Database** | **Explore**. In the window that shows up, select the database to explore and click on **OK.**

Whichever way you choose, the following window appears:

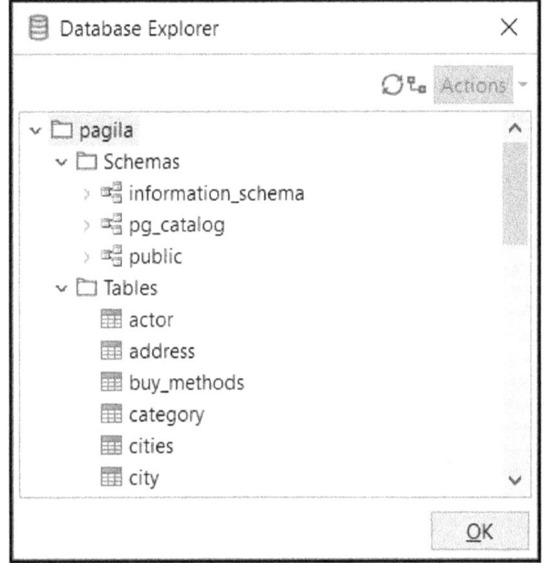

Database Explorer

When you open the **Database Explorer**, the first thing that you see is a tree with the different objects of the database. When you right-click on a database table, a contextual menu appears with several available options for you to explore that table. The following is a full list of options and their purpose:

Option	**Description**
Preview first 100	Returns the first 100 rows of the selected table, or all the rows if the table has less than 100. Shows all the columns of the table.
Preview x Rows	Same as the previous option but you decide the number of rows to show.
Row Count	Tells you the total number of records in the table.
Show Layout	Shows you the metadata for the columns of the table.
DDL | Use CurrentConnection	Shows you the DDL statement that creates the selected table.
DDL | Select Connection	Lets you select another existent connection, then shows you the DDL just like the previous option. In this case, the DDL is written with the syntax of the database engine of the selected connection.
View SQL	Lets you edit a `SELECT` statement to query the table.
Truncate Table	Deletes all rows from the selected table.
Data Profile	Collects and displays some statistics for the fields in the selected table: maximum or minimum values, averages, and so on.

As an example, let's try one of the options on the sample database:

1. Right-click on the `actors` table and select **View SQL**. The following SQL editor window appears:

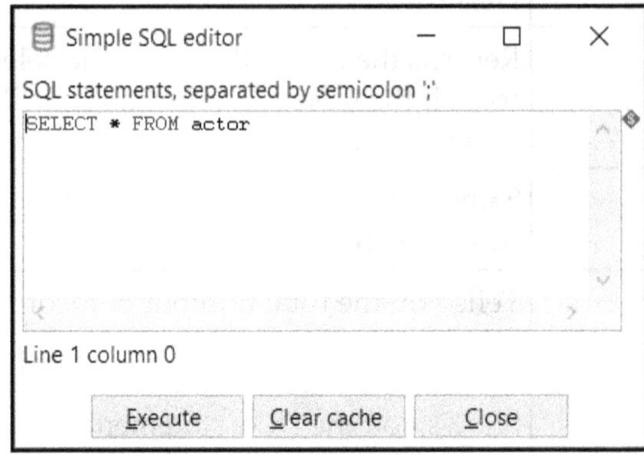

Simple SQL editor

2. Modify the text in there so you have the following:

```
SELECT first_name, last_name
FROM actor
```

3. Click on **Execute**. You will see this result:

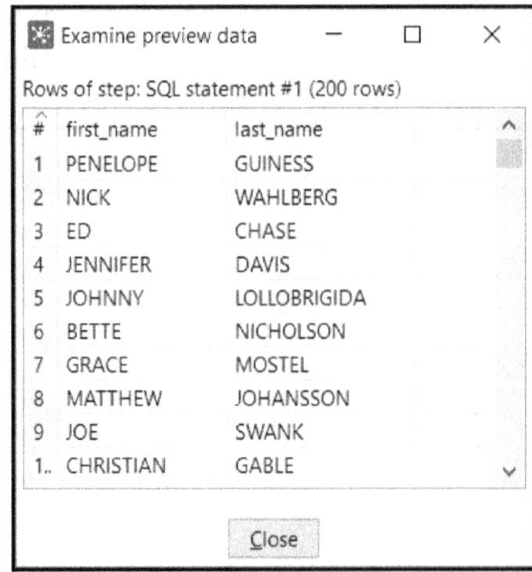

Previewing the result of a SELECT statement

4. Close the **Preview** window—the one that tells the result of the execution as well as the **Results of the SQL statements** window, which is the window that tells us the SQL statements are executed. Finally, close the **Simple SQL editor** window.
5. Click on **OK** to close the **Database Explorer** window.

Previewing and getting data from a database

Now that you have a database ready to use, let's start by querying. In this section, you will learn how to run both simple and advanced queries.

Getting data from the database with the Table input step

The **Table input** step is the main step to get data from a database. To run very simple queries, the use of this step is straightforward, as explained in this example:

1. Create a new Transformation.
2. From the **Input** category of steps, select and drag to the work area a **Table input** step.
3. Double-click on the step.
4. As **Connection**, you should see the `pagila` connection selected by default. If not, select it.

The `pagila` connection appears by default because it's the only connection in your environment. In case you have more connections, you should choose the one that you will use.

5. Click on the **Get SQL select statement...** button. The **Database Explorer** window appears.
6. Expand the tables list, select **city**, and click on **OK**.
7. PDI asks you if you want to include the field names in the SQL. Answer **Yes**.

8. The **SQL** box gets filled with a `SELECT` SQL statement:

```
SELECT
  city_id
, city
, country_id
, last_update
FROM city
```

9. Click on **Preview** and then **OK**. The following window appears:

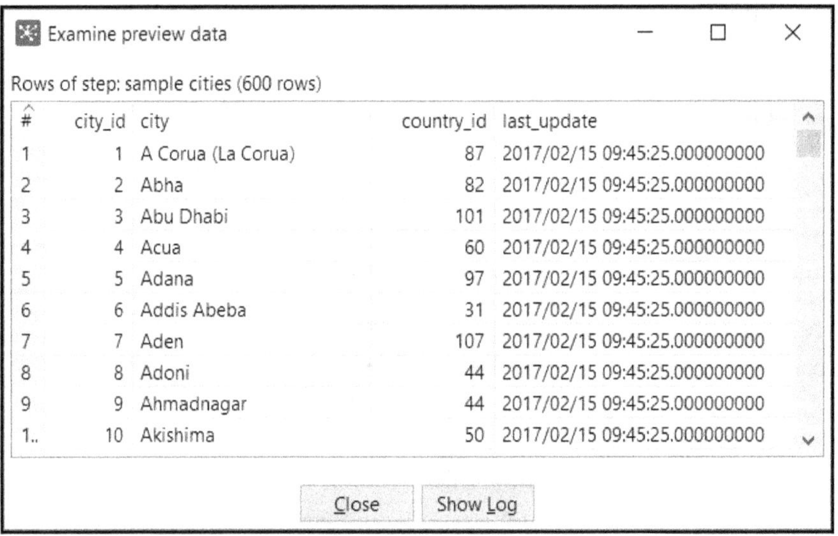

#	city_id	city	country_id	last_update
1	1	A Corua (La Corua)	87	2017/02/15 09:45:25.000000000
2	2	Abha	82	2017/02/15 09:45:25.000000000
3	3	Abu Dhabi	101	2017/02/15 09:45:25.000000000
4	4	Acua	60	2017/02/15 09:45:25.000000000
5	5	Adana	97	2017/02/15 09:45:25.000000000
6	6	Addis Abeba	31	2017/02/15 09:45:25.000000000
7	7	Aden	107	2017/02/15 09:45:25.000000000
8	8	Adoni	44	2017/02/15 09:45:25.000000000
9	9	Ahmadnagar	44	2017/02/15 09:45:25.000000000
1..	10	Akishima	50	2017/02/15 09:45:25.000000000

Previewing a Table input step

The output of a **Table input** step is a regular dataset. Each column of the SQL query leads to a new field and the rows generated by the execution of the query become the rows of the dataset.

As the data types of the databases are not exactly the same as the PDI data types, when getting data from a table, PDI implicitly converts the metadata of the new fields. For example, consider the `city` table:

1. Open the **Database Explorer** and look at the DDL definition for the `city` table.
2. Right-click on the **Table input** step and select **Show output fields** to see the metadata of the created dataset. You will see the PDI metadata for the city fields.

You will see that the output of (1) and (2) differs. The following table shows you how the metadata was translated:

Fields	Database data type	PDI metadata
city_id	Integer	Integer(9)
city	VARCHAR(50)	String(50)
country_id	SMALLINT	Integer(4)
last_update	TIMESTAMP	Timestamp(6)

Once the data comes out of the **Table input** step and the metadata is adjusted, PDI treats the dataset just as regular data, no matter whether it came from a database or any other data source.

Using the Table input step to run flexible queries

As shown earlier, the **Table input** step is the option to read data from a database. The **SQL** area is where you write the `SELECT` statement that will generate your dataset.

When you add a **Table input** step, it comes with a default `SELECT` statement for you to complete:

```
SELECT <values> FROM <table name> WHERE <conditions>
```

If you need to query a single table, you can take advantage of the **Get SQL select statement...** button, which generates the full statement for you. After you get the statement, you can modify it at your will. If you need to write more complex queries, you definitively have to do it manually.

You can write any `Select` query as far as it is a valid SQL statement for the selected type of database.

Although SQL is standard, each database engine has its own version of the SQL language.

When you type SQL statements in PDI, try to keep the code within the standard. If you do, your transformations will be reusable in case you have to change the database engine.

Whether simple or complex, you may need to pass the query some parameters. You can do this in a couple of ways as explained next.

Adding parameters to your queries

One of the ways you can make your queries more flexible is by passing it some parameters. For example, suppose that you want to list the films that belong to a given category and you have that category in a properties file. If the category in your file is `Comedy`, the query to run will look as follows:

```
SELECT f.title
 FROM public.film f
 JOIN public.film_category fc ON f.film_id = fc.film_id
 JOIN public.category ca ON fc.category_id = ca.category_id
WHERE ca.name = 'Comedy';
```

In your Transformation, you want to replace `Comedy` with a parameter, so the category changes according to the content of your file. This is done in two parts:

- You have to prepare a stream with the parameter(s) that the query will receive
- You adapt the query to receive these parameters

This is how you do the first part:

1. Create a Transformation, and add to the work area the following steps: a **Property Input**, a **Filter rows**, and a **Select values** step. Link them as follows:

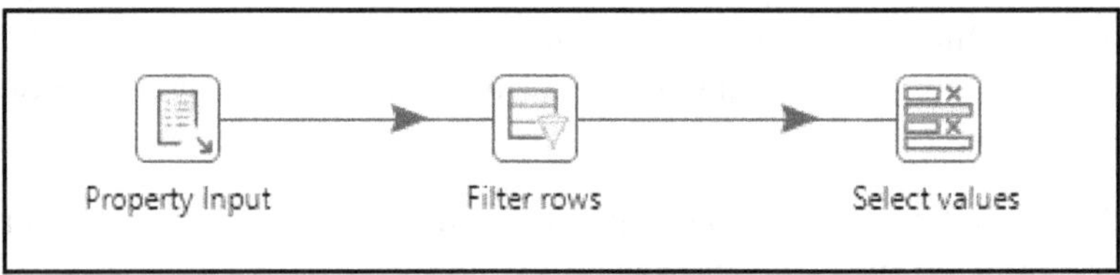

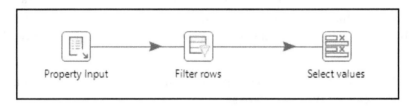

Preparing the parameters for a query

2. Use the preceding steps to read the properties file, filtering the `category` key and selecting only the column that contains the category. If you preview the last step, you should see something like this:

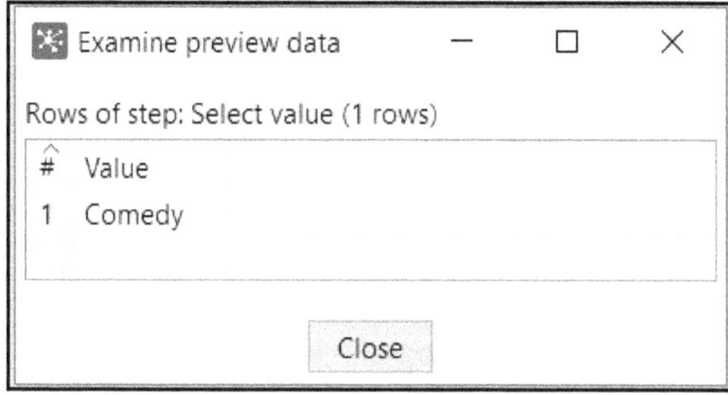

Previewing the parameters

In this case, the source was a file. You can get the fields from any source using any number of steps, as long as the output of the last step gives you the values for the parameters to inject in the query.

For testing purposes, you can avoid doing the previous steps and just create a very simple stream with a **Generate rows** step, containing the `category` field with a sample value.

Now that you have a stream with the field that will be plugged as a parameter, we are ready to adapt the query:

1. After the **Select values** step, add a **Table input** step.
2. Edit the **Table input** step and type the query introduced previously, but replacing the last line with the following:

```
WHERE ca.name = ?;
```

Where `?` is the placeholder for the category.

3. In the **Insert data from step** option, select the name of the step from which the parameters will come; in this case, **Select values**.

4. Close the window. You will see that the hop that links the **Select values** step with the **Table input** step changes its look and feel, showing that the **Select values** step feeds the **Table input** with data.
5. With the **Table input** selected, run a preview. You will see the following:

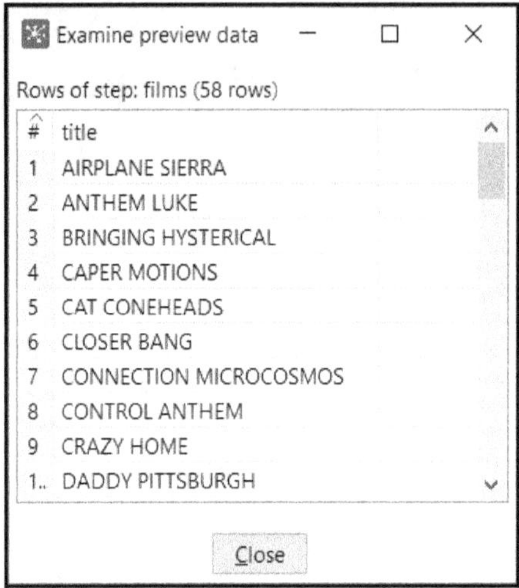

Previewing a query with parameters

In this case, you had a single parameter. In general, you have to put a question mark (`?`) for each incoming parameter. When you execute the Transformation, the question marks are replaced one by one with the data that comes to the **Table input** step.

The replacement of the markers respects the order of the incoming fields. When you use question marks to parameterize a query, don't forget that the number of fields coming to a **Table input** must be exactly the same as the number of question marks found in the query.

Using Kettle variables in your queries

As an alternative to the use of positional parameters, you can use Kettle variables. Instead of getting the parameters from an incoming step, you check the **Replace variables in script?** option and replace the question marks with names of variables. This is how you create a new version of the preceding Transformation but using variables:

1. Create a Transformation and add a **Table input** step.

2. Double-click on the **Table input** step and type the preceding query used, this time, replacing the last line with the following:

```
WHERE ca.name = '${CATEGORY}';
```

3. Check the **Replace variables in script?** checkbox.
4. Save the Transformation.
5. With the **Table input** selected, click on the **Preview** button.
6. Click on **Configure**.
7. Fill in the **Variables** tab in the dialog setting window by providing a value for the `CATEGORY` variable, as shown in this screenshot:

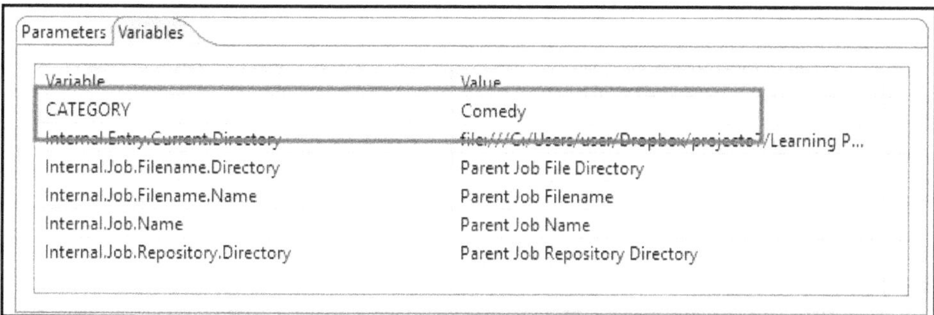

Introducing variables before previewing

8. Click on **OK**. If you type `Comedy`, you should see the same result as in the previous example.

You can also preview the SQL statement in the **Table input** configuration window--the window where you type the query—but you have to make sure that the variables already have values. One way to assign them values is with the options **Edit | Set Environment Variables...** available from the main menu.

When you use variables, PDI replaces the name of the variables with their values. Only after that, it sends the SQL statement to the database engine to be executed.

Kettle variables have several advantages over the use of question marks:

- You can use the same variable more than once in the same query.
- You can use variables for any portion of the query and not just for the values; for example, you could have the following query:

```
SELECT ${COLUMNS} FROM public.film
```

- Then the result will vary upon the content of the `${COLUMNS}` variable. For this particular example, the variable could be `title` or `title, description` among other options.
- A query with variables is easier to understand and less error-prone than a query with positional parameters.

Note that in order to provide parameters to a statement in a **Table input** step, it's perfectly possible to combine both methods: positional parameters and Kettle variables.

Inserting, updating, and deleting data

By now, you know how to get data from a database. Now you will learn how to perform other basic operations. The next sections explain different ways to insert, update, and delete data from a database.

Inserting new data into a database table

The **Table output** step is the main PDI step to insert new data into a database table.

The use of this step is simple. You have to create a stream of data with the data that you want to insert. At the end of the stream, you will add a **Table output** step and configure it to perform the operation.

The following screenshot shows the dialog window for the step:

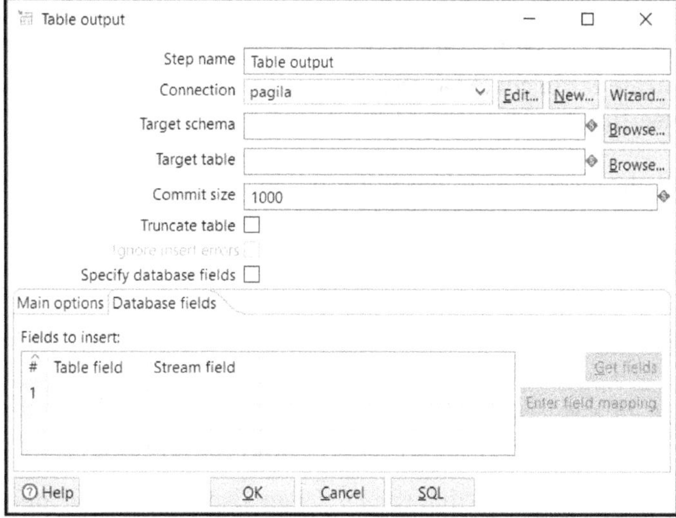

Table output dialog window

As you can see, there is the main area where you enter the name of the database connection and the name of the table where you want to insert data. These fields are mandatory.

Then you have the **Database Field** tab where you specify the mapping between the dataset stream fields and the table fields. In order to fill this tab, you have to check the **Specify database fields** option.

The rest of the settings in the step are optional and the configuration depends on your needs or the properties of your table.

The following are some important tips and warnings about the use of the **Table output** step:

- If the names of the fields in the PDI stream are equal to the names of the columns in the table, you don't have to specify the mapping. In that case, you have to leave the **Specify database fields** checkbox unchecked and make sure that all the fields coming to the **Table output** step exist in the table.
- Before sending data to a **Table output** step, check your Transformation against the definition for the table. All the mandatory columns that don't have a default value must have a correspondent field in the PDI stream coming to the **Table output** step.

- Check the data types for the fields that you are sending to the table. It is possible that a PDI field type and a table column data type don't match. In that case, fix the problem before sending the data to the table. You can, for example, use the **Metadata** tab of a **Select values** step to change the data type of the data.
- The **Truncate table** check, as the name implies, causes the truncation of the table before inserting the incoming data.

The truncation of a table is done as soon as the Transformation starts. It's really important to know that even when the stream that comes into the step is disabled, the truncation will be done.

In the **Table output** step, as well as in many of the steps that we will see in this chapter, there is a button named **SQL**. This button generates the DDL to create or alter the output table in order to execute the inserts successfully. If you want to create a table from scratch, this button allows you to do it based on the database fields that you provided in the step.

It's important to note that the DDL can also propose the deletion of some columns. This may happen if the table exists and has some columns that you don't have in your stream. So be careful before confirming the execution of the script.

For performance reasons, **bulk loading** is the recommended option when you have a big amount of data to insert. For a limited set of database engines, PDI has steps that allow you to bulk load data into a database as an alternative to insert data with the **Table output** step. You will find them under the bulk loading category of steps. There are also a couple of job entries that allow you to bulk load data into a database.

Inserting or updating data with the Insert / Update step

While the **Table output** step allows you to insert brand new data, the **Insert / Update** step allows you to do both, insert and update data in a single step.

The rows directed to the **Insert / Update** step can be new data or data that already exists on the table. Depending on the case, the **Insert / Update** step behaves differently. Before explaining each case, let's introduce the step. The following image corresponds to the **Insert / Update** configuration window:

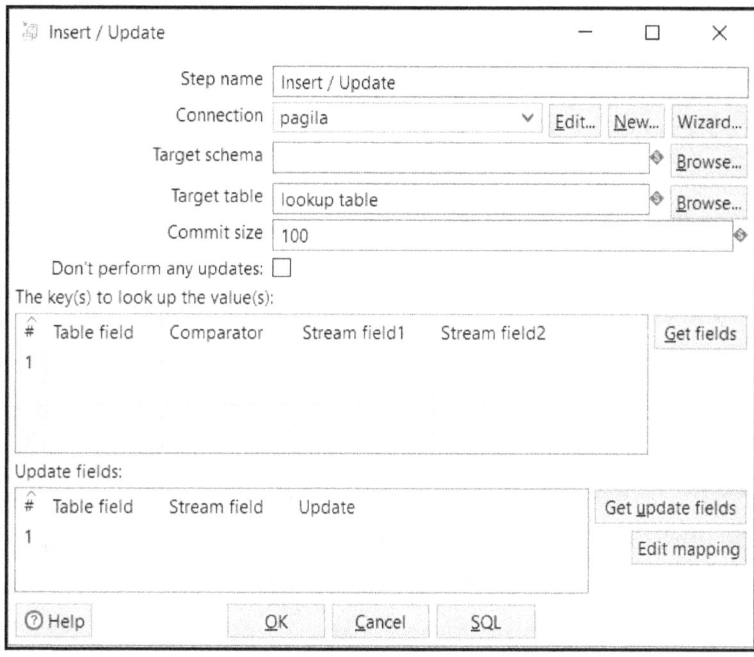

Insert / Update window

As you can see, the upper section is identical to the **Table output** window. Here, you select the database connection and provide the table name where you will insert or update rows.

Then we have two grids. While the upper grid is meant to define the conditions for the inserts or updates, the lower grid is where you define the fields to be inserted or updated.

Let's see each case in detail:

- For each incoming row, the step uses the lookup condition you put in the upper grid to check whether the row already exists in the table.
- If the lookup fails, that is, the row doesn't exist, the step inserts the row in the table using the mapping you put in the lower grid.
- If the lookup succeeds, the step updates the table, replacing the old values with the new ones. This update is made only for the fields where you put `Y` as the value for the **Update** column in the lower grid.

If you don't want to perform any `Update` operation, you can check the **Don't perform any updates** option.

This insert operation is exactly the same as you could have done with a **Table output** step. This implies that here also you have to be careful about the following:

- All the mandatory columns that don't have a default value must be present in the **Update Field** grid, including the keys you used in the upper grid
- The data types for the fields that you are sending to the table must match the data type for the columns of the table

If you only want to perform updates, you can use the **Update** step instead. The configuration window is almost identical to the **Insert / Update** one.

Deleting records of a database table with the Delete step

The **Delete** step allows you to delete records of a database table based on a given condition. As shown following, the configuration window for the **Delete** step is really simple and very similar to the others explained previously:

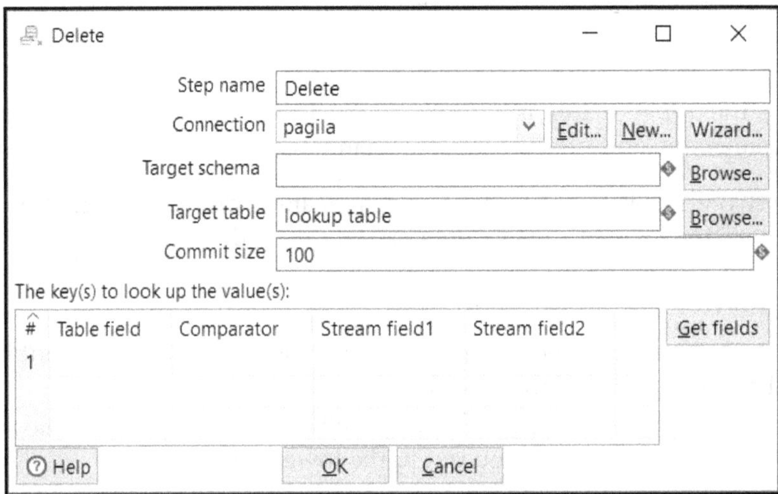

The Delete step configuration window

Exactly as in the other windows explained, the upper section is where you define the database connection and the table involved.

Then, in the grid is where you define the conditions for the delete operation. The definitions you put in the grid represent the WHERE in a DELETE statement.

For each row that comes to the step, PDI deletes the records that match the condition set in its configuration window.

Performing CRUD operations with more flexibility

In the previous paragraphs, you learned how to use the basic steps to perform **CRUD**--Create, Read, Update, and Delete operations. For simple use cases, these steps should be enough. There are, however, some situations where you may need a bit more flexibility. For example, suppose that you want to insert rows under one of the following conditions:

```
WHERE upper(column1) > column2 OR column1 is null
```

This looks like a very common statement but the **Insert** step doesn't allow us to enter such a condition.

This and other similar situations can be implemented with the **Execute row SQL script** step. To use this step, you just create a new string field and use it to define the SQL statement to execute. After that, you add an **Execute row SQL script** step and the step will execute for every input row. Alternatively, there is another step, the **Execute SQL script** step. If you check its **Execute for each row?** checkbox, the behavior is similar. Compared to the previous step, this one allows you to include parameters in your statements.

The **Execute SQL script** step has another useful purpose. With the **Execute for each row?** option unchecked, it can be dropped alone in the work area--that is, unlinked from any other step. The statements that you write in its configuration window will execute once during the initialization phase of the Transformation. Common uses for this is to clear status and flags in configuration tables, delete records from tables that will be loaded in the current Transformation, among others.

Verifying a connection, running DDL scripts, and doing other useful tasks

When you work with databases, before performing CRUD operations, you may want to run other useful tasks, for example, verify if a database is accessible, clean up some tables before execution, and more. Look at the following sample job:

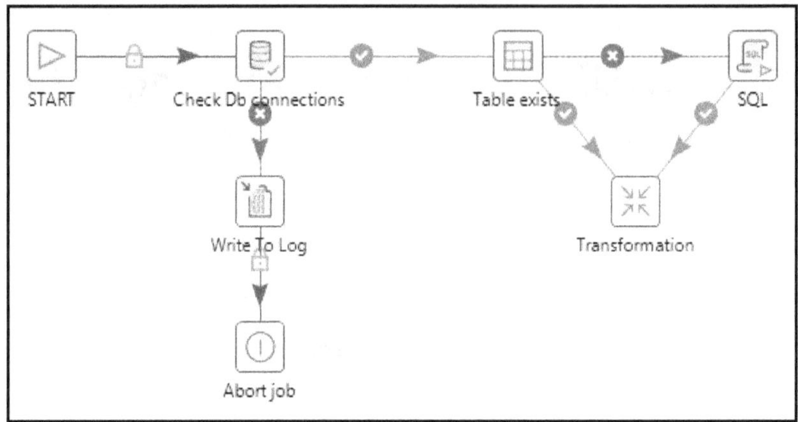

Sample job that runs some database-related tasks

This job verifies the connectivity with a database connection. If the database is accessible, it creates a table—as soon as the table doesn't exist. After that, it executes a Transformation. If the database is not available, a message is written to the log.

Besides these, there are some other job entries that can be useful for database-related tasks. The following table summarizes them:

Job entry	Purpose
Check Db connections	Verifies the connectivity with one or several databases.
Table exists	Verifies that a specified table exists on a database.
Columns exist in a table	Verifies that one or more columns exist in a database table.
Truncate tables	Truncates one or several tables.

Evaluate rows number in a table	Evaluates the number of rows in a table and succeeds when a specified condition is true. (For example, the number of rows is greater than zero). Alternatively, you can evaluate the result of a custom SQL statement.
Wait for SQL	Similar to **Evaluate rows number in a table**, but in this case, the entry waits for the condition to be true. The evaluation is done every given amount of time. The execution of the entry ends either when the condition is true or a given timeout period is reached.
SQL	Executes one or more SQL statements. You can use this entry to perform procedure calls, create tables, refresh views, disable constraints, and more.

The job entries **Table exists** and **Columns exist in a table** have their correspondent Transformation steps: **Table exists** and **Check if a column exists**. The functionality is the same. The difference is that you use the Transformation when you have to do the operation for every row in a dataset, for example, the list of columns that you want to verify is in a dataset, one per row.

This is not the first time you see equivalences between job entries and Transformation steps. Remember we learned the email options or the operations on files (create, move, among others). In general, when you have steps and entries that provide the same functionality, in order to decide which one applies, you have to take into account one of the following:

- If the operation will run once for fixed values or values stored in a Kettle variable, you will use the job entry
- If the operation should be executed once for every row in a list of values, you will use a Transformation step.

Looking up data in different ways

You already know how to read, insert, update, and delete data from a database. You're ready to learn how to look up data. Let's call lookup as the act of searching information in a database. You can lookup a column of a single table or you can do more complex lookups. In this section, you will learn to perform both the simplest and the more complex kinds of lookups.

Doing simple lookups with the Database Value Lookup step

The **Database Value Lookup** step allows you to lookup values in a database table based on data you have in your main stream.

The following screenshot shows the **Database Value Lookup** configuration window, which looks very similar to the **Stream lookup** step you already know:

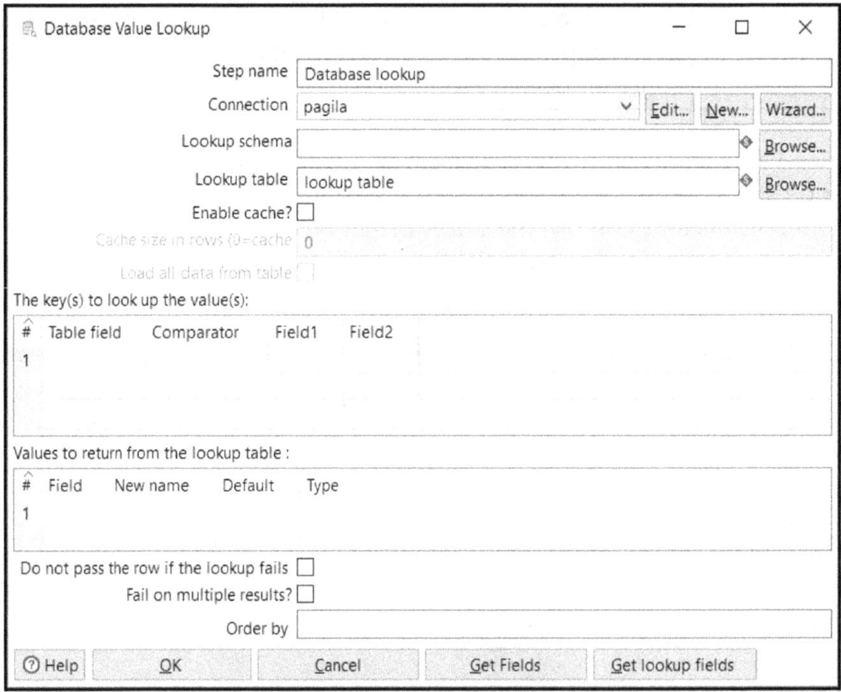

Database Value Lookup configuration window

In the upper section, you have the database connection and the table where you will look for data.

Then you have two grids:

- In the upper grid, you specify the keys to look up.
- In the lower grid, you put the name of the table columns you want back. These fields are added to the output stream.

Let's put the step into practice with a simple example. Suppose that you have a list of names and want to list actors with those names.

For simplicity, we will start with a simple stream, containing only one field with sample data. You can replace this stream with any stream, with any number of fields, coming from different kinds of sources.

1. Create a Transformation.
2. Add a **Data Grid** step and configure it with a single string field called `name`.
3. Fill in the **Data** tab of the **Data Grid** with some sample names, for example, `DANY`, `MORGAN`, `RALPH`.
4. After the **Data Grid**, add a **Database lookup**. You will find it under the **Lookup** category of steps.
5. Double-click on the step. Select the **Pagila** connection. As **Lookup schema**, type `public`. As **Lookup table**, type `actor`. Then fill in the grids as follows:

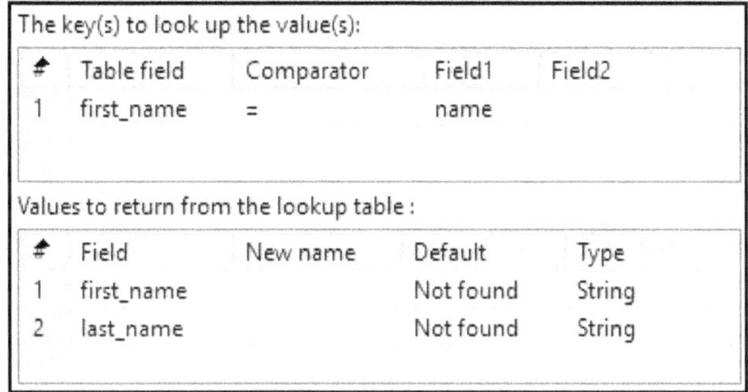

The key(s) to look up the value(s):

#	Table field	Comparator	Field1	Field2
1	first_name	=	name	

Values to return from the lookup table :

#	Field	New name	Default	Type
1	first_name		Not found	String
2	last_name		Not found	String

Configuring a Database lookup step

Remember that, as in all grids in PDI, you always have the option to populate the grids using the **Get Fields** and **Get lookup** fields respectively.

6. Close the window.

7. With the step selected, run a preview. You will see this:

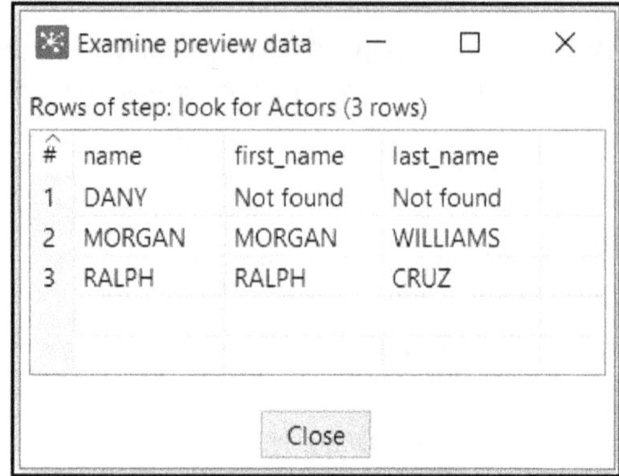

Previewing the output of a Database lookup

As you can see, the behavior is quite similar to the **Stream lookup** step's behavior. You search for a match and, if a record is found, the step returns the specified fields. If there are no matches, the new fields are filled with default values. Besides the fact that the data is searched in a database, the new thing here is that you specify the comparator to be used: =, <, >, and so on. The **Stream lookup** step only looks for equal values.

Some important note about the result of a **Database Value Lookup** step. The step returns only one row even if it doesn't find a matching record or if it finds more than one. You can somehow change the default behavior:

- If the step doesn't find results, you can either provide default values for the new fields or you can filter the row by checking the option, **Do not pass the row if the lookup fails**.
- If there are two or more rows as a result, you can choose to fail by checking the option, **Fail on multiple results?** If you don't mind and just want to keep one row out of all the found rows, you can provide a value in the **Order by** textbox, for example, `last_name desc`. If you do so, PDI returns the first row after sorting the results by that criteria.

Making a performance difference when looking up data in a database

Database lookups are costly and can severely impact Transformation performance. However, performance can be significantly improved using the cache feature of the **Database lookup** step. In order to enable the cache feature, just check the **Enable cache?** option.

This is how it works. Think of the cache as a buffer of high-speed memory that temporarily holds frequently requested data. By enabling the cache option, PDI will look first in the cache and then in the database:

- If the table that you look up has few records, you could preload the cache with all of the data in the lookup table. Do this by checking the **Load all data from table** option. This will give you the best performance.
- On the contrary, if the number of rows in the lookup table is too large to fit entirely into memory, instead of caching the whole table, you can tell PDI the maximum number of rows to hold in the cache. Do this by specifying the number in the **Cache size in rows** textbox. The bigger this number, the faster the lookup process.

The cache options should be set with care. If you have a large table or don't have much memory, you risk running out of memory. Another caveat to using the cache is if this lookup data changes frequently—not the typical scenario for lookup data—but a possible pitfall.

Performing complex database lookups

The **Database lookup** step is very useful and quite simple, but it is quite limited. Taking as an example our `Pagila` database, suppose that you want to do the following lookups:

- You want to look for films with a given category, for example, `Comedy`. In our database, the films and the category names are in different tables. As the **Database Value Lookup** works with a single table, it's not suitable for this search.
- You want to look for films where the name contains the word, `House`. You can do this search with a **Database Value Lookup** step but the step will return maximum one film, even if there are more in the films table containing that word.

- You want to look for an actor whose name or the last name begins with `J`. The **Database Value Lookup** step doesn't have the possibility to put OR conditions, so it is not the step to use in this case.
- You want to get the number of times a given film was hired. You cannot get this with the **Database Value Lookup** step as the step doesn't allow you to get aggregated results, just plain values.

These are only some examples where the step you learned is not useful and you have to look for a different way to look up. Fortunately, there are other steps prepared to perform more complex searches as mentioned. The steps are as follows:

- **Database join** step
- **Dynamic SQL row** step

The purpose of both steps is quite similar. They execute a statement that combines fields in the main stream with fields in one or more database tables, and return one or more new fields. As an option, as part of the statement, you can use variables and provide conditions. You can conclude that both steps are used to solve any of the given examples.

The next subsections show you how to use each of these steps. Both sections will implement the same example so you can compare and decide which step suits best for your needs.

Looking for data using a Database join step

The Transformation that we will create takes pairs of words as input and looks for films whose description contains both words. For example, if the words are `robot` and `rocket`, what we want is the same as the output of the following SQL statement:

```
SELECT title, description
FROM public.film
WHERE description like '%robot%' and description like '%rocket%'
```

Just for simplicity, as input, we will write the words in a **Data Grid** but the source of the lookup can be any stream.

This is how we do this:

1. Create a Transformation.
2. Add a **Data Grid** step. Define two `String` fields named `word1` and `word2`.

3. Fill in the **Data** tab as follows or with your own set of words:

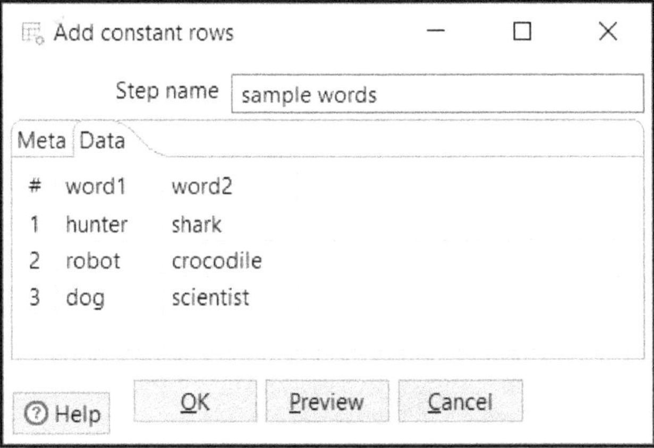

Sample input data

4. After the **Data Grid**, add a **Database join** step. You will find it under the **Lookup** category of steps.
5. Double-click on the step and select the connection to the `pagila` database.
6. In the **SQL** box, type the following:

```
SELECT title, description
 FROM public.film
 WHERE upper(description) like UPPER(concat('%', ?, '%'))
 AND upper(description) like UPPER(concat('%', ?, '%'))
```

The question marks in the query are the parameters that we will provide in the lower grid.

7. Fill the lower grid as follows:

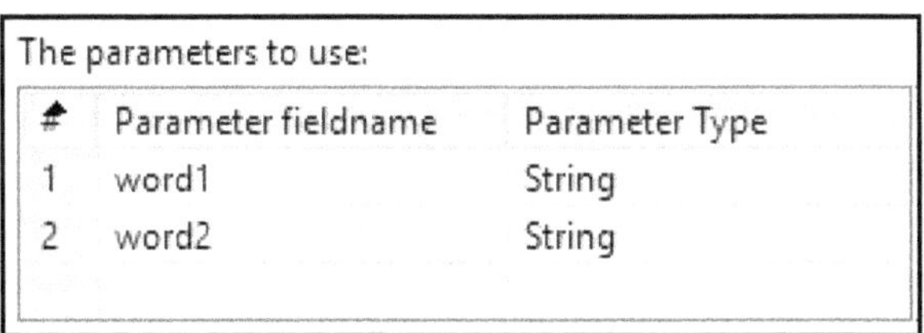

Configuring parameters in a Database join

8. As **Number of rows to return**, type `3`.
9. Close the window.

10. With the **Database join** selected, run a preview. You will see this:

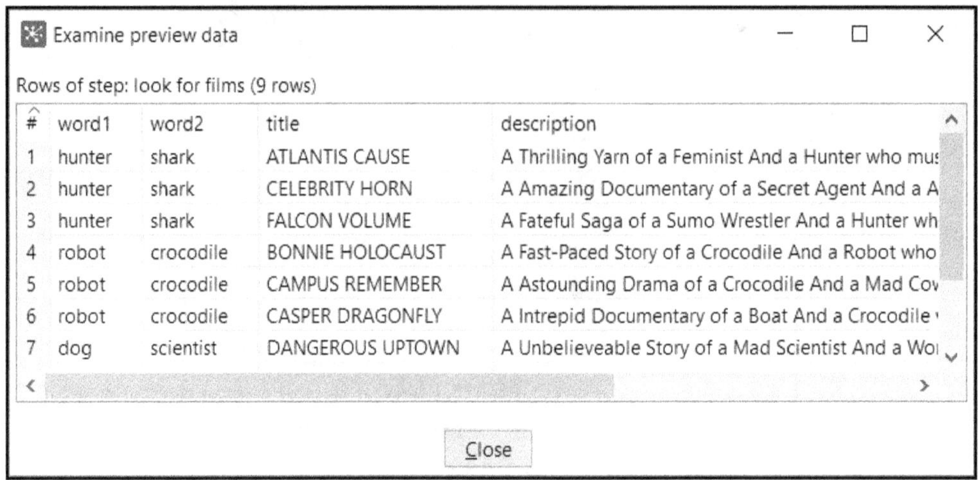

Previewing the output of a Database join

Note that this step doesn't involve a database join as the name suggests. In fact, it is the joining of data from the database to the stream data.

The output of the **Database join** step shows the expected result. For each incoming row, that is, each pair of words, the result is a list of up to three films. This limit was forced in the **Number of rows to return** option.

If you had left the **Number of rows to return** empty, the step would have returned all found rows.

In the example, we set the parameters as question marks. These work like the question marks in the **Table input** step that you learned at the beginning of the chapter—the parameters are replaced according to the position. The difference is that here, you define the list and the order of the parameters. You do it in the small grid at the bottom of the setting window. This means that you aren't forced to use all the incoming fields as parameters and that you may also change the order.

Just as you do in a **Table input** step, instead of using positional parameters, you can use Kettle variables by checking the **Replace variables** checkbox and using the `${}` notation.

As you cannot preview the statement in the **Database join** configuration window, you can write and try your query inside a **Table input** step or in an external tool, for example, PgAdmin if you work with PostgreSQL. When you are done, just copy and paste the query here and do the needed adjustments, for example, inserting variables or parameters.

Looking for data using a Dynamic SQL row step

The previously implemented example can also be implemented with the **Dynamic SQL row** step, as explained here:

1. Create a new Transformation.
2. From the Transformation created in the previous tutorial, copy and paste the **Data Grid** into the sample words.

The **Dynamic SQL row** step needs the query to run already defined in a field in the dataset. So, in order to create this field, we will use a **JavaScript** step.

3. After the **Data Grid** step, add a **JavaScript** step.
4. Use the **JavaScript** step to add a new field named `STATEMENT`. In the scripting area, type the following:

```
var STATEMENT;
STATEMENT = "SELECT title, description FROM public.film" +
            " WHERE upper(description) like '%" + upper(word1) +
"%'" +
            " AND upper(description) like '%" + upper(word2) + "%'"
+
            " LIMIT 3";
```

5. With the **JavaScript** step selected, run a preview. You will see all the statements that will run, as follows:

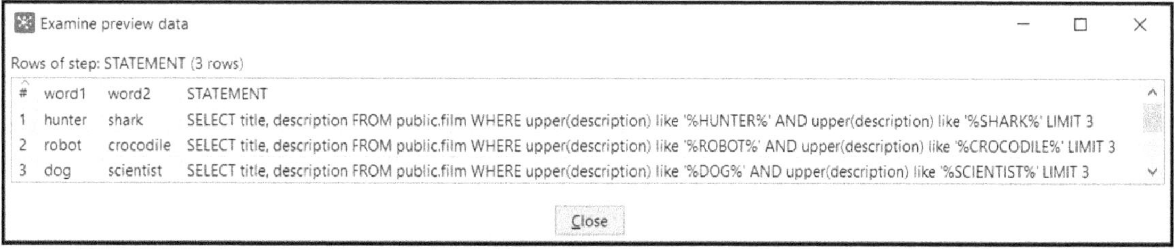

Examine preview data

Rows of step: STATEMENT (3 rows)

#	word1	word2	STATEMENT
1	hunter	shark	SELECT title, description FROM public.film WHERE upper(description) like '%HUNTER%' AND upper(description) like '%SHARK%' LIMIT 3
2	robot	crocodile	SELECT title, description FROM public.film WHERE upper(description) like '%ROBOT%' AND upper(description) like '%CROCODILE%' LIMIT 3
3	dog	scientist	SELECT title, description FROM public.film WHERE upper(description) like '%DOG%' AND upper(description) like '%SCIENTIST%' LIMIT 3

Close

Statements to run

6. Finally, after the **JavaScript** step, add a **Dynamic SQL row**. This step is also located under the **Lookup** category.
7. Double-click on the step and fill it as follows:

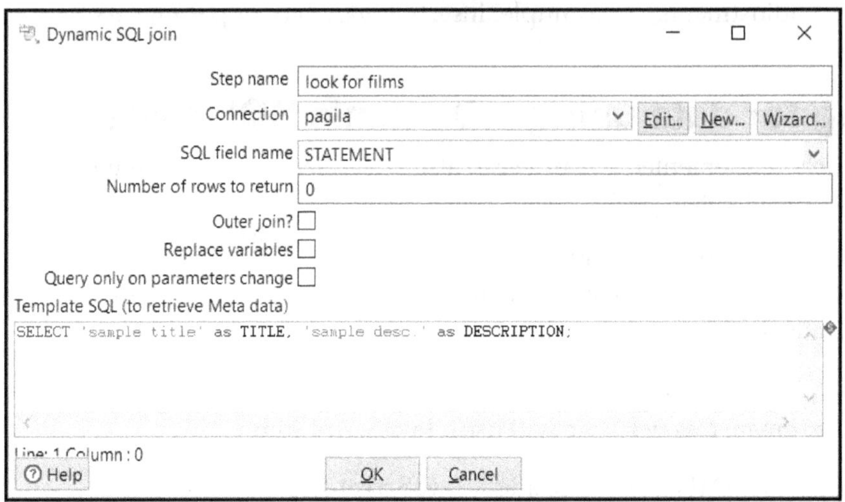

Configuring a Dynamic SQL row step

8. Close the window.
9. Run a preview of this last step. You should see the same output as before.

The **Tempate SQL** field may seem a bit confusing, but its concept is simple: Here, you just type any SQL statement that returns the same metadata as the queries that will run.

The sample Transformation implemented with both lookup steps should serve you as a base to implement any other complex lookup.

Summary

This chapter discussed how to use PDI to work with relational databases. You learned how to create connections from PDI to different database engines and to explore databases with the PDI **Database Explorer**. Then, you learned how to perform insert, update and delete operations on databases.

You also learned to search for data on databases. First, you were introduced to the simplest way to search by using the Database lookup step. As that step has limitations, you were also introduced to other options that PDI offers for performing more complex lookups.

Finally, you also performed useful tasks such as checking a connection, verifying the existence of a table, running some DDLs, and more. In the next chapter, you will continue working with databases. Specifically, you will learn how to load a data mart.

11
Loading Data Marts with PDI

Performing **Create**, **Read**, **Update** and **Delete** (**CRUD**) operations on databases is just the beginning in your database-learning journey. Besides that, there are other interesting things that you can do with databases, for example, addressing data warehouse concepts. This chapter is fully devoted to data warehouse-related concepts. The list of the topics that will be covered includes the following:

- Introducing dimensional modeling
- Learning the basics of dimensions
- Loading a different kind of dimensions including time, junk and mini dimensions
- Loading slowly changing dimensions Type I and Type II
- Learning the basics of fact tables
- Loading cumulative and snapshot fact tables

Preparing the environment

Before getting into the details of building a data mart with PDI, we will perform the following:

- Present the data that will be used for all the tutorials and examples through the rest of the chapter
- Create and populate the database so that it's ready to run the tutorials

Exploring the Jigsaw database model

The following information allows you to understand the organization of the data in our sample `Jigsaw` database. In the first place, you have the **entity relationship diagram** (**ERD**) for the `js` database:

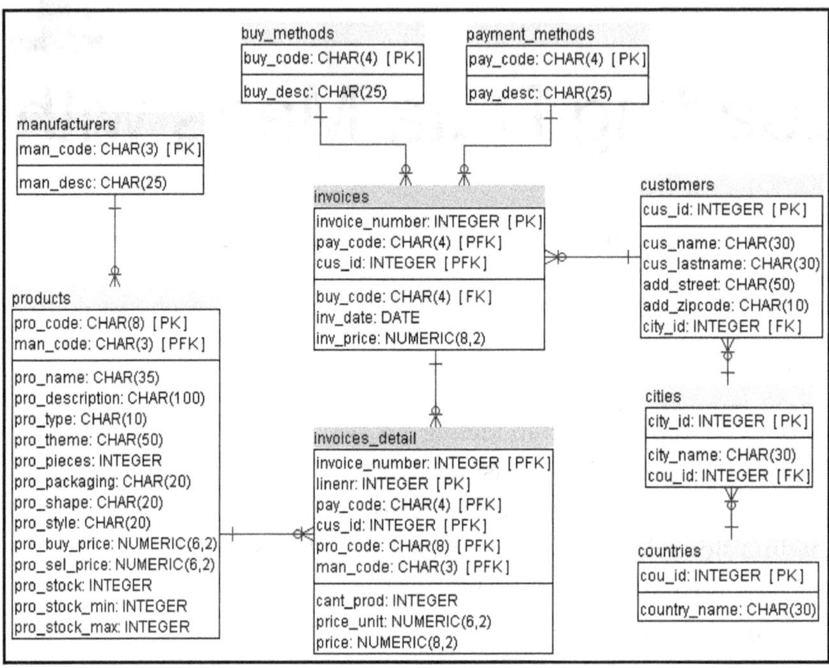

ERD for the Jigsaw database

The following table contains a brief explanation of what each table is for:

Table	Content
`manufacturers`	Information about manufacturers of the products.
`products`	It contains information about products such as puzzles and accessories. The table has descriptive information and data about prices and stock. The `pro_type` column has the type of product—puzzle, glue, and so on. Several of the columns only apply to puzzles, for example, shapes or pieces.
`buy_methods`	It contains information about the methods for buying, for example, in-store and by telephone.

Table	Content
`payment_methods`	Information about methods of payment such as cash, check, and credit card.
`countries`	List of countries.
`cities`	List of cities.
`customers`	List of customers. A customer has a number, a name, and an address.
`invoices`	The header of invoices including date, customer number, and total amount. The invoice dates range from 2004 to 2010.
`invoices_details`	Detail of the invoices including invoice number, product, quantity, and price.

Creating the database and configuring the environment

In order to run the tutorials in the chapter, you will need to do some preparatory tasks.

In the first place, you will need the Jigsaw operational database installed and populated:

1. From the book's website, download the material for the chapter.
2. In the bundle material, you will find a folder with some SQL scripts. Use them to create and populate the operational database as well as to create the data mart tables.

There are two versions of the scripts—one for PostgreSQL and one for MySQL. Use the one that fits your environment or adapt them to your own engine.

As a final task, open Spoon and perform the following:

1. Create a database connection named `js` that connects PDI with the Jigsaw puzzle operational database.
2. Create another database connection named `js_dw` to connect PDI with the data mart.
3. Make both connections shared so that they are ready to be used through all the exercises in the chapter.

If you are not sure about how to do this, you'll find the instructions in `Chapter 10`, *Performing Basic Operations with Databases*.

Introducing dimensional modeling

Databases used for daily operational work are maintained by an **Online Transaction Processing** (**OLTP**) system. The users of an OLTP system perform operational tasks; they sell products, process orders, control stock, and so on.

As a counterpart, a data warehouse is a non-operational database; it is a specialized database designed for decision support purposes. Users of a data warehouse analyze the data, and they do it from different points of view.

The most used technique to deliver data to data warehouse users is **dimensional modeling**. This technique consists of building a star-like schema with dimension tables surrounding a fact table, making databases simple and understandable.

The primary table in a dimensional model is the fact table. A **fact table** stores numerical measurements of the business as a quantity of products sold, amount represented by the sold products, discounts, taxes, number of invoices, number of claims, and anything that can be measured. These measurements are referred to as **facts**.

A fact is useless without the **dimension** tables. Dimension tables contain the textual descriptors of the business. Typical dimensions are product, time, customers, and regions. As all surrounding dimension tables get formed in a star-like structure, we often call it a **star schema**.

Data warehouse is a very broad concept. In this book, we will deal with data marts. While a data warehouse represents a global vision of an enterprise, a **data mart** holds the data from a single business process. You could have data marts focused on customer relationship management, inventory, human resources management, budget, and more.

Data stored in data warehouses and data marts usually comes from the different sources—the operational database being the main one. The process that takes the information from the source, transforms it in several ways, and finally loads the data into the data mart or data warehouse is the **ETL process**. PDI is a perfect tool to accomplish this task. In the rest of this chapter, you will learn how to load dimension and fact tables with PDI.

Through the tutorials, you will learn more about this. However, the terminology introduced here constitutes just as a preamble to dimensional modeling. There is much more than you can learn.

If you are really interested in the data warehouse subject, you should start by reading *The Data Warehouse Toolkit*, Ralph Kimball and Margy Ross, Wiley Computer Publishing. This book is undoubtedly the best guide to dimensional modeling.

Loading dimensions with data

A dimension is an entity that describes your business; customers and products are examples of dimensions. A dimension table, no surprises here, is a table that contains information about one or more dimensions. In this section, you will learn to load dimension tables, that is, fill dimension tables with data. The following are the topics covered:

- Learning the basics of dimensions
- Loading a time dimension
- Loading slowly changing dimensions
- Loading other kinds of dimensions

Learning the basics of dimensions

Dimensions are sets of attributes used to describe a business. A list of products along with their shape, color, or size is a typical example of dimension. Dimensions are one of the basic blocks of a data warehouse or data mart.

A dimension has the purpose of grouping, filtering, and describing data. Think of a typical report you would like to have—sales grouped by region, by customer, and method of payment that are ordered by date. The **by** word lets you identify potential dimensions—regions, customers, methods of payment, and dates.

If we look at our sample `Jigsaw` database, we can think of many dimensions, for example:

Dimension	**Description**
Time	The date on which the sales occurred
Regions	The geographical area where the products were sold
Manufacturers	The name of the manufacturers that build the products that were sold
Payment method	Cash, check, and so on
Buy method	Internet, by telephone, and so on
Product type	Puzzle, glue, frame, and so on

Depending on the way we use the dimensions or the kind of data they hold, dimensions fall into one of a list of categories. The next subsections describe the most common kinds of dimensions and explain how to load them. Before going into these details, let's explain some technical details common to all of them.

Understanding dimensions technical details

No matter the kind of dimension, when you implement them, there are some best practices to take into account:

- A dimension table must have its own technical key column different to the business key column used in the operational database. This technical key is known as a **surrogate key**. While in the operational database, the key may be a string--for example, in an alphanumeric code, surrogate keys are always integers.
- Dimensions should have a special record for the unavailable data. This implies that besides one record for every member of the dimension, you should have a record with the key equal to zero, and `N/A` or `unknown`, or something that represents invalid data for all the descriptive attributes. Having this record, data that is unavailable or invalid in the operation database will not be inserted in the data warehouse; it will be represented by this special record instead.
- Finally, along with the descriptive attributes that you save in a dimension, you usually keep the **business key** so that you can match the data in the dimension table with the data in the source database.

The following screenshot depicts typical columns in a dimension table:

surrogate key — business key

id	name	theme	id_js_prod
488	Fire!	Comedy/Cartoon	FAL428G
489	Tour de France	Comedy/Cartoon	FAL45Q7
490	Princesses and Horses - Cinderella	Horses	FAL46IO
491	Christmas Carriage	Christmas	FAL4ATQ
492	At The Beach	Comedy/Cartoon	FAL4DJ4
493	Christmas Spirits	Christmas	FAL4FGA
494	Pick a Friend	Dogs	FAL4H54
495	German Beer Festival	Comedy/Cartoon	FAL4HMU
496	Mickey and Friends	Disney	FAL4LC9
497	Hidden Lake Chateau	Castles	FAL4MME
498	The Airshow	Comedy/Cartoon	FAL4MVE

Relation between dimensional data and source data

Loading a time dimension

The **time dimension** is a special dimension used to describe a business in terms of when things happened. Time dimensions are meant to answer questions related to time, for example, do I sell more on Mondays or on Fridays? Am I selling more this quarter than the same quarter last year? Depending on the kind of question you want to answer, is the list of attributes you need to include in your time dimension. Typical fields in a time dimension are year, month (a number between 1 and 12), description of month, day of month, weekday, and quarter.

In terms of databases, a time dimension table has one row for every date in a given range of dates and one column for each attribute describing the date.

In `Chapter 2`, *Getting Started with Transformations*, you created a Transformation that generated a dataset with one row by date in a date range. In the following tutorial, we will reuse that work.

The following instructions guide you in populating a time dimension with the following attributes: year, month, day of month, and day of week:

1. Open the Transformation created in the *Running Transformations in an Interactive Fashion* section in `Chapter 2`, *Getting Started with Transformations*. Save it under a new name.
2. Edit the **Generate rows** step and change the value of `start_date` to `2000-01-01`.
3. Right-click on the **Delay row** step and select **Detach step**. Then, delete the step. You should have this:

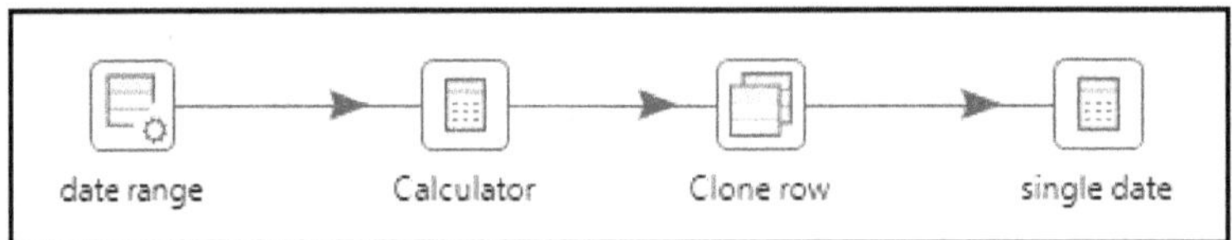

Transformation with a range of dates

4. Double-click on the second **Calculator** and define the new fields `year`, `month`, `day`, and `week_day`, as shown in the following screenshot:

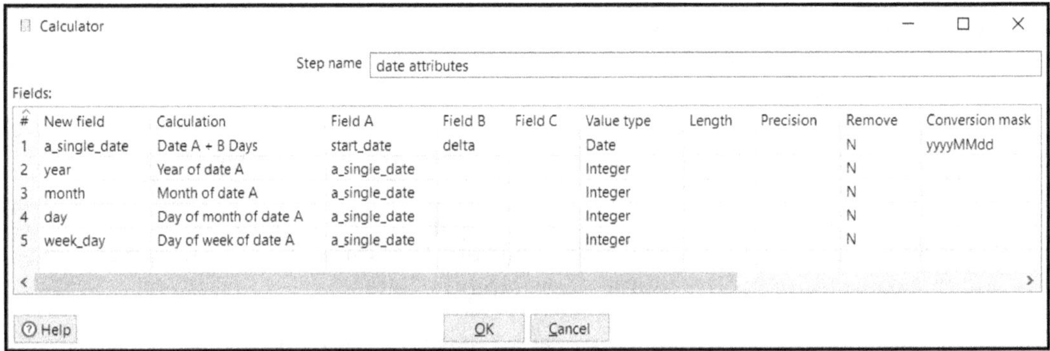

Calculating date attributes

5. Run a preview of this last step. You will see this:

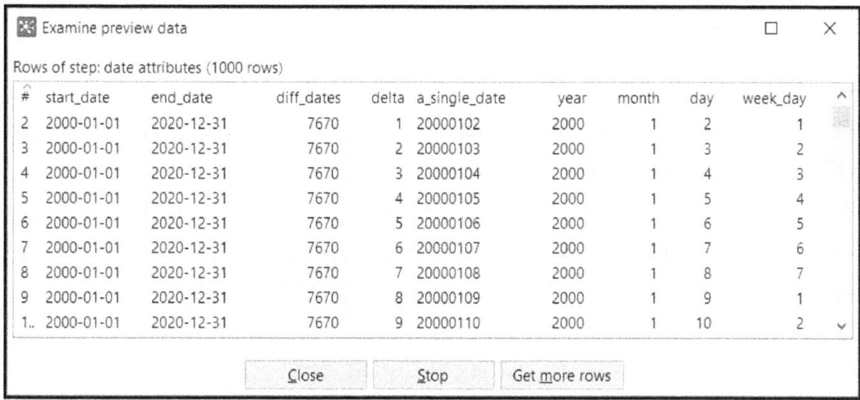

Previewing a dataset with date attributes

As mentioned before, it's recommended to have a number as the key of a dimension. Also, in the case of a time dimension, it's convenient that the key be the date itself represented as a number. For example, for the date `2017-08-15`, the key could be the number `20170815`. In order to have this, we will convert the date field to a number with the following trick:

6. Add two **Select values** steps. Use the first to change the metadata of the date from `Date` to `String`, using `yyyyMMdd` as the mask. Use the second step to change the metadata from `String` to `Number` using `#` as the mask.
7. Finally, at the end of the stream, add a **Table output** step. We will use it to insert the data into the time lookup table. As a table, type `lk_time_simple`, click on **Truncate table**, click on **Specify database fields**, and fill the **Database fields** grid as follows:

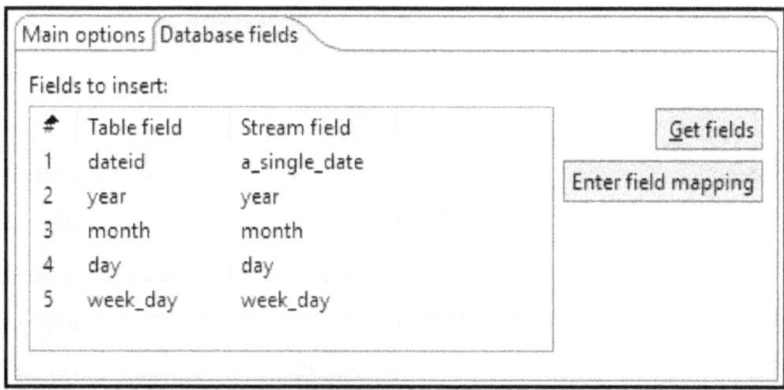

Configuring a Table output step

8. Save and run the Transformation.
9. With the **Database explorer** or an external tool, run a `SELECT` on the lookup table. You should see the table populated with the dates and their attributes.

This example showed a very simple version of the dimension. Depending on your business, you may need many more fields describing a date. You shouldn't have any problems in calculating new fields in this Transformation and adapting the dimension table to store them.

The *Operating with Dates* section from `Chapter 5`, *Manipulating PDI Data and Metadata,* will be of much help in creating new date attributes for the time dimension.

Introducing and loading Type I slowly changing dimensions

Besides the time dimension, **Slowly Changing Dimension** (**SCD**) is the most common kind of dimension used. SCD are dimensions where changes may occur from time to time. Typical examples of SCD are regions, customers, and products.

Suppose that you have a dimension with products. It may happen that the description of a product changes. If you don't care about the old description and, in your dimension, you just overwrite the attribute with the new description, then your product dimension is called a **Type I SCD**.

In general, if you don't preserve historical values when you update an SCD dimension, the dimension is called **Type I slowly changing dimension** (**Type I SCD**).

The next tutorial explains how to load this kind of dimension with PDI.

Loading a Type I SCD with a combination lookup/update step

We will explain the loading process of a Type I SCD by example. We will load the region dimension, which contains geographical information—cities and countries. The source of our dimension will be the `cities` and `countries` tables, and the dimension table to be loaded is `lk_regions`.

Note that we will take information from the operational database `js` and load a table in another database `js_dw`.

We load Type I SCDs with the **Combination lookup/update** step. Before loading the dimension, it's a good idea to take a look at the definition of the table so that we can identify the different kinds of fields needed to configure the **Combination lookup/update** step properly:

```
CREATE TABLE LK_REGIONS (
    id INT(4) NOT NULL,
    city CHAR(30) DEFAULT 'N/A' NOT NULL,
    country CHAR(30) DEFAULT 'N/A' NOT NULL,
    region CHAR(30) DEFAULT 'N/A' NOT NULL,
    id_js INT(4) NOT NULL,
    lastupdate DATE,
    PRIMARY KEY (id)
    );
```

Among the fields, we have the surrogate key (`id`), the business key (`id_js`), and the fields for the different attributes: `city`, `country`, and `region`. We also have a field named `lastupdate`, not mandatory as we will shortly see.

This is how we proceed. First of all, we have to gather the region information from the source:

1. Launch Spoon and create a new Transformation.
2. Drag a **Table input** step to the work area and double-click on it.
3. As **Connection**, select `js`.
4. In the **SQL** area, type the following query and click on the **OK** button:

```
SELECT ci.city_id, city_name, country_name
FROM cities ci, countries co
WHERE ci.cou_id = co.cou_id
```

Now that you have all the data to populate the dimension, do the following:

5. After the **Table input** step, add a **Combination lookup/update** step. You will find it in the **Data Warehouse** category of steps.
6. Double-click on the step; as **Connection**, select `dw`. As **Target table**, browse and select **lk_regions** or simply type it. Set **Commit size** to `1`.

7. Fill the grid, as shown in the following screenshot:

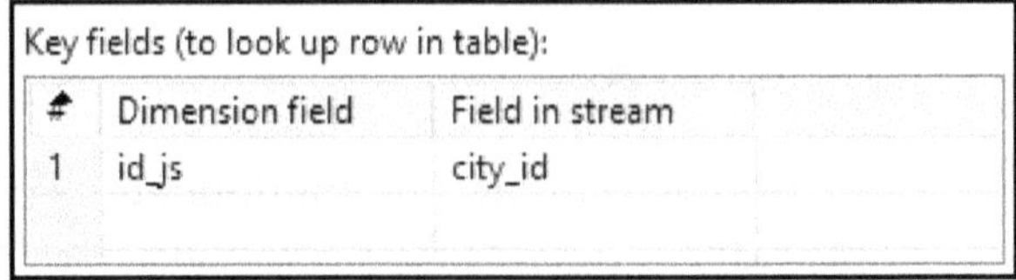

Configuring a Combination lookup/update step

8. As **Technical key field**, type `id`, and as **Date of last update field (optional)**, type `lastupdate`.
9. Close the window.
10. After the **Combination lookup/update** step, add an **Update** step and double-click on it.
11. As **Connection**, select `js_dw` and as **Target table**, type `lk_regions`.
12. Fill the upper grid by adding the condition `id = id`. The `id` attribute to the left is the table's id, while `id` to the right is the stream id.
13. Fill the lower grid. Add one row with the **city** and **city_name** values. Add a second row with the **country** and **country_name** values. This will update the table columns `city` and `country` with the values `city_name` and `country_name` coming in the stream.
14. Save the Transformation and run it.
15. Explore the `js_dw` database and preview the `lk_regions` table. You should see this:

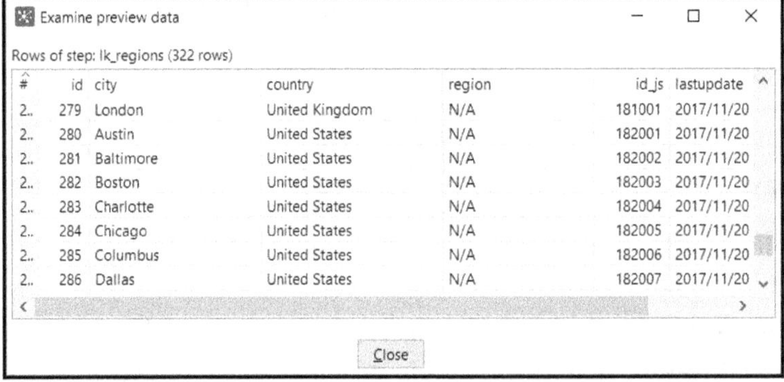

#	id	city	country	region	id_js	lastupdate
2..	279	London	United Kingdom	N/A	181001	2017/11/20
2..	280	Austin	United States	N/A	182001	2017/11/20
2..	281	Baltimore	United States	N/A	182002	2017/11/20
2..	282	Boston	United States	N/A	182003	2017/11/20
2..	283	Charlotte	United States	N/A	182004	2017/11/20
2..	284	Chicago	United States	N/A	182005	2017/11/20
2..	285	Columbus	United States	N/A	182006	2017/11/20
2..	286	Dallas	United States	N/A	182007	2017/11/20

Region dimension populated

Be aware that in the **Combination lookup/update** step, the **Dimension field**, **Technical key field**, and **Date of last update field** options do not refer to fields in the stream, but to columns in the table. In those cases, where you see the word **field**, you should know that it refers to a column: **Dimension** column, **Technical key** column, and **Date of last update** column. Also, note that the term **Technical** refers to the surrogate key.

How does this work? The **Combination lookup/update** (**Combination L/U**) looks in the dimension table for a record that matches the key fields that you put in the upper grid in the setting window:

- If the combination exists, the step returns the surrogate key of the found record.
- If it doesn't exist, the step generates a new surrogate key and inserts a row with the key fields and the generated surrogate key. In this case, the surrogate key is also added to the output stream.

This behavior implies that the **Combination lookup/update** step merely inserts the row for each city, whereas the **Update** step is the one that adds the city and country information.

Note that the dimension table `lk_regions` has a column named `region` that you didn't update because you don't have data for this column. The column is filled with a default value set in the DDL definition of the table.

In the **Combination lookup/update** step, we set the commit size to `1`. This is the only way in which this Transformation will run successfully and reliably every time. There are conflicts in timing if the commit size is larger as we are attempting to update a row that may not have been committed yet. Of course, if you don't have fields to update, you don't have to change the commit size.

A commit size equal to 1 certainly degrades the performance when loading dimensions of high cardinality. If that's the case, you have an alternative way to load Type I SCD, which is explained in the next section.

Now you may wonder why we update the attributes with a separate step. We do it because they are not part of the key. In our example, if we put the city and country in the **Combination lookup/update** step, the first time that we run the Transformation, the row would be inserted without problem. If some change is applied to the `city` or the `country` fields in the source system, the next time we run the Transformation, PDI would assume that the key changed and would insert a new record for the same city, which would be wrong.

As the **Combination L/U** only maintains the key information, if you have non-key columns in the table, you must update them with an extra **Update** step. These values must have a default value or must allow null values. If none of these conditions is true, the insert operation will fail.

In our sample database, there is another Type I SCD: manufacturers. The process to load this dimension is exactly the same as the one explained for the REGION dimension.

Introducing and loading Type II slowly changing dimension

The REGION dimension is a typical Type I SCD dimension. If some description changes, it makes no sense to keep the old values. The new values simply overwrite the old ones. Sometimes you would like to keep a history of the changes. This is when **Type II Slowly Changing Dimensions** come into play. A **Type II SCD** keeps the whole history of the data of your dimension. Some typical examples of attributes for which you would like to keep history are sales territories that change over time, categories of products that are reclassified from time to time, promotions that you apply to products, which are valid in a given range of dates.

There are no rules that dictate whether or not you keep the history in a dimension. It's the final user who decides this based on his requirements.

Now you will learn how to load a dimension that keeps a history.

Loading Type II SCDs with a dimension lookup/update step

As we did for a Type I SCD, we will load a Type II SCD by example. We will load the PUZZLE dimension, which contains name and category for puzzles. As the puzzles are regrouped from time to time, we want to keep the history of the category or theme to which each puzzle belonged in time. The source of our dimension will be the product table, and the dimension table that we will load is `lk_puzzle`.

We load SCD Type II with a **Dimension lookup/update** step. The main difference between this step and the **Combination lookup/update** step that you saw before is that the **Dimension L/U** step has the ability to keep a history of changes in the data.

Before loading the dimension, take a look at the definition of the table so that you can identify the different kinds of fields needed to configure the **Dimension lookup/update** step properly:

```
CREATE TABLE LK_PUZZLES (
    id INT(10) NOT NULL,
    name CHAR(35) DEFAULT 'N/A' NOT NULL,
    theme CHAR(50) DEFAULT 'N/A' NOT NULL,
    id_js_prod CHAR(8) DEFAULT 00000000 NOT NULL,
    id_js_man CHAR(3) DEFAULT 000 NOT NULL,
    start_date DATE,
    end_date DATE,
    version INT(4) DEFAULT 1 NOT NULL,
    current CHAR(1) DEFAULT 'Y' NOT NULL,
    lastupdate DATE,
    PRIMARY KEY (id)
   );
```

In the definition, we have the surrogate key (`id`), the business key--in this case, represented with two fields, `id_js_prod` and `id_js_man`--and the fields for the attributes, `name` and `theme`.

Besides these puzzle-related fields, there are some fields that are specific to the Type II SDC. These fields are specially designed to keep the history and you will see them every time you load this kind of dimension:

Field	Purpose
`start_date`	The date from which the record is valid.
`end_date`	The date until which the record is valid.
`version`	An auto-numeric field to keep track of all versions of the same record (the same puzzle in our example).
`current`	A flag indicating if, out of all versions for a record (a puzzle in our example) this record is the valid one. For any given date, only one of the records will have the `current` flag in `true`. This field is optional.

In the dimension table, there is also a field named `lastupdate`, which is not mandatory.

For better understanding the way the **Dimension L/U** step works, we will split the explanation into two:

- Loading a dimension for the first time
- Loading a dimension after some changes occurred in the source

Loading a Type II SDC for the first time

In this tutorial, we will load the PUZZLE dimension for the first time. This is how we proceed:

1. Create a new Transformation.
2. Drag a **Table input** step to the work area and double-click on it.
3. As **Connection**, select `js`. In the **SQL** area, type the following query:

```
SELECT pro_code
     , man_code
     , pro_name
     , pro_theme
FROM  products
WHERE pro_type LIKE 'PUZZLE%'
```

4. Click on **OK**.
5. Add an **Add constants** step and create a hop from the **Table input** step toward it.
6. Use the step to add a **Date** field named `changedate`. As format, type `dd/MM/yyyy` and as value, type `01/10/2017`.
7. After the **Add constants** step, add a **Dimension lookup/update** step. You will find it in the **Data Warehouse** category of steps.
8. Double-click on the **Dimension lookup/update** step. As **Connection**, select `js_dw`. As **Target table**, type `lk_puzzles`.
9. Fill the **Key** fields, as shown in the following screenshot:

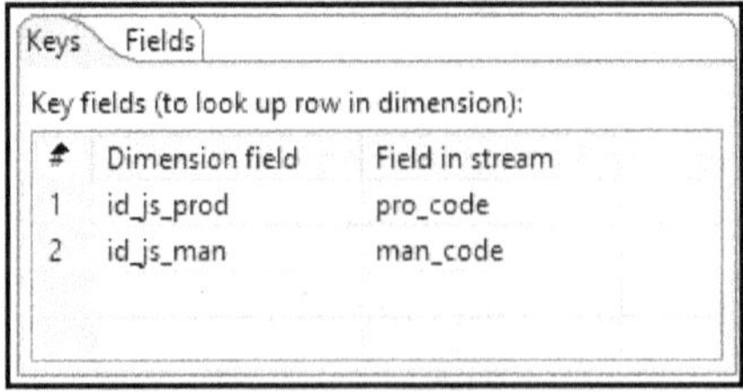

Filling the Key fields in a Dimension L/U step

10. Fill the lower section of the configuration window as follows:

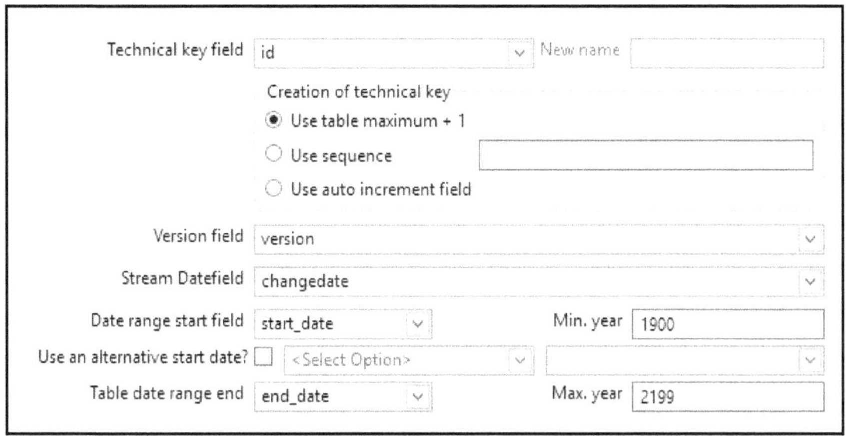

Configuring a Dimension L/U step

11. Select the **Fields** tab and fill it in with the following information:

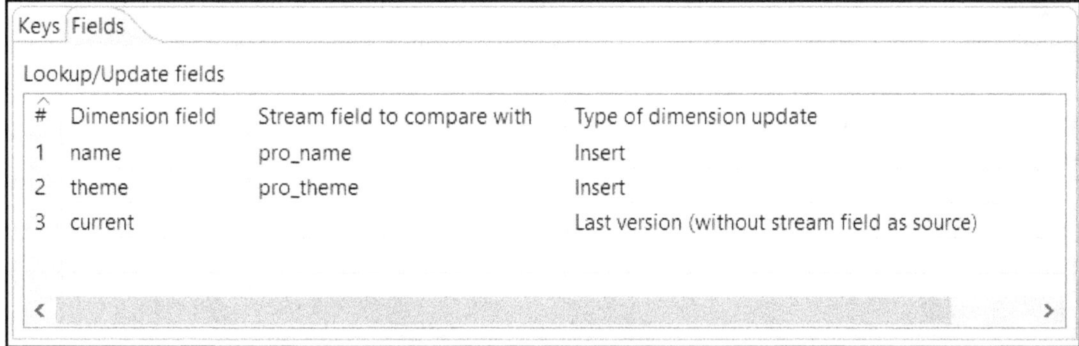

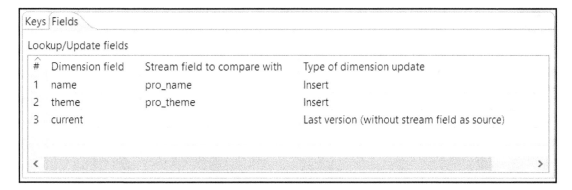

Filling the Fields data in a Dimension L/U step

12. Close the setting window.
13. Save the Transformation and run it.

14. Explore the `js_dw` database and do a preview of the `lk_puzzles` table. You should see this:

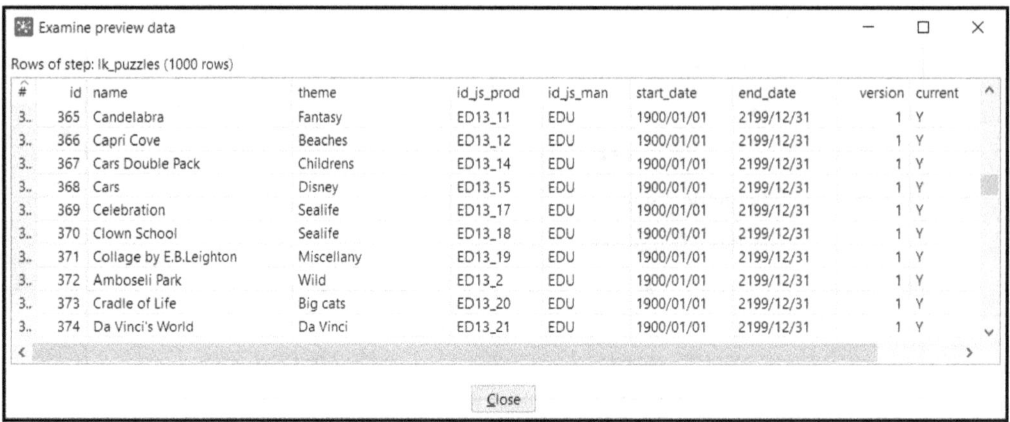
Examine preview data

Rows of step: lk_puzzles (1000 rows)

#	id	name	theme	id_js_prod	id_js_man	start_date	end_date	version	current
3..	365	Candelabra	Fantasy	ED13_11	EDU	1900/01/01	2199/12/31	1	Y
3..	366	Capri Cove	Beaches	ED13_12	EDU	1900/01/01	2199/12/31	1	Y
3..	367	Cars Double Pack	Childrens	ED13_14	EDU	1900/01/01	2199/12/31	1	Y
3..	368	Cars	Disney	ED13_15	EDU	1900/01/01	2199/12/31	1	Y
3..	369	Celebration	Sealife	ED13_17	EDU	1900/01/01	2199/12/31	1	Y
3..	370	Clown School	Sealife	ED13_18	EDU	1900/01/01	2199/12/31	1	Y
3..	371	Collage by E.B.Leighton	Miscellany	ED13_19	EDU	1900/01/01	2199/12/31	1	Y
3..	372	Amboseli Park	Wild	ED13_2	EDU	1900/01/01	2199/12/31	1	Y
3..	373	Cradle of Life	Big cats	ED13_20	EDU	1900/01/01	2199/12/31	1	Y
3..	374	Da Vinci's World	Da Vinci	ED13_21	EDU	1900/01/01	2199/12/31	1	Y

Close

Previewing the Puzzles Dimension

Note that a special record was automatically inserted for unavailable data. In order to insert the special record with a key that equals zero, all fields must have default values or should allow nulls. If none of these conditions is true, the automatic insertion will fail.

This is how it works. The **Dimension lookup/update** step looks in the dimension table for a record that matches the information you put in the **Keys** grid of the setting window. Also, the period from `start_date` to `end_date` of the record must contain the value of the `datefield` stream, which in our sample Transformation is `01/10/2017`:

- If the lookup fails, it inserts a new record
- If a record is found, the step inserts or updates records depending on how you configured the step

As this was the first time we run the Transformation and the table was empty, the lookup failed in all cases. As a result, the step inserted all the products.

Note the values that were set for the special fields. The version for the new record is `1`, the current flag is set to `true`, and the `start_date` and `end_date` fields take as values the dates you put in the **Min. year** and **Max. year**, that is, `01/01/1900` and `31/12/2199` in this case.

Regarding the `stream date`, the field you put here is key to the loading process of the dimension, as its value is interpreted by PDI as the effective date of the change. In this section, you put a fixed date `01/10/2017`. In real situations, you should use the effective or last changed date of the data, if that date is available. If it is not available, leave the field blank. PDI will use the system's date.

Loading a Type II SDC and verifying how history is kept

In the preceding section, you loaded a dimension with products using a **Dimension lookup/update** step. You ran the Transformation once, caused the insertion of one record for each product, and a special record with `N/A` values for the descriptive fields. In order to effectively see how history is kept, we will make some changes in the operational database and run the Transformation again to see how the **Dimension lookup/update** step stores history:

1. Among the downloaded material, locate the `update_jumbo_products.sql` script and run it. This script will change the category to a list of products.
2. Switch to Spoon.
3. Open the Transformation created in the last tutorial and run it.
4. Explore the `js_dw` database again. Right-click on the `lk_puzzles` table and click on **View SQL**. Modify the proposed statement so that it looks like the following:

```
SELECT   *
FROM     lk_puzzles
WHERE    id_js_man = 'JUM'
ORDER BY id_js_prod
       , version
```

5. You will see this:

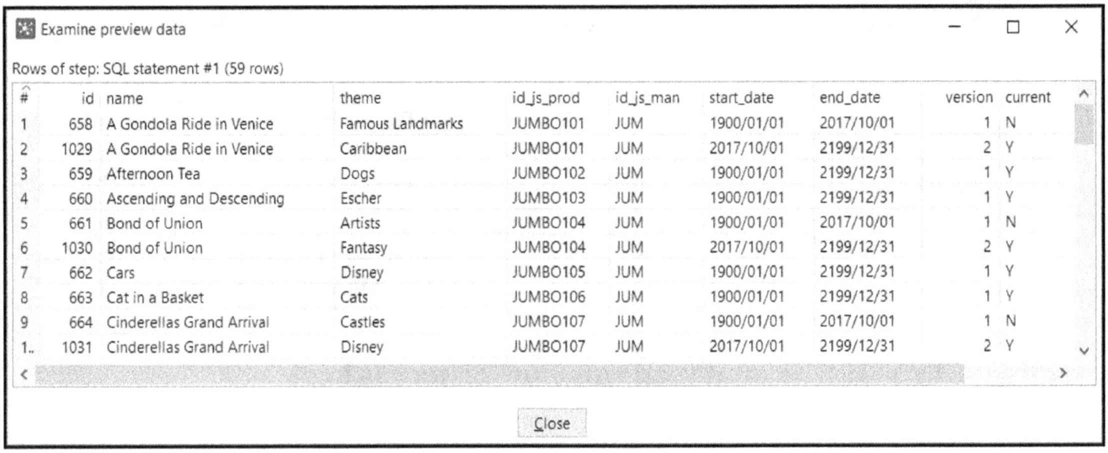

Examine preview data

Rows of step: SQL statement #1 (59 rows)

#	id	name	theme	id_js_prod	id_js_man	start_date	end_date	version	current
1	658	A Gondola Ride in Venice	Famous Landmarks	JUMBO101	JUM	1900/01/01	2017/10/01	1	N
2	1029	A Gondola Ride in Venice	Caribbean	JUMBO101	JUM	2017/10/01	2199/12/31	2	Y
3	659	Afternoon Tea	Dogs	JUMBO102	JUM	1900/01/01	2199/12/31	1	Y
4	660	Ascending and Descending	Escher	JUMBO103	JUM	1900/01/01	2199/12/31	1	Y
5	661	Bond of Union	Artists	JUMBO104	JUM	1900/01/01	2017/10/01	1	N
6	1030	Bond of Union	Fantasy	JUMBO104	JUM	2017/10/01	2199/12/31	2	Y
7	662	Cars	Disney	JUMBO105	JUM	1900/01/01	2199/12/31	1	Y
8	663	Cat in a Basket	Cats	JUMBO106	JUM	1900/01/01	2199/12/31	1	Y
9	664	Cinderellas Grand Arrival	Castles	JUMBO107	JUM	1900/01/01	2017/10/01	1	N
1..	1031	Cinderellas Grand Arrival	Disney	JUMBO107	JUM	2017/10/01	2199/12/31	2	Y

Close

Previewing data in a Type II Dimension

In the final preview, you can observe that there are products with more than one version. Take as an example the product with the name `A Gondola Ride in Venice`. Before `2017/10/01`, the puzzle was classified as `Famous Landmarks`. After that date, the new classification is `Caribbean`.

Let's analyze how this update process worked.

As explained before, when a record arrives at the **Dimension L/U** step, a lookup is made by the keys in the first grid, and also using the period of validity. For this particular product, the lookup succeeds. There is a record for which the keys match and the period from `start_date` to `end_date` of the record `01/01/1900` to `31/12/2199` contains the value of the **Stream Datefield**, that is, `01/10/2017`.

Once found, the step compares the fields you put in the **Fields** tab, `name` and `theme`, in the dimension table against `pro_name` and `pro_theme` in the incoming stream.

As there is a difference in the `theme` field, the step inserts a new record and modifies the current—it changes the validity dates and sets the current flag to `false`. Now this puzzle has two versions in the dimension table. These update and insert operations are made for all records that changed.

For the records that didn't change, the step finds records in the dimension table but as nothing changed, nothing is inserted nor updated.

Explaining and loading Type III SCD and Hybrid SCD

In the preceding example, in which you loaded a Type II SCD, you filled the **Type of dimension update** column with the **Insert** option for every field. By doing this, you loaded a pure Type II dimension, that is, a dimension that keeps track of all changes in all fields. In the sample puzzles dimension, you kept history of changes both in the theme and name fields. If you want to track sales by theme, keeping a Type II SCD is the option you should choose. On the other hand, if the name of the puzzle changes, you may not be interested in the previous name. Fortunately, you are not forced to keep track of every change in your dimension. In a situation like this, you may change the configuration and create a **Hybrid SCD**. Instead of selecting `Insert` for every field, you may select `Update` or `Punch through`:

- When there is a change in a field for which you choose `Update`, the new value overwrites the old value in the last dimension record version. This is the usual behavior in Type I SCDs.
- When there is a change in a field for which you choose `Punch through`, the new data overwrites the old value in all record versions.

Note that if you select `Update` for all the fields, the **Dimension L/U** step allows you to load a Type I SCD. As for a Type I, you are not interested in range dates; you can leave the **Stream Datefield** textbox empty. The current date is assumed by default.

Besides Type I and Type II, there is also the **Type III Slowly Changing Dimension**. This type of SCD stores the immediately preceding and current value for a descriptive field of the dimension. Each entity is stored in a single record. The field for which you want to keep the previous value has two columns assigned in the record: one for the current value and other for the old. Sometimes it is possible to have a third column holding the date of effective change.

Type III SCD is appropriate to use when you don't want to keep all of the history and mainly when you need to support two views of the attribute simultaneously—the previous and current. Suppose that you have an Employees dimension. Among the attributes, you have their position. People are promoted from time to time and you want to keep these changes in the dimension; however, you are not interested in knowing all the intermediate positions the employees have been through. In this case, you may implement a Type III SCD. PDI doesn't have an ad hoc step to load Type III SCD but you can still load these types of dimensions. You can use a **Database lookup** step to get the previous value. Then with a **Dimension L/U** step or a **Combination L/U** step, you insert or update the records.

You may have read about several types of SCDs besides these. In practice, the most common are both Type I and Type II along with Hybrid SCD. The choice of the type of SCD depends on the business needs.

Loading other kinds of dimensions

In terms of database tables, dimensions may be represented with tables in a one-to-one relationship. This was the case of the dimensions explained so far. Despite being the common situation, this is not always the case.

A one-to-one relationship between a dimension and a dimension table is not required, but may coincidentally exist.

In real situations, we can have database tables that hold information for several dimensions, as well as dimensions that are not stored in any dimension table. In this section, you will learn a bit about these special dimensions.

Loading a mini dimension

A **mini dimension** is a dimension where you store the frequently analyzed or frequently changing attributes of a large dimension. Look at the products in the `Jigsaw` puzzles database. There are several puzzles attributes you may be interested in, for example, when you analyze the sales, that is, number of puzzles in a single pack, number of pieces of the puzzles, material of the product, and so on. Instead of creating a big dimension with all puzzles attributes, you can create a mini dimension that stores only a selection of attributes. There would be one row in this mini dimension for each unique combination of the selected attributes encountered in the products table.

Here, you have the definition of a sample table that could serve as a mini dimension table with puzzles attributes:

Column	**Description**
`id`	Surrogate key
`glowsInDark`	Y/N
`is3D`	Y/N
`wooden`	Y/N

isPanoramic	Y/N
nrPuzzles	Number of puzzles in a single pack
nrPieces	Number of pieces of the puzzle

Loading this kind of table is really simple. For this sample mini-dimension, you could take the following query as a starting point:

```
SELECT DISTINCT pro_type
              , pro_packaging
              , pro_shape
              , pro_style
FROM  products
WHERE pro_type like 'PUZZLE%'
```

Then, you use the output stream of the **Table Input** to create the fields you need for the dimension, for example, for the `is3D` field, you'll have to check the value of the `pro_shape` field.

Once you have all the fields you need, the records can be inserted into the dimension table using a **Combination L/U** step. In this mini dimension, the key is made by all the fields of the table. As a consequence, you don't need an extra **Update** step.

Loading junk dimensions

A **junk dimension** is an abstract dimension that groups unrelated low-cardinality flags, indicators, and attributes. Each of these items could technically be a dimension on its own, but grouping them into a junk dimension has the advantage of keeping your database model simple. It also saves space and contributes to better performance.

An example of a junk dimension in our model could be one that puts together the payment and buy method. The way to load the dimension is quite the same as the one explained for mini dimensions.

Explaining degenerate dimensions

When the fact table's grain is at the transaction level, we could also have columns with ticket number, check number, or transaction ID. As these fields allow filtering or grouping, they can also be seen as dimensions. As they are part of the fact table, they are called **degenerate dimensions**. These particular dimensions don't fall in any of the categories explained, as there is no associated dimension table.

Loading fact tables

Fact tables contain the central information of star models. In this section, you will learn to load these kinds of tables. This is the list of topics covered:

- Introducing different kinds of fact tables
- Translating business keys into surrogate keys
- Loading fact tables with PDI

Learning the basics about fact tables

As explained in the introduction, fact tables are the central tables in a dimensional model. While the dimensions serve to group, filter, and describe data, the fact tables contain the measures of the business. There are basically two types of fact tables:

- **Cumulative**: They describe what happened over a period of time—a `Sales` fact table is a typical example of this. The measures for these types of fact tables are mostly additive, that is, measures that can be added across all dimensions.
- **Snapshots**: They describe the activity of a business process, with pictures taken at a given instant of time. Examples of this kind of fact table are postal tracking systems, order processing, or claims. You can take one snapshot every X period of time (hourly, daily, and so on). Then you insert new pictures into the fact table, along with the timestamp in which the picture was taken, or you can overwrite the fact with the latest status of everything. In snapshots, fact tables measures are mainly semi-additive—they can be added only across a subset of the dimensions, and not additive—they cannot be added through dimensions.

Deciding the level of granularity

The level of detail in your star model is called **grain**. The granularity is directly related to the kind of questions you expect your model to answer. Let's see some examples.

Suppose that we build a fact table with sales along with the following dimensions: product type, manufacturer, region, and time. With this model, we would be able to answer the following questions:

- Beyond puzzles, which kind of product is the best sold?
- Do you sell more products manufactured by Ravensburger than products manufactured by Educa Jigsaws?

What if you want to know the names of the top ten products sold? You simply cannot, because that level of detail is not stored in the proposed model. The dimensions contain information about the type of product, but don't have the detail at the product level. To answer this type of question, you need a lower level of granularity. You could have that by adding a product dimension where each record represents a particular product.

Now let's see the time dimension. Each record in that dimension represents a particular calendar day. This allows you to answer questions such as, how many products did you sell every day in the last four months?

If you were not interested in daily, but in monthly information, you could have designed a model with a higher level of granularity by creating a time dimension with just one record per month.

Understanding the level of granularity of your model is key to the process of loading the fact table.

Translating the business keys into surrogate keys

No matter the kind of fact table to load, the loading process has much in common for all of them. The source data for the fact table comes from an OLTP system where data contains business keys. In the fact table, you have foreign keys to surrogate keys, the primary keys in the dimension tables. So, before inserting the data into the fact table, for each business key used in your data, you have to find the proper surrogate key. Depending on the kind of dimensions referenced in the fact table, you get the correspondent surrogate keys in a different way.

In the following subsections, we will see how you obtain the surrogate key in each case.

Obtaining the surrogate key for Type I SCD

To get the surrogate key in case of Type I SCD, you use a **Database lookup** step. The following image shows you an example.

In this case, the step is used to get the surrogate key for the REGION dimension:

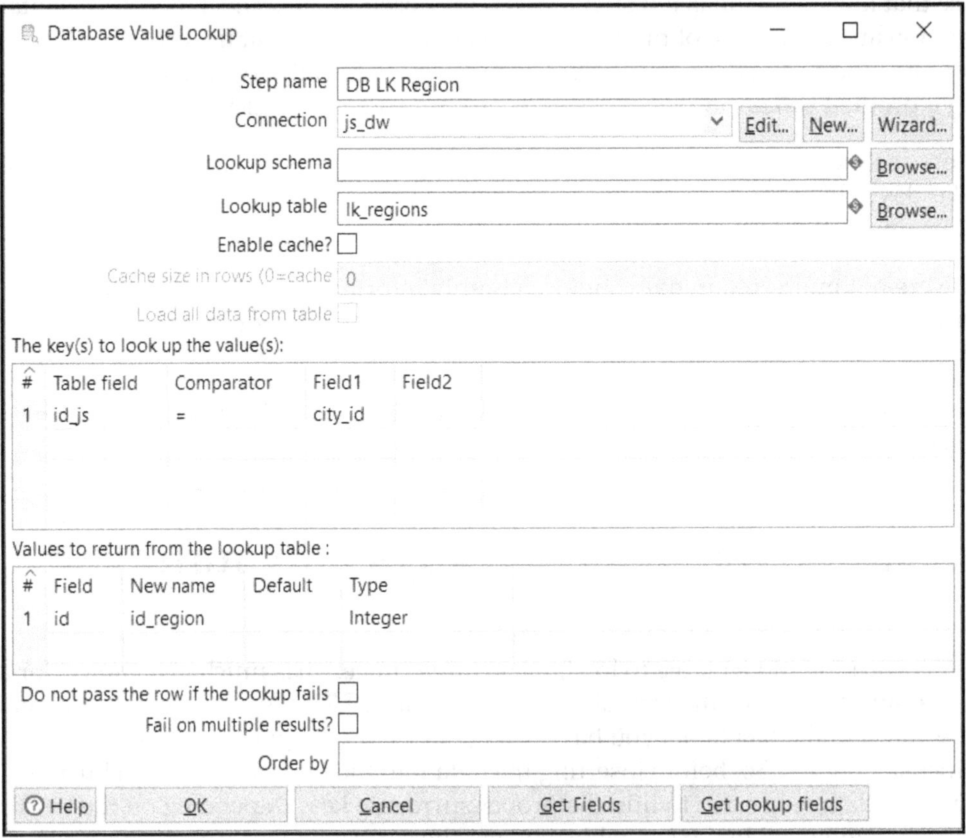

Obtaining the surrogate key for Type I SCD

In the upper grid, you look for the business key. As **Table field**, you put the dimension field that contains the business key, and as **Field1**, you put the field coming from your source data.

In the lower grid, you get the surrogate key and rename it with the name of the field in the fact table that you will populate. If the key is not found, you should use `0` as default, that is, the record in the dimension reserved for unknown values.

Obtaining the surrogate key for Type II SCD

In the case of a Type II SCD, you use the same step that you used to load the table dimension—a **Dimension L/U** step. The difference is that here you unchecked the **Update the dimension?** option. By doing that, the step behaves quite as a database lookup—you provide the keys to look up and the step returns the fields you put in both the **Fields** tab and the **Technical key field** option. The difference with this step is that here you have to provide time information. Using this time information, PDI finds and returns the proper record in time from the Type II SCD.

The following image shows you how to configure the step for the sample PUZZLES dimension:

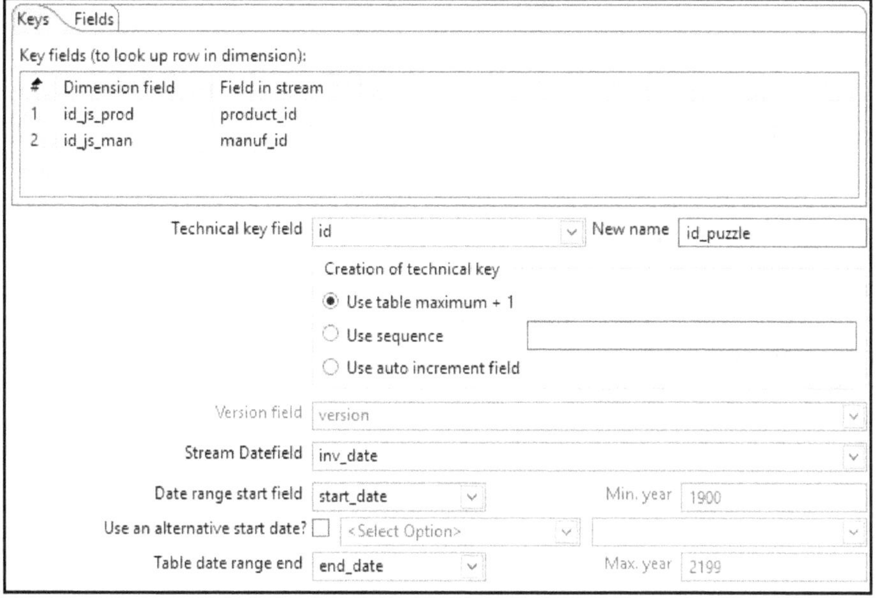

Obtaining the surrogate key for a Type II SCD

Here, you give PDI the names of the columns that store the validity date range—`start_date` and `end_date`. You also give it the name of the field stream to use in order to compare the dates—in this case, `inv_date`, that is, the date that you will store in your fact.

Remember the sample puzzle we looked when we loaded the PUZZLE dimension. It had two records:

id	name	theme	id_js_prod	id_js_man	start_date	end_date	version	current
658	A Gondola Ride in Venice	Famous Landmarks	JUMBO101	JUM	1900/01/01 ...	2017/10/01 ...	1	N
1029	A Gondola Ride in Venice	Caribbean	JUMBO101	JUM	2017/10/01 ...	2199/12/31 ...	2	Y

Sample data for a Type II SCD

If we load a fact table with a date before `1/10/2017`, the **Dimension L/U** will return the first key, `658`, when the product belonged to the `Famous Landmarks` category.

If, when loading the fact, we provide a date greater than `1/10/2017`, the step will return the second key, `1029`, for which the product was classified as belonging to the `Caribbean` theme.

If no record is found for the given keys on the given date, the step retrieves the ID `0`, which is used for unknown data.

Obtaining the surrogate key for the junk dimension

As said before, the payment and buy methods could be stored in a junk dimension. A junk dimension can be loaded using a **Combination L/U** step. As all the fields in a junk dimension are part of the primary key, you don't need an extra **Update** step to load it. The following image shows you how to load this sample dimension:

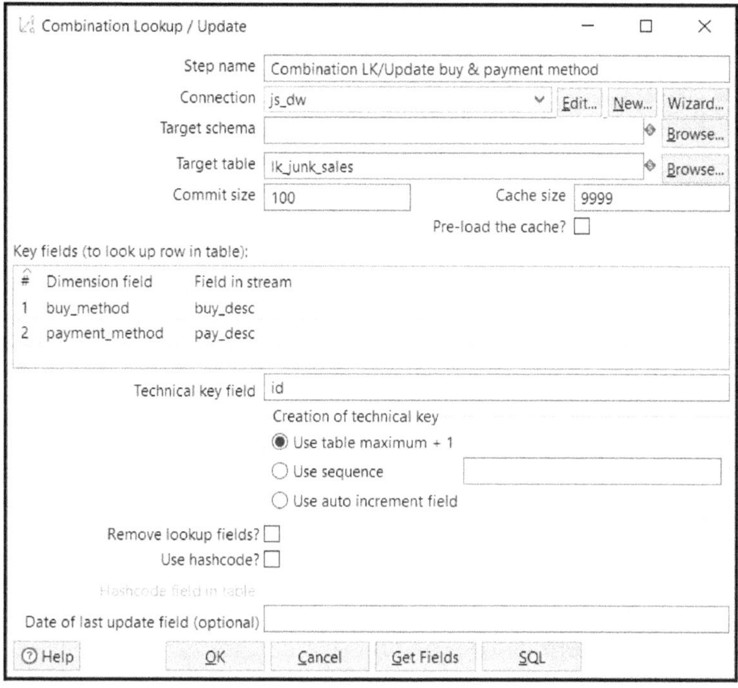

Loading a Junk dimension

When you use a **Combination L/U** step, the step returns the generated key to you. So, the use of the step here to load and get the key at the same time fits perfectly.

If the dimension had been loaded previously, instead of a **Combination L/U** step, you could use a **Database lookup** step by putting the key fields in the upper grid and the key in the lower grid of the **Database lookup** configuration window.

Obtaining the surrogate key for a time dimension

In the case of a time dimension, if the key is the date in numeric format, the method to get the surrogate key is simply changing the metadata for the date, in the same way we did when loading the dimension: from date to string first, and then from string to number.

If, instead of the date you have a regular surrogate key, you can use a **Database lookup** step to get the surrogate key.

The following table summarizes the different possibilities to get surrogate keys:

Dimension type	**Method to get the surrogate key**	**Sample dimension**
Type I SCD	**Database lookup** step.	REGIONS
Type II SCD	**Dimension L/U** step.	PUZZLES
Junk and Mini	**Combination L/U** step if you load the dimension at the same time as you load the fact (as in the section). **Database lookup** step if the dimension is already loaded.	Sales Junk dimension
Degenerate	As you don't have a table or key to translate, you just store the data as a field in the fact. You don't have to worry about getting surrogate keys.	Product type
Time	Change the metadata to the proper format if you use the date as the key (as in the section). **Dimension L/U** step if you use a normal surrogate key.	Time

Loading a cumulative fact table

In order to load a fact table, you have to look at the grain, or level, of detail. For example, looking at our model, you can see that the maximum level of detail is a city for the REGION dimension; the maximum level of detail is a day for the time dimension. This information is then used to aggregate the measures. For example, suppose that we want to load a sales fact table with the following definition:

```
CREATE TABLE FT_SALES (
    date integer NOT NULL,
    id_region integer NOT NULL,
    id_puzzle integer NOT NULL,
    quantity integer default 0 NOT NULL,
    sales numeric(8,2) default 0 NOT NULL
   );
```

In this sample fact table, we have foreign keys to three dimensions—`TIME`, `REGION`, and `PUZZLES`—and two measures—`quantity` representing the number of products sold and `sales` representing the amounts. In order to feed the table, what you need to take from the source is the sum of `quantity` and the sum of `sales` for every combination of `day` and `city` as well as the `puzzle`.

You do this with a regular query using a **Table input** step. The output of the step will be the aggregated data by business keys.

As this is a cumulative load, as part of the query, you should also limit the results with a WHERE constraint specifying a data range for the sales.

After getting the data from the source, you have to translate the business keys into surrogate keys. You do it in different ways depending on the kind of each related dimension.

Finally, you are ready to insert the data into the fact table using a regular **Table Output** step.

The following screenshot shows you a draft of what you would have in the main Transformation:

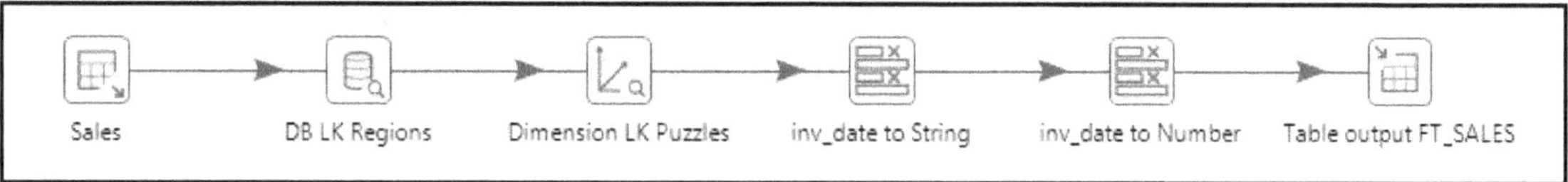

Loading a cumulative fact table

Loading a snapshot fact table

As explained, a snapshot fact table keeps pictures of the current status of a business process. Let's suppose that we keep track of the status of orders. The orders may be waiting, ready to deliver, delayed, cancelled, and so on. Now we want to reflect this information in a fact table.

The main process to load the snapshot fact table doesn't differ from the one for a cumulative fact table. You have to look at the grain, get the information from the source, and obtain the surrogate keys that will be used in the fact. The main difference is at the time of saving the data into the fact table, as explained in the following section.

Loading a fact table by inserting snapshot data

For the proposed example, suppose that every day you take a picture of the orders aggregated by manufacturer. For each manufacturer, you want to know the quantity of orders in each status. You want to have this picture into the fact table along with a timestamp. The objective of this fact table is to be able to filter by date and know the status of your business on that particular date.

In order to load this fact table, you just add a field with the timestamp, and then you insert the data with a **Table Output** step.

Loading a fact table by overwriting snapshot data

Now suppose that you want to track individual orders. In the fact table, you have columns where you want to save the date in which the order was in each state. In this case, when you take the picture, you want to not only insert new orders into the fact table, but also update the status in the orders that already were saved in the fact in a previous load.

The way we do this is with an **Insert/Update** step. As an alternative and for better performance, you can do as follows:

1. In the fact, define a primary key as the `order id`.
2. Update the fact table with a **Table output** step. The primary key will cause the orders already in the fact table to be rejected by the **Table output**.
3. Capture the error in the **Table output** and redirect the failed inserts to an **Update** step.

The part that inserts the fact table would look like this:

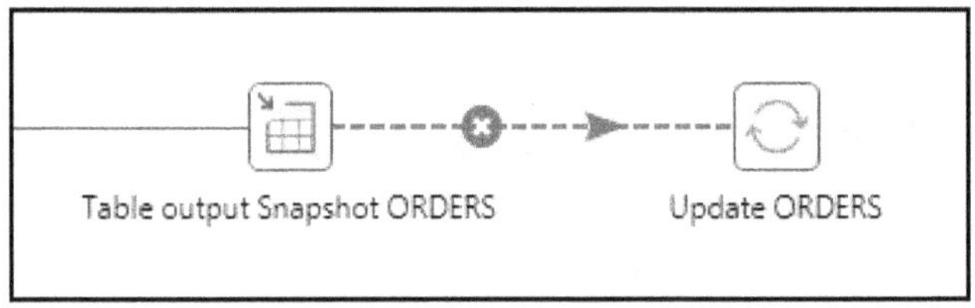

Updating a snapshot fact table

Summary

This chapter was fully devoted to datawarehousing concepts. First of all, there was a brief introduction to dimensional concepts. You learned about facts and dimensions, and also learned about technical terms as for example business keys and surrogate keys. Then you learned about the different kind of dimensions—including time dimensions and slowly changing dimensions—and how to load them with PDI. Finally, you were introduced to different kind of fact tables, and also learned to load those tables with data.

Starting from the next chapter, we will see advanced concepts that will allow you to use PDI to address any complicated challenge.

12
Creating Portable and Reusable Transformations

When you design and implement jobs and transformations in PDI, you not only want certain tasks to be accomplished, but also want a work that can be reused, easy to maintain, and more. This chapter explains several techniques meant to accomplish these objectives. We will cover the following topics:

- Using Kettle variables to give flexibility to your transformations
- Reusing part of your transformations using mappings
- Copying and getting rows as part of a process flow
- Iterating the execution of transformations

The basics about Spoon have already been covered. Therefore, in this chapter, we will not give much space to details such as how to configure a **Text file input** step. Instead, we will focus on the techniques you will learn.

If you get into trouble, you can refer to earlier chapters, browse the Pentaho *Transformation Step Reference* at `https://help.pentaho.com/Documentation/8.0/Products/Data_Integration/Transformation_Step_Reference`, or simply download and browse the material for the chapter from the book's site.

Defining and using Kettle variables

In `Chapter 3`, *Creating Basic Task Flows,* you were introduced to Kettle variables. This section resumes the subject by explaining to you all the kinds of Kettle variables, how to define them, and all the ways to use them.

Introducing all kinds of Kettle variables

Kettle variables can be defined in several ways, and with the different scope. You already know about predefined variables and variables defined in the `kettle.properties` file, but there are more options. The following subsections summarize them all.

Explaining predefined variables

Predefined variables are Kettle variables mainly related to the environment in which PDI is running. These variables are ready to be used both in Jobs and Transformations and their scope is the **Java Virtual Machine** (**JVM**).

The following table lists some of the most used predefined variables:

Subject	Predefined variables
Operating system	`${os.name}`, `${os.version}`
Current user	`${user.home}`, `${user.name}`, `${user.timezone}`, `${user.language}`
Java installation	`${java.home}`, `${java.io.tmpdir}`, `${java.version}`
Kettle (aka PDI) installation	`${Internal.Kettle.Build.Date}`, `${Internal.Kettle.Build.Version}`, `${Internal.Kettle.Version}`

Among the internal or predefined variables, there is one that we will use in several places in the rest of this chapter `${Internal.Entry.Current.Directory}`. This variable indicates the current filename or repository directory in a Transformation step or Job entry.

The `${Internal.Entry.Current.Directory}` variable is meant to be used in place of the following, which are deprecated since PDI 7: `{Internal.Job.Filename.Directory}`, `${Internal.Job.Repository.Directory}`, `${Internal.Transformation.Filename.Directory}`, and `${Internal.Transformation.Repository.Directory}`.

If you look for some environmental information and don't find it among the predefined variables, you can try the **Get System Info** step, which doesn't retrieve variables but fields. The **Get System Info** step allows you to get information related to dates (for example, Yesterday or Today), Kettle information (version, build version, and build date), IP address, JVM information (max memory, total memory, and JVM free memory), among other options.

Revisiting the kettle.properties file

The `kettle.properties` file is used to define variables with JVM scope. If a variable meets the following conditions:

- It is going to be used in several places in your project
- Its value is fixed—you don't expect it to change—and known beforehand

Then it is a perfect candidate to be defined in the `kettle.properties` file. Examples of variables that you define here are paths to common directories, for example, directories for logs, temporary files, or input files, SMTP settings, or database connection settings.

Defining variables at runtime

There are a couple of ways to define a variable at runtime, as explained in the following subsections.

Setting a variable with a constant value

Setting a variable with a constant value is really simple. The following instructions explain to you how to do it:

1. Create a Job and add a **START** entry.
2. From the **General** category of entries, add a **Set variables...** Job entry. Create a hop from the **START** entry toward this one.

3. Double-click on the **Set variables...** entry and fill the lower grid as shown:

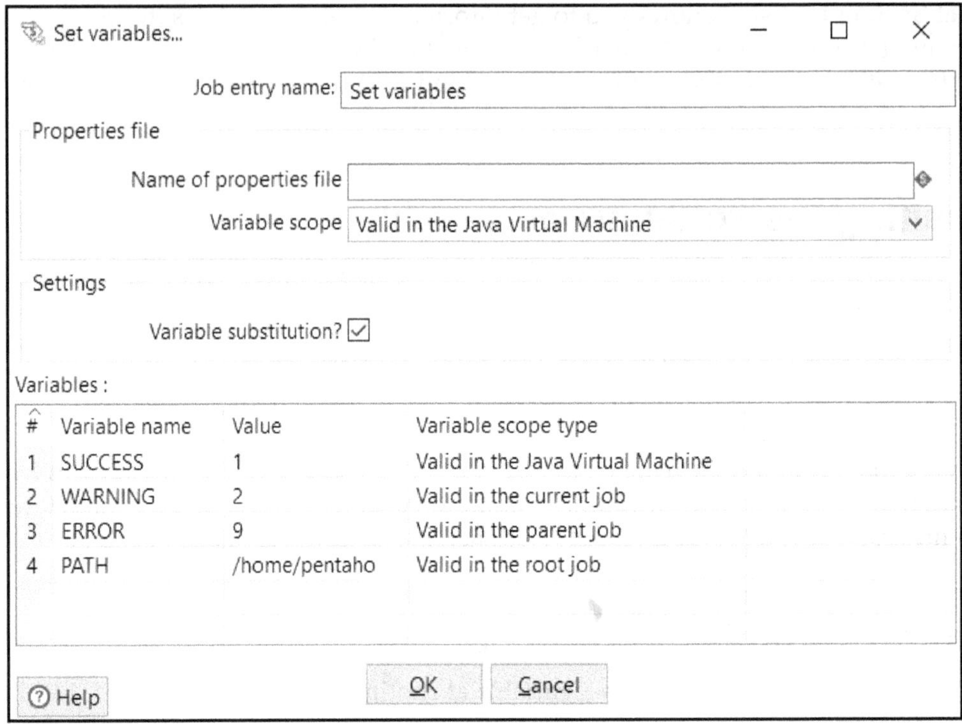

Setting variables with fixed values

4. Close the window.

Once the **Set variables...** entry is executed, the variable or variables defined are ready to be used in any of the entries that follow it.

As you can see in the preceding screenshot, when you define a variable, you have to provide the value and the scope. There are four scopes available. For the moment, we are only interested in the first two:

- A variable with **Java Virtual Machine** scope will be available in all Jobs and Transformations you run.

- A variable with **Valid in the current Job** scope will be valid in the Job where you define it and also in all the Transformations that the job executes.

We will go back to these definitions and we will also explain the other two scopes in `Chapter 14`, *Creating Advanced Jobs*.

To demonstrate the use of the **Set variables...** entry, we put it just after the **START** entry, but you can use it anywhere in a Job.

You can also set variables defined in a properties file. For this, you use the same entry, but fill the **Properties file** box instead. In this case, you provide the full path to the properties file and the scope you want to give to all the variables in the file.

Setting a variable with a value unknown beforehand

You just saw how to set a variable with a fixed value. Now you will learn to set a variable with a value that you don't know beforehand. There are many examples of this:

- The result of a query against a database
- The result of a call to a web service
- The current date
- The name of a file

In all these cases, the solution involves creating a Transformation. The idea here is to create a dataset with a single row where the fields contain the values that you want to set to the variables. Let's see it as an example. Suppose that you want to set a variable with the current date, and a second variable with the date before, both in the format `yyyy-MM-dd`. This is how you do it:

1. Create a Transformation.
2. From the **Input** category, add a **Get System Info** step to the work area.

3. Double-click on the step and fill the grid as shown:

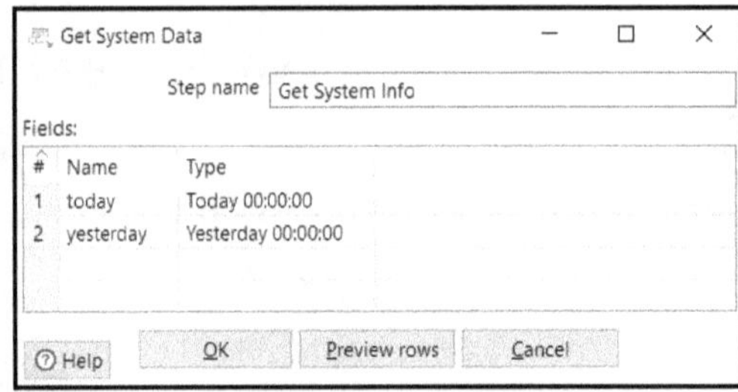

Configuring a Get System Info step

4. After the **Get System Info** step, add a **Select values** step.
5. Double-click on the **Select values** step and use it to change the **Type** and **Format** for the dates, as shown in the following screenshot:

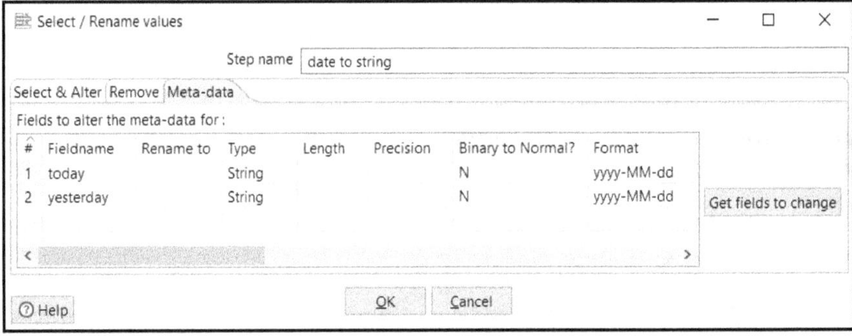

Changing the metadata

6. With the **Select values** step selected, run a preview. You should see something like this:

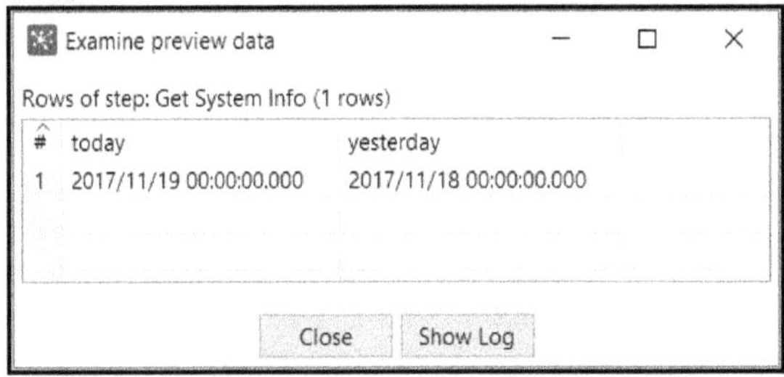

Previewing data

7. After the **Select values** step, add a **Set Variables** step. You will find it in the **Job** category of steps.
8. Double-click on the step and configure it like this:

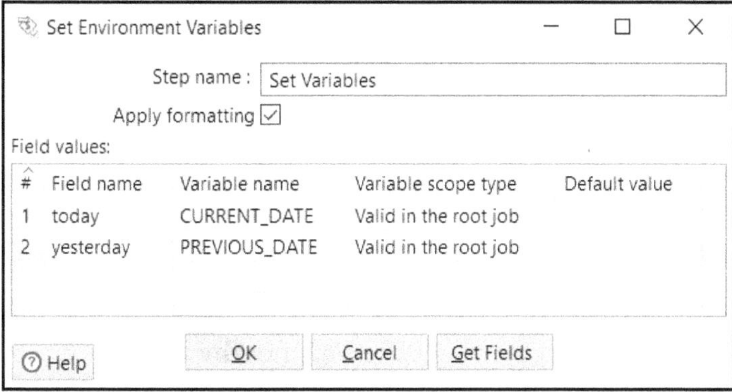

Configuring a Set Variables step

9. Click on **OK**. You will see the following **Notice** window:

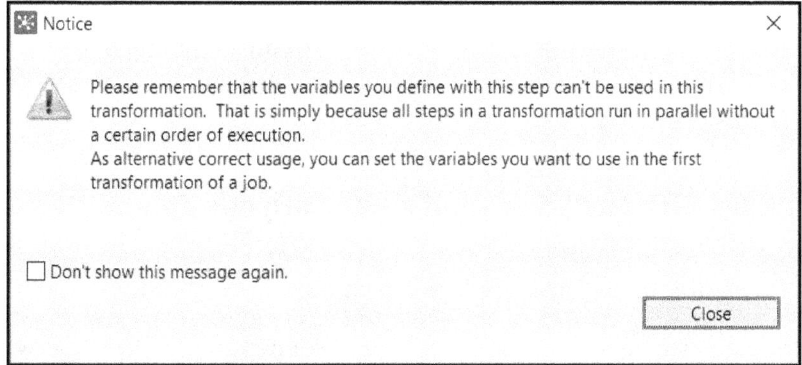

Variables warning window

10. Click on **Close**.
11. Save the Transformation and run it.

12. In the **Logging** tab of the **Execution Result** window, you will see something like this:

```
2017/11/19 09:07:37 - Set Variables.0 - Set variable CURRENT_DATE
to value [2017-11-19]
2017/11/19 09:07:37 - Set Variables.0 - Set variable PREVIOUS_DATE
to value [2017-11-18]
```

In this case, you only set values for two variables, but you can set values to any number of variables.

If you have several values to set, you may save time using the **Get Fields** button located in the configuration window of the **Set Variables** step. This button populates the grid with one row per variable. By default, the name of each variable will be equal to the name of the correspondent field but in uppercase, and the scope will be **Valid in the root job**.

The variables you define with a **Set variables** step can be used in the same way and in the same places where you use any Kettle variable. Just take precautions to avoid using these variables in the same Transformation where you have set them.

As stated in the warning window that appears when you close the **Set Variables** configuration window, the variables defined in a Transformation are not available for use until you leave that Transformation.

Setting variables with partial or total results of your flow

There is still another common situation in which you may want to set variables—at the end of a flow in a Transformation. These are some examples:

- Setting a variable with `OK` or `ERROR` values depending on the flow where the rows go
- Setting a variable with the total number of rows inserted in a table
- Setting a variable with the total number of valid rows coming from a file

To set these variables, you use the **Set Variables** step in the same way. The only thing that you have to take into account is that the **Set Variables** step may receive only one row. So, before linking any flow with this step, you have to add the proper PDI steps in order to keep just one row. You may use a **Group by** step, a **Unique** step, a **Filter row** step, among others. The choice will depend on the nature of your dataset and the value you want to set.

Defining and using named parameters

PDI Transformations can receive parameters, which makes Transformations more flexible and reusable. The parameters that you provide to Transformations are called **named parameters**. Inside a Transformation, a named parameter can be used exactly as a Kettle variable, and its scope is local to the Transformation.

Why would you define a named parameter over another kind of variable? The main advantage of a named parameter is that, at the time you define them, you can set default values. Doing this way, you are not forced to provide values when running the Transformation.

The named parameters are defined in the **Transformation Properties** window in the following way:

1. Create a Transformation.
2. Open the **Transformation Properties** window by double-clicking on the work area or by pressing *Ctrl* + *T*.
3. Select the **Parameters** tab and fill the grid with the named parameters, as shown in the following example:

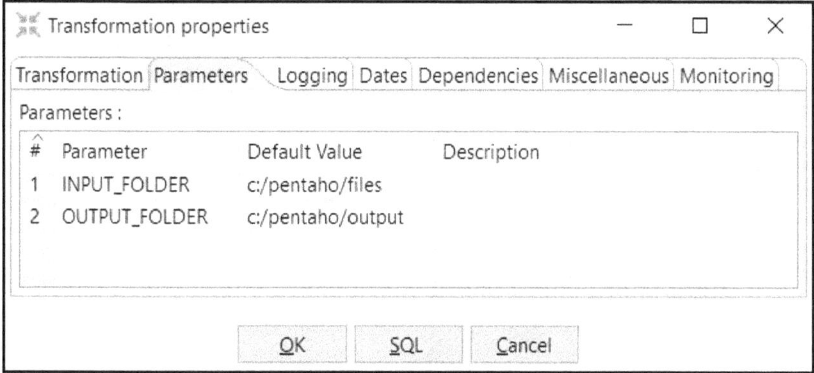

Defining named parameters

4. Close the window.

These named parameters are ready to be used inside the Transformation as any other Kettle variable. Now we will create a stream that uses them to demonstrate how you provide values for these parameters. We will read a file from `${INPUT_FOLDER}` and write the first 10 lines of that file in a new file in the `${OUTPUT_FOLDER}`. For this exercise, we will read a file named `exam1.txt` that comes with the bundle code, but you can read any file of your choice, as the content of the file is not important in this exercise.

1. Drag a **Text file input** step to the work area and use it to read the `exam1.txt` file. As **File/Directory**, type `${INPUT_FOLDER}/exam1.txt`.
2. In the **Content** tab, set the **Limit** textbox to `10`.
3. Drag a **Text file output** step and create a hop from the **Text file input** step toward this one.
4. Configure the **Text file output** step to write the fields to a new file. As **Filename**, type `${OUTPUT_FOLDER}/first_10_students`.
5. Save the Transformation.
6. Press *F9* to run the Transformation.
7. In the **Run Options** window, you will be prompted for the values. In the **Parameters** tab, fill the grid with the values of your choice—you type them in the **Value** column. If the default values are fine, you don't have to type anything. The following screenshot shows you an example where only the output folder needs to be changed:

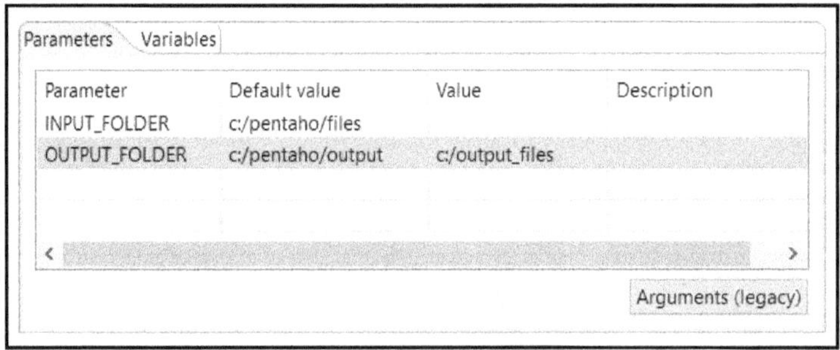

Providing values for named parameters

8. Click on **Run**.
9. When the execution finishes, the output folder that you specified as the named parameter should have been created, if it didn't exist. Inside that folder, there should be a file named `first_10_students.txt`.

It's not mandatory to define default values for named parameters. In that case, make sure to provide proper values when you run the Transformation.

Using variables as fields of your stream

As you already know, Kettle variables can be used in Jobs and Transformations wherever you see a dollar sign. There is one more way to use variables—getting their values as fields of your stream. For this, you have to use the **Get Variables** step.

With the **Get Variables** step, you can get the value for one or more variables. The kind of variable can be any of the Kettle variables types you just learned the variables defined in the `kettle.properties` file, internal variables, for example, `${user.dir}`, named parameters, or other Kettle variables.

Let's see how to use this step by modifying a Transformation from `Chapter 2`, *Getting Started with Transformations*. At that moment, you created a Transformation that generated a dataset with one row by date in a date range. Later, in `Chapter 11`, *Loading Data Marts with PDI*, you reused and modified the Transformation to load a *Time Dimension* table. In both cases, the date range was defined with fixed values in a **Data Grid** step. Now you will learn to enhance these Transformations using variables for the date range:

1. Open the `date_range.ktr` Transformation that you created in `Chapter 2`, *Getting Started with Transformations* and save it with a different name.
2. Open the **Transformation properties** window and define two named parameters: `DATE_FROM` with default value `2010-01-01` and `DATE_TO` with default value `2020-12-31`. Close the window.
3. Now delete the **Data Grid** step.
4. From the **Job** category of steps, add a **Get Variables** step to the work area. Create a hop from this step toward the first **Calculator** step. Your Transformation will look as follows:

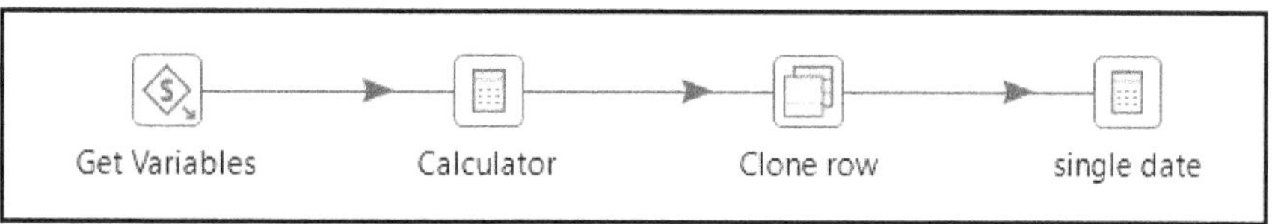

Sample Transformation that gets variables

5. Edit the **Get Variables** step and fill it in, as shown in the following screenshot:

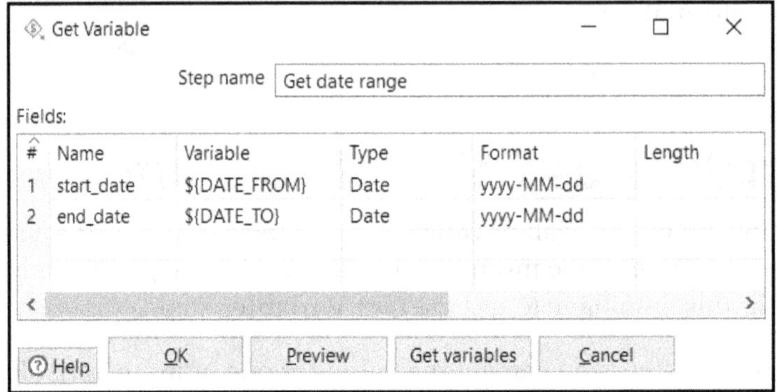

Configuring a Get variables step

6. Note that the **Variable** column is to specify the variable to read, while the **Name** column is the name of the new field that will be populated with the value of that variable.
7. Close the window.
8. With the last **Calculator** step selected, click on **Preview**, and then click on **Configure**. This will allow us to provide values for the named parameters just defined.
9. In the **Parameters** tab, fill the grid providing the values: `2017-01-01` and `2017-12-31` for the `DATE_FROM` and `DATE_TO` variables respectively.
10. Click on **Launch**. You will see this:

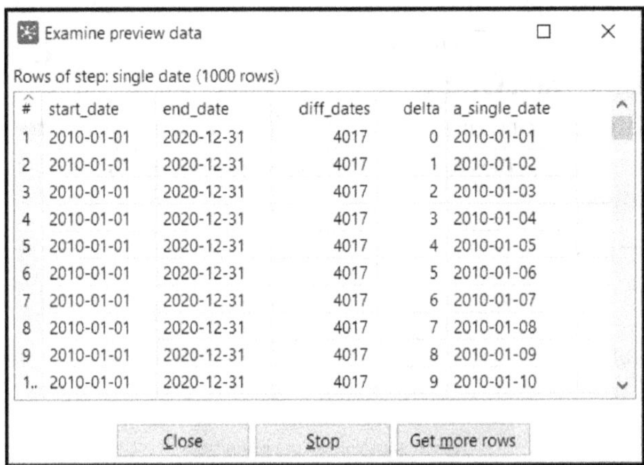

Previewing a Transformation

As you can see, using variables as part of the stream by adding a **Get Variables** step is really simple. Let's just highlight some aspects of the use of this step:

- You can put the **Get Variables** step as the first step of a stream as in this example, or in the middle of the stream. In the first case, the **Get Variables** step creates a dataset with one single row and as many fields as read variables. When the step is inserted in the middle of a stream, it adds to the incoming dataset as many fields as the variables it reads.
- The type of Kettle variables is `String` by default. However, at the time you get a variable, you can change its metadata. As an example of that, you converted `${START_DATE}` to a `Date` value using the `yyyy-MM-dd` mask.
- The full specification of the name of a variable allows you to mix variables with plain text. As an example, you can use a variable named `YEAR` instead of the `DATE_FROM` variable. Then in the **Variable** column of the **Get Variables** step, you may specify `${YEAR}-01-01`. When you execute the Transformation, this text will be expanded to the year you enter plus the string `-01-01`.

Note that the purpose of using the **Get Variable** step is to have the values of variables as fields in the dataset. Otherwise, you don't need to use this step when using a variable. You just use it wherever you see a dollar sign icon.

Creating reusable Transformations

On occasions, you have bunches of steps that do common tasks and you notice that you will need them in other contexts. That is, you would copy, paste, and reuse part of your work unless you work with sub-transformations.

Creating and executing sub-transformations

Sub-transformations are, as the name suggests, Transformations inside Transformations.

The PDI proper name for a sub-transformation is **mapping**. However, as the word mapping is also used with other meanings in PDI—an example of that is the mapping of table fields with stream fields in a **Table output** step—we will use the more intuitive name sub-transformation.

A common reason to create sub-transformations is to isolate functionality that is likely to be needed more than once, in a single Transformation or in different places of your project. You implement the functionality once, and then you use it any number of times by calling the sub-transformation with a single PDI step.

Sub-transformations are also a way to isolate a subset of steps that accomplish a specific purpose. By moving these steps to a sub-transformation, your main Transformation becomes cleaner and easier to understand.

Creating and testing a sub-transformation

To explain how to develop a sub-transformation, we will create a very simple one. Our sub-transformation will have the purpose of taking a text as the input and splitting it into two fields in the following way: if the text is `Pentaho Data Integration`, the sub-transformation will split it into two—the first field will be `Pentaho` and the second field will be `DATA INTEGRATION`. Very simple but enough for demonstrating purposes.

First of all, we will create a regular Transformation that implements this functionality:

1. Create a new Transformation.
2. Add a **Data Grid** and a **JavaScript** step to the work area. Create a hop from the grid toward the other step.
3. Use the **Data Grid** step to define a field named `word`. Then fill the grid with sample data, for example, `dog`, `cat`, `bird`, `african elephant`, and `australian sea lion`.
4. Double-click on the **JavaScript** step and type the following code:

```
var first_word;
var other_words;
pos=indexOf(word," ");
if (pos>0) {
 first_word = substr(word,0,pos);
 other_words = substr(word, pos+1);
 }
else {
 first_word = word;
 other_words = "";
}
first_word = initCap(first_word);
other_words = upper(other_words);
```

5. Click on the **Get variables** button to fill the lower grid. Then close the window.

6. With the **JavaScript** step selected, run a preview. You will see this:

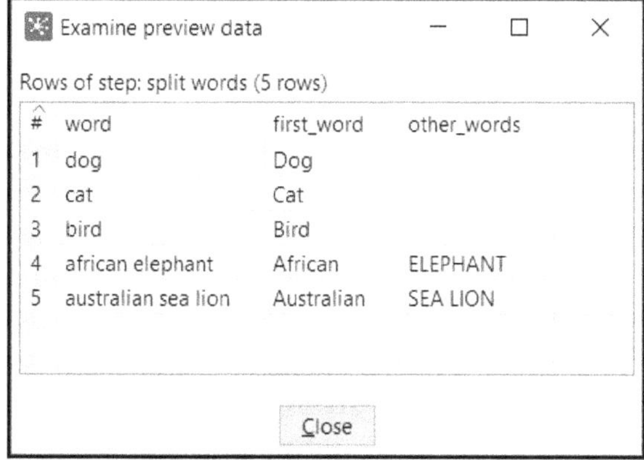

Previewing a Transformation

7. Close the window.

We have a Transformation that does what we expected. Now we have to do a couple of changes to convert it into a sub-transformation. A sub-transformation is like a regular Transformation but it has input and output steps that connect it to the Transformations that call it:

STEP	PURPOSE	CONFIGURATION
Mapping Input Specification	It defines the entry point to the sub-transformation	In this step, you specify just the fields needed by the sub-transformation
Mapping Output Specification	It defines where the flow ends	There is nothing to configure in this step

The presence of the **Mapping Input Specification** and **Mapping Output Specification** steps is the only fact that makes a sub-transformation different from a regular Transformation.

This is how we modify our Transformation:

1. From the **Mapping** category of steps, add a **Mapping Input specification** and a **Mapping output specification** step to the work area.

2. Link the steps as shown:

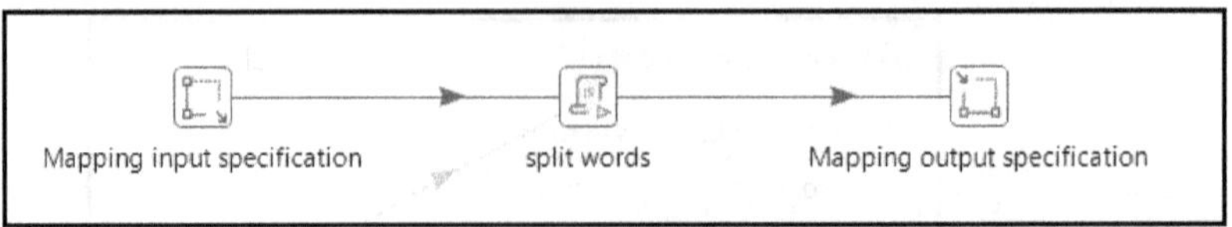

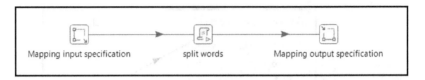

Building a sub-transformation

3. Don't remove the **Data Grid**. Just disable the hop that connects it to the **JavaScript** step. This way, you can enable it later if you need to test the sub-transformation isolated.
4. Double-click on the **Mapping Input Specification** step and fill it with the metadata expected as input:

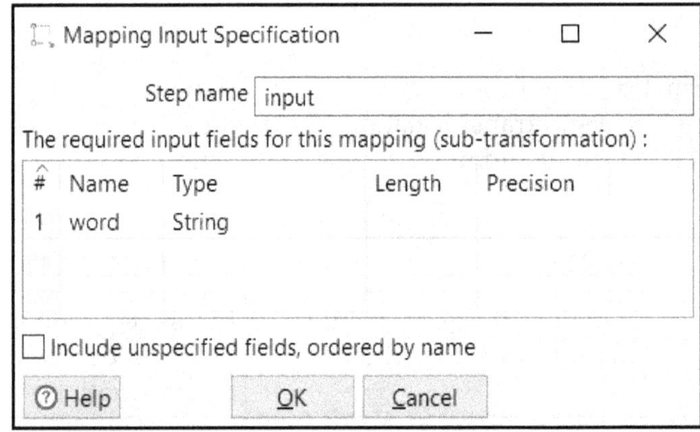

Configuring a Mapping Input Specification step

5. Close the window and save the Transformation.

The sub-transformation is ready to be used.

Executing a sub-transformation

There are two dedicated steps to use or execute a sub-transformation: **Mapping (sub-transformation)** step and **Simple Mapping (sub-transformation)** step. To execute a sub-transformation like the one created earlier, we will use the second one.

In this example, we will read a file that looks like the following one:

```
student_code;name;writing;reading;speaking;listening
80711-85;William Miller;81;83;80;90
20362-34;Jennifer Martin;87;76;70;80
75283-17;Margaret Wilson;99;94;90;80
83714-28;Helen Thomas;89;97;80;80
61666-55;Maria Thomas;88;77;70;80
...
```

After reading the file, we will call the sub-transformation to split the student's name.

Before starting, get the sample files from the book site. You will find several files, all of them with the same structure. Alternatively, you can create your own file with any sample data.

Here are the instructions:

1. Create a Transformation.
2. With a **Text file input** step, read the `exam1.txt` file that comes with the code bundle for the chapter.
3. From the **Mapping** category of steps, drag to the work area a **Simple Mapping** (sub-transformation) step (we will call it **Mapping** for short). Create a link from the **Text file input** step toward this new step.
4. Double-click on the **Mapping** step to configure it.
5. In the **Transformation:** textbox, type the full path for your sub-transformation, for example, `${Internal.Entry.Current.Directory}/subtransformations/split_word.ktr`.

6. Select the **Input** tab, and fill the grid as shown:

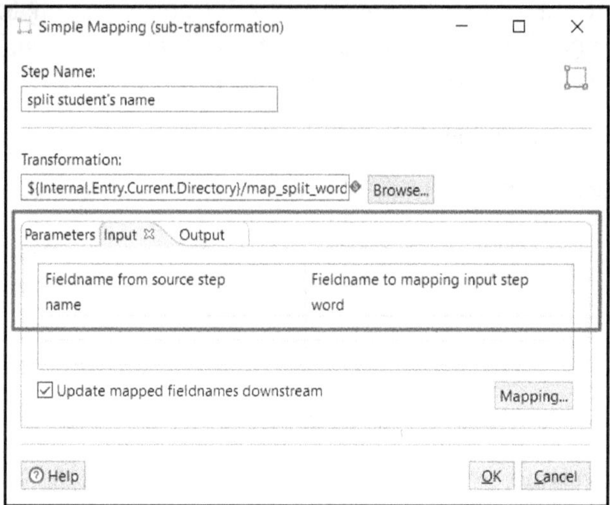

Configuring an Input tab

7. Select the **Output** tab, and fill the grid as shown:

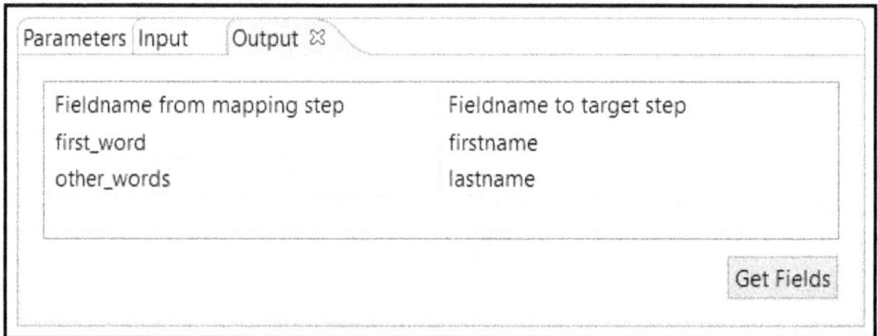

Configuring an Output tab

8. Close the window.
9. After the **Mapping** step, add a **Dummy** step.

10. With the **Dummy** step selected, run a preview. You will see this:

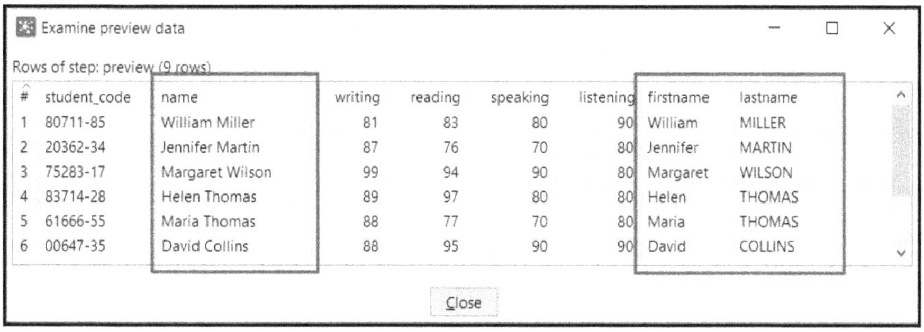

Examine preview data

Rows of step: preview (9 rows)

#	student_code	name	writing	reading	speaking	listening	firstname	lastname
1	80711-85	William Miller	81	83	80	90	William	MILLER
2	20362-34	Jennifer Martin	87	76	70	80	Jennifer	MARTIN
3	75283-17	Margaret Wilson	99	94	90	80	Margaret	WILSON
4	83714-28	Helen Thomas	89	97	80	80	Helen	THOMAS
5	61666-55	Maria Thomas	88	77	70	80	Maria	THOMAS
6	00647-35	David Collins	88	95	90	90	David	COLLINS

Close

Previewing the output of a sub-transformation

As you can deduce, the key to call a sub-transformation is to establish a relationship between the fields in your main Transformation and the fields in the sub-transformation. You do it by filling the **Input** and **Output** tabs in the **Mapping** step dialog window.

Let's start by explaining the input. In the input specification of the sub-transformation, you can see that it expects a field named `word`. In your Transformation, the field that you want to transform is called `name`. Therefore, in the **Input** tab of the **Mapping** step dialog window, you defined the mapping between `name` and `word`.

On the other end, the sub-transformation creates two new fields: `first_word` and `other_words`. These fields will be added as fields to the main Transformation. If you want to give them a different name, you do it in the **Output** tab of the **Mapping** step dialog window, just as you did in the tutorial.

Before going on with advanced features, let's remark two things about sub-transformations:

- In the sample sub-transformation, you used a single input field, but you can use any number of fields. Even more, the **Mapping Input Specification** step has a checkbox named **Include unspecified fields, ordered by name**. If you check this option, all of the fields in the dataset of the main Transformation will be passed to the sub-transformation, and will be available to be used.
- As said, sub-transformations are a special kind of transformation. This means that all the things you do in a transformation can be done in a sub-transformation. One of those things is to define named parameters. When you call a sub-transformation, you provide the values for the named parameters in the **Parameters** tab of the **Mapping** step.

Introducing more elaborate sub-transformations

The sample sub-transformation that we developed and used is the simplest kind of sub-transformation. It has a **Mapping input** step, it implements some functionality, and its flow ends with a **Mapping output** step. This sub-transformation can be called using a **Simple Mapping (sub-transformation)** step exactly as we just did.

There are some other possibilities:

- If you want the sub-transformation to simply transform the incoming stream without adding new fields, or if you are not interested in the fields added to the sub-transformation, there is no need to create a **Mapping output** step.
- You can have a sub-transformation that serves to create your starting dataset. In that case, you don't need a **Mapping input** step. As your flow starts in the sub-transformation, your main Transformation would look like this:

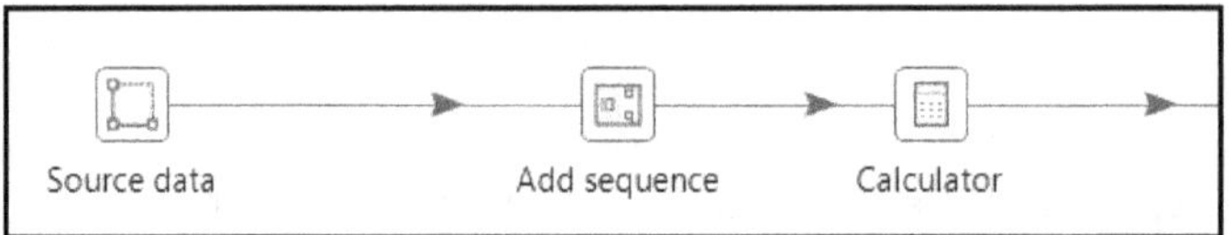

Sample use of a sub-transformation

- Finally, you can also have more than one **Mapping input specification** or **Mapping output specification** steps. One example of that is a sub-transformation that performs a lookup. It can receive two flows: one with the main data and the other with the data that serves as the lookup.

In all these cases, you execute the sub-transformation with a **Mapping (sub-transformation)** step. Compared to the **Simple Mapping (sub-transformation)** step, this one allows you to remove the **Input** or the **Output** tab, and it also allows you to add as many **Input** and **Output** tabs as needed.

For examples of sub-transformations using the Mapping (sub-transformation) step, you can browse *Chapter 7, Understanding and Optimizing Data Flows*, and *Chapter 8, Executing and Reusing Jobs and Transformations*, in the *Pentaho Data Integration Cookbook - Second Edition* book by Packt Publishing.

Making the data flow between transformations

In this section, you will learn a very simple but useful technique to allow the data flow from one Transformation to another. In other words, you will learn to create a very simple process flow.

For this tutorial, we will continue using the sample file that we just used to learn about sub-transformations.

Transferring data using the copy/get rows mechanism

The copy/get rows mechanism allows you to transfer data between two Transformations, creating a process flow. The following figure shows you how it works:

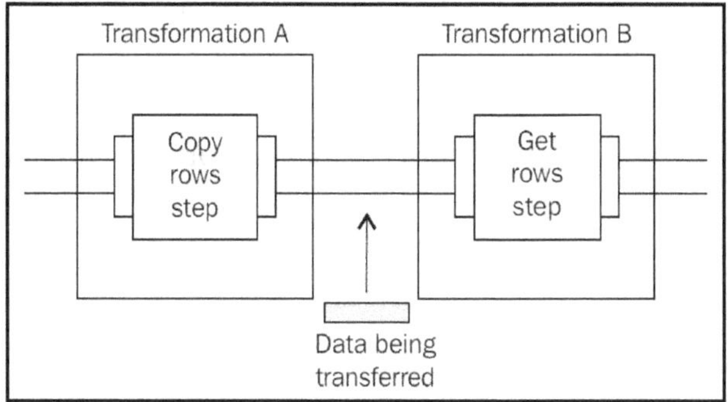

Copying and getting rows

There is a **Copy rows to result** step that transfers your rows of data to the outside of the Transformation. Then you can pick that data using another step named **Get rows from result**. By calling the Transformation that gets the rows right after the Transformation that copies the rows, you get the same result as having all steps in a single Transformation.

Let's see how this works with a simple example. We will read a file, copy all the rows out of the Transformation, pick the rows in a second Transformation, and send the rows to a new file:

1. Open Spoon and create a new Transformation.
2. Read the `exam1.txt` file with a **Text file input** step.

3. Expand the **Job** category of steps and drag a **Copy rows to result** step to the canvas.
4. Create a hop from the **Text file input** step toward this step.
5. The Transformation should look as shown:

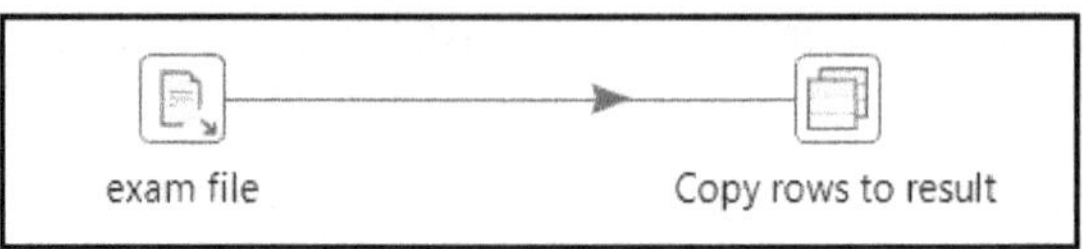

Copying rows to result

6. Save the Transformation as `first_transformation.ktr`.
7. Create a new Transformation.
8. From the **Job** category, drag a **Get rows from result** step to the canvas.

Please be careful when selecting and dragging the step. Do not choose the **Get files from result** step, which is just next to it, but serves a totally different purpose.

9. In the **Get rows from result** step, you have to provide the metadata for the incoming data. For doing this, double-click on the step and fill the window as follows:

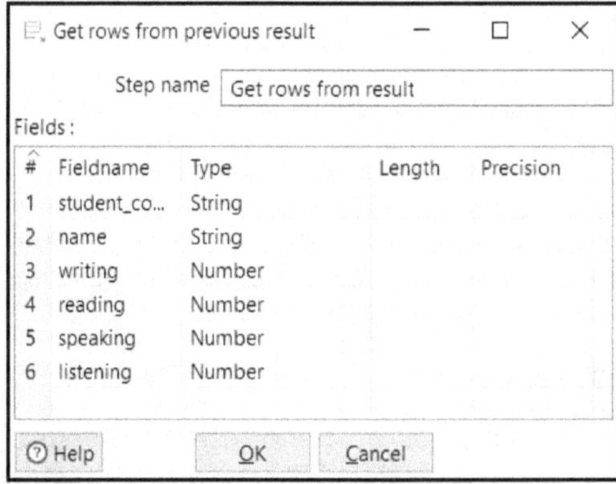

Configuring the Get rows from result step

10. To save time filling the grid in this window, you can do the following: select the **Copy rows to result** step in the previous Transformation and press space. This will bring a window with the metadata of fields that come out of the step. Select all the rows, copy them to the clipboard, and past them in the grid of the **Get rows from result** step.
11. Close the window.
12. After the **Get rows from result** step, add a **Text file output** step. Configure the step to send all the rows to a new file.
13. Save the transformation as `second_transformation.ktr`.

Now we will put the pieces together:

1. Create a job.
2. Drag a **START** and two **Transformation** Job entries to the canvas.
3. Link the entries so that you have the following:

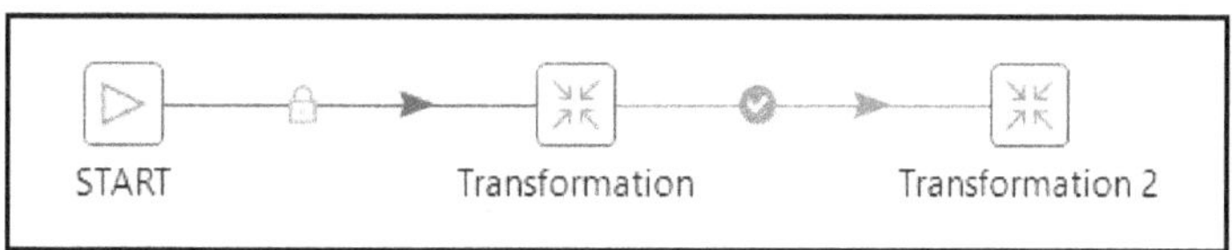

Sample job

4. Configure the **Transformation** entries to run `first_transformation.ktr` in the first place, and `second_transformation.ktr` in the second place.
5. Save the Job and run it.
6. Check your filesystem. The file generated by the second Transformation should have the same content as the file read in the first Transformation.
7. Take a look at the log. You will confirm that the first Transformation copied all the rows from the file, and the second Transformation read the same number of rows:

```
... - first_transformation - Dispatching started for transformation
[first_transformation]
...
... - Copy rows to result.0 - Finished processing (I=0, O=0, R=9,
W=9, U=0, E=0)
... - second_transformation - Dispatching started for
transformation [second_transformation]
... - Get rows from result.0 - Finished processing (I=0, O=0, R=9,
W=9, U=0, E=0)
...
```

The only purpose of this example is to show how data is transferred from one Transformation to another. This Job, as is, is not useful but serves as the basis to develop more interesting work. A simple use case would be to split some task into these two Transformations.

For example, you could validate and filter some data in the first Transformation, and do extra processing and manipulation in the second one. You not only split the data manipulation, but also create Transformations that can be reused in a different place.

The copy of the dataset is made in the memory. It's useful when you have small datasets. For bigger datasets, you should prefer saving the data in a temporary file or database table in the first Transformation, and then create the dataset from the file or table in the second Transformation. Another option is to use the **Serialize to file/De-serialize from file** steps, which are very useful for this, as the data and the metadata are saved together.

In the preceding example developed, the second Transformation just reads the data and sends it to a file. What if you want to perform more tasks? You can't test the Transformation or preview data coming from a **Get rows from result** step. The trick here is the same as the one explained in the section about sub-transformations. You disable the hop that leaves that step, and supply some sample data, for example, using a data grid or a text file input.

The copy/get rows mechanism is used to perform several particular tasks. One of them is iterating the execution of Transformations, as you will learn in the next section. In `Chapter 14`, *Creating Advanced Jobs*, you will see more examples where the copy/get rows mechanism is used.

Executing transformations in an iterative way

If you have to execute the same Transformation several times, once for each row or subset of your data, you can do it by iterating the execution. This section shows you how to do it.

Using Transformation executors

The **Transformation Executor** is a PDI step that allows you to execute a Transformation several times simulating a loop. The executor receives a dataset, and then executes the Transformation once for each row or a set of rows of the incoming dataset.

To understand how this works, we will build a very simple example. The inner Transformation, that is, the Transformation that will be executed iteratively, will receive a row with a student code and a student name and will create a file with some message for the student. The main Transformation will generate a list of students and then it will execute the inner Transformation once for every student, that is, once for every row.

Let's start by creating the Transformation that will run iteratively, once for each student:

1. Create a Transformation.
2. Drag a **Get rows from result**, a **UDJE**, a **Delay row**, and a **Text file output** steps to the work area.
3. Link the steps one after the other. You should have this:

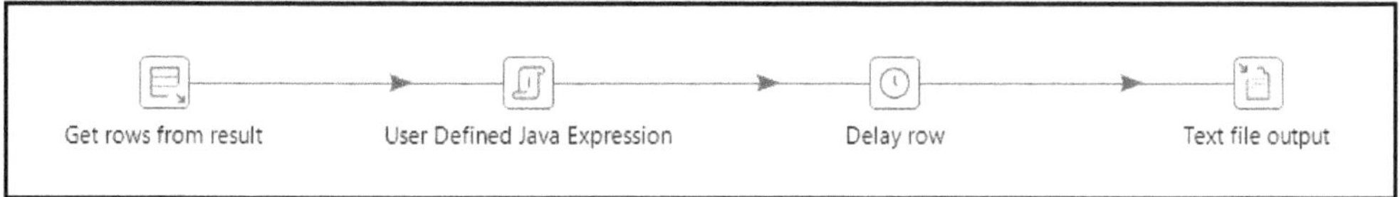

Creating a Transformation

4. Double-click on the **Get rows from result** step. Fill in the grid with two string fields: `student_code` and `name`.
5. Double-click on the **UDJE** step. Add a string named `message` with the following expression: `"Hello! You'll have to take the examination again, " + name + "."`.
6. Configure the **Text file output** step. As **Filename**, type `${Internal.Entry.Current.Directory}/output/hello_`.
7. Click on the **Specify Date time format** option. As **Date time format**, type `HH_mm_ss`.
8. In the **Content** tab, uncheck **Header**.
9. Select the **Fields** tab and fill the grid with the `message` field.
10. Save the Transformation with the name `hello_each.ktr`.

If you want to test this Transformation alone, do just as you learned in the previous section. Disable the **Get rows from result** step, and generate a sample row of data, for example, using a **Generate rows** step.

Now we will create the main Transformation:

1. Create a Transformation.
2. Using a **Text file input** step, read all the files included in the bundle code whose names start with `exam`.
3. After that step, add a **Filter rows** step. Use it to filter the rows with the condition `writing < 60`. By doing this, only a subset of the rows will be used for our main task of running the inner Transformation in a loop.
4. From the **Flow** category of steps, add a **Transformation Executor** step.
5. Create a hop from the **Filter row** toward the **Transformation Executor** step. When prompted for the kind of hop, select **Main output of step**.
6. Save the Transformation.

You just build the main skeleton. Now we will configure the Executor so that it executes the `hello_each.ktr` Transformation, once for every row that passes the filter:

1. Double-click on the **Transformation Executor** step.
2. As **Transformation**, select the path to the `hello_each.ktr` Transformation, for example, `${Internal.Entry.Current.Directory}/hello_each.ktr`.
3. Close the window and save the Transformation.
4. Run the Transformation. The **Step Metrics** in the **Execution Results** window reflects what happens:

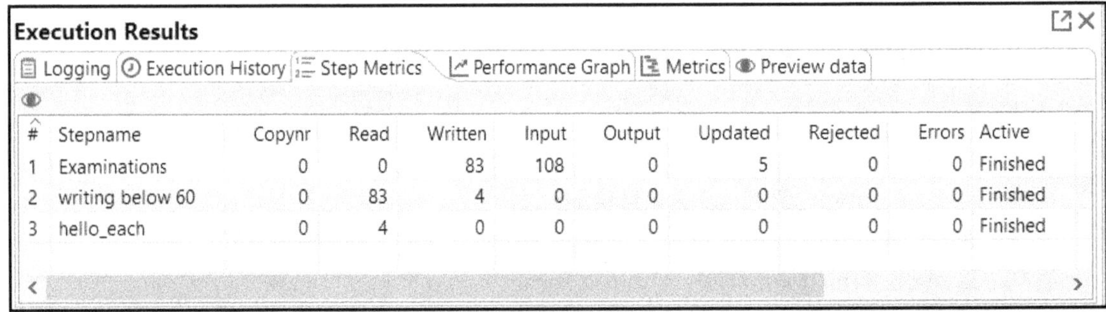

#	Stepname	Copynr	Read	Written	Input	Output	Updated	Rejected	Errors	Active
1	Examinations	0	0	83	108	0	5	0	0	Finished
2	writing below 60	0	83	4	0	0	0	0	0	Finished
3	hello_each	0	4	0	0	0	0	0	0	Finished

Step Metrics

5. Click on the **Logging** tab. You will see the full log of the inner Transformation.
6. Browse your filesystem. You will find one different file for every execution of the inner Transformation.

PDI executes the `hello_each.ktr` Transformation as many times as the number of rows that arrives to the **Transformation Executor** step, once for every row. Each time the `hello_each.ktr` Transformation executes, it gets the incoming row with the **Get rows from result** step. Then it uses it to generate a new file with a message for a different student.

Note that in the inner transformation, you don't limit the number of incoming rows. You simply assume that you are receiving a single row.

Configuring the executors with advanced settings

In the previous example, you used the **Transformation Executor** in the simplest possible way: you just provided the name of the Transformation. The Transformation then executed once for each incoming row, which is the default behavior. There are some settings that allow you to configure the behavior and the output of the Transformation to be executed.

To avoid confusion, we will call **inner transformation** to the Transformation that is executed in a loop—in our example, this is the `hello_student.ktr` Transformation—and **outer transformation** to the Transformation that builds the list of rows and executes the loop.

Let's summarize the options.

Getting the results of the execution of the inner transformation

Regarding the execution of the inner transformation, you have the option of capturing the results. You can collect just the step metrics (number of rows read, rejected, and more) or you can have the complete log of the execution. For this, proceed as follows:

1. Drag to the work area a step where you want to redirect the results. It could be any step, for example, a **Text file output** or a **Write to log** step.

2. Create a hop from the **Transformation Executor** toward this new step. You will be prompted for the kind of hop. Choose the **This output will contain the execution results** option, as shown here:

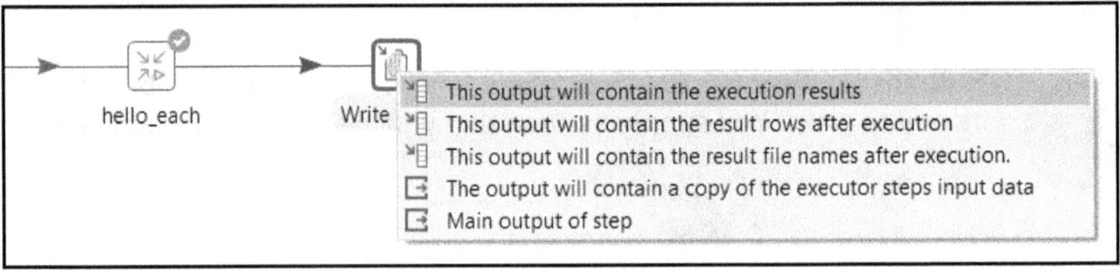

Creating a hop for the execution results

3. Double-click on the **Transformation Executor** and select the **Execution results** tab. You will see the list of metrics and results available. The **Field name** column has the names of the fields that will contain these results.
4. If there are results you are not interested in, feel free to delete the value in the **Field name** column. For the results that you want to keep, you can leave the proposed field name or type a different name. The following screenshot shows an example that only generates fields for the log and the exit status:

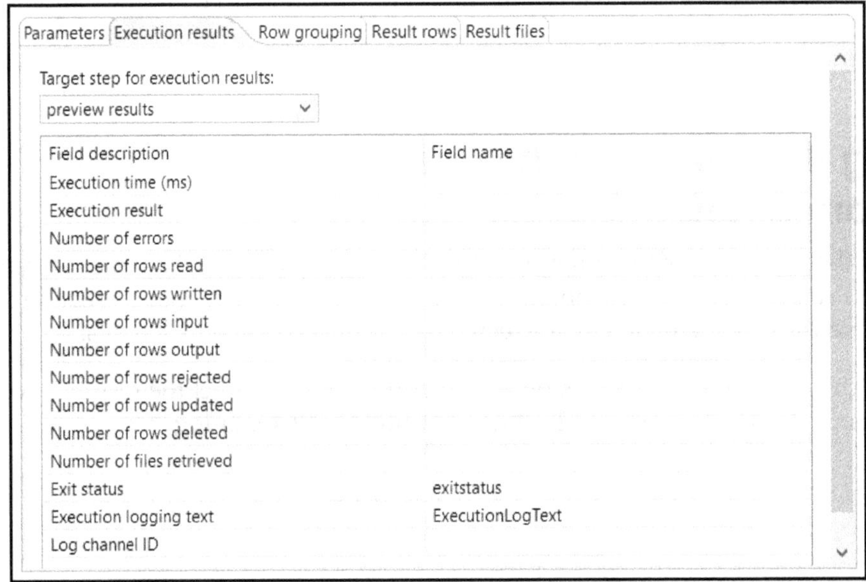

Configuring the execution results

5. When you are done, click on **OK**.
6. With the destination step selected, run a preview. You will see the metrics and results that you just defined, as shown in the next example:

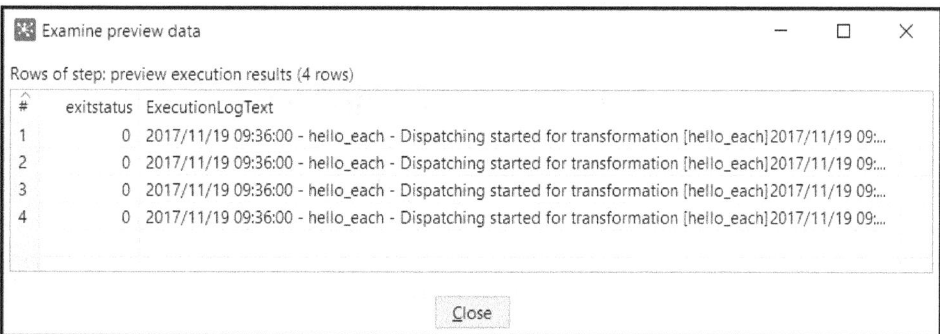

Previewing the execution results

The **Transformation Executor** doesn't abort if the Transformation that it runs has errors. If you want to detect if it has errors and then abort or keep processing rows accordingly, you do it by getting the execution results.

Working with groups of data

In the preceding example, we run the inner transformation once for every row in the list. As said, this is the default behavior. There is also the possibility to run the inner transformation for a group of rows. You may consider creating a Transformation that processes rows grouped by client number, by product line, by date, just to mention some examples. Also, you may just want to process groups of `N` rows instead of the whole dataset at once.

Once you have the inner transformation ready, you can use a **Transformation Executor** to execute it with the proper groups of rows. The way you group the rows is configured in the **Row grouping** tab of the **Executor**. There are several possibilities.

You can send groups of `N` rows, where `N` is greater than `1`. You set that value by changing the **Number of rows to send to transformation** to `N`.

You can also pass a group of rows based on the value in a field. Then all the rows with the same value will pass to the inner transformation together as a group. In order to enable the **Field to group rows on:** option and select the grouping field, you have to delete the value of the **Number of rows to send to transformation** option.

Finally, there is an option of sending groups of rows based on the time the step collects rows before executing the inner transformation.

Be aware that in all these cases, the inner transformation has to be prepared to receive a list of rows and not a single row as the one in our example.

Using variables and named parameters

If the inner transformation has named parameters, you can provide values for them in the **Parameters** tab of the **Transformation Executor** step. For each named parameter, you can assign the value of a field, or a fixed-static-value. Even more, when you run this Transformation for a single row of data, it's not mandatory to get the data with a **Get rows from result** step. You can pass the fields as variables or named parameters if that suits best to your Transformation.

In case you execute the Transformation for a group of rows instead of a single one, the parameters will take the values from the first row of data sent to the Transformation.

Continuing the flow after executing the inner transformation

In our example, the flow of data of the outer transformation ends in the Transformation `hello_student.ktr`. It may happen that you want to continue the treatment of data after that. There are two options here:

- You want the data as it ended in the inner transformation
- You want the dataset just as it entered the **Executor** step

Suppose that you want the data as it ended in the inner transformation, that is, you want the data flowing from the inner transformation towards the outer one. You do it as follows:

1. In the inner transformation, add a **Copy rows to result** step to the end of the stream.
2. In the outer transformation, drag the step to the work area where you want to redirect the rows.
3. Create a hop from the **Transformation Executor** toward this new step. You will be prompted for the kind of hop. Choose the option. **This output will contain the result rows after execution**.

4. Double-click on the **Transformation Executor** and select the **Result rows** tab. You will see a grid to fill with the metadata of the rows. You configure this grid in the same way you do in a **Get rows from result** step. The following screenshot shows an example:

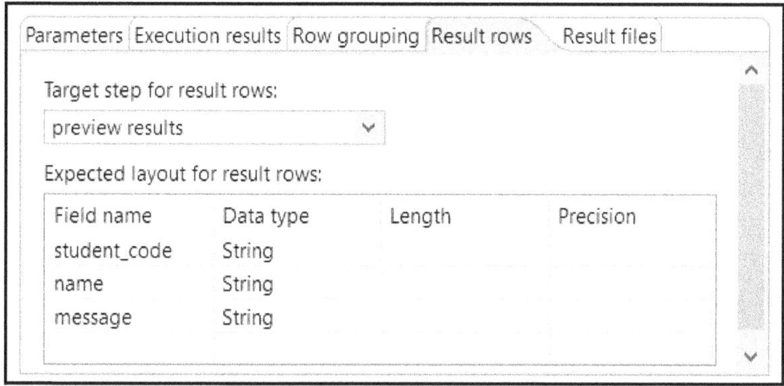

Configuring the Result Rows tab

5. When you are done, click on **OK**.
6. With the destination step selected, run a preview. You will see all the fields coming from the inner transformation.

On the contrary, if you just want the data as it arrived in the **Executor**, create the hop and, when prompted for the kind of hop, select **This output will contain a copy of the executor steps input data**. In this case, you don't have to apply any extra configuration.

Note that you may combine the different options. You can continue the flow of data in one direction and, in the same **Executor**, configure another stream where you redirect the execution results.

There is one more option not explained here—the one that captures the result filenames. We will talk about it in `Chapter 14`, *Creating Advanced Jobs*.

Summary

In this chapter, you learned techniques to construct Transformations in different ways. First, you learned all about Kettle variables. By understanding how to define and use them, you can develop more flexible and reusable Transformations. After that, you created and used sub-transformations or mappings, another way to create reusable work. Then you were introduced to the mechanism of copying and getting rows, which you will revisit in the next chapters. Finally, you learned to iterate over transformations using the Transformation Executors.

There are still more possibilities to give power to your Transformations. One of them is about creating dynamic **Extracting, Transforming, Loading** (**ETL**) processes. You will learn about this in the next chapter.

13
Implementing Metadata Injection

This chapter is about a powerful feature of **Pentaho Data Integration** (**PDI**): metadata injection, which is basically about injecting metadata into a template Transformation at runtime. In this chapter, we will explain the motivation behind this feature and then we will give a couple of practical examples for you to learn how to implement this feature.

We will be covering the following topics in this chapter:

- Introducing metadata injection
- Discovering metadata and injecting it
- Identifying use cases to implement metadata injection

Introducing metadata injection

Throughout the book, we have been talking about PDI metadata, the data that describes the PDI datasets. Metadata includes field names and data types, among other attributes. Inside PDI, metadata not only refers to datasets, but also to other entities. For example, the definition of an input file—name, description, columns--is also considered as metadata.

You usually define the metadata in the configuration windows of the different steps. You do this manually while you are developing or modifying a Transformation in Spoon. This works perfectly when you know exactly how the data looks like—for example, when you are reading a file—or how you want it to be—for example, when you are creating new fields. There are situations where this is not the case, and you don't know the metadata until runtime. This is a kind of situation where metadata injection can help.

Explaining how metadata injection works

Let's see how metadata injection works through a very simple example. Suppose that you have an Excel file with sales data. There are several sheets in the file, but only one has the data you want to read. The name of the sheet is not fixed, so you have it in a Kettle variable. The quick solution to read the spreadsheet would be to explicitly declare the sheet name.

Unfortunately, PDI is not prepared to put a field or variable as the name of the sheet. Which other options do you have? As you know, the **Sheet** tab in the Excel configuration window can be left empty and PDI will read the sheets anyway. However, this would cause an error as, by default, PDI reads all the sheets, and in this case, the rest of the sheets may have a different kind of data.

In a few words, in a development stage, you don't have the means to create the final Transformation that reads the Excel file. The solution is to inject the variable information at execution time.

The general idea is as follows. You should have two transformations:

- A template Transformation, here you will implement all the tasks needed, but the Transformation will lack some metadata information. In our example, the missing metadata information will be the sheet name.
- A Transformation that injects data, the purpose of this one is to inject the missing metadata into the template, generating a working Transformation.

The following screenshot depicts this idea:

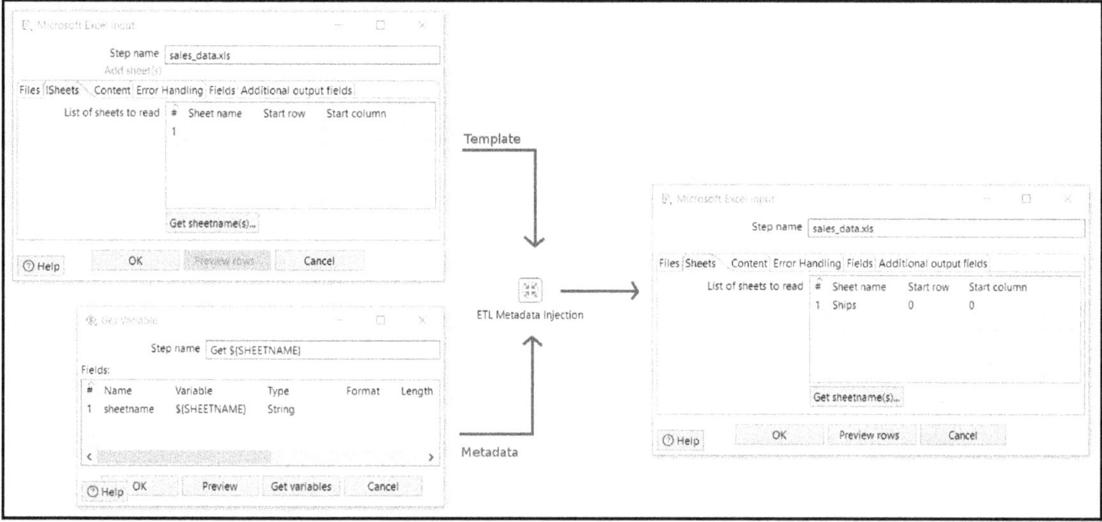

Metadata injection

With this concept in mind, let's implement this example.

In order to follow the instructions for the following examples, you will need the sample Excel files that come with the code bundle for the chapter.

Creating a template Transformation

For this exercise, you will need the `sales_single_productline.xls` file. The sheet that has the data looks as follows:

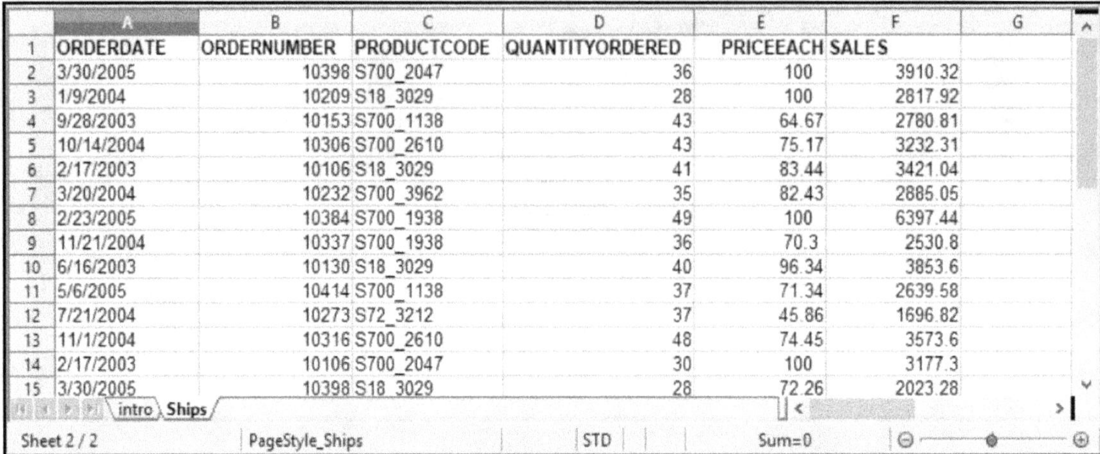

	A	B	C	D	E	F	G
1	ORDERDATE	ORDERNUMBER	PRODUCTCODE	QUANTITYORDERED	PRICEEACH	SALES	
2	3/30/2005	10398	S700_2047	36	100	3910.32	
3	1/9/2004	10209	S18_3029	28	100	2817.92	
4	9/28/2003	10153	S700_1138	43	64.67	2780.81	
5	10/14/2004	10306	S700_2610	43	75.17	3232.31	
6	2/17/2003	10106	S18_3029	41	83.44	3421.04	
7	3/20/2004	10232	S700_3962	35	82.43	2885.05	
8	2/23/2005	10384	S700_1938	49	100	6397.44	
9	11/21/2004	10337	S700_1938	36	70.3	2530.8	
10	6/16/2003	10130	S18_3029	40	96.34	3853.6	
11	5/6/2005	10414	S700_1138	37	71.34	2639.58	
12	7/21/2004	10273	S72_3212	37	45.86	1696.82	
13	11/1/2004	10316	S700_2610	48	74.45	3573.6	
14	2/17/2003	10106	S700_2047	30	100	3177.3	
15	3/30/2005	10398	S18_3029	28	72.26	2023.28	

intro Ships

Sheet 2 / 2 PageStyle_Ships STD Sum=0

Sample data

We will start by creating the template Transformation:

1. Create a Transformation.
2. Add a **Microsoft Excel Input** step, and configure it to read your file.

In order to configure the **Fields** tab properly, you can use the sample file and supply a temporary sheetname. Remember that the name of the sheet can be different at runtime.

3. Make sure that the **Sheets** tab remains empty, and close the configuration window.
4. After the Excel step, add a **Dummy** step. We will use it later to preview the incoming data.
5. Save the Transformation.

You may append the word `TEMPLATE` to the filename so that it's easier to distinguish a regular Transformation from a template one.

Just to confirm what we explained in the introduction about the possibilities to read the file, run a preview of the last step. You should get an error as the file has sheets with a different format.

Injecting metadata

Now that we have the template, we are ready to create a Transformation that injects the missing data. In our example, the missing data is the content of the **Sheetname** tab of the Excel configuration window. In this Transformation, we will complete this gap. We will do it with an **ETL Metadata Injection** step. The configuration of the step may seem complicated at first, but the idea is simple. In the configuration window of this step, we just tell which data has to be injected in which part of the template Transformation. This is how we do it:

1. Create a Transformation.
2. With a **Get Variables** step, read the `${SHEETNAME}` variable.
3. After that step, add an **ETL Metadata Injection** step. You will find it under the **Flow** category of steps.
4. Double-click on the step.
5. In the **Transformation:** textbox, type the full path for the Transformation in which we will inject data—the one created earlier.
6. Press *Tab*. The **Inject Metadata** window will be filled with the metadata available in the template Transformation. The following screenshot shows you how it looks like:

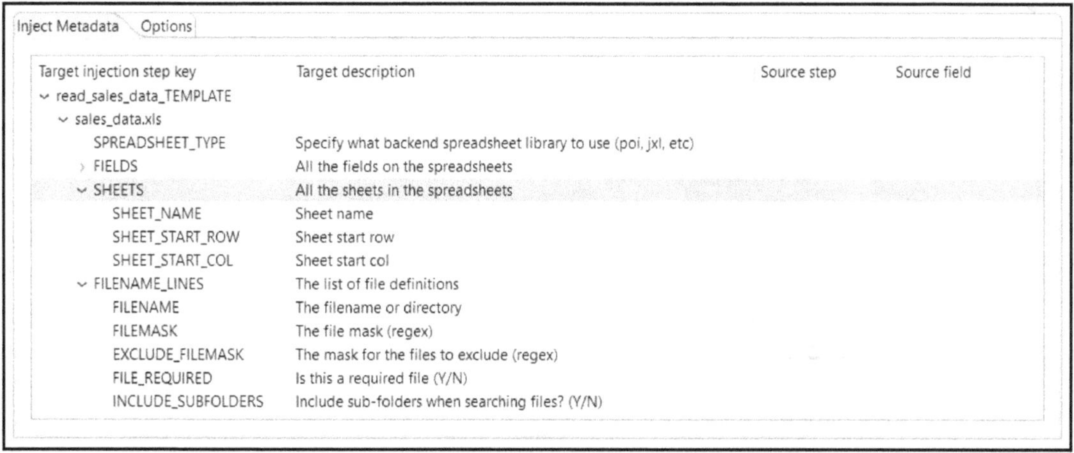

Inject Metadata tab

7. Now you have to provide the metadata for the **SHEETS** tree in this list.
8. Click on **SHEET_NAME**. A pop-up window will appear showing the only source field available for the injecting:

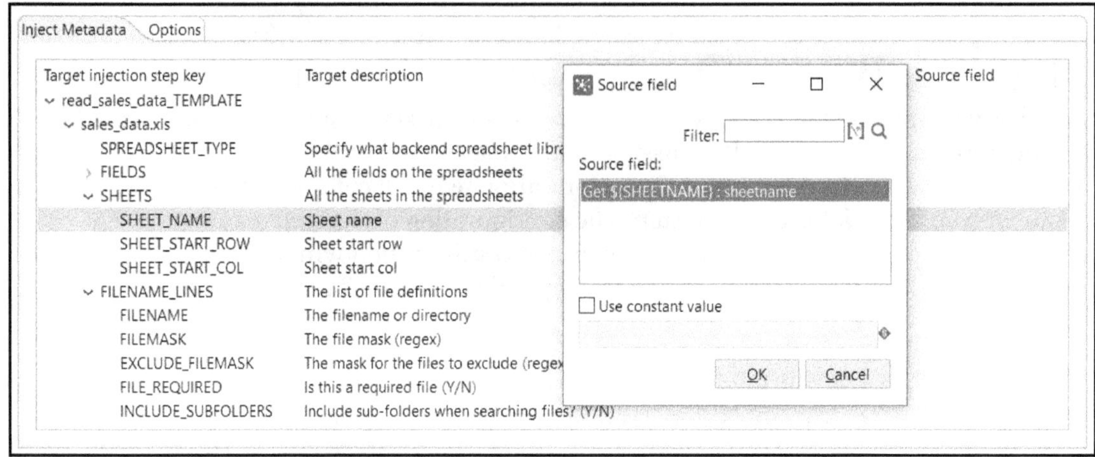

Filling the source field

9. Select the option, and click on **OK** to confirm.
10. Click on `SHEET_START_ROW`. In the pop-up window, check the **Use constant value** option. In the following textbox, type `0`.
11. Repeat the preceding instruction for the **SHEET_START_COL** value. The final configuration will look as follows:

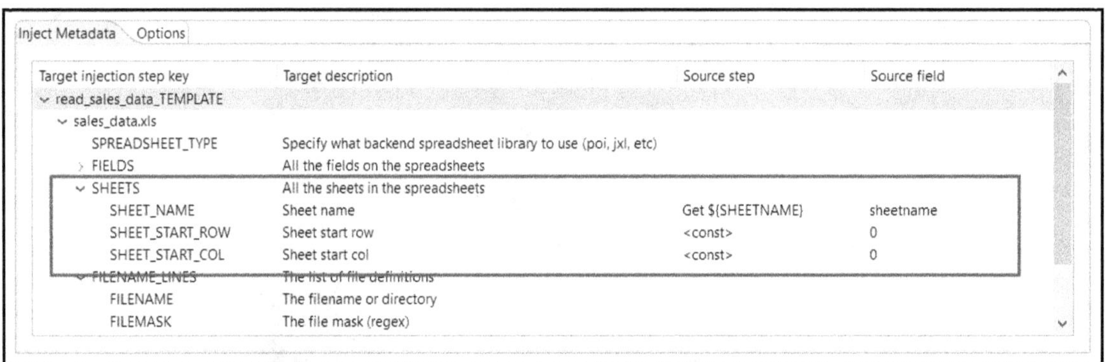

Injection sample

The last thing to do is to provide some options settings. We will configure the step to generate a working Transformation based on the template, but with the final data injected:

1. Select the **Options** tab.
2. There is a textbox labeled **Optional target file (ktr after injection):**. Fill it with the full path for a Transformation with the data injected, for example, `${Internal.Entry.Current.Directory}/read_sales_data_injected.ktr`.
3. Uncheck the **Run resulting transformation** option.
4. Click on **OK** to close the window and save the Transformation.
5. Press *F9* to run the Transformation.
6. Select the **Variables** tab. As **SHEETNAME**, type `Ships`.
7. Click on **OK**.

Now let's check what happened:

1. Browse your filesystem. The `read_sales_data_injected.ktr` Transformation should have been created.
2. Open the generated Transformation with Spoon.
3. Double-click on the **Microsoft Excel File input** step, and click on the **Sheet name** tab. You should see the data injected, as shown here:

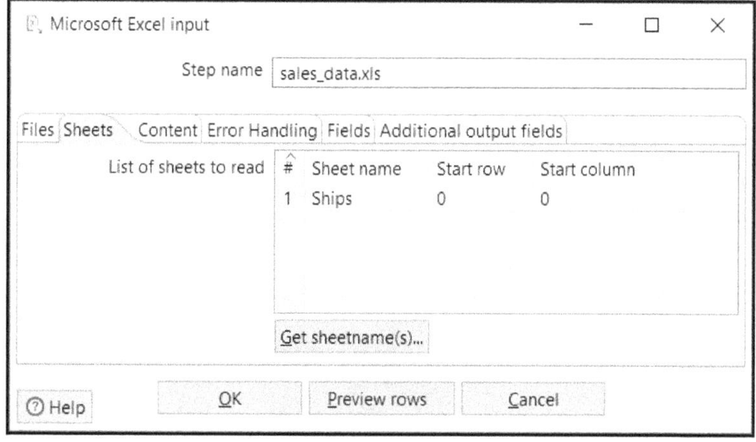

Data injected

4. Close the window, select the last step of the Transformation, and run a preview. You should see the data coming from the `Ship` sheet, as expected.

In the **Options** tab, we explicitly asked to generate the running Transformation, and not to run it. This is the best idea when you are developing. Doing this way, you can see if the data has been injected correctly. When you are done with this, you can avoid generating the Transformation and can run it just after injecting the metadata. For this, just leave the name of the target file empty and leave the **Run resulting transformation** option checked.

Discovering metadata and injecting it

Let's move to a use case a bit more elaborate than the previous one. We will continue working with sales data. In this case, we will work with an Excel file named `sales_data.xls`, which has a single sheet. There are several fields in this file, but we are only interested in the following: `PRODUCTLINE`, `PRODUCTCODE`, and `QUANTITYORDERED`. The problem is that the fields can be in any order in the Excel file. We will only know the order when we read the file.

In the same way as before, we need to create a template with missing data and then a Transformation that injects that data.

Let's start with the template. As we don't have the list of fields, we will fill the **Fields** grid with generic names—`HEADER1`, `HEADER2`, and so on. We have to select and keep only three fields. For this, we will use a **Select Values** step and leave the task of filling it to the Transformation that injects the missing data:

1. Create a Transformation.

2. Add a **Microsoft Excel input** step, and configure it like this—provide the name of the Excel file to read. Complete the grid in the **Fields** tab, as follows:

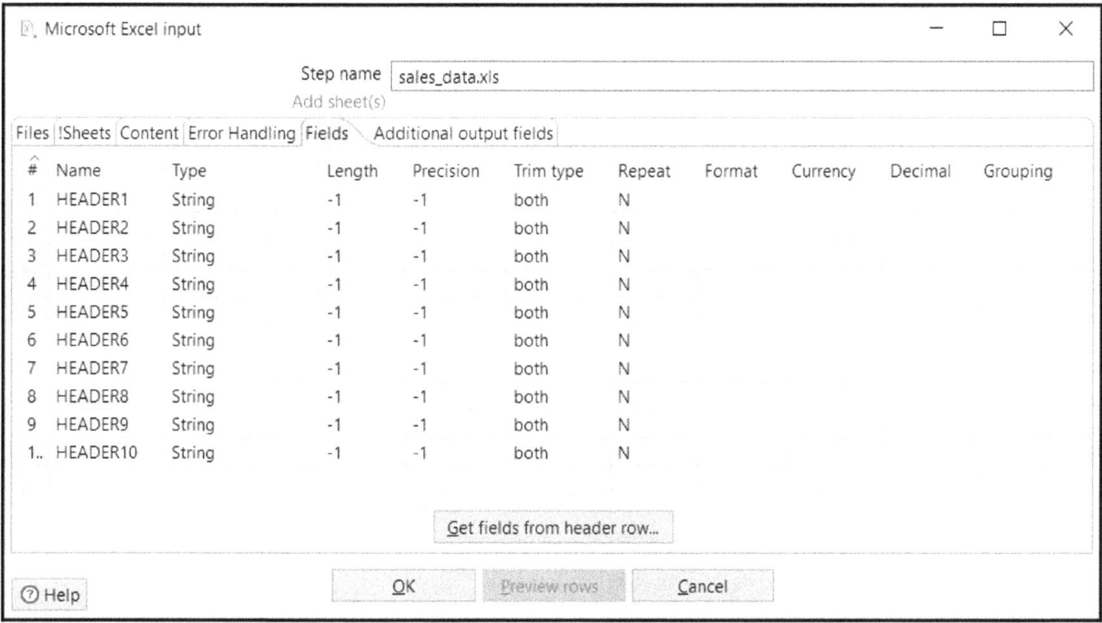

Generic Fields tab

3. After the input step, add a **Select Values** step. Leave its window empty--with no configuration.
4. At the end of the stream, add a **Dummy** step.
5. Save the Transformation.

Now comes the tricky part: finding out where the fields of interest are, and injecting that information into the template, that is, into the **Select Values** step. For this, we will read only the headers of the Excel file and use them to deduce the order of the fields. Then, we will complete the metadata using a couple of PDI steps:

1. Create a Transformation.
2. Add a **Microsoft Excel input** step, and configure it like this: provide the name of the Excel file to read. In the **Content** tab, uncheck the **Header** option and set the value **Limit** to 1.
3. Complete the grid in the **Fields** tab exactly as you did in the template Transformation, as shown in the screenshot *Generic Fields tab*.

4. Run a preview. You should see this:

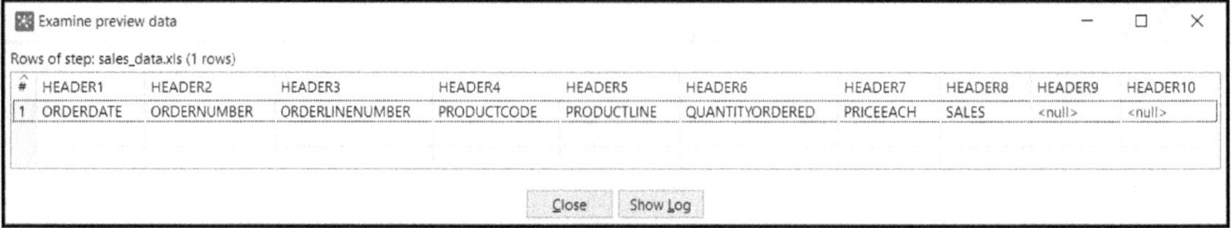

Previewing the headers of a file

5. From the **Transform** category, drag a **Row Normaliser** step to the work area and create a hop from the previous step toward this one. Configure the step as follows:

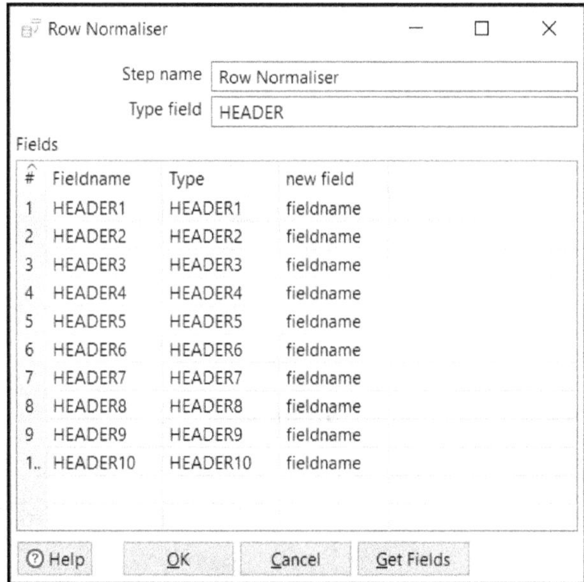

Normalizing data

To understand how this step works, refer to `Chapter 9`, *Transforming the Dataset*.

6. Run a preview. You should see this:

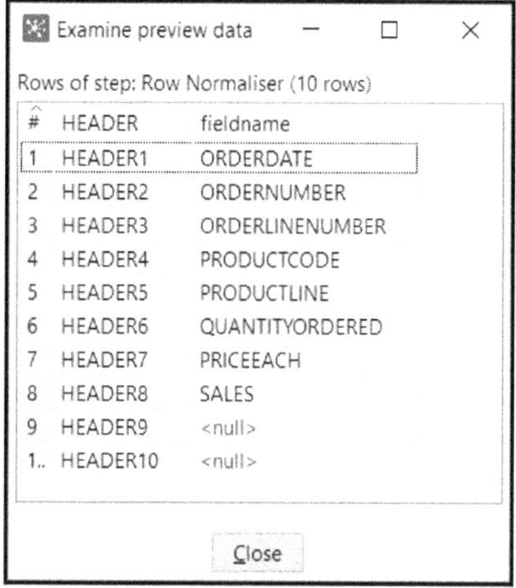

Previewing normalized data

7. Use a **Filter rows** step to filter the headers of interest. That is, as **Condition**, enter `fieldname IN LIST QUANTITYORDERED;PRODUCTCODE;PRODUCTLINE`.
8. After the filter, add an **ETL Metadata Injection** step.
9. Double-click on the step, and fill the **Transformation:** textbox with the full path of the template Transformation.
10. In the **Inject Metadata** tab, there is a tree with fields. Each branch corresponds to a different step in the template. Look for the Select Values step branch, and fill the **FIELDS** items as shown:

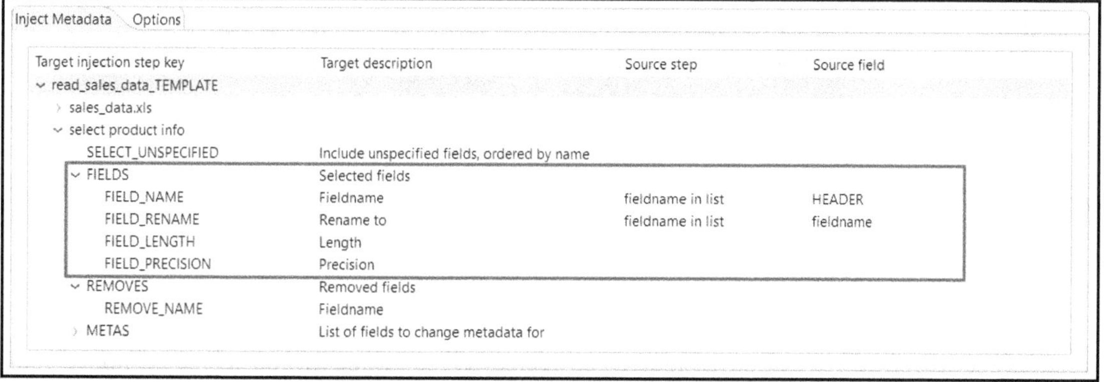

Filling the Inject Metadata tab

11. The names in the **Source** step column may differ, depending on the name you gave to the **Filter rows** step. In our example, the name of the **Filter rows** step is fieldname in list.
12. Select the **Options** tab.
13. Complete the **Optional target file (ktr after injection):** textbox with the full path for a Transformation with the data injected. Also, uncheck the **Run resulting transformation** option.
14. Click on **OK** to close the window and save the Transformation.
15. Run the Transformation so that PDI generates a Transformation with the injected data.

Now verify the results:

1. Open the injected Transformation.
2. Double-click on the **Select values** step. You should see this:

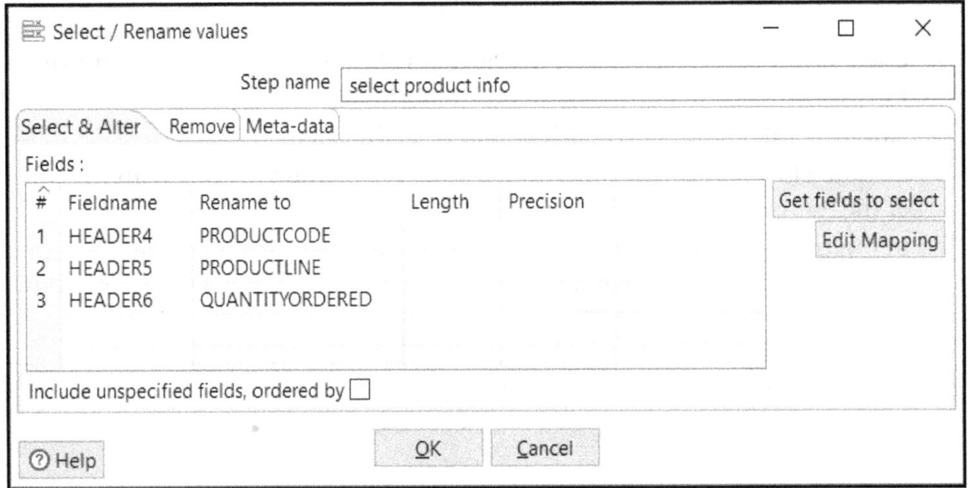

Select values step injected

3. Preview or run the Transformation just to confirm that it selects only the three fields of interest.

Compared with the previous example, we had two main differences. In the first place, we had to work a bit harder to build the data to inject. In the first example, we just read a variable. In this case, we had to analyze a bit the same data source that we intended to read. The second difference has to do with the template. In this example, the template Transformation had more fields available to be injected with metadata.

Not all PDI steps support metadata injection. In the **Inject Metadata** tree, we will only see the steps and fields that are prepared to be injected. To see a list of steps that support metadata injection, follow this link: `https://help.pentaho.com/Documentation/8.0/Products/Data_Integration/Transformation_Step_Reference/ETL_Metadata_Injection/Steps_Supporting_MDI`.

Despite the differences, the idea of the injection was exactly the same in both examples. In the next and last section, we will talk about more generic use cases for the use of metadata injection.

Identifying use cases to implement metadata injection

So far, we used injection to deal with dynamic sources. The opposite could have been dealing with dynamic targets. An example of this is generating files with a variable number of fields.

Metadata injection can also be used to reduce repetitive tasks. A typical example is the loading of text files into staging tables. Suppose that you have a text file that you want to load into a staging table. Besides the specific task of loading the table, you want to apply some validations—for example, checking for non-null values, storing audit information such as user and timestamp for the execution, counting the number of processed rows and log in a result table, among other tasks.

Now suppose that you have to do this for a considerable quantity of different files. You could take this process as the base and start copying and pasting, adapting the process for each file. This is, however, not a good idea for a list of reasons:

- It is time-consuming
- It is difficult to maintain

Your process clearly follows a pattern. So, instead of creating a different process for each file, you could define a single template, and then just inject the data that is specific to the input files and the target tables.

This was just an example. You can think of any repetitive process that follows a pattern, and evaluate the possibility of solving the **Extracting, Transforming, Loading** (**ETL**) with injection. The solution would be convenient as far as you really have a lot of files or tables to process. If you have just a few, applying injection may not be the solution and you may stick to a simple traditional implementation.

Summary

In this chapter, you learned the basics about metadata injection. You learned what metadata injection is about and how it works. After that, you developed a couple of examples with PDI, which will serve as patterns for implementing your own solutions. Finally, you were introduced to use cases where injection can be useful.

By learning metadata injection, you already have all the knowledge to create advanced transformations. In the next chapter, we will switch back to jobs to continue learning advanced concepts.

14
Creating Advanced Jobs

This chapter explains techniques to create complex processes, for example, iterating over jobs or manipulating lists of files. You will learn about the following topics:

- Enhancing your processes with the use of variables
- Accessing copied rows for different purposes
- Working with file lists
- Executing jobs in an iterative way

This chapter is closely related to `Chapter 12`, *Creating Portable and Reusable Transformations*. Many concepts that apply to transformations are revised but this time applied to jobs. So if you skipped that chapter, it's a good idea to read it before reading this one.

Enhancing your processes with the use of variables

You already know a lot about Kettle variables. This time, you will learn how those variables can help you create more flexible and reusable work.

Running nested jobs

Before explaining the different ways in which variables can be used to enhance your processes, it's important to introduce the concept of **nested jobs**, which is closely related to the scope of variables.

In the same way that you can run a Transformation inside a Job, you can also run a Job from a Job, which allows you to nest the execution of jobs. In order to do this, you use the **Job** Job entry, located in the **General** category of job entries. A Job with nested jobs will look like this:

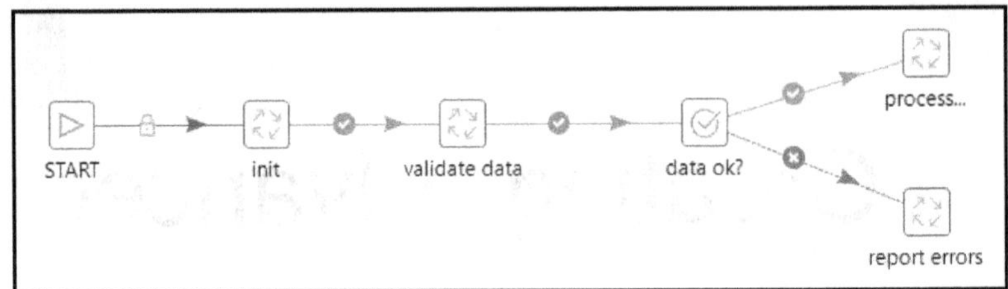

Nested jobs

Just like any job entry, the **Job** Job entry may end successfully or may fail. Based on this result, PDI decides which of the entries that follow it will execute. None of the entries following the **Job** Job entry start until the nested Job ends its execution.

You nest jobs mainly for organization purposes. If your Job does a lot of different things, you better break the functionality into parts, creating different jobs and calling them in order from a main Job. There is no limit to the levels of nesting. You may call a Job that calls a Job that calls a Job and so on. Usually, you will not need more than two or three levels of nesting.

Understanding the scope of variables

By nesting jobs, you implicitly create a relationship among the jobs. Look at the following screenshot:

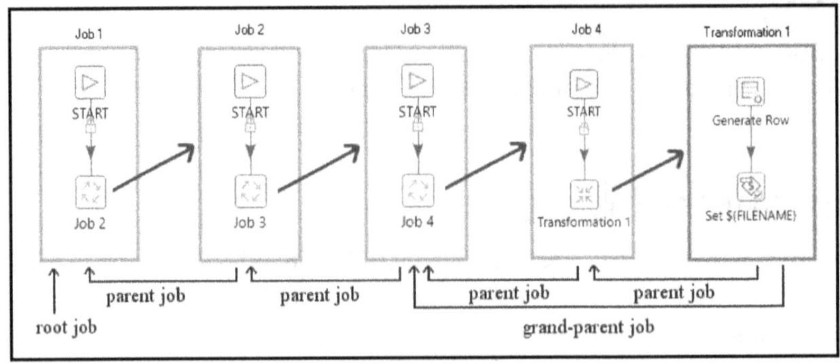

Job that executes jobs

Here, you can see how a Job and even a transformation may have parents and grandparents. The main Job is called **root job**. This hierarchy is used to understand the scope of variables, that is, the places where the variables are visible. In `Chapter 12`, *Creating Portable and Reusable Transformations*, you learned about two scopes: **Java Virtual Machine** and **Valid in the current Job**. Now that you know about nested jobs, you are ready to understand all the scopes, which are summarized in the next table:

Scope	Explanation
Java Virtual Machine	The variable will be available in all jobs and transformations you run.
Valid in the current Job	The variable will be valid in the Job where you define it and also all its child jobs and transformations.
Valid in the parent Job	The variable will be valid in the Job that calls the current Job and also all its child jobs and transformations.
Valid in the root Job	The variable will be valid in the root Job and also all its child jobs and transformations.

In general, if you have doubts about which scope type to use, you can use **Valid in the root job** and you will be good.

Using named parameters

Just as transformations, jobs can also have **named parameters**. You define them in the same way as you do in transformations, that is, in the **Parameters** grid in the **Job properties** window. Once defined, the named parameters will be available to be used as regular Kettle variables.

Now let's go a step forward. If a Job or Transformation that has named parameters is called by a Job—using a **Job** or **Transformation** Job entry—it's in the calling Job where you provide the values. To explain how you do this, we will develop a Job that calls a Transformation with named parameters.

In this example, we will use the transformation named `cutting_exam_file.ktr` created in `Chapter 12`, *Creating Portable and Reusable Transformations*. So before continuing, make sure you have that transformation handy.

These are the instructions to provide named parameters to a Transformation from a Job:

1. Create a Job.
2. Add **START** and **Transformation** entries, link them in that order, and save the Job.

It's not mandatory to save the Job at this moment. We just do it in order to have a value for the `${Internal.Entry.Current.Directory}` variable, used in the following steps.

3. Double-click on the **Transformation** entry. Change the **Transformation filename:** textbox to point to the `cutting_exam_file.ktr` transformation, for example, `${Internal.Entry.Current.Directory}/transformations/cutting_exam_file.ktr`.
4. Select the **Parameters** tab and click on the **Get Parameters** button. The grid will be filled with the named parameters defined in the Transformation. Fill the grid as shown:

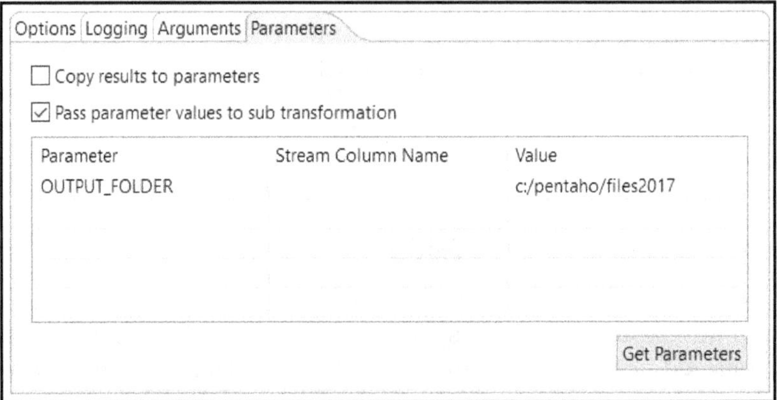

Configuring a Transformation entry with named parameters

5. Click on **OK** to close the window.
6. Save the Job and press *F9* to run the Job.
7. Then click on **Launch**.
8. When the execution finishes, the `first_10_students.txt` file should have been created in the output folder specified.

In this exercise, we called a Transformation that had named parameters. If you want to call a Job with named parameters, the procedure is exactly the same.

Just a couple of observations regarding the use of named parameters in a Transformation (or a Job) that is called by a Job:

- As named parameters, you can provide fixed values as you did in this case, but you can also provide variables.
- If the main Job itself has named parameters with the same names as the named parameters of the called Transformation or Job, you can leave the grid of the **Parameters** tab empty. Just make sure that the **Pass parameter values to sub transformation** option is checked. The values for the named parameters will be passed from the Job to the transformation or sub-Job automatically.
- If, in the main Job, exists a variable—not a named parameter—with the same name as a named parameter of the called Transformation or sub-job, this Transformation (or sub-job) will not recognize it unless you explicitly provide the value in the **Transformation** (or **Job**) Job entry. This means that you have to fill the **Parameters** tab anyway, for example, as shown in the following screenshot:

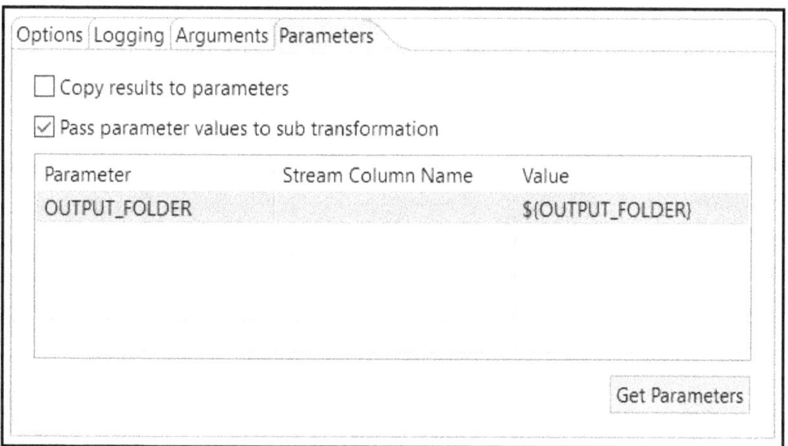

Providing named parameters from a Job to a Transformation

If you don't provide values for the named parameters in the **Parameters** tab in a **Transformation** or **Job** Job entry—either by filling the grid or by checking the **Pass parameter values to sub transformation** option—the Transformation/sub-job will use its default values.

Using variables to create flexible processes

In addition to all the ways you have been using variables until now, there is an interesting use of variables that helps in the creation of flexible ETL processes. It's about using variables as part of the Transformation or Job names or location. The following are just two examples that will give you ideas to create your own variants.

Using variables to name jobs and transformations

Suppose that you have to process several files with sales, each file coming from a different branch of your business. You have three branches: A, B, and C. You load each file into a staging area, then you validate the data and load it into a final table. Supposing that you read one file at a time, a simplified version of your main Job could be as follows:

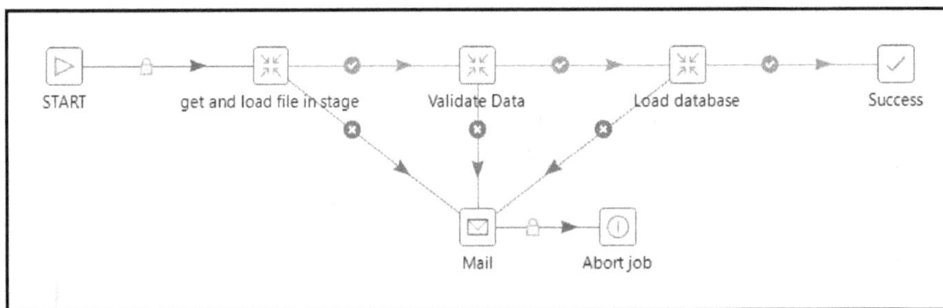

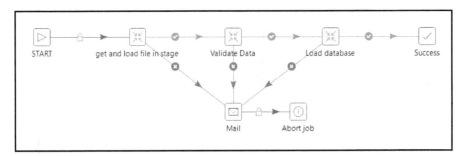

Sample ETL that loads sales data

Now let's add some complexity to the Job. Despite having the same kind of data, the files are in different locations and have different structure for each branch. For example, you could have Excel files or CSV files, and the files may be in a local disk or in a remote server. So, you have a process that is common to all branches except for the way you get and read the source.

A simplistic solution would be to add the branch name as a parameter and change the Job, as shown in this screenshot:

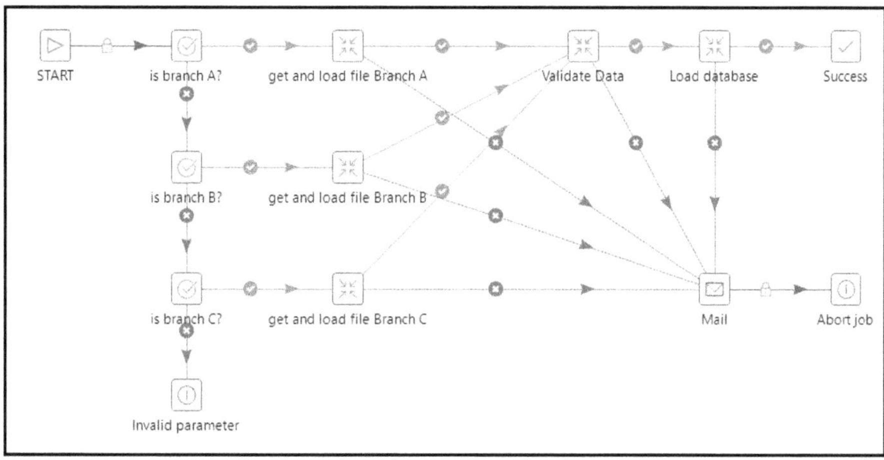

Sample ETL that loads sales data

What if there are new branches? There are at least two cons:

- Continuing adding logic to the Job will cause an endless chain of Job entries asking for the branch and changing the flow. Visually, this will soon become very difficult to understand.
- Every time a new branch is added, you will have to modify the main Job.

There is a very simple trick to avoid this. You name the Job that gets and reads the file after the name of the branch. For example, `get_and_load_source_branch_A.kjb`, `get_and_load_source_branch_B.kjb`, and so on.

If a new branch is added, you just create the Job that gets and reads its file, and name it as `get_and_load_source_branch_<branch name>.kjb`.

Then in your main Job, you call the sub-job as `${Internal.Entry.Current.Directory}/get_and_load_source_branch_${BRANCH_NAME}.ktr`

The main Job doesn't need to ask for the branch all the time. The look and feel would be as simple as follows:

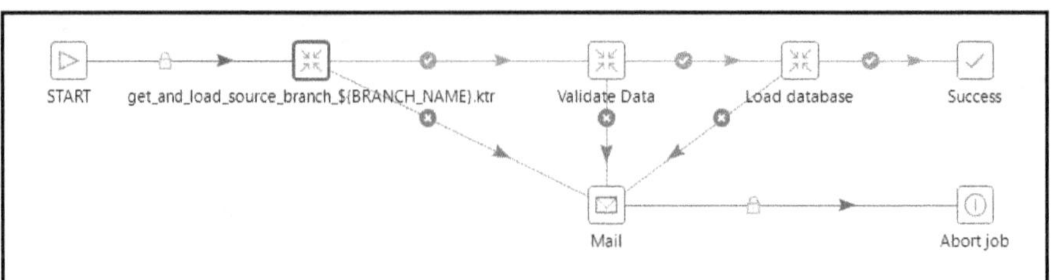

Simplified ETL that loads data from different sources

The Job that gets and reads the file will be different depending on the branch, and its name will be resolved at runtime.

Using variables to name Job and Transformation folders

Let's continue with the same preceding case: an ETL that processes sales files coming from different branches of a business. This time, we will add one more task: after loading the file, you should generate a report with the result of the process. Each branch may decide how it wants the report. Some may want a report by email, others may want that you generate a simple text file with the results and save it in a given folder, and so on.

Now for each branch, you have two specific jobs: one to get and read the file, another to report the results.

We could continue with the idea of naming the jobs/transformations differently for each branch, for example, `report_results_A.kjb`, `report_results_B.kjb`, and so on. The Job will still be clean and simple, but the folder with jobs will not. We will have everything mixed in a single place, as follows:

```
get_and_load_source_branch_A.kjb
get_and_load_source_branch_B.kjb
get_and_load_source_branch_C.kjb
report_results_A.kjb
report_results_B.kjb
report_results_C.kjb
...
```

To avoid this, we could implement a different approach. Instead of naming the jobs and/or transformations after the name of the branch, we could create a different folder for each branch. Inside each folder, the jobs/transformations will share the names. The following listing shows the idea:

```
C:\Pentaho\project
|____ BRANCH_A
|       |__ get_and_load_source.kjb
|       |__ report_results.kjb
|____ BRANCH_B
|       |__ get_and_load_source.kjb
|       |__ report_results.kjb
|____ BRANCH_C
        |__ get_and_load_source.kjb
        |__ report_results.kjb
 ...
```

Then, supposing that the folders are inside the current directory, you call the Job that reads the file:
`${Internal.Entry.Current.Directory}/${BRANCH_NAME}/read_and_get_source_branch.kjb`.

In the same way, you call the Job that report the results as follows:

```
${Internal.Entry.Current.Directory}/${BRANCH_NAME}/report_results.kjb
```

If new branches are created, you just add a new folder, and nothing in the existing ETL has to be modified or adapted.

In these examples, we worked with sub-jobs, but the same logic applies if you have to call transformations.

Accessing copied rows for different purposes

In `Chapter 12`, *Creating Portable and Reusable Transformations*, you learned to copy a set of rows in one Transformation, and to access the copied rows using the **Get rows from result** step. Doing this allowed the rows to flow from one transformation to another. This is only one of the uses of the copied rows.

In general, when you copy rows using the **Copy rows to result** step, the copied rows become available to be used by the entries that are executed afterward. The next subsections shows you the possibilities.

Using the copied rows to manage files in advanced ways

In `Chapter 3`, *Creating Basic Task Flows*, you learned to manage files by copying, moving, and zipping files among other operations. At that time, you were introduced to the different steps and Job entries meant to do these operations. There are still two more ways to manage files:

- Copying rows to the arguments of an entry
- Using result filelists

We will explain the first of these options. In the section, *Working with file lists*, you will learn about the other method.

As you know, when configuring a Job entry, you have the possibility to type fixed text or use variables. Look at the following sample Job entry:

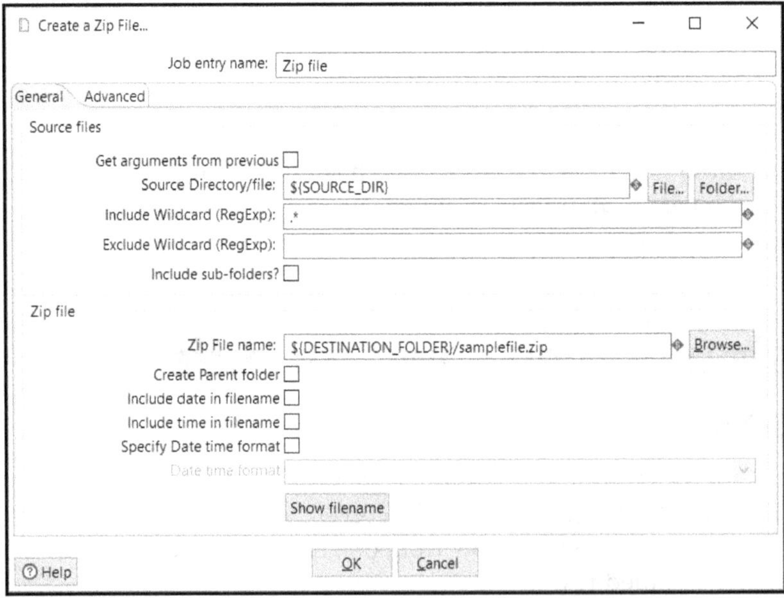

Sample zip file entry

Using variables for the arguments of the entry is a flexible option. However, this may not always solve your requirements. Suppose that you want to create some ZIP files, but you don't know beforehand how many ZIP files would be. In this case, using variables doesn't help. Instead of that, you can build a dataset with the arguments to the **Zip file** entry, and then copy them to its arguments. The following step-by-step instructions show you how you do this:

First of all, let's investigate the configuration options of a **Zip file** entry:

1. Create a Job.
2. Drag a **Zip file** entry to the canvas and double-click it.
3. Move the cursor over the option, **Get arguments from previous**. The following tooltip shows up:

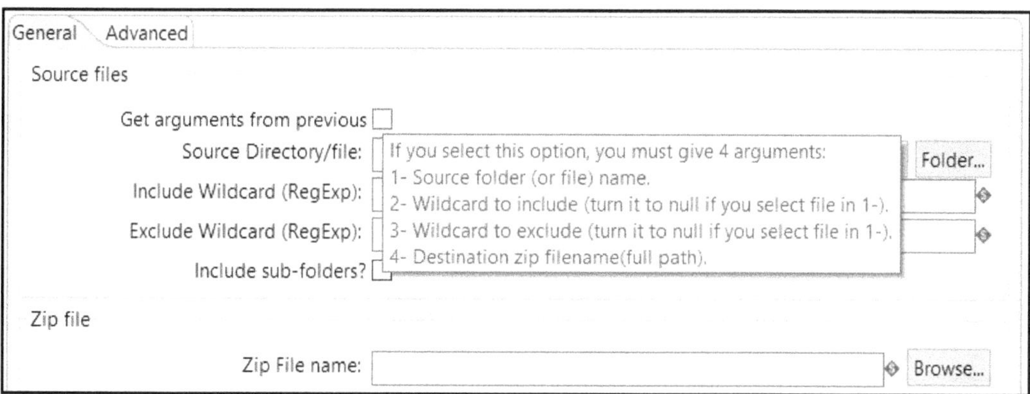

Arguments for a Zip file entry

What you see in the tooltip is the list of arguments that you can provide from outside the step, instead of typing fixed values. In this case, if you decide to provide arguments, you should build a dataset with the following:

- The folder where the files to ZIP are located
- A wildcard (a regular expression) describing the files to include
- A wildcard (a regular expression) describing the files to exclude
- The full path to the destination ZIP file

You build this list in a transformation. As usual, we will keep the example simple and create the dataset with a grid, but you can use all the steps you want or need. To create the dataset, take for example the following:

1. Create a Transformation.
2. Drag a **Data Grid** step to the work area.
3. Double-click the step and configure it with the following fields:

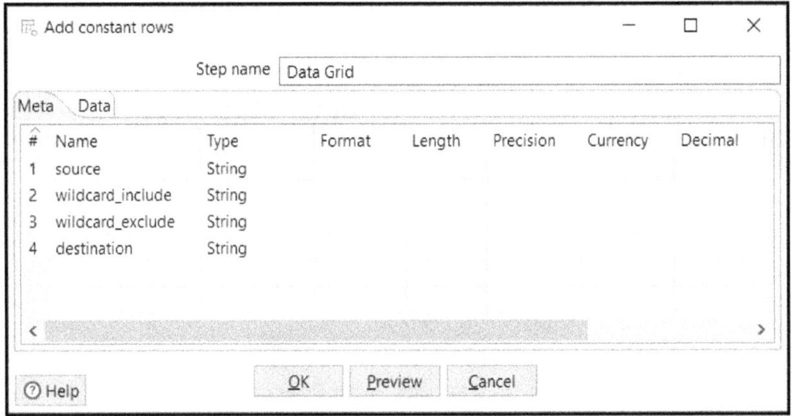

4. Defining a dataset
5. Complete the **Data** tab with some sample data, as shown in the next example:

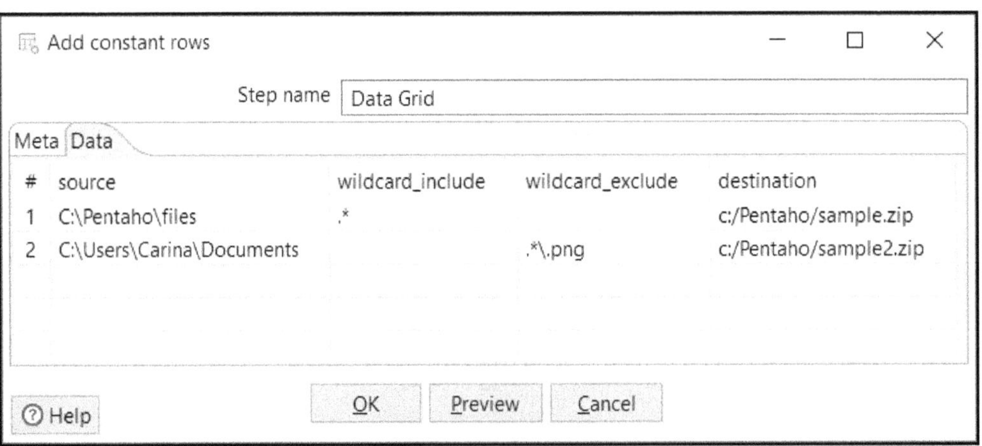

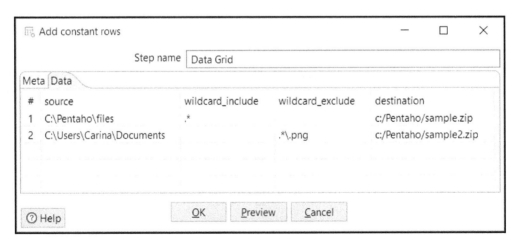

Sample data with files to zip

6. Drag a **Copy rows to result** step to the work area and create a hop from the grid toward this step.
7. Save the Transformation.

We are ready to build the main Job:

1. Open the Job created earlier.
2. Drag **START** and **Transformation** entries to the canvas. Link all the entries as shown:

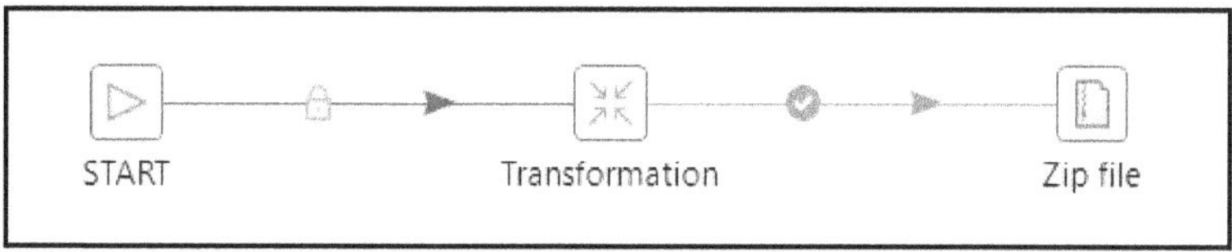

Job that zips files with arguments

3. Configure the **Transformation** entry to execute the transformation you just created.
4. Double-click the **Zip file** entry.
5. Check the option, **Get arguments from previous**. You will notice that the texboxes below are disabled. This means that they will be populated with the data coming from the Transformation.
6. Close the window and save the Job.
7. Run it.
8. Browse the filesystem. You should see the ZIP created according to the arguments you built in the Transformation.

In general, wherever you see a checkbox named **Copy previous results to args?**, you can use it like you did in the example. Currently, the Job entries that allow copying the results to the arguments are **Zip file**, **Unzip file**, **Delete files**, **Move Files**, **Copy Files**, **Delete folders** and **Add filenames to result**, all of them located under the **File management** category of entries. Additionally, you can also copy the results to the arguments of the **Truncate tables** entry from the **Utility** category.

Not all the entries have the tooltip telling you the list of arguments expected. You can, however, deduce them easily. The fields that should be passed as arguments are the ones that are disabled when you check the **Copy previous results to args?** option.

Using the copied rows as parameters of a Job or Transformation

Recall the Job that we created in the *Using Named Parameters* section at the beginning of the chapter. We had a Transformation with named parameters and you learned how to pass the parameters both with fixed values or using Kettle variables. There is one more way to pass named parameters to a Transformation or Job. We can do it by copying rows. To show how to do this, we will recreate the same example but this time, we will use this new method.

First, we will create a transformation that builds a dataset with the values for the parameters:

1. Create a Transformation.
2. Using the steps of your choice, create a dataset with the following structure—the image shows sample data:

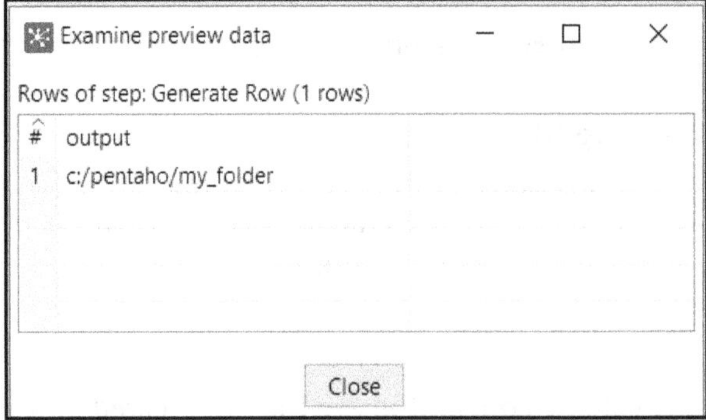

Sample dataset

3. At the end of the stream, add a **Copy rows to result** step.
4. Save the Transformation.

Now we will create the main Job:

1. Create a Job.

2. Drag a **START** and two **Transformation** entries to the canvas, and link them as shown:

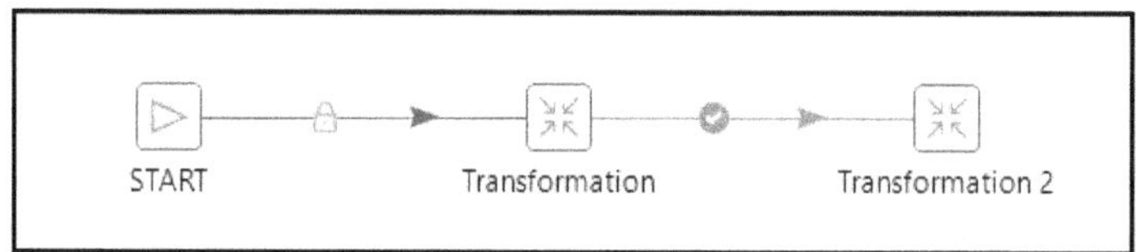

Sample Job

3. Use the first **Transformation** entry to run the Transformation that you just created.
4. Double-click the second **Transformation** entry.
5. Configure it to execute the Transformation `cutting_exam_file.ktr`—the same that we used in the *Using Named Parameters* section.
6. Click on the **Parameters** tab.
7. Check the **Copy results to parameters** option.
8. Fill the lower grid as shown:

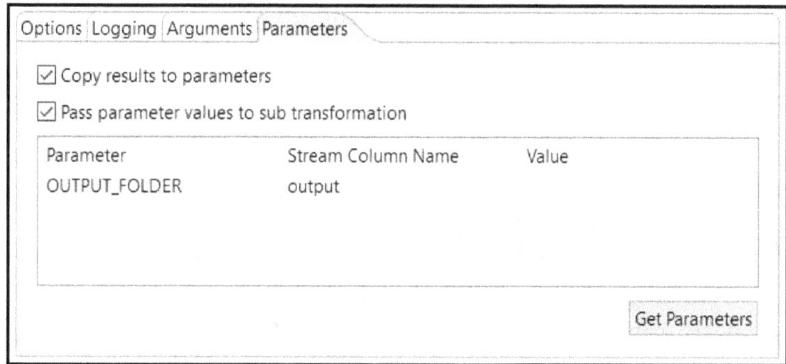

Configuring a Parameters tab

9. Click on **OK** and save the Job.
10. Run the Job.
11. Browse your file disk. You should see a new file created in the specified location.

How does this work? You already know the copy rows mechanism. In this case, the copied rows are used for set values to the named parameters. Each name parameter specified in the **Parameters** grid is set with the value specified in the **Fields** column, which is taken from the copied row.

In this case, we copied just one row. It is possible to embed this into a loop: you can copy several rows and then, in the **Options** tab of the **Transformation setting** window, check the option, **Execute every input row**. Doing this, the Transformation is executed once for every copied row. The result is equivalent to the execution of the Transformation with a **Transformation Executor** step.

In the same way as we copy rows to the parameters of a Transformation, we can copy rows to the parameters of a Job.

Working with filelists

In this section, you will learn about the **result filelist**, which is a list of files in memory. The purpose of having a result filelist is to apply some operation on the whole set of files in a single step. The kind of operation you can apply ranges from copying the list of files to a new location, to sending the files attached in an email.

In this section, you will learn the ways PDI offers to add or remove files from that custom list, and then you will see a couple of use cases where you can use it.

Maintaining a filelist

You might have noticed that most of the output PDI steps have a checkbox named **Add filenames to result**, which is checked by default. What this checkbox does, as the name implies, is it adds the name of the generated file to the filelist in memory.

Besides this automatic behavior, there are other ways to add files to the list, and also to remove them. The following table summarizes the steps used to add files to the list:

Transformation step	Description
All of the steps that generate files, for example, **Text file output** and **Microsoft Excel Output**	By default, PDI adds the generated file to the result filelist. In order to avoid that behavior, you have to uncheck the **Add filenames to result** option.

Job category | **Set files in result**	Adds files to the filelist. The step takes the names of the files from a field of your dataset.

The following table summarizes the Job entries that you may use to add or remove files from the list:

Job entry	**Description**
File management category | **Add filenames to result**	Adds files to the filelist.
File management category | **Unzip file**	If you check the option **Add extracted file to result**, the step adds the extracted files to the filelist.
File management category | **Delete filenames from result**	It deletes all the filenames that are in the result filelist. Alternatively, you can only delete from the filelist the files that match or that doesn't match a regular expression.
General category | **Transformation**	By checking the option, **Clear results files before execution**, PDI deletes all the filenames that are in the result filelist.

Note that the last two options don't remove the files. They just remove the filenames from the result filelist.

The next section explains where and how you can use the list.

Using the filelist for different purposes

There are a couple of ways in which you can use the result filelist. Here are some examples.

Attaching files in an email

The most common use for a filelist is to attach the files in the list in an email. This is a very straightforward task, as shown in this simple example:

1. Create a Transformation.

2. Use the Transformation to generate a sample file to be attached in an email. The following screenshot shows you a very simple stream to generate the file. Feel free with generating any file you like:

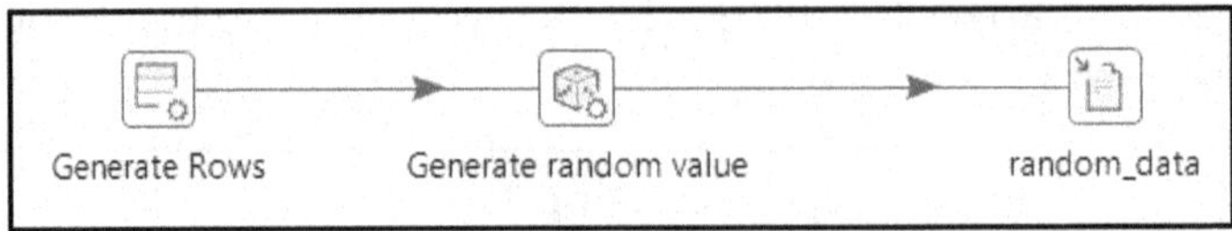

Generating a sample file

3. Make sure that the **Add filenames to result** option in the output step is checked.
4. Save the transformation.
5. Create a Job and add a **START**, a **Transformation**, and a **Mail** entry to the work area. Link them as follows:

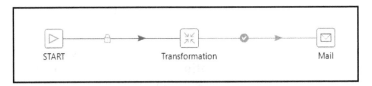

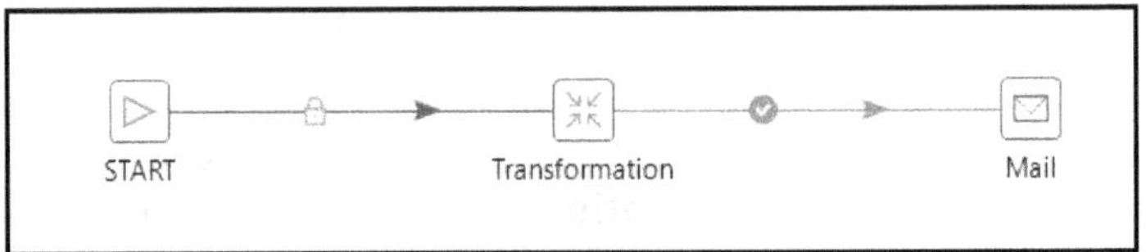

Job that sends an email

6. Use the **Transformation** entry to execute the preceding transformation created.
7. Configure the **Mail** entry to send an email with the subject, content, and destination of your choice.

If you have doubts about the configuration of the **Mail** entry, refer to `Chapter 3`, *Creating Basic Task Flows*.

8. Select the **Attached Files** tab in the **Mail** entry configuration window and configure it as follows:

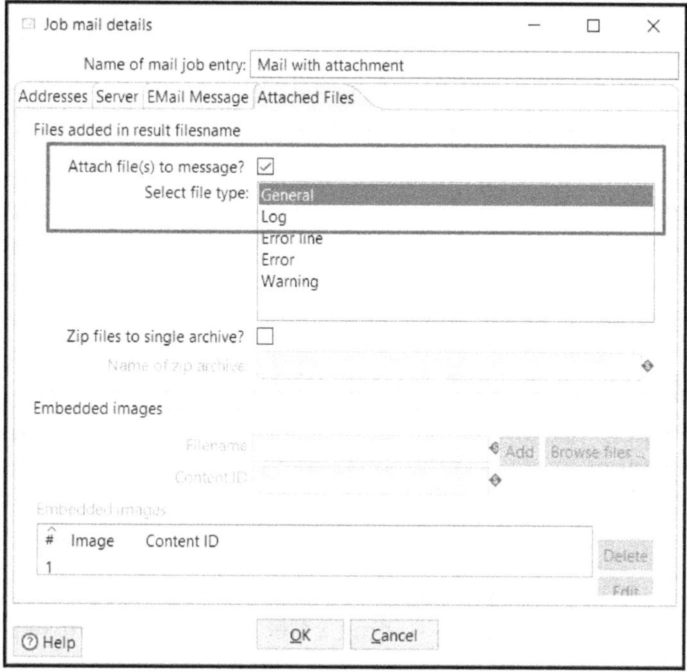

Configuring the attached Files tab in a Mail entry

9. Close the window and save the Job.
10. Run the Job, and check the mail inbox of the account to which you sent the email. You should see the mail with the generated file attached.

As you noticed, in order to attach files in an email, you configure the correspondent tab in the **Mail** entry. By selecting the **General** option, you are asking PDI to attach the files in the result filelist.

Copying, moving, and deleting files

As mentioned earlier, you can copy, move, and delete files whose names are in a result filelist. Some situations where you would do this are as follows:

- Deleting all the temporary files you created in your ETL process
- Moving a file to a different place after sending it by email
- Creating a backup of the files generated in the process

In order to do any of these operations, you use a **Process result filenames** Job entry located under the **File management** category of Job entries. The configuration of the step is quite straightforward. You just specify the action to apply to the files in the result filelist: **Copy**, **Move**, or **Delete**. Then there are some extra settings that you will configure depending on the action selected and your particular needs.

If you use the entry to copy or move files, the entry itself allows you to modify the result filelist by removing the source files from the list and/or adding the destination files to the list.

Introducing other ways to process the filelist

In addition to the options listed, you can get the list of files of the result filelist and process the files in any way, for example, opening them and processing their content somehow. The following is a simple Transformation that demonstrates how to list the content of the result filelist in the log:

1. Create a Transformation.
2. From the **Job** category of steps, drag a **Get files from result** step to the work area.
3. After this step, add a **Write to log** step. You will find it under the **Utility** category.

You don't need to configure any of these steps. The **Get files from result** step doesn't require any configuration and the **Write to log** step, if you don't change the default configuration, writes all the incoming fields.

4. Save the transformation.
5. Open the Job that you created before, the one that sends an email. Save it under a new name.
6. Remove the **Mail** entry and, in its place, add a new **Transformation** entry.
7. Configure this entry to execute the transformation that you just created.
8. Save the Job and run it.
9. Look at the **Logging** tab in the **Execution Results** window. You will see something like this:

```
...
2017/10/26 20:57:36 - Get files from result.0 - Finished processing
(I=0, O=0, R=1, W=1, U=0, E=0)
2017/10/26 20:57:36 - Write to log.0 -
2017/10/26 20:57:36 - Write to log.0 - ------------> Linenr 1------
```

```
------------------------
2017/10/26 20:57:36 - Write to log.0 - type = General
2017/10/26 20:57:36 - Write to log.0 - filename = random_data.txt
2017/10/26 20:57:36 - Write to log.0 - path =
file:///c:/pentaho/files/random_data.txt
2017/10/26 20:57:36 - Write to log.0 - parentorigin =
generate_sample_file
2017/10/26 20:57:36 - Write to log.0 - origin = random_data
2017/10/26 20:57:36 - Write to log.0 - comment = This file was
created with a text file output step
2017/10/26 20:57:36 - Write to log.0 - timestamp = 2017/10/26
20:57:36.478
2017/10/26 20:57:36 - Write to log.0 -
2017/10/26 20:57:36 - Write to log.0 - ====================
2017/10/26 20:57:36 - Write to log.0 - Finished processing (I=0,
O=0, R=1, W=1, U=0, E=0)
...
```

Executing jobs in an iterative way

For a long time, PDI developers used to ask, can I run a Job inside a transformation? The answer was definitely a no. In order to solve the requirement, the solution was to create jobs and transformations nested in complex ways. Now you can avoid all that unnecessary work by looping jobs in an easier way. There is a **Job Executor** step—analogous to the **Transformation Executor** that you know—that can easily be configured to loop over the rows in a dataset.

Using Job executors

The **Job Executor** is a PDI step that allows you to execute a Job several times simulating a loop. The executor receives a dataset, and then executes the Job once for each row or a set of rows of the incoming dataset.

To understand how this works, we will build a very simple example. The Job that we will execute will have two parameters: a folder and a file. It will create the folder, and then it will create an empty file inside the new folder. Both the name of the folder and the name of the file will be taken from the parameters.
The main transformation will execute the Job iteratively for a list of folder and file names.

Let's start by creating the Job:

1. Create a new Job.
2. Double-click on the work area to bring up the **Job properties** window. Use it to define two named parameters: `FOLDER_NAME` and `FILE_NAME`.
3. Drag a **START**, a **Create a folder**, and a **Create file** entry to the work area and link them as follows:

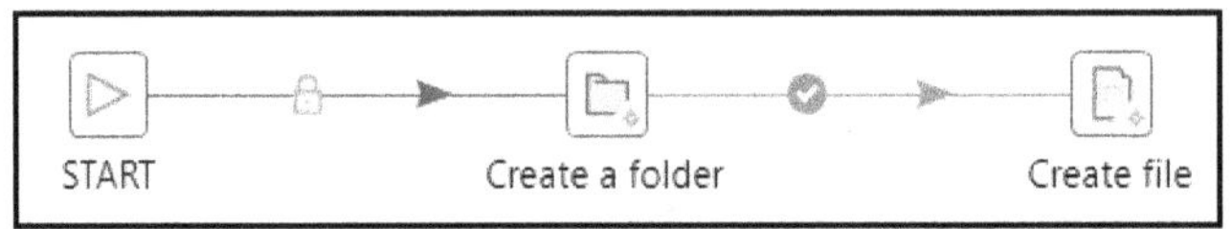

Sample Job

4. Double-click the **Create a folder** entry. As **Folder name**, type `${FOLDER_NAME}`.
5. Double-click the **Create file** entry. As **File name**, type `${FOLDER_NAME}/${FILE_NAME}`.
6. Save the Job and test it, providing values for the folder and filename. The Job should create a folder with an empty file inside, both with the names that you provide as parameters.

Now create the main Transformation:

1. Create a Transformation.
2. Drag a **Data Grid** step to the work area and define a single field named `foldername`. The type should be `String`.
3. Fill the **Data Grid** with a list of folders to be created, as shown in the next example:

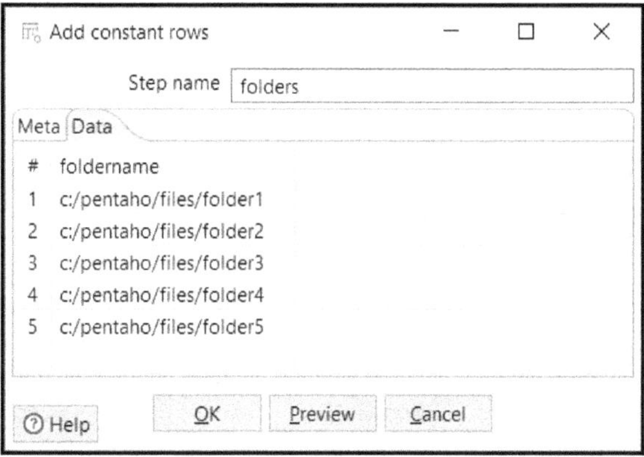

Sample data

4. As the name of the file, you can create any name of your choice. As an example, we will create a random name. For this, we use a **Generate random value** and a **UDJE** step, and configure them as shown:

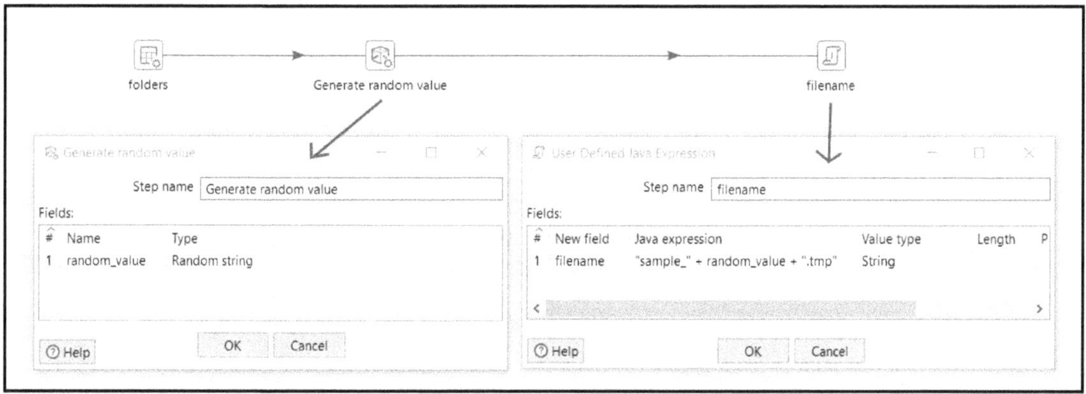

Generating a sample filename

5. With the last step selected, run a preview. You should see the full list of folders and filenames, as shown in the next sample image:

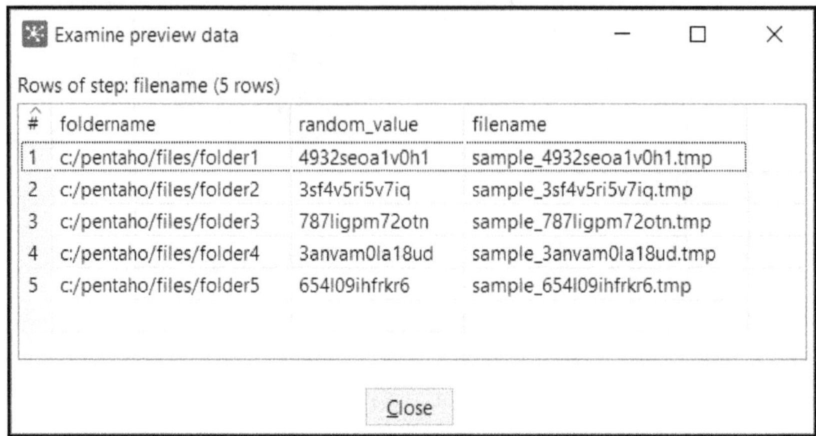

Sample folder and file names

6. At the end of the stream, add a **Job Executor** step. You will find it under the **Flow** category of steps.
7. Double-click on the **Job Executor** step.
8. As **Job**, select the path to the Job created before, for example, `${Internal.Entry.Current.Directory}/create_folder_and_file.kjb`
9. Configure the **Parameters** grid as follows:

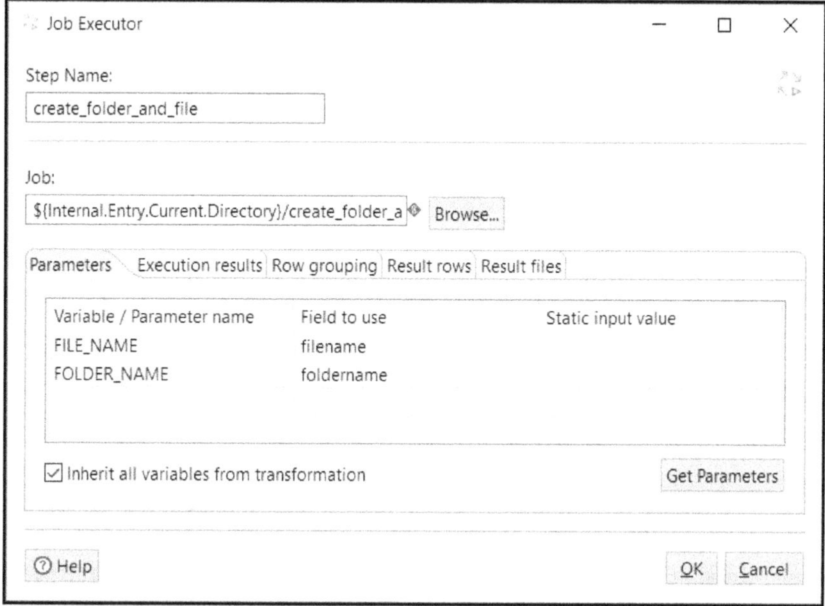

Configuring the parameters in a Job Executor

10. Close the window and save the transformation.
11. Run the transformation. The **Step Metrics** in the **Execution Results** window reflects what happens:

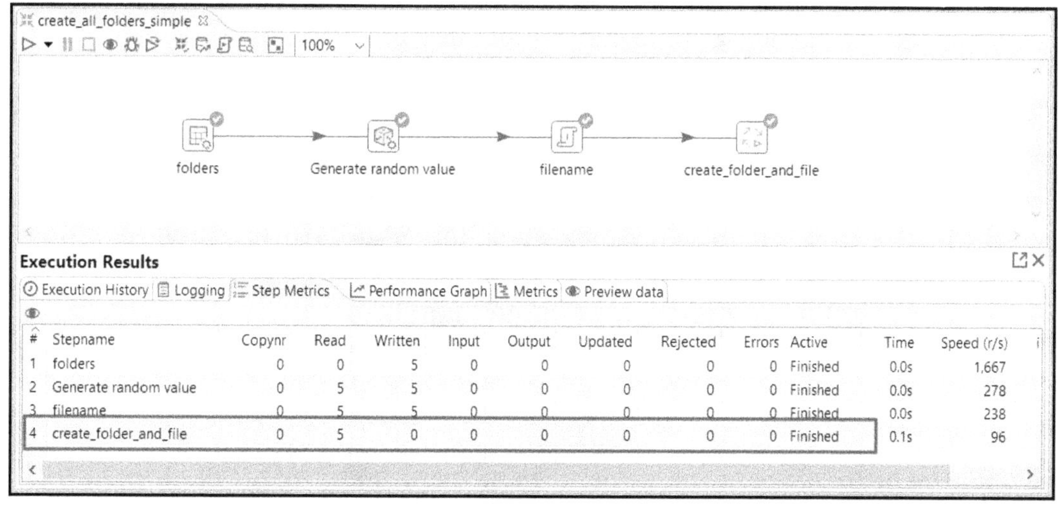

#	Stepname	Copynr	Read	Written	Input	Output	Updated	Rejected	Errors	Active	Time	Speed (r/s)
1	folders	0	0	5	0	0	0	0	0	Finished	0.0s	1,667
2	Generate random value	0	5	5	0	0	0	0	0	Finished	0.0s	278
3	filename	0	5	5	0	0	0	0	0	Finished	0.0s	238
4	create_folder_and_file	0	5	0	0	0	0	0	0	Finished	0.1s	96

Step Metrics

12. Click on the **Logging** tab. You will see the full log for the Job.
13. Browse your filesystem. You will find all the folders and files just created.

As you see, PDI executes the Job as many times as the number of rows that arrives to the Job Executor step, once for every row. Each time the Job executes, it receives values for the named parameters, and creates the folder and file using these values.

Configuring the executors with advanced settings

Just as it happens with the Transformation Executors that you already know, the Job Executors can also be configured with similar settings. This allows you to customize the behavior and the output of the Job to be executed. Let's summarize the options.

Getting the results of the execution of the job

The Job Executor doesn't cause the Transformation to abort if the Job that it runs has errors. To verify this, run the sample transformation again. As the folders already exist, you expect that each individual execution fails. However, the Job Executor ends without error. In order to capture the errors in the execution of the Job, you have to get the execution results. This is how you do it:

1. Drag a step to the work area where you want to redirect the results. It could be any step. For testing purposes, we will use a **Text file output** step.
2. Create a hop from the **Job Executor** toward this new step. You will be prompted for the kind of hop. Choose the **This output will contain the execution results** option as shown here:

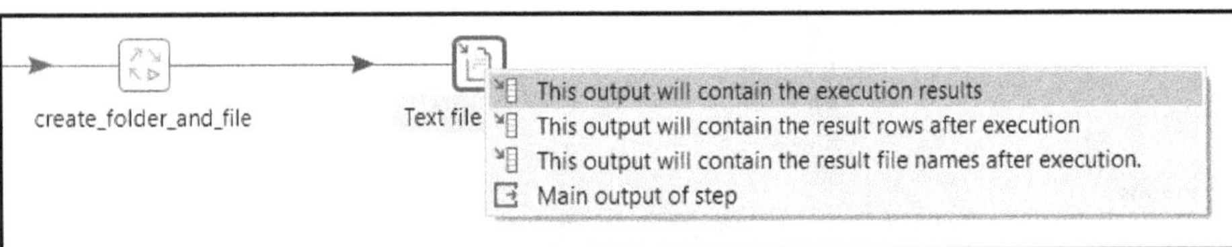

Creating a hop for the execution results

3. Double-click on the **Job Executor** and select the **Execution results** tab. You will see the list of metrics and results available. The **Field name** column has the names of the fields that will contain these results. If there are results you are not interested in, delete the value in the **Field name** column. For the results that you want to keep, you can leave the proposed field name or type a different name. The following screenshot shows an example that only generates a field for the log:

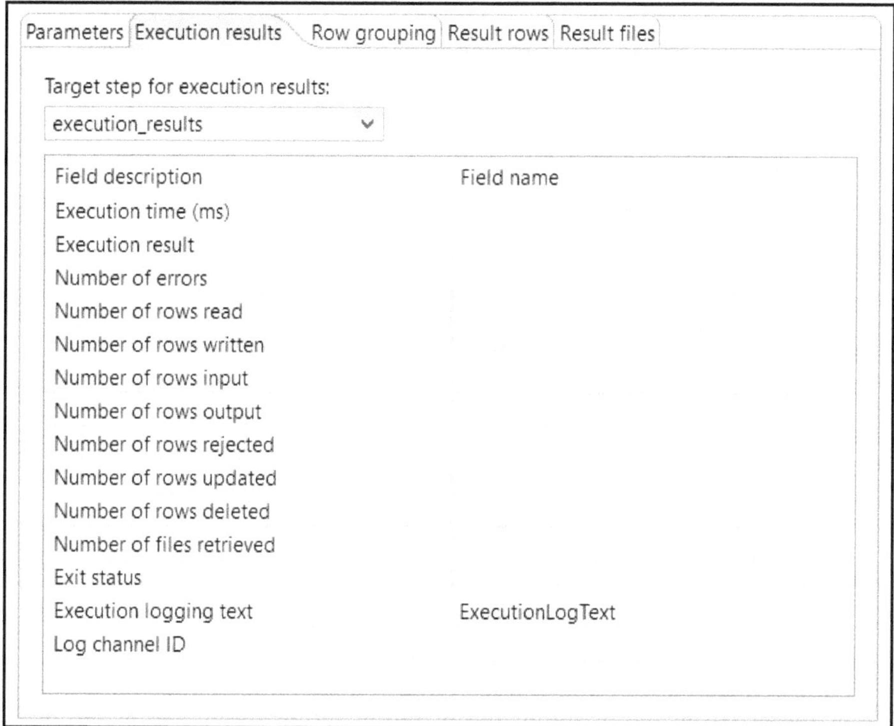

Configuring the execution results

4. When you are done, click on **OK**.

5. With the destination step selected, run a preview. You will see the results that you just defined, as shown in the next example:

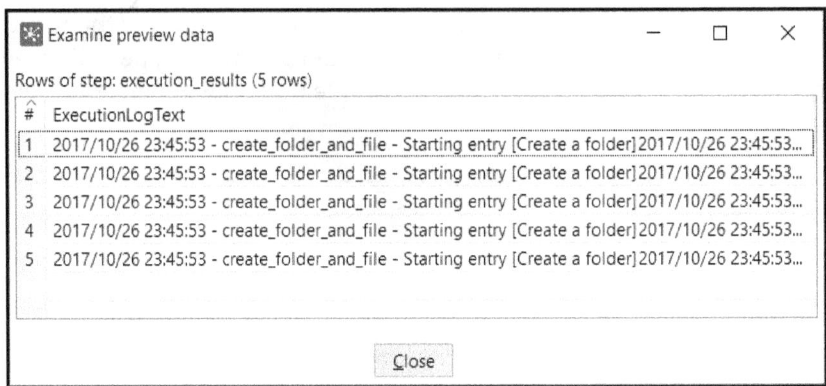

Previewing the execution results

6. If you copy any of the lines and paste it into a text editor, you will see the full log for the execution, as shown in the following example:

```
2017/10/26 23:45:53 - create_folder_and_file - Starting entry
[Create a folder]
2017/10/26 23:45:53 - create_folder_and_file - Starting entry
[Create file]
2017/10/26 23:45:53 - Create file - File
[c:/pentaho/files/folder1/sample_50n9q8oqsg6ib.tmp] created!
2017/10/26 23:45:53 - create_folder_and_file - Finished job entry
[Create file] (result=[true])
2017/10/26 23:45:53 - create_folder_and_file - Finished job entry
[Create a folder] (result=[true])
```

Working with groups of data

As you know, jobs don't work with datasets. Transformations do. However, you can still use the **Job Executor** to send the rows to the Job. Then, any transformation executed by your Job can get the rows using a **Get rows from result** step.
By default, the **Job Executor** executes once for every row in your dataset, but there are several possibilities where you can configure in the **Row Grouping** tab of the configuration window:

- You can send groups of N rows, where N is greater than 1
- You can pass a group of rows based on the value in a field

- You can send groups of rows based on the time the step collects rows before executing the Job

Using variables and named parameters

If the Job has named parameters—as in the example that we built—you provide values for them in the **Parameters** tab of the **Job Executor** step. For each named parameter, you can assign the value of a field or a fixed-static-value. In case you execute the Job for a group of rows instead of a single one, the parameters will take the values from the first row of data sent to the Job.

Capturing the result filenames

At the output of the **Job Executor**, there is also the possibility to get the result filenames. Let's modify the Transformation that we created to show an example of this kind of output:

1. Open the transformation created at the beginning of the section.
2. Drag a **Write to log** step to the work area.
3. Create a hop from the **Job Executor** toward the **Write to log** step. When asked for the kind of hop, select the option named **This output will contain the result file names after execution.** Your transformation will look as follows:

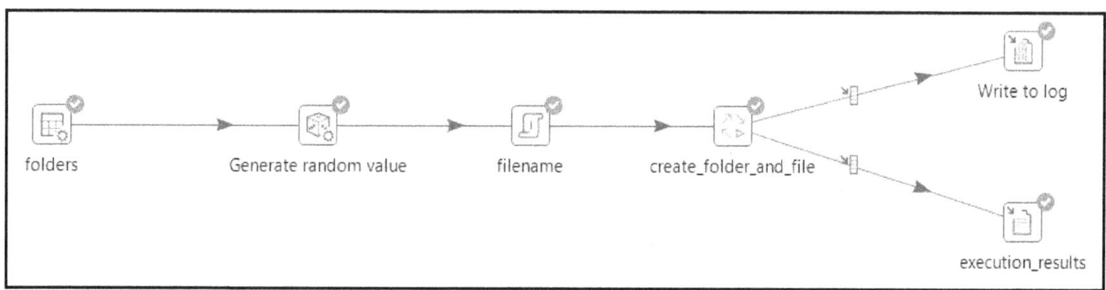

Redirecting the output of an executor

4. Double-click the **Job Executor** and select the **Result files** tab.

5. Configure it as shown:

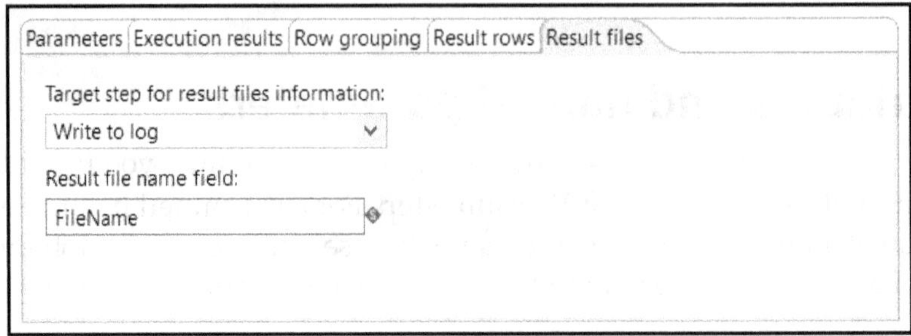

Capturing the result filenames

6. Double-click the **Write to log** step and, in the **Fields** grid, add the `FileName` field.
7. Close the window and save the transformation.
8. Run it.
9. Look at the **Logging** tab in the **Execution Results** window. You will see the names of the files in the result filelist, which are the files created in the Job:

```
...
... - Write to log.0 -
... - Write to log.0 - ------------> Linenr 1----------------------
--------
... - Write to log.0 - filename =
file:///c:/pentaho/files/folder1/sample_5agh7lj6ncqh7.tmp
... - Write to log.0 -
... - Write to log.0 - ====================
... - Write to log.0 -
... - Write to log.0 - ------------> Linenr 2----------------------
--------
... - Write to log.0 - filename =
file:///c:/pentaho/files/folder2/sample_6n0rhmrpvj21n.tmp
... - Write to log.0 -
... - Write to log.0 - ====================
... - Write to log.0 -
... - Write to log.0 - ------------> Linenr 3----------------------
--------
... - Write to log.0 - filename =
file:///c:/pentaho/files/folder3/sample_7ulkja68vf1td.tmp
... - Write to log.0 -
... - Write to log.0 - ====================
...
```

The example that you just created showed the option with a **Job Executor**. This also applies to the **Transformation Executor** step explained in `Chapter 12`, *Creating Portable and Reusable Transformations*.

Summary

In this chapter, you learned techniques to create advanced jobs and also to combine jobs and transformations in different ways.

First, you learned all about the different scopes for variables. You saw how to define named parameters in jobs, and also learned how to supply parameters from a parent Job to sub-jobs and transformations. Besides, you saw several ways to get a smart use of Kettle variables so that your work looks cleaner and more organized.

Then, you were presented new ways to use the copied rows. In this opportunity, you used them to manage files in advanced ways, and also as parameters of jobs and transformations.

After this, you learned what result filelists are, how to create and modify them, and of course, how to use them for different purposes such as zipping files or attaching files to an email.

Finally, you learned how to nest jobs and iterate the execution of jobs.

You already have all the knowledge to develop both simple and complex ETL processes. You are now ready for the next chapter, where you will see in detail how to launch transformations and jobs from the command line.

15

Launching Transformations and Jobs from the Command Line

Despite having used Spoon as the tool to run jobs and transformations, you may also run them from a Terminal. In fact, running them like this is the chosen method for production environments.

This chapter is a reference not only to run jobs and transformations from the command line, but also to deal with the output of the executions. The topics covered are as follows:

- Using the Pan and Kitchen utilities
- Checking the exit code
- Using command-line arguments
- Generating log files with the output of executions

Using the Pan and Kitchen utilities

Pan is a command-line program used to launch the transformations designed in Spoon. The counterpart to Pan is **Kitchen**, which allows you to run Jobs. In this first section, you will learn the basics about these utilities.

Running jobs and transformations

Kitchen, the program that executes Jobs from a Terminal window, comes in two versions:`kitchen.bat` and `kitchen.sh`. You will use one or the other depending on the platform—Windows or Unix-like systems respectively. Pan, the program that executes transformations from a Terminal window, also comes in two versions: `pan.bat` and `pan.sh`.

You will find all these files—`kitchen.bat`, `kitchen.sh`, `pan.bat`, and `pan.sh`—in the PDI installation directory.

The simplest way to run a Job or Transformation with these utilities is just providing the full path of the `kjb` or `ktr` file that you intend to execute. You will execute Pan or Kitchen according to the following table:

Task	**Windows**	**Unix-based system**
Running a Transformation	`pan.bat /file:<ktr file name>`	`pan.sh /file:<ktr file name>`
Running a Job	`kitchen.bat /file:<kjb file name>`	`kitchen.sh /file:<kjb file name>`

Suppose that you want to execute a Job named `hello_world.kjb`, located in `c:/pdi_labs/` (Windows) or `/home/pentaho_user/pdi_labs/` (Unix-based system). In order to run this Job from a Terminal window, follow these instructions:

1. Open a Terminal window.
2. Go to the directory where PDI is installed.
3. Depending on your operating system, proceed as explained:
    - On Windows systems, type the following:

    ```
    kitchen /file:c:/pdi_labs/hello_world.kjb
    ```

    - On Unix, Linux, and other Unix-like systems, type the following:

    ```
    ./kitchen.sh
    /file:/home/pentaho_user/pdi_labs/hello_world.kjb
    ```

In the same way, if you want to run a Transformation named `hello_world.ktr` located in the same folder as the previous Job, you have to follow these instructions:

1. Open a Terminal window.
2. Go to the directory where PDI is installed.
3. Depending on your operating system, proceed as explained:
    - On Windows systems, type the following:

```
pan /file:c:/pdi_labs/hello_world.ktr
```

    - On Unix, Linux, and other Unix-like systems type as follows:

```
./pan.sh /file:/home/pentaho_user/pdi_labs/hello_world.ktr
```

When specifying the `.ktr` or `.kjb` filename, you must include the full path. If the name contains spaces, surround it with double quotes.

The log of the execution—the same log that you see in the **Execution Results** window in Spoon—will be written in the same Terminal.

Checking the exit code

Both Pan and Kitchen return an error code based on how the execution went. To check the exit code of Pan or Kitchen under Windows after running the command, type as follows:

```
echo %ERRORLEVEL%
```

To check the exit code of Pan or Kitchen under Unix-based systems, type as follows:

```
echo $?
```

If you get a zero, it means that there are no errors. A value greater than zero means a failure. The following table shows the meanings of the possible exit codes:

Exit Code	Meaning
0	The Transformation/Job ran without problem
1	Errors occurred during processing
2	An unexpected error occurred during loading/running of the Transformation/Job
3	Unable to prepare and initialize the Transformation (only in Pan)
7	The Transformation/Job couldn't be loaded from XML or the repository
8	Error loading steps or plugins (error in loading one of the plugins mostly)
9	Command line usage printing

Supplying named parameters and variables

In `Chapter 12`, *Creating Portable and Reusable Transformations*, you learned how to parameterize transformations with **Named Parameters**. In `Chapter 14`, *Creating Advanced Jobs*, you revisited the concept but used the parameters in Jobs.

In Spoon, you specify the named parameters in the **Parameters** box. The window shows you the name of the defined named parameters for you to fill in the values or leave the defaults. From the Terminal window, you provide the values as part of the Pan or Kitchen command line. The syntax that you have to use is as follows:

```
/param:<parameter name>=<parameter value>
```

For example, you have a named parameter called `REPORT_FOLDER` and you want to give the parameter the value `my_reports`. The following screenshot shows you how you can provide that value in Spoon:

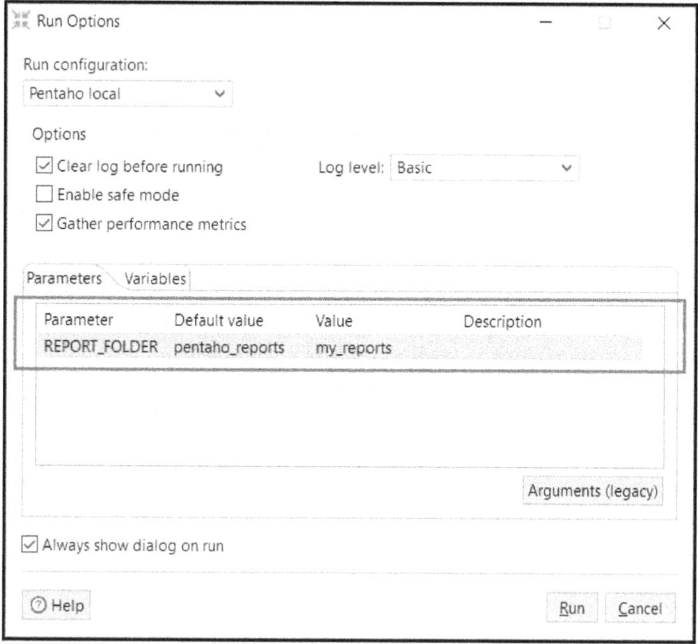

Providing named parameters in Spoon

This is how you do the same as part of a Pan or Kitchen command:

```
/param:"REPORT_FOLDER=c:\my_reports"
```

As you know, named parameters are a subset of Kettle variables. In general, when you use Kettle variables in your Jobs or transformations, you expect that they already exist and have a value. In Spoon, you have the option to set them on the fly. When you execute a Job or Transformation, the grid named **Variables** shows the variables used in the Transformation/Job as well as their current values. At the time of the execution, you can type different values, which is useful for developing and testing purposes.

In Spoon, you can also set variables from the menu option, **Edit** | **Set Environment Variables...**.

When you run Jobs and transformations from the Terminal, you don't have the opportunity to set variables. If you need to provide values for Kettle variables, you should use some tricks, for example, set them in the first Job that you call, or define them in the `kettle.properties` file.

Using command-line arguments

Besides the use of named parameters, there is another way to provide external values to a Transformation: **command-line arguments**, that is, arguments that you supply in the command line when you run Pan or Kitchen. In this section, you will learn how to implement the use of command-line arguments in Spoon and how to provide the values in Spoon and also when running Pan.

First, let's create a new version of the *Hello World* Transformation that we created in `Chapter 1`, *Getting Started with Pentaho Data Integration*. The purpose of the Transformation is to read your name from the command line and then write it to the log:

1. Create a new Transformation.
2. Drag to the work area a **Get System Info** step, a **UDJE** step, and a **Write to log** step. Link the steps in this order.
3. Double-click on the **Get System Info** step and use it to add a field called `name` that will hold the **command line argument 1**. Use the following screenshot as reference:

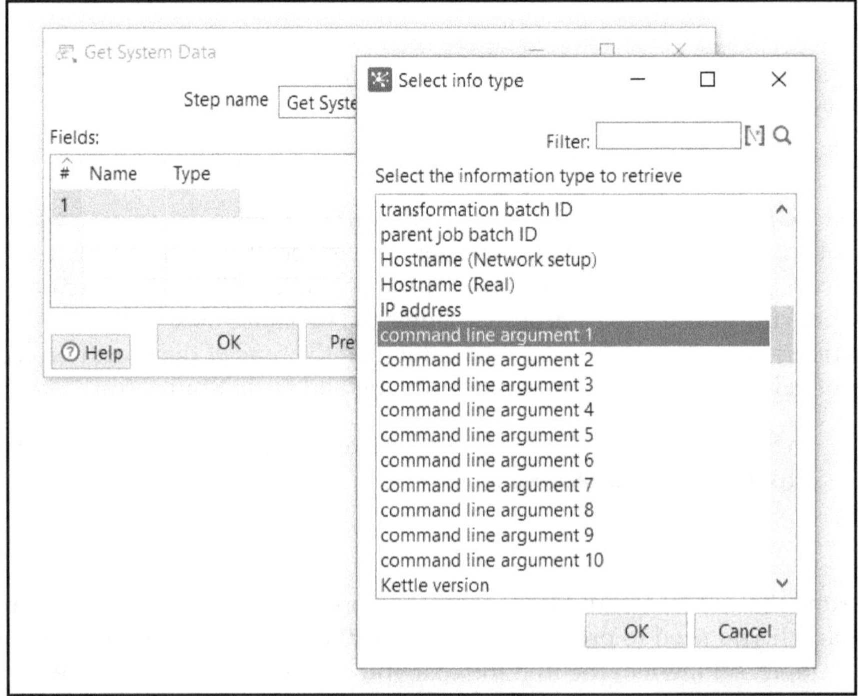

Using command line arguments

4. Click on **OK**.
5. Use the a **UDJE** step to add a `String` field named `message`. For **Java expression**, type `"Hello, " + name + "!"`.
6. Click on **OK**.

Without applying any configuration to the **Write to log** step, it will write to the log the values for all the incoming fields.

7. Save the Transformation with the name `hello_world_argument.ktr`.
8. Run the Transformation. In the dialog window, click on the **Arguments (legacy)** button. Fill the grid with your name, as shown in the following screenshot:

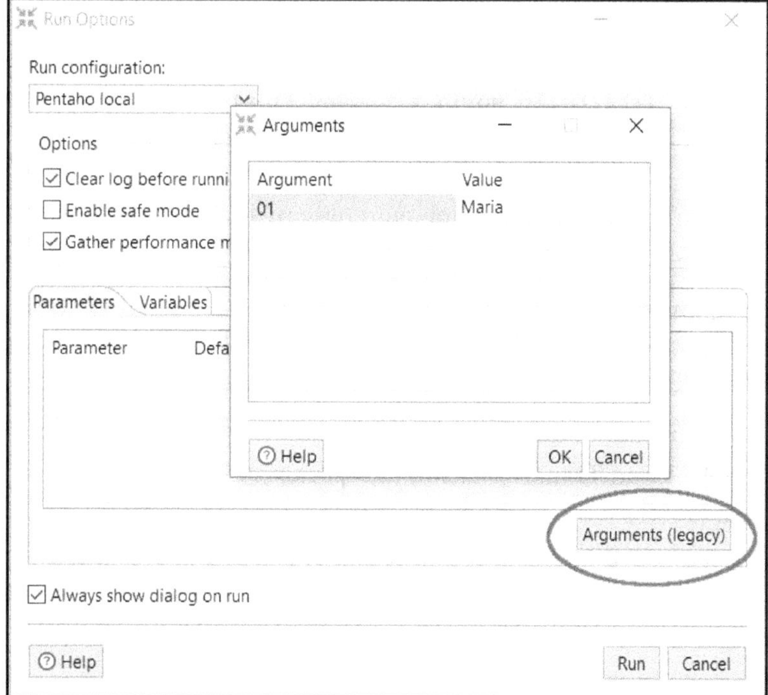

Providing arguments

9. Close the window and click on **Run**.

10. Look at the **Logging** tab in the **Execution Results** window. You will see this:

```
... - Write to log.0 - ------------> Linenr 1----------------------
--------
... - Write to log.0 - name = Maria
... - Write to log.0 - hello_message = Hello, Maria!
... - Write to log.0 -
... - Write to log.0 - ====================
```

In this Transformation, you used just one argument. You can use up to 10, by selecting the options `command-line argument 2`, `command-line argument 3`, and so on.

To run the same Transformation with Pan, you just write the arguments after the name of the Transformation.

For example, if your system is Windows, the command will look like this:

```
pan /file:c:/pdi_labs/hello_world_argument.ktr Maria
```

The execution of this command will generate the same output as it did in Spoon.

If this Transformation is embedded in a Job, you may provide the arguments in the same way but use `kitchen` instead.

Command-line arguments don't come necessarily from the Terminal. If you call a Transformation that uses command-line arguments from a Job, you can provide fixed values, as explained in the next instructions:

1. Create a Job and name it `Hello.kjb`.
2. Add **START** and **Transformation** Job entries.
3. Create a hop from the **START** towards the **Transformation** entry.
4. Double-click on the **Transformation** entry, provide the full path to the Transformation `hello_world_argument.ktr`, and fill in the **Argument** tab as follows:

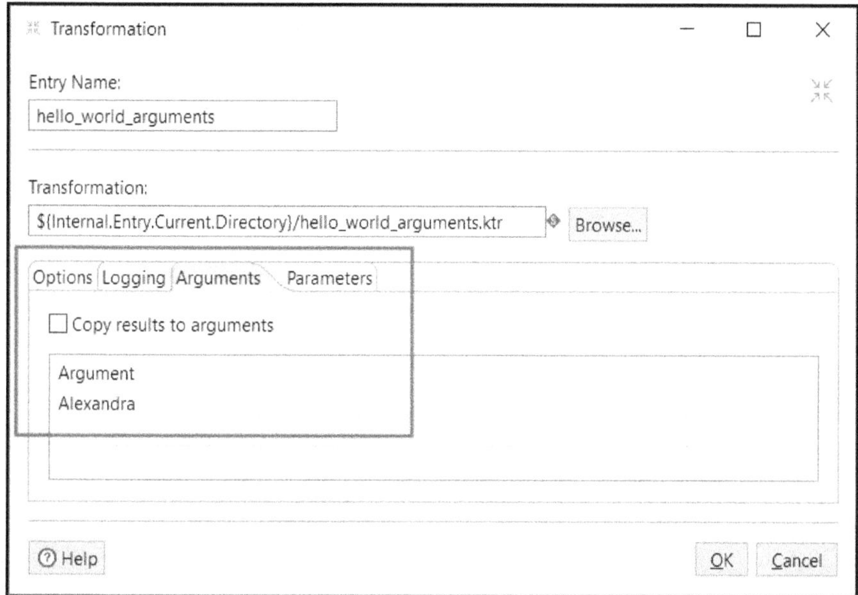

Configuring a Transformation entry with arguments

5. Click on **OK** and save the Job.
6. Run the Job.
7. Look at the **Logging** tab. Among the lines of logs, you will see the following:

```
... - hello_world_arguments - Dispatching started for
transformation [hello_world_arguments]
... - Get name.0 - Finished processing (I=0, O=0, R=1, W=1, U=0,
E=0)
... - Write to log.0 -
... - Write to log.0 - ------------> Linenr 1----------------------
--------
... - Write to log.0 - name = Alexandra
... - Write to log.0 - hello_message = Hello, Alexandra!
... - Write to log.0 -
... - Write to log.0 - ====================
... - hello_message.0 - Finished processing (I=0, O=0, R=1, W=1,
U=0, E=0)
```

If you run this Job from the command line, you don't have to provide any argument.

Deciding between the use of a command-line argument and named parameters

Both command-line arguments and named parameters are a means of creating more flexible jobs and transformations. The following table summarizes the differences and reasons to use one or the other.

In the first column, the word argument refers to the external value that you will use in your Job or Transformation. This argument could be implemented as a named parameter or as a command-line argument.

Situation	**Solution using named parameters**	**Solution using arguments**
It is desirable to have a default for the argument.	Named parameters are perfect in this case. You provide default values at the time you define them.	Before using the command-line argument, you have to evaluate if it was provided on the command line. If not, you have to set the default value at that moment.
The argument is mandatory.	You don't have the means to determine if the user provided a value for the named parameter.	To know if the user provided a value for the command-line argument, you just get the command-line argument and compare it to a null value.
You need several arguments but it is probable that not all of them are present.	If you don't have a value for a named parameter, you are not forced to enter it when you run the Job or Transformation.	Let's suppose that you expect three command-line arguments. If you have a value only for the third, you still have to provide values for the first and the second.
You need several arguments and it is highly probable that all of them are present.	The command line with all the named parameters would be too long. The purpose of each parameter will be clear, but typing the command line would be tedious.	The command line is simple as you just list the values one after the other. However, there is a risk you may unintentionally enter the values unordered, which could lead to unexpected results.
You want to use the argument in several places.	You can do it, but you must ensure that the value will not be overwritten in the middle of the execution.	You can get the command-line argument using a **Get System Info** step as many times as you need.

You need to use the value in a place where a variable is needed.	Named parameters are ready to be used as Kettle variables.	First, you need to set a variable with the command-line argument value. Usually, this requires creating additional transformations to be run before any other Job or Transformation.

Depending on your particular situation, you will prefer one or the other solution. Note that you can mix both.

Sending the output of executions to log files

You are already familiar with the log that PDI generates every time you run a Job or Transformation. In Spoon, you see it in the **Logging** tab of the **Execution Results** window. When launching a Job or Transformation with Pan/Kitchen, you see the log in the terminal.

In `Chapter 2`, *Getting Started with Transformations*, you also learned about the different levels o the log. In Spoon, you specify the level in the **Log level** drop-down list inside the **Options** box in the **Run Options** window. To do the same when using Pan/Kitchen, you append the `/level:<logging level>` option, where the logging level can be one of the following: `Error`, `Nothing`, `Minimal`, `Basic`, `Detailed`, `Debug`, or `Rowlevel`.

The next sample screenshot shows you how to run a Job with minimal details in the log:

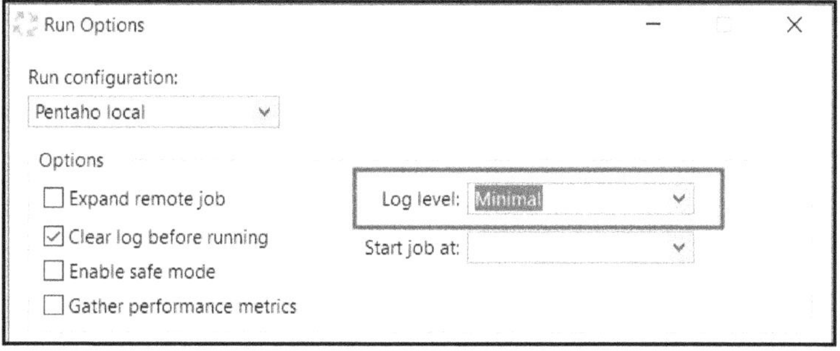

Setting the log level in Spoon

The following sample shows how you provide the same selection as an option in the Pan/Kitchen command line:

```
/level:Minimal
```

Besides sending the log to the Terminal, you can send it to a file. In Pan/Kitchen, just redirect the output to a file:

```
pan.bat /file:"c:\pdi_labs\sales_report.ktr" /level:Detailed >
c:\pdi_labs\logs\sales_report.log
```

The sample command generates a detailed log and redirects it to the `c:\pdi_labs\logs\sales_report.log` file.

It is also possible to generate log files only for a subset of your jobs and transformations. You define this in Spoon as follows:

1. Open the `Hello.kjb` Job generated earlier.
2. Double-click on the **Transformation** entry.
3. Select the **Logging** tab and fill it as shown:

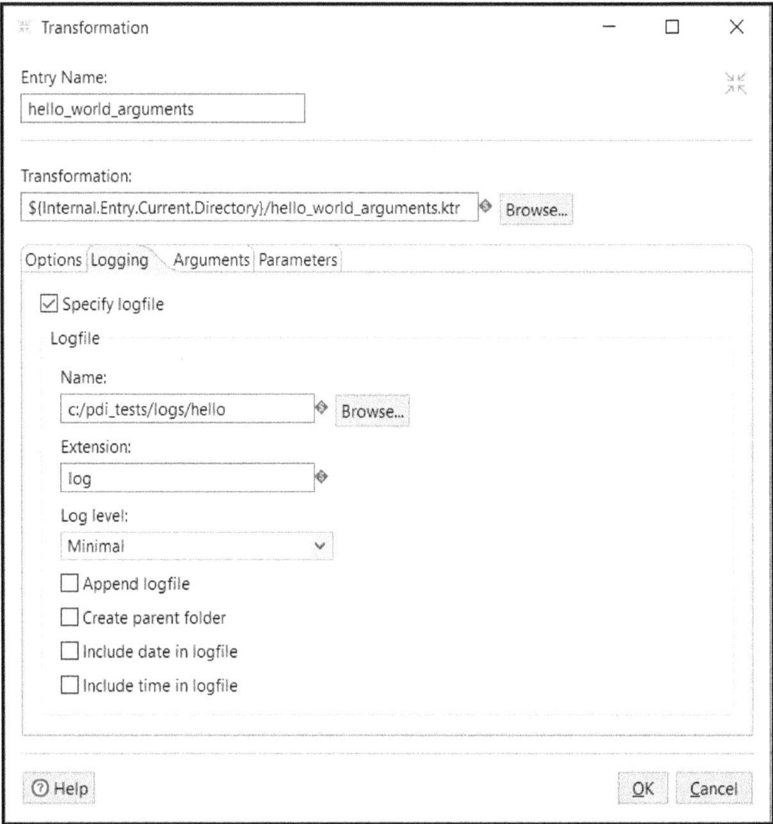

Configuring a Logging tab

4. Close the window and save the Job.
5. Run the Job.
6. Browse your filesystem for the `hello.log` file. It should contain the log for the execution of the Transformation with minimal information.

To configure a log file for the output of a Job execution, proceed in the same way but select the **Logging** tab of the correspondent **Job** entry.

Note that for a given root Job, you can not only select which sub-jobs or the sub-transformation PDI will generate logs, but you can also mix levels of logs.

As a final note, in all the examples provided, the options are specified using the syntax `/option:value`, for example, `/file:"Hello"`. Instead of a slash (/), you can also use a hyphen (-). Between the name of the option and the value, you can also use an equal to (=). This means that the `/file:"Hello"` and `-file="Hello"` options are equivalents.

As for the values, if spaces are present, you can use quotes (`''`) or double quotes (`""`) to keep the value together. If there are no spaces, the quotes are optional.

You may use any combination of a slash (/) and a hyphen (-) or a colon (`:`) and an equal to (=).

As in Windows, the use of - and = may cause problems, it's recommended that you use the `/option:value` syntax.

Besides all the options explained in this chapter, both Pan and Kitchen have additional options.

For a full list and more examples, visit the Pan and Kitchen documentation at `https://help.pentaho.com/Documentation/8.0/Products/Data_Integration/Command_Line_Tools`.

Automating the execution

As you just learned, running Pan and Kitchen not only involves providing the name of the `ktr` or `kjb` file, but also typing several options, for example, parameters or names of log files. You can type the full command manually when you are developing or testing, but when your work is ready for production, you want to keep things simple and automated. The following tutorial explains how to embedd the execution of Kitchen inside a script. Once you have the script, you can schedule its execution using a system utility, for example, `cron` in Unix or `scheduler` in Windows.

Suppose that you have a Job named `process_sales.kjb` located in the `c:\project\etl` folder (Windows) or `/home/project/etl` folder (Unix), and you want to run it every day. You want to keep a history of logs, so the log of the execution will be written in a folder named `C:\project\logs` (Windows) or `/home/project/logs` (Unix-like systems). This is how you do it:

1. Open a Terminal window.
2. Create a new file with your favorite text editor.
3. Under Windows systems, type the following in the new file:

```
for /f "tokens=1-3 delims=/- " %%a in ('date /t') do set
XDate=%%c%%b%%a
for /f "tokens=1-2 delims=: " %%a in ('time /t') do set
XTime=%%a.%%b

set path_etl=C:\project\etl
set path_log=C:\project\logs

c:\
cd ..
cd pdi-ce
kitchen.bat /file:%path_etl%\process_sales.kjb /level:Detailed >>
%path_log%\sales_"%Xdate% %XTime%".log
```

4. Save the file as `process_sales.bat` in a folder of your choice. Schedule the execution as needed.
5. Under Linux, Unix, and similar systems, type the following:

```
UNXETL=/home/project/etl
UNXLOG=/home/project/logs

cd /pdi-ce
kitchen.sh /file:$UNXETL/process_sales.kjb /level:Detailed >>
$UNXLOG/sales_'date +%y%m%d-%H%M'.log
```

6. Save the file as `process_sales.sh` in a folder of your choice. Add a cron entry for scheduling the execution as needed.

Regardless of your system, to create your own script, replace the names of the folders with the names of your own folders, that is, the folder where your main Job is, the folder for the logs, and the folder where PDI is installed.

When you execute the script with either `process_sales.bat` or `process_sales.sh`, a log file will be generated named `sales_` followed by the date and hour. The file will contain the full log for the execution of the Job.

In the same way, you can create a script to run a Transformation instead of a Job.

Summary

This chapter explained in detail how to run Jobs and transformations from a Terminal window using the Kitchen and Pan command-line programs respectively. You learned how to use the Kitchen and Pan utilities and saw the most commonly used command-line options available. You also learned how to check the exit code to know the end status of an execution. In addition, you learned how to generate log files both with the command-line utilities and by configuring Job and Transformation entries.

The lessons learned so far gave you the basis of PDI. In the next chapter, you will find useful information to go further, ranging from applying best practices to deploying a project in a production environment.

16

Best Practices for Designing and Deploying a PDI Project

This chapter covers the setup of a new project and also the best practices that make it easier to deploy a project in different environments. It also gives you some advice to take into account in your daily work with PDI.

The topics covered are as follows:

- Setting up a new project
- Best practices to design jobs and transformations
- Maximizing the performance
- Deploying a project in different environments

Setting up a new project

When you start a new PDI project, there are several aspects that we have to take into account. In this section, we will talk about the following:

- Setting up of the environment
- Defining a folder structure for the project
- Availability of resources
- Versioning

Setting up the local environment

When you run Spoon for the first time, a folder named `.kettle` is created by default in your home directory. This folder is referred to as the **Kettle home directory**. As you already know, it's in this folder where the `kettle.properties` file is located. The folder contains additional configuration files, which are summarized in the following table:

FILE	**DESCRIPTION**
`kettle.properties`	Definition of Kettle variables with Java Virtual Machine scope.
`shared.xml`	Definition of shared objects as for example database connections.
`.spoonrc`	User interface settings. This file contains the settings that you defined in the **Tool** | **Options...** setting window in Spoon, as well as the history of your work, for example the last jobs and transformations opened.
`.languageChoice`	User language settings defined in the **Tool** | **Options...** window in Spoon.
`db.cache`	Database cache.

As you can see, most of the files are specific to your local environment and are independent of the project you are working on. There is, however, the `kettle.properties` file that we should care about when it's time to start up a new project.

As you already know, the `kettle.properties` file contains a definition of variables visible in all jobs and transformations. Therefore, it's the perfect place to define general settings, for example:

- Database connection settings: host, database name, and so on
- SMTP settings: SMTP server, port, and so on
- Common input and output folders
- Directory where to send temporary files

Both Spoon and the command-line scripts, Pan and Kitchen, recognize the variables defined in this file.

Take care if you are involved in more than one project at the same time. In that case, you should prefer either using a regular properties file for the definition of general variables, or having a different Kettle home directory for each project. By the end of the chapter, we will explain how to implement this.

Through the rest of the chapter, we will continue talking about the `kettle.properties` file.

Defining a folder structure for the project

There is no general rule regarding the folder structure for a PDI project, but in general terms, we suggest a structure that is easy to understand, maintain, and also port when it's time to take the project to a different environment. The following is a suggested list of folders that you should have:

- Input files
- Output files
- Temporary files
- Log files
- Database scripts
- Properties files
- Scripts (`bat` / `sh` files)
- PDI files (jobs and transformations)

Then, in the `kettle.properties` file, you could add variables pointing to each of these folders, for example:

```
INPUT_FOLDER = /home/pentaho/input
OUTPUT_FOLDER = /home/pentaho/output
TEMP_FOLDER=/tmp
...
PROJECT_PATH=/home/pentaho/my/project
```

Finally, in your jobs and transformations, you don't have to worry about the name of the folders. You just use the variables as shown in the following example:

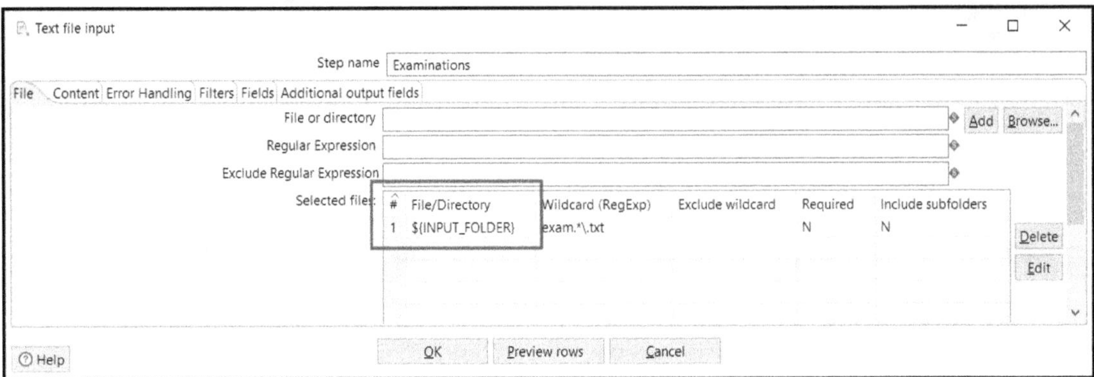

Sample use of variables for reading files

Dealing with external resources

Before starting with the development, make sure that you have access to all the external resources needed for your project. For example, if you work with a database, you will need the connection settings, the proper JDBC drivers to connect from PDI, and permissions to perform create, read, update, and delete known as **CRUD** operations. If you will access a remote server, for example, to upload or download files, verify the full paths to the remote folders and check for permissions to read and write. If you will send emails, verify the settings of the SMTP server.

Then, in the `kettle.properties` file, you could add variables pointing to all these resources:

```
# source data base
DB_HOST=
DB_NAME=
...

# warehouse
DW_HOST=
DW_NAME=
...

# SMTP
SMTP_SERVER=
SMTP_PORT=
```

```
...

# S3 access
S3_ACC_KEY=
S3_SEC_KEY=
...
```

Finally, in your jobs and transformations, you just use the variables, as shown in the following example:

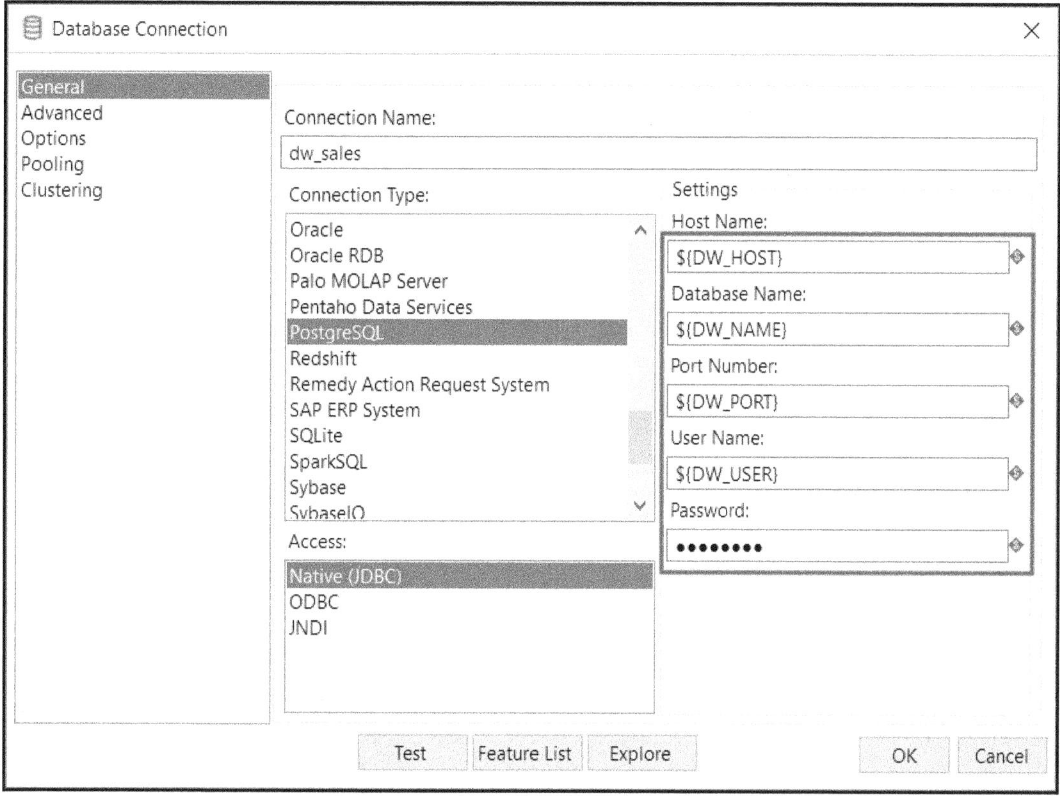

Sample use of variables in a database connection

Defining and adopting a versioning system

When you are working with a team, you definitely need to keep track of the new developments or the changes that are applied to the current work. This is the main reason why you should use a version control system.

Doing so, you can not only examine the history of changes, but you can also recover old versions of your jobs and transformations. Among the versioning systems available, you could try some of the most popular, namely the following:

- **Subversion**, an open source version control system developed as a project of the Apache Software Foundation. For more on Subversion, visit `https://subversion.apache.org/`.
- **Git**, a free and open source distributed version control system. For more on Git, visit the official site, `https://git-scm.com/`.

Best practices to design jobs and transformations

Best practices not only make the development process easier, but also improve the quality of your ETL processes and facilitate their maintenance. By considering the following list of best practices, your projects will have more chances of success.

Styling your work

The following is a simple list of practices to take into account while working with Spoon:

- Outline your ideas on paper before creating a Transformation or Job. Don't drop steps randomly on the canvas trying to get things to work; otherwise, you will end up with a Transformation or Job that is difficult to understand and might not be of any use.
- Document your work:
    - Write at least a simple description of the Transformation and Job properties windows.
    - Replace the default names of the steps and Job entries with meaningful ones.
    - Use notes to clarify the purpose of transformations and jobs. Color-code your notes for a better effect; for example, use a color for notes explaining the purpose of a Transformation, and a different color or font for technical notes.
- Make your jobs and transformations clear to understand. Arrange the elements on the canvas so that it does not look like a puzzle to solve. Memorize the shortcuts for arrangement and alignment and use them regularly.

The following is a sample screenshot of a Transformation that somehow represents the preceding list of best practices:

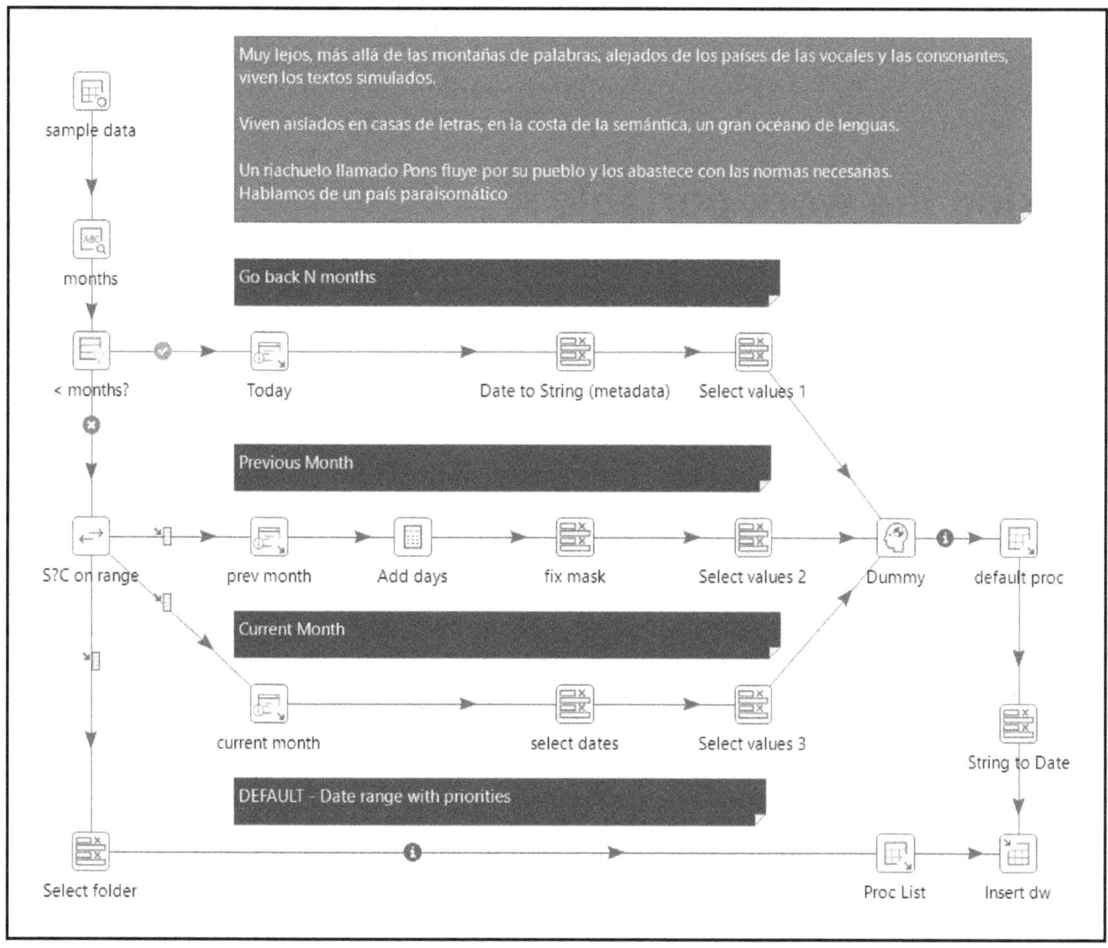

Sample well-documented Transformation

Leaving Spoon aside for a moment, there are still more good practices to apply while designing and developing:

- Organize the PDI elements in folders. Don't save all of the transformations and jobs in the same folder, but organize them according to the purpose that they have.
- Use name conventions. This applies to a broad range of elements: variable names, fields, step and Job entries, Job and transformations files, and project folders.

- Give the database connections meaningful names. Don't name the connections after the engine, for example, instead of `customers_mysql`, use just `customers`.

Finally, don't forget to handle errors. Try to figure out the kind of errors that may occur and trap them by validating, handling, and acting accordingly—fixing data, taking alternative paths, sending friendly messages to the log files, reporting the errors by email, and so on.

Making the work portable

Making your work portable is one of the best advice to keep things simple when it's time to deploy the work into a different environment. If you move your work to another machine or another folder, or the path to source or destination files changes, or the connection properties to the databases change, the idea is that everything keeps working without or with minimal changes. There are a couple of things that you can do when you pursue this objective:

- Don't use fixed names but variables. As mentioned before, this applies to database connections, project folders, remote servers, among others. If you know the values of the variables beforehand, define the variables in the `kettle.properties` file.
- For the location of transformations and jobs, use relative paths, as shown in the following example:

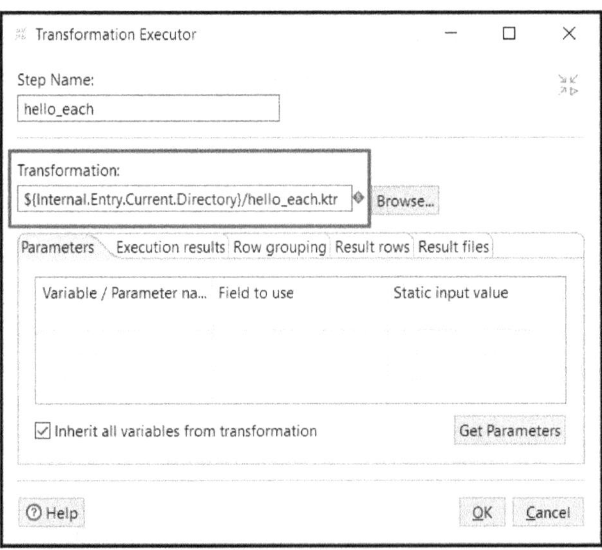

Using relative paths

Designing and developing reusable jobs and transformations

Besides applying the different practices already explained, there is one more valuable factor while you design ETL processes: reusability. This feature not only benefits your current project, but also saves development time if you end up using your work in other projects. There are a couple of ways to design and develop reusable jobs and transformations:

- Make heavy use of variables and named parameters.
- If you identify tasks that are going to be used in several situations, create sub-transformations.
- If you identify patterns to manipulate data, use metadata injection.
- Avoid overloading your transformations. If a Transformation does much more than a specific task, think of splitting it into two or more. Small pieces of work are better candidates to be reused.

In general, a good recommendation for your daily work is to bookmark the forum page and visit it frequently. The PDI forum is available at `https://community.hds.com/community/products-and-solutions/pentaho/data-integration`. If you are stuck with something, search for a solution in the forum. If you don't find what you're looking for, create a new thread, expose your doubts or scenario clearly, and you'll get a prompt answer as the Pentaho community and particularly the PDI one is quite active. Alternatively, you can meet Pentaho people on the IRC server, `www.freenode.net`, channel `#pentaho`. On the channel, people discuss all kinds of issues related to all the Pentaho tools, and not just Kettle.

Maximizing the performance

A PDI Transformation may be colorful, organized, full of pretty notes, but at the end, the most important thing is that it meets its purpose within a reasonable time of execution. Therefore, it's important to test your work with real data in order to detect if there are things that can be affecting the performance.

There are many factors involved both internal—for example, bad configuration of sort steps—and external—for example lack of indexes in a database table. Fortunately, PDI offers some means to analyze and improve the performance of your transformations.

Analyzing Steps Metrics

You are already familiar with the **Step Metrics** tab, which shows statistics for each step in your Transformation. There are some columns that we haven't mentioned until now, which are useful to monitor the performance:

STEP METRIC	DESCRIPTION
Time	The time of execution of the step
Speed (r/s)	The processing speed in rows per second
input/output	The number of rows in the input and output buffer relative to the step

The first two metrics are self-explanatory. The **input/output** field requires an extra explanation. This field shows the number of rows in the buffers entering and coming out of the current step.

The input and output buffers have a maximum size defined in the **Miscellaneous** tab in the **Transformation properties** window. None of the values in the **input/output** field will be greater than the buffer size.

To understand how the **input/output** metric is useful, you could see it as a ratio between the input and the output:

- If the ratio **input/output** is closer to `1/0`, this is because the rows are being accumulated in its input buffer. This means that this step is not processing the rows at a good speed, thus causing a bottleneck.
- If the ratio **input/output** is closer to `0/1`, it means that the step is not receiving rows to process. This could be because there is a bottleneck prior to the step in the stream.
- If the input and output are similar, this means that the step is handling the rows at a reasonable speed.

The following screenshot shows you an example of a step performing slow—the **Delay row** step:

Execution Results

Logging | Execution History | Step Metrics | Performance Graph | Metrics | Preview data

#	Stepname	Copynr	Read	Written	Input	Output	Updated	Rejected	Errors	Active	Time	Speed (r/s)	input/output
1	date range	0	0	1	0	0	0	0	0	Finished	0.0s	59	-
2	diff_dates	0	1	1	0	0	0	0	0	Finished	0.0s	26	-
3	Clone row	0	1	4017	0	0	0	0	0	Finished	0.1s	58,217	-
4	clone	0	24	23	0	0	0	0	0	Running	8.6s	3	3993/0
5	calc	0	23	23	0	0	0	0	0	Running	8.6s	3	0/0
6	single date	0	23	23	0	0	0	0	0	Running	8.6s	3	0/0

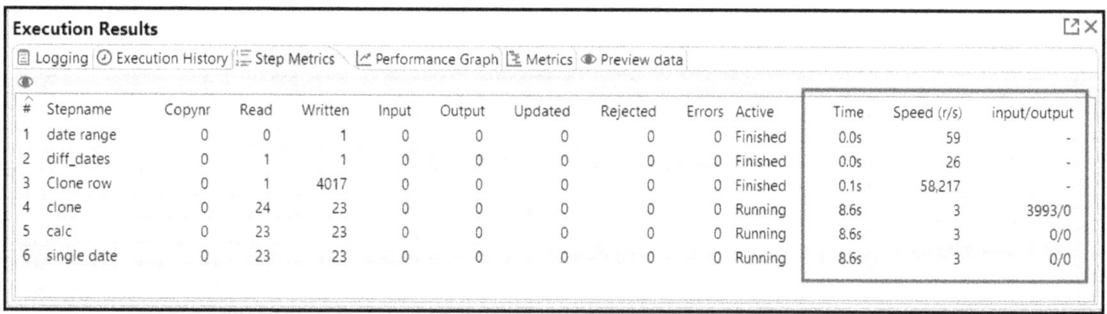

Sample Step Metrics

By identifying the step or steps that are causing performance issues, you can decide how to revert the situation either by revising the configuration of the steps or by refactoring the Transformation.

Analyzing performance graphs

If you look at the **Execution Results** window, you will see a **Performance Graphs** tab. This tab shows you a performance evolution graph based on the Step Metrics. By analyzing this graph, you can fine-tune the performance.

In order to see the performance graphs, you have to enable the step performance monitoring, as explained here:

1. Open the **Transformation Properties** window by double-clicking anywhere in the work area.
2. Select the **Monitoring** tab and check the **Enable step performance monitoring?** option.

> TIP: By default, a performance snapshot is taken every second for all the running steps, but you can change the value in the same tab window. You can also change the default value for the number of snapshots in memory.

3. Once the monitoring has been configured, you will be able to show the performance graph and analyze the execution per step and metric. The following screenshot is a sample performance graph showing the input buffer size for the selected step:

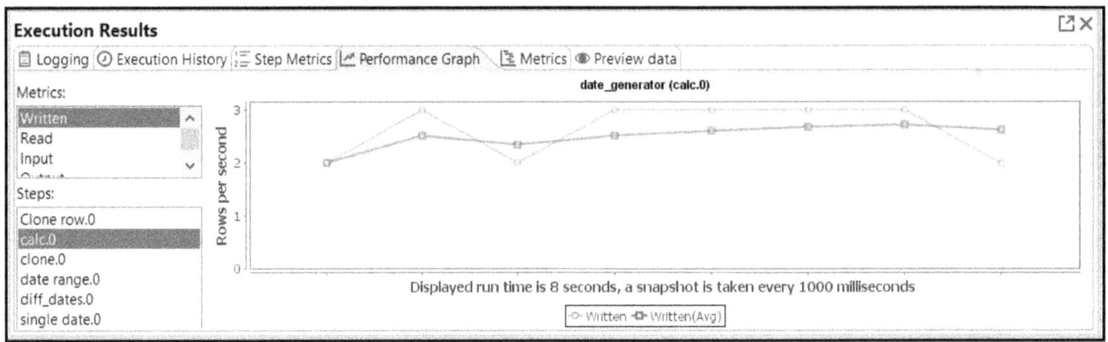

Sample performance graph

If you are working with an earlier version of PDI you may not see the graph. After PDI 5.4 a bug was introduced and the performance graph was not displayed. The bug was not fixed until PDI 8.0.

We just explained the basics about performance issues. In different chapters, we mentioned some possible performance problems and their solutions, but there are many more factors involved.

For a detailed guide to factors that can affect the performance and possible ways to address them, you can read the following article: `https://support.pentaho.com/hc/en-us/articles/205715046-Best-Practices-Pentaho-Data-Integration-Performance-Tuning`.

Deploying the project in different environments

If you take into account all of the best practices explained so far, deploying a project to a different environment shouldn't be a painful task.

The complexity of the deployment will vary from project to project, but in all cases, there are common tasks as follows:

1. Get all the information and settings related to the new environment. This includes information about external resources such as servers, folders, and database settings.
2. Edit a copy of the `kettle.properties` files and update the values of variables with the information of the new environment. Save the file in the right location—the Kettle home of the environment where you are deploying.
3. If you have more properties files besides the `kettle.properties` one, review and update them.
4. Regarding the PDI installation, make sure that it contains all the drivers needed for your project, for example, the JDBC drivers. Also, if in your project, you used plugins installed from the Marketplace, make sure to install them here as well.
5. Check out the project from the versioning system into the new location.

All of this works for a single project. Now suppose that for testing, you have a machine with a single PDI installation shared by several projects. You don't want the projects to share the Kettle home. The next subsection gives a solution to this and similar situations.

Modifying the Kettle home directory

As explained, PDI takes the general configuration files from the Kettle home directory located by default in the user home folder. There are several situations where you would like to have multiple Kettle directories or a single one in a different location. These are some examples:

- You have a PDI installation shared by several projects. You need a separate `kettle.properties` files, one for each different project.
- In the same machine, you want to switch between development and production. You want to have two `kettle.properties` files, one for each environment.
- You have a single project but the project is run by different users. As the default Kettle home directory changes depending on the user who is logged on, you would have to replicate the same directory once for each user.

The solution to all these scenarios is to change the value of the `KETTLE_HOME` variable so that it points to the new location of the Kettle home directory. If for example, the new location is `c:/pentaho/test/.kettle`, you will want to set the `KETTLE_HOME` variable to `c:/pentaho/test`. You can do this permanently, or just before starting PDI. Depending on your system, you proceed differently.

Modifying the Kettle home in Windows

If you want to modify the Kettle home directory permanently, you can do as follows:

1. Access the **Control Panel** | **System and Security** | **System window**.
2. Click on **Advanced system settings**. In the window that shows up, click on **Environment Variables...**.
3. In the **System Variables** section, find the `KETTLE_HOME` variable. If it exists, select it and click on **Edit...**.
   If it does not exist, click on **New...**.
4. In the **Edit System Variable** or **New System Variable** window, specify the value for the `KETTLE_HOME` environment variable, as shown in the following example:

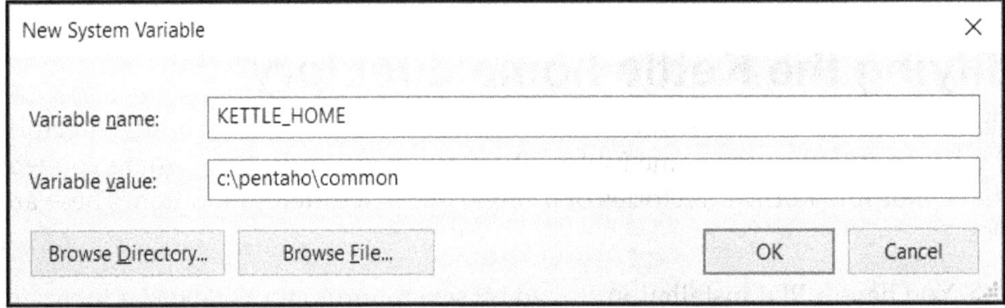

Changing the KETTLE_HOME variable

5. Click on **OK** and close all the setting windows.

These instructions apply to Windows 10. The name of the options to access the **Environment Variables** window may vary for different Windows versions.

If you just want to set the value for the current execution, edit Spoon.bat and add the following line (replacing <kettle_home_value> with the proper value):

```
set KETTLE_HOME=<kettle_home_value>
```

Modifying the Kettle home in Unix-like systems

If you want to modify the Kettle home directory permanently, proceed as follows:

1. Edit the startup file (for example, ~/.bashrc)
2. Add the following lines (replacing <kettle_home_value> with the proper value):

    ```
    KETTLE_HOME=<kettle_home_value>
    export KETTLE_HOME
    ```

3. Save and close the file.

If you just want to set the value for the current execution, add the same lines to the Spoon.sh file.

Summary

Knowing how to accomplish different tasks with PDI is as important as doing it in the right way. This chapter had the purpose of guiding you in that direction. First of all, you learned about the purpose and content of the Kettle home directory. Then you received directions to set up a new project. You also learned about best practices to design, develop, and deploy PDI solutions. You also received some instructions to analyze and enhance the performance of your work.

Following all the guidelines proposed here, your work will be useful, easy to maintain, reusable, and of high quality.

Index

E

F

G

H

Q

R

S

T

U

V

W

X

www.ingramcontent.com/pod-product-compliance
Lightning Source LLC
Chambersburg PA
CBHW060641060326
40690CB00020B/4476

* 9 7 8 1 7 8 8 2 9 2 4 3 6 *